Bad Girls and Boys Go to Hell
(or not)

Bad Girls and Boys Go to Hell (*or not*)

Engaging Fundamentalist Evangelicalism

GLORIA NEUFELD REDEKOP

WIPF & STOCK · Eugene, Oregon

BAD GIRLS AND BOYS GO TO HELL *(OR NOT)*
Engaging Fundamentalist Evangelicalism

Wipf & Stock
An Imprint of Wipf and Stock Publishers
199 W. 8th Ave., Suite 3
Eugene, OR 97401
www.wipfandstock.com

ISBN 13: 978-1-62032-061-7
Manufactured in the U.S.A.

I dedicate this book to Vern Neufeld Redekop,
my partner for life, who has walked the journey
out of fundamentalist evangelicalism with me.

Contents

List of Illustrations

Foreword

GLORIA NEUFELD REDEKOP GREW up in Saskatchewan in the Mennonite Brethren Church some years after I had grown up in Philadelphia in the Plymouth Brethren. But, as I discovered while reading the book, we sang the same hymns, learned the same attitudes, shared the same certainties, and made the same promises (no movies, no smoking, no making friends with unbelievers, and so forth). So it was like coming home to read Gloria's description of her gradual recovery from fundamentalism and the extensive study she has made of seventy-three others who have experienced a similar recovery. Because my own case was one of the seventy-three, I was able to observe that Gloria's report on my journey was accurate—and hence, I have felt free to trust the accuracy of her reports concerning the others.

Now that I am over eighty years old and living in a secular retirement community with people of all religious traditions and no religious tradition, I have met a great many friends who can hardly *comprehend* the nature of fundamentalist evangelicalism. Because certain politicians are now admitting their desire to make their own convictions the moral standard for all Americans—and some of those politicians are fundamentalist—I find myself being asked repeatedly to explain the tone of arrogant certainty that frightens many of my fellow senior citizens. This book, with its careful history of the origins, developments, and tenets of fundamentalism, will be an excellent resource for many of my elderly friends—and for younger folks as well.

Gloria's extensive analysis of hymns is helpful, especially her insight that fundamentalist hymns rarely mention the human life of Jesus: the focus is on his death and "cleansing blood." There is also plenty of militaristic imagery. And the emotions in the hymns are almost always extreme. Those who are "lost" (who have not asked Jesus to be their personal Savior from sin) are described as utterly miserable and in desperate darkness. Conversely, those who are "saved" are full of joy, free from sin, and apparently on a constant emotional "high," except for the rare cases when they are tired or lonely, in which case the Lord is always there to lift them up. These hymns are a vital part of fundamentalist childhood, instilling by tune, tone, and repetition a belief pattern that is absolutely unforgettable. Like Gloria, I still sing the old hymns of the faith on a frequent basis, even though I interpret some of them differently from when I was a child.

One thing I noticed about many of the "recovering fundamentalists" described in this book is that a fair number of them apparently continue to seek for authoritative guidance from some source external to themselves. In fundamentalism, of course, that external source is the Bible as interpreted by the fundamentalist community. And I wonder whether relying on a "chapter and verse" to achieve certainty remains an unconscious habit even after one has broken one's addiction to bibliolatry. Fortunately for me, my freedom came about precisely through learning to interpret the Bible in liberating ways—for instance, learning to believe that God really is not only *above* all, but also *through* all and *in us all* (Eph 4:6). So for me, authoritative guidance is not located "somewhere out there" but is to be contacted in the depths of my own spirit, which is in unbroken connection with the Divine Spirit. True to my evangelical training, I would love to share this good news with everyone. But I can rest in the confidence that everyone will be gathered into Eternal Love at the time that is right for them. What a contrast to the driven feeling I had as an undergraduate at Bob Jones University, feeling responsible for the "twenty-three souls a minute" that I was told were passing into eternal torment without having heard the gospel!

I commend Gloria Neufeld Redekop for her thoroughness in providing historical context for every topic she explores, including the insistence on a literal hell of fire and brimstone. (Charitably, she chalks up that insistence to the need to know that eventually justice will be meted out to evildoers.) She reveals exactly how and why advances in biblical scholarship have been withheld from the majority of church-goers on the theory that what they don't know won't hurt them.

As I read, I realized that a sense of liberation does indeed emerge from knowing that what one was taught as a child is not an eternal reality, but rather a brand of Christianity born out of specific political and theological disputes in the nineteenth and twentieth centuries. Gloria has also provided liberating help by describing several theories of spiritual development as well as methods of self-analysis. So to my sister Gloria Neufeld Redekop, I say, thank you for helping to set captives free from fear, and for clarifying their predicament to those who have never before understood fundamentalist evangelicalism. And to her readers I say, here's hoping you will enjoy the honest and scrupulous inquiry that lies open before you.

Dr. Virginia Ramey Mollenkott is Professor of
Literature Emeritus at The William Paterson University
of New Jersey. She authored *Omnigender: A Trans-
Religious Approach* and many other books and articles.
Visit her at www.virginiamollenkott.com

Preface

THIS BOOK HAS BEEN a lifetime in the living and many years in the making. Ever since I was young girl, I had questions about the fundamentalist evangelical belief system, although I didn't know it by that name. I only knew that I wasn't living up to what God and the church expected of me. I pleaded with God for the emotional high that others seemed to have when they were converted, but I never got it.

After high school I attended a Bible college where I took a Koine Greek language course so that I would be able to see for myself what the New Testament had to say. After college I attended a Bible school, an institution that I understood to be more "spiritual" than a liberal arts college. Maybe I would find peace with God there. But I remained confused about my faith, and it wasn't until after I was married and had a family of my own that I had the courage to confront the doubts and questions I had had all along. In my two years at seminary I came a long way to understanding the human dimensions of the writing of the Bible and I developed a hermeneutics of suspicion with respect to biblical texts. A courageous step was to translate for myself a biblical text that was used to prevent women from taking leadership roles in the church. The results of this exegetical work forms chapter 6 in this book.

The moment I knew I needed to write this book was while waiting for our luggage in a hotel room in Jacksonville, Florida. As I tried repeatedly to reach the airline, my partner, Vern, decided to get out the Gideon Bible and find something to read. It was Sunday. He turned to Matthew 13, remarking, "it's quite a long chapter." It had fifty-eight verses. We had time. We read them all. When it came to the "furnace of fire" and the "weeping and gnashing of teeth" in verse forty-two, I knew it was time to look seriously at the teachings I had received. I took out my computer print-out from the airlines baggage services, entitled "Property Irregularity Report," and scribbled chapter titles on the other side of the three by eight inch slip of paper. I may have missed a few hours of sun, but I had the ideas for a book that I just *had* to write.

When I realized that fundamentalist evangelicalism was my faith foundation, I asked the question, "Where and when did it originate?" I also wanted to know more about the fundamentalist evangelical approach to the interpretation of the Bible. And how others had coped with the same kind of religious teaching I had received. What prompted them to leave? What were the consequences of their decision? And how did they feel once they left the movement? What was left when they gave up their fundamentalist evangelical faith? I started reading their stories and I started writing.

I wish to acknowledge all those who have supported me in this writing project. First, I express my thanks to my project editor, Christian Amondson, at Wipf and Stock Publishers. I also wish to thank Ellen Shenk, who carefully edited the entire manuscript. Her attention to detail and helpful suggestions were greatly appreciated. I am profoundly grateful to Virgina Ramey Mollenkott for the care she took in reading my manuscript and writing the Foreword. Special thanks goes to Gilbert and Adeline Berg, Brian Cornelius, and Sonia Williams who reviewed chapters and offered helpful feedback. I thank those whom I interviewed and who spoke candidly about their experiences in the fundamentalist evangelical movement. I am indebted to my partner, Vern, for the many hours of conversation about the fundamentalist evangelical movement and my experience within it. His insights and support were invaluable. I was also fortunate to have the support of my three children and their families who encouraged me on this journey. My dear grandchildren provide me with hope for the future.

Introduction

I HAD A DREAM. I dreamed I was in Regina, Saskatchewan, having arrived there by train. After some days, I decided to go to my childhood home in Saskatoon. I went back to the train station and boarded the train. After we had travelled for ten minutes or so I realized I was on the wrong train, going the wrong direction. In a panic, I asked the conductor if he would take me back to the station. I pled with him. I told him I was afraid to walk back by myself. After much persuasion he agreed to take me back part of the way. He said that if we would see others walking that direction, I would have to disembark and walk back with them. As we travelled back I noticed just how desolate the surroundings were. No houses, roads or people could be seen. On the left was an ocean with huge fierce-looking waves. I had never seen waves so high. And on the right were stacks and stacks of silver-coloured metal tanks, like large oil tanks. There were countless numbers of them, stack after stack.

When the conductor saw a group of four people standing among the stacks, I had to get off the train. I soon realized this was a tour group that was finding out about the stacks. The tour guide told us that her parents had died and had left the stacks to her, but she didn't know what to do with them. She said they were full of toxic chemicals. She didn't want them, but she didn't know how to dispose of them. She was crying.

Then we were led to an open railway car that was to take us back to the Regina train station. The ride was scary, almost like a rollercoaster ride. My grandson was sitting on my lap at that point and he almost fell over the edge. I screamed and held him closer.

When I awoke, I knew that the dream had to do with my journey out of fundamentalist evangelicalism and the writing of this book. I interpreted the dream like this: Early in my life, I was directed onto a spiritual path that was not right for me. I went the wrong direction. It took many years before I realized that the direction I was going was not the way "home," not the way to a place of safety and comfort where I could live a life that was free from guilt and fear. So I turned around. The crashing waves signified my fear of hell. The large metal stacks with harmful chemicals represented the toxicity of fundamentalism to my being. Each stack in my dream stood for one of the fundamentalist evangelical church's beliefs. The tour guide, who was crying because she didn't know how to get rid of the toxic stacks, was actually me. I had been given the stacks of fundamentalist evangelical belief; I didn't want them anymore, but to get rid of them would not be easy. Luckily the dream didn't stop there. Even though the rollercoaster-type ride was scary, it nonetheless took me back to the train station. Though the process out of fundamentalist evangelicalism is painful and full of challenges, the practice of remembering, the researching and the writing is one key to the way out.

The day before I had the dream I had read Susan Campbell's account of her journey in *Dating Jesus: A Story of Fundamentalism, Feminism, and the American Girl*. Campbell describes her experience in fundamentalism as having been pierced with a sword that got broken off in her body with the broken piece staying in the body and continuing to cause discomfort, "We were thrust with the sword of faith, and then it broke off in us, and we cannot pull it out and we cannot be free of the discomfort of its presence. . . . We will never, ever heal from the wound."[1] Those stacks of toxic chemicals can be like that sword; they are difficult to remove for fear of doing damage. The challenge is for fundamentalists who wish to have the "sword of faith" removed from their inner beings to find a way out that doesn't do damage to themselves. How can the toxicity of fundamentalist evangelicalism be removed?

There is strong evidence that many today are in need of help as they attempt to be free from the burden of fundamentalist thought. Fundamentalists Anonymous (F.A.), founded in the United States in 1985, had a membership of 30,000 within two years of its conception.[2] This phenomenal growth attests to the fact that people have been negatively affected by fundamentalism to such a degree that they need a regular system of deprogramming in order to escape its hold.

I approach this topic from the perspective of growing up in the Mennonite Brethren Church in the 1960s, a church that was strongly

1. Campbell, *Dating* Jesus, 161, 165–66.
2. Evans and Berent, *Fundamentalism: Hazards and Heartbreaks*, 153.

influenced by the fundamentalist movement. The Mennonite Brethren denomination stemmed from the Anabaptist tradition with its roots in the Radical Reformation in Europe in the 1500s. It was in 1860 that Mennonite Brethren broke away from the larger Mennonite community in Russia. The purpose of this new denomination was to "restore a New Testament believers' church in both pattern and polity."[3] The Mennonite Brethren Church emphasized closed Communion (Communion only for those who were church members), church discipline, and adult baptism by immersion. At its inception, meetings were held in people's homes and were quite informal with lively singing. The Mennonite Brethren saw their break with the other Mennonites as a spiritual awakening, a revival of New Testament Christianity. It is interesting that this happened at the same time as there were religious awakenings in North America. It was in the 1870s that some Mennonite Brethren people went to North America, settling predominantly in Kansas. In the 1880s they went to Manitoba; and in the early 1900s, they went to Saskatchewan, British Columbia, Alberta, and Ontario. The Mennonite Brethren denomination was influenced by both Pietism and the fundamentalist evangelical movement, which was developing in North America in the late 1800s.

In this book, I use the term fundamentalist evangelicalism to describe a Christian evangelicalism that was strongly influenced by the North American fundamentalist movement of the late 1800s and early 1900s. I place "evangelical" after "fundamentalist" because the phenomenon I describe began with evangelicalism, an evangelicalism that became fundamentalist. Thus, fundamentalist describes the kind of evangelicalism it is.

As I conducted my research I came across two other writers who also use the term fundamentalist evangelicalism. Timothy Weber, in his chapter, "Premillennialism and the Branches of Evangelicalism" in the book *The Variety of American Evangelicalism*, describes four branches of evangelicalism, one of them being fundamentalist evangelicalism.[4] He includes in this branch all those who were "shaped by the debates of the fundamentalist-modernist controversy" of the late 1800s and early 1900s; they "focused on a few fundamentals, in opposition to liberal,

---

3. Toews, *A History of the Mennonite Brethren Church*, 51.
4. Weber, "Premillennialism and the Branches of Evangelicalism," 12–14.

critical and evolutionary teaching."[5] My understanding of the term is similar to that of Weber's. In this book I describe the ways in which fundamentalist evangelicals were affected by that controversy and I look at how this influenced their religious experience and doctrinal beliefs.

Another author who uses the term fundamentalist evangelicalism is George Marsden; he uses it with reference to the politicized Religious Right that arose in the late 1970s.[6] While the Religious Right of the late 1970s could well share much with the fundamentalist evangelicals of the early twentieth century, my focus is on the history and character of the movement before it became politicized.

A major academic work to examine fundamentalist movements within religious traditions was *The Fundamentalist Project*, published in the 1990s in five edited volumes: *Fundamentalisms Observed, Fundamentalisms and Society, Accounting for Fundamentalisms, Fundamentalisms and the State*, and *Fundamentalisms Comprehended*. In the first volume, the writers approach fundamentalisms from historical and phenomenological viewpoints, looking at how fundamentalisms evolved, their goals and their leaders.[7] In the first chapter of this volume, Nancy Ammerman traces the development of the fundamentalist movement through to 1975.[8] Her approach to exploring fundamentalism within Protestantism is similar to my own. But what sets mine apart is that methodologically I look at a historical deconstruction of fundamentalist evangelical origins.

In Volume 4, *Accounting for Fundamentalisms,* Robert Wuthnow and Matthew P. Lawson point out that Christian fundamentalism can be accounted for not only through a descriptive history of the movement, but also by examining its social and cultural environment, an environment that demanded that the community of believers remain separate from unbelievers and live morally upright lives.[9] My book shows the importance of tight boundaries in fundamentalist evangelicalism, boundaries that were to keep the community separate from what were thought to be worldly influences.

---

5. Ibid., 13.

6. Marsden, *Understanding Fundamentalism and Evangelicalism*, 235.

7. Marty, *Fundamentalism Observed*, x–xi.

8. Ammerman, "North American Protestant Fundamentalism."

9. Wuthnow and Lawson, *Accounting for Fundamentalisms*, 4–8.

Many argue that evangelicalism has changed a lot since the early 1900s. While this may be the case, and while I am aware of the emergence of other related "isms," such as neo-evangelicalism and neo-fundamentalism in the later twentieth century, I leave the discussion of those developments to others. This book does not address the ways in which that may have happened, nor does it deal at length with the differences between Canadian and American fundamentalist evangelicalism.

The study of fundamentalist evangelicalism is complex. It is a populist phenomenon that engaged a host of people who contributed to it becoming a significant movement in the western expansion of Christianity in North America. First, such a study involves interaction between a historical tradition—evangelicalism that had its roots even before the Reformation in Europe—and certain other phenomena, including scientific discoveries and the rise of biblical criticism. Second, adding to its complexity is the fundamentalist evangelical approach to the Bible as infallible and credible for use as the basis for any theological argument. This means that in order to do justice to this phenomenon, one needs to be well versed in the Bible and in methods of exegesis. And third is the complexity of the level of fervent devotion of its adherents, intense emotional involvement that was all encompassing. One cannot look at fundamentalist evangelicalism without engaging all three aspects. And that is what I aim to do in this book. Mine is a three-fold methodology, involving social history, biblical studies, and the narrative analysis of the experience of former fundamentalist evangelicals.

My own background includes expertise in social history, biblical exegesis and analytic methods. The fact that I was part of the fundamentalist evangelical movement and subsequently left it, enables me to ask the questions that address the root of people's involvement. I play different roles in the book. First I am a historian and analyst. I am also a participant observer. Since I experienced fundamentalist evangelicalism firsthand, I am able to make observations from inside the movement, from my own personal history. I then observe how this affected both me and others.

In Part I, I discuss the history of the fundamentalist evangelical movement—its origins and its growth in North America. Chapter 1 sets the stage for the historical engagement by providing a summary of the personal beliefs I held as a teenager. I also examine the characteristics of both evangelicalism and fundamentalism and show how the two relate to each other. In chapter 2, I discuss the emergence of evangelicalism in the sixteenth century Reformation in Europe and in chapter 3, I talk about the influences that gave rise to the fundamentalist evangelical movement in North America in the nineteenth and early twentieth century. I also discuss the factors that caused the movement to grow substantially. Chapter 4 is dedicated to the crucial role music played in the emergence and growth of the movement. I look at the kinds of songs that were written, their themes, and how they were used in tandem with preaching in order to further the fundamentalist evangelical movement.

Part II is the engagement with the way fundamentalist evangelicals interpret the Bible. In chapter 5, we see how the absolute authority of the Bible is a foundation for fundamentalist evangelicalism. Their approach to the text is key to understanding their religious worldview. In keeping with the methodology of historical deconstruction, I explore how the books in the Bible came to be viewed as sacred text. Chapter 6 offers a case study of an exegesis of a biblical text that has been traditionally interpreted to keep women silent in the church. My exegesis is evidence of what happens when one examines a biblical text in its literary form, its historical context, and its comparative study of the use of words. Chapter 7 discusses a second primary fundamental, which I believe to be one of the pillars that kept (and continues to keep) fundamentalist evangelicals "spreading the Word," so to speak. This is the belief in hell. It is because of this belief that there is a passion to "save" others, as expressed in the song:

> Give me a passion for souls dear Lord,
> A passion to save the lost
> Oh that thy love were by all adored
> And welcomed at any cost.

The belief in hell is crucial for fundamentalist evangelicals, since, if there were no hell, there would be no need for salvation and no need to believe in the atonement of sin through Jesus' death. And because the belief in hell has instilled so much fear in former fundamentalist evangelicals, I am devoting this chapter to the history of the concept of hell, as well as an examination of biblical texts that have traditionally been used to affirm the belief in hell.

Part III is an engagement with the experience of fundamentalist evangelicalism, in particular, the experience of leaving the movement. I examine the experiences of former fundamentalist evangelicals and the impact that leaving had on them. Chapter 8 analyzes seventy-three personal accounts of individuals who have left the movement. Chapter 9 discusses the process of leaving the movement with respect to levels of consciousness and stages of faith.

Those who have left fundamentalist evangelicalism may be deeply affected and even traumatized when they leave the movement. Even though they have given up believing the fundamentals of the movement, the old tapes of fear and guilt and the "what if" factor ("what if it's true after all?") can still plague ex-fundamentalist evangelicals. In chapter 10, I focus on the emotional effects of leaving the movement.

There are several audiences for this book. First, it is for those who have left the fundamentalist evangelical movement and want to understand more about what they have gone through. They may still be struggling to make sense of the movement. It is also for those within the movement who have questions about it, its history, the way the Bible is interpreted, and the reasons why some of us have left the movement.

The book is also useful for those in other religious traditions who wish to know the origins of fundamentalist evangelicalism and the reasons why those in the movement understand the world as they do. They will come to see that the movement has significant historical roots and will gain a deeper understanding of how it came to be, the reasons why it evolved as it did, and why adherents exhibit such strong devotion.

Students of religion will gain knowledge of the movement and learn how it is that people come to hold their beliefs in a militant way.

This book is also valuable for anyone who has experienced fundamentalism within any religion or ideology and has been struggling with the hold that a fundamentalist mindset can have on them. Methodologically, the book can be seen as a way to study fundamentalisms of any kind, as it combines history, rethinking of the interpretation of the sacred text, and the ways people have come to terms with their own fundamentalist experience.

If you desire to take this journey, come with me as we explore the fundamentalist evangelical movement—historically, with respect to approaches to biblical interpretation, and from the perspective of those who experienced it and left.

PART I

Engaging Fundamentalist Evangelical History

To set the stage for a historical look at fundamentalist evangelicalism, I begin with a personal history. Then, after offering definitions of both evangelicalism and fundamentalism, I situate the movement within the history of evangelicalism, going back to the Reformation in Europe in the 1500s. The evangelical movement was transplanted to North America along with European immigration. And it was in North America, then, that fundamentalism emerged, with the purpose of maintaining orthodoxy and rejecting evolution, modernism, and liberalism. This resulted in two Protestant streams, the mainline evangelical tradition and the fundamentalist evangelical stream, the latter with an emphasis on salvation, prophecy, and the return of Christ. Believers in the movement held firmly to what they considered to be fundamentals of the faith. In the early 1900s, the movement was nurtured through literature, preaching, teaching, and music. The singing of gospel songs written during that time was crucial to the spread of the movement in that it reinforced the fundamentals in a way that encouraged emotionally charged responses.

1

Setting the Stage: A Personal History

ONE WAY TO UNDERSTAND the meaning of fundamentalist evangelicalism is to enter the belief system experientially. Since I grew up in the fundamentalist evangelical church, I will open a window into my world as a teenager, focusing on how I understood my religion. Methodologically, I am treating my earlier experience as an object of critical examination and reflection.

While I have found that many share the same experiences, I cannot speak for others who grew up in evangelical churches. Evangelical churches vary in their emphases and the degree of fundamentalist influence varies from church to church and from denomination to denomination. My experience comes out of belonging to an evangelical denomination that was strongly influenced by fundamentalism, the Mennonite Brethren. It could easily have been the story of someone in any other fundamentalist Protestant or Anabaptist tradition with the same worldview, such as people belonging to the Baptist, Church of the Nazarene, or Pentecostal traditions.

As I identify each belief, I will explain how I understood it and sometimes follow it with a song that served to reinforce the belief. Italics are used to identify my personal thoughts.

When we went to Sunday School each Sunday morning, all ages of children and youth would first meet together to sing a few hymns and choruses. One of the books we used was a little four-by six-inch red, white, and navy spiral-bound book called *Sunday School Sings:*

A Praise Book of Favorite Sunday School Hymns and Choruses.[1] These songs served to reinforce the core beliefs of the church and many of the songs referenced in this chapter are in that songbook.

BELIEFS OF A SIXTEEN YEAR OLD RAISED IN A FUNDAMENTALIST EVANGELICAL CHURCH

What follows is a reconstruction of the belief system I had as a teenager, using words, concepts, and songs as I understood them then.

One of the most important beliefs is the inspiration of the Bible, which means that the words in the Bible are God-breathed. People have different ways of describing this. It seems that writers of the Bible were mysteriously directed by God to write the words in the Bible as they held their pens (or quills or whatever they wrote with). They hardly even knew what they were writing because they were led by God's Spirit to write what they did. Everything in the Bible is there because God planned it to be there. If there is anything that seems to contradict a text found elsewhere in the Bible, that doesn't matter. It is a mystery that we will not understand in this life. Our finite minds are not able to grasp the texts that seem to contradict other texts.

We sing songs that talk about the importance of the Bible:

> The B I B L E, yes that's the book for me,
> I stand alone on the Word of God, the B I B L E.

The word "Scripture" has a holy ring to it and you always spell it with a capital "S." If you don't, it means you are not showing proper respect for the Bible. When you refer to the Bible as Scripture, it means that it came from God and is the special Word of God (and Word has a capital letter too because sometimes it refers to Jesus). Sometimes you call it the "Holy Bible." The New Testament (the part written after Jesus died) is more important than the Old Testament because it is the fulfillment of the Old Testament.

We are encouraged to memorize large portions of the Bible so that we can call up verses in our minds when we need encouragement or advice. I am on a Youth for Christ quiz team that competes with other teams across the province. We are given several chapters in New Testament books to memorize and then compete at Youth for Christ gatherings.

1. Nelson, *Sunday School Sings.*

When a question is asked, the first person to step on the pedal under their chair jumps up and repeats the Bible verse that answers the particular question being asked. If answered correctly, that team gets a point.

The term, Bible-believing Christian, is a short phrase that means someone is a true Christian. Bible-believing means that you believe in the "word for word" inspiration of the Bible. In other words, whatever it says in the Bible is taken literally, exactly what it says. And the Bible calls the shots of everything you need to know about being a Christian, or most other things for that matter.

Sin refers to all the bad things you do. You are born in sin. This is called original sin. Sin began with Adam and Eve. Actually it was Eve who sinned first. Poor Adam, he got into trouble with God because Eve seduced him to taste the apple God had said they should not eat. It was Eve's fault that sin came into the world. Everyone born after Adam and Eve is sinful from the get-go, as soon as they are born. They can't help it. Although even babies are born in sin, they are not accountable for their sin until the age of reason. But I'm not exactly sure what age is the age of reason.

There are a lot of songs that send the message of our sinfulness. One of these is:

> Search me O God and know my heart today;
> Try me, oh Savior, know my thoughts I pray.
> See if there be some wicked way in me.
> Cleanse me from ev'ry sin and set me free.

Because you are born in sin, you are not worthy to be loved by God just as you are, even though the song says, "Just as I am." You only become worthy through God's grace. By grace is meant a favor that you don't deserve; the favor is that God loved you so much that God sent his son, Jesus, to die for your sins. Like the song says:

> Marvelous grace of our loving Lord,
> grace that exceeds our sin and our guilt,
> Yonder on Calvary's mount outpoured.
> There where the blood of the Lamb was spillt.
> Grace, grace, marvelous grace.
> Grace that will pardon and cleanse within.
> Grace, grace, infinite grace.
> Grace that is greater than all our sin.

Conversion and salvation are terms used to describe what happens when you become a Christian. You ask Jesus to forgive your sin and accept him into your heart. Then you are converted; you are saved. Saved from what? Saved from hell. Many songs talk about this, like:

> I am the Door I am the Door, I am the Door.
> By Me if any man [*sic*] enter in, he [*sic*] shall be saved,
> he [*sic*] shall be saved, he [*sic*] shall be saved.

Since "Door" refers to Jesus, it is capitalized. And whenever the pronoun "he" is used for Jesus, it also has a capital letter.

When we are told about being saved, it is often referred to as "letting Jesus into our hearts," as the song says:

> Into my heart, into my heart, come into my heart Lord Jesus.
> Come in today, come in to stay. Come into my heart Lord Jesus.

I am puzzled about what this means, Jesus in my heart. How does that happen anyway? I guess it is just one of those mysteries you can't understand.

When you are converted, you are a changed person. You are "saved" from hell. You are not bad anymore. Jesus can accept you now. I was saved when I was seven years old. That's what it says in my little white New Testament.

When you accept Jesus, he becomes your personal Savior. From now on you will be happy and not sin so much, as the song says:

> If you want joy, real joy, wonderful joy,
> let Jesus come into your heart.
> Your sins He'll wash away,
> your night He'll turn to day, your life He'll make it over anew.
> If you want joy, real joy, wonderful joy,
> let Jesus come into your heart.

Conversion is supposed to change you. The problem with me is that being "saved" doesn't seem to make much difference. At first I was happy, but soon I realized that I was still a bad girl. Things were not as different as the song said they would be:

> Things are different now, something happened to me, when I
> gave my heart to Jesus.
> Things are different now, I was changed it must be when I gave
> my heart to Him.

Another way to talk about salvation is that you are born again, born a second time. The first time is your natural birth and the second time is by the Holy Spirit; you are born into the family of God. And just simply going to church or being born into a Christian family does not make you a Christian. You have to make a personal decision to be born again, as the song says:

> A ruler once came to Jesus by night,
> to ask him the way of salvation and light.
> The Master made answer with words kind and true,
> "Ye must be born again.
> Ye must be born again. Ye must be born again.
> I verily, verily say unto thee, Ye must be born again."

Everyone who has not accepted Jesus as their personal Savior is lost. This means they are cut off from God. They will definitely go to hell when they die. If they are not Mennonite Brethren, they don't have much of a chance, except for Baptists, because they believe a lot like we do and they baptize the "right" way, by immersion. I'm not quite sure about Mennonites who are not Mennonite Brethren. I've heard, for instance that some General Conference Mennonites smoke cigarettes and they don't baptize by immersion. Does that mean they are "lost"? Roman Catholics are definitely lost because they pray to the saints and to Mary and they don't believe in a personal salvation experience.

Sometimes preachers talk about putting Jesus on the throne of your life. This means that Jesus needs to be the most important person in your life; you have to put him in charge of everything in your life, all your thoughts and actions. Another way of talking about this is that Jesus is Lord of your life. He is in charge. He is in the driver's seat. You have to let him drive. Does this mean that I should not decide anything for myself?

Atonement means that Jesus took the punishment for our sins on the cross. It was a sacrifice. Before Jesus time, the Jewish people had to sacrifice animals to atone for their sins. Then Jesus became the final sacrifice for sin. Because of his death, animal sacrifices were no longer needed. Jesus became the one sacrifice for the sins of everyone in the world if they accept him. The ransom was paid when Jesus died on the cross, like the song says:

> The children's friend is Jesus. He calls them to his side.
> He gave His life a ransom, heaven's gate to open wide.
> The children's friend is Jesus, Jesus, Jesus.

His life He gave their souls to save. The children's friend is He.

Every Christian should live a Spirit-filled life. After you accept Jesus as your Savior, the Holy Spirit comes to live in you, and then you are filled with the fruits of the Holy Spirit (love, joy, peace, etc.). If you are Spirit-filled you don't sin so easily:

My desire to be like Jesus, my desire to be like Him.
His Spirit fill me, His love o'erwhelms me.
In deed and word to be like Him.

Having devotions or "quiet time" (as it is sometimes called) is one of the ways you stay in touch with God. This is a daily time you set aside to read the Bible and pray, like the song says:

Whisper a prayer in the morning, whisper a prayer at noon,
Whisper a prayer in the evening, 'twill keep your heart in tune.

If there are days when you don't read your Bible, you feel guilty because you have not done what every good Christian should do.

Figure 1. I Must Have Daily Devotions

After you are saved, you will want to tell others about what God has done for you. Sometimes at Sunday evening church services there is something called "testimony time." The minister asks if anyone wants to tell their testimony of what God has done for them recently. People stand up and talk about how God has spoken to them or how they acted on what God asked them to do. I always feel "convicted" to stand up and say something. Testimony time makes me very nervous and I don't really want to do get up and say anything, but to prove to myself and others in the church that I am a good Christian, I always feel I have to stand up and talk about what God has done for me, even though I am never sure if God has done anything for me. I dread testimony time. First, I have nothing truthful to say, and second, every time I get up I start to cry and then I weep right through everything I say. That is really embarrassing and in the end I wonder what good it does for either me or the congregation.

"Right with God" means that you have done everything necessary to be in the right relationship with God. You are saved, you are telling others about Jesus, and you read your Bible and pray daily. You live as much as possible like Jesus lived. If you do this, you are walking with the Lord. Sometimes I hear people ask each other, "How is your walk with the Lord?" Whatever would I answer if someone asked me that question? This song talks about walking with the Lord:

> When we walk with the Lord in the light of His Word,
> What a glory He sheds on the way.
> While we do His good will, He abides with us still
> And with all who will trust and obey.

People who are not Christians are worldly. Preachers talk about how we are "in the world" but not "of the world." By "of the world" they mean you should not participate in worldly activities such as drinking, dancing, and going to movie theatres. Nor should you get too friendly with those who are not Christians, the non-Christians. They might be a bad influence on you. This includes Roman Catholics as well as "liberal" Christians who do not agree with all the fundamentals of the faith.

There is a lot of pressure to get baptized when you reach fifteen or sixteen years old. When you are baptized, you show that you have decided to follow Jesus and to live separate from the world. Baptism is done by immersion. There is a big tank at the front of the church, a tank that is usually not seen because it has a curtain in front of it. Before you get baptized, you have to prove that you are truly saved. You do this by giving your "testimony" to church members at a meeting of church members. I was petrified to get baptized. First, I had a phobia of putting my head under water. Second, I was anxious about getting up in front of the whole church to give my testimony. And third, I was afraid that church members would be able to see through my testimony, see all the doubts and questions I had, and then refuse me for baptism.

The dreaded evening arrived, and one by one, baptismal candidates gave their testimonies. We were not allowed to hear each other's testimonies; all baptismal candidates waited in the church basement and were called up one at a time. Well, I did make it through my testimony and then the minister asked if anyone in the congregation had any questions to ask me. One of the well-respected elderly men had a question. He asked, "How do you know you are saved?" Oh, oh. The very question I feared, but I pulled from my memory a Bible verse that I thought would provide a satisfactory answer. And it worked. He didn't see the doubt within; he accepted my answer. And so I was baptized the next Sunday. After each one was baptized, the choir, sitting in the balcony at the back of the church, sang one verse of the song, "Thou Wilt Keep Him in Perfect Peace." It was an emotional experience.

Thou wilt keep him in perfect peace (3x)
Whose mind is stayed on Thee.

Marvel not that I say unto you (3x)
Ye must be born again.

Though your sins as scarlet be (3x)
They shall be white as snow.

If the Son shall make you free (3x)
You shall be free indeed.

They that wait upon the Lord (3x)
They shall renew their strength.

Once you are baptized, you have given a public witness of your salvation experience. You can now participate in the Lord's Supper (Eucharist) and your way to heaven is even more secure.

There is a lot said about eternal life. There is an afterlife and the choice is yours, will it be heaven or hell?

Heaven is the place Jesus has prepared for those who love him, for those who have accepted him as their personal Savior. Heaven is somewhere above the clouds, a mansion with many rooms, as Jesus said in John 14:2–3: "In my Father's house are many mansions. If it were not so, I would have told you. I go to prepare a place for you. And if I go and prepare a place for you, I will come again, and receive you unto myself; that where I am, there ye may be also" (King James Version). In heaven Jesus sits on a throne beside God. Elders bow down to worship Jesus. The streets are gold. No one gets hungry there or cries. There is no night. People will recognize each other in heaven; you will see all the Bible characters and all your friends and relatives who made it there. This song tells you that even children can know they will be going to heaven when they die:

> Jesus loves me, He who died, Heaven's gate to open wide,
> He will wash away my sin, let His little child come in.

If you don't go to heaven, you will definitely go to hell. Hell is a place of fire and the fire never goes out. It is located under the earth. The people in hell burn forever. They feel they are burning but they never die; they just keep on feeling burned. This is the place you don't want to go. It is for all the people who have not accepted Jesus into their hearts. It is for people who have lied, stolen, and done other bad things for which they have not asked forgiveness. Hell is a scary place and this is a scary song:

> One door and only one and yet its sides are two:
> "Inside" and "outside," on which side are you?
> One door and only one and yet its sides are two;
> I'm on the inside, on which side are you?

What if I am on the outside of the door? How can I know for sure?

Another part of the afterlife that is scary is the "judgment." This is a future event that will take place before you get into either heaven or hell. At this time everyone will be judged for what they have done on earth. If they have asked Jesus to be their personal Savior and have been forgiven of their sins, they will go to heaven; if they have not, they will go to hell. The things they have done in their lives will also be judged, whether they were good or bad. What I can't figure out is, if Jesus forgives what you have done wrong, why are you still judged for it at the end of your life? And when does this actually happen? Do all the bodies pop out of the graves at some point in time and everyone all line up for the sentence?

If a Christian has either stopped believing or if they have done something that goes against what a Christian should do, this is called backsliding. Telling lies or talking back to your parents is considered backsliding. I talk back to my parents a lot. I even stole money from my brother.

If you have backslidden, there is an easy solution. You simply have to rededicate your life to Jesus. This means you can just say a prayer, asking Jesus to forgive you. Then you are back in good standing with God. I rededicate myself to Jesus a lot, but nothing ever seems different. It is hard to believe that any of this makes me a better Christian.

A lot of rededication takes place at evangelistic services. These events happen at least once a year. Sometimes they are in the church and other times the services take place in one of the larger buildings in the city, like the arena. A speaker from out of town, the evangelist, comes to preach, with the goal of getting people "saved." Services take place every night for two weeks straight. I usually attend them all. A mass choir with people from across the city sing each night. There is a special choir conductor who travels with the evangelist. I always sing in the choir. It is an amazing experience, singing under a professional conductor. It is very emotional. I love singing in the choir.

At the end of each evening service there is always an altar call. After the sermon, the evangelist asks people to come forward to the front of the church to be saved, or if they have backslidden, they can rededicate themselves to God. The choir usually sings "Just as I am" while the evangelist asks people to come to the front of the auditorium for prayer.

After the choir sings a couple of verses, the evangelist says, "Now while the choir hums the next verse, and every head is bowed and every eye closed . . . " Then the evangelist encourages people to leave their places and go to the front of the auditorium, where they will later be paired up with a counsellor, who will pray with them about whatever they need, whether that is salvation, forgiveness for specific sins, rededication, or anything that is bothering them. (Counsellors are selected in advance. Often they will start walking to the front of the auditorium as soon as they see others going forward for prayer. That way, there will be one counsellor for everyone who goes forward.)

There are six verses to the song, "Just as I am," and the choir sings them all, sometimes even repeating verses, while the evangelist keeps calling for people to come to the front. He even encourages people in the audience to nudge people next to them if they feel those people are under conviction to go forward.

> Just as I am without one plea
> But that Thy blood was shed for me
> And that Thou bidst me come to Thee
> O Lamb of God, I come, I come.

> Just as I am, and waiting not
> To rid my soul of one dark blot,
> To Thee whose blood can cleanse each spot,
> O Lamb of God, I come, I come.

> Just as I am, though tossed about
> With many a conflict, many a doubt,
> Fightings and fears within, without,
> O Lamb of God, I come, I come.

> Just as I am, poor, wretched, blind;
> Sight, riches, healing of the mind,
> Yea, all I need in Thee to find,
> O Lamb of God, I come, I come.

> Just as I am, Thou wilt receive,
> Wilt welcome, pardon, cleanse, relieve;
> Because Thy promise I believe,
> O Lamb of God, I come, I come.

> Just as I am, Thy love unknown
> Hath broken every barrier down;
> Now, to be Thine, yea, Thine alone,
> O Lamb of God, I come, I come.

Lots of people cry at these services, me too. I used to go forward at least once every year because I always had some sin that made me backslide. I always cried while walking to the front. I even started crying before I started to walk to the front. That's how I knew I was being "convicted" to "go forward." If I was crying, it meant I was really sorry for my sins. But after it was over, I wasn't sure what difference it made. It didn't seem to help me be a good girl. I was still bad. I still talked back to my parents and I still wasn't sure I would go to heaven after I died.

One time, when there was an altar call in our church, people who came forward were instructed to go downstairs to Sunday School rooms, each person with a counsellor. I went forward. And there I was in the Sunday School room with a counsellor. She said to me, "So tell me about your problem." And at that moment I realized I didn't know what my problem was. Through my tears I said, "I don't know." And the counsellor said, "Well, I'll pray for you anyway." After this experience I never went forward again. It was just too embarrassing to not know how to express what was wrong with me.

Besides evangelistic services, another way that people can find out about Jesus is by Christians witnessing to them. Witnessing means that Christians tell others about Jesus. In fact, that is one of the reasons we are saved, as the song says:

> We're saved, saved to tell others of the Man of Galilee
> Saved, saved to live daily for the Christ of Calvary.
> Saved, saved to invite you to His salvation free.
> We're saved, saved, saved by His blood for all eternity.

We are told that all Christians automatically want to witness because they want others to know about Jesus. They won't be able to keep quiet about it. Jesus told his followers to tell others the good news of salvation when he said, "Go and make disciples of all nations" (Matt 28:19). If you are not witnessing, there is something dreadfully wrong with your "walk with the Lord." Because I don't feel comfortable witnessing, I wonder whether I really am a Christian.

When you are witnessing, it is helpful to carry some tracts with you. Tracts are little brochures that explain the way of salvation in just a few small pages. Tracts often talk about heaven and hell. The tracts about hell are scary. There is one tract that says, "Hell and the LAKE OF FIRE are Waiting for YOU! WARNING: If you aren't Biblically saved AT THIS MOMENT, you are a heartbeat away from Hell."[2] Then the tract tells you how to "get forgiven and escape eternal torment."[3] Some tracts even have pictures of the flames of hell. Of course I believe all of this is true. And the scariest thing for me is that I am not sure I'll be going to heaven when I die.

Because we believe that even children will go to hell if they are not saved, child evangelism is seen as a very important activity. After all, you

2. "Hell and the LAKE OF FIRE are Waiting for YOU!", Evangelical Outreach, 1999, http://www.evangelicaloutreach.org/heavenhell.pdf.

3. Ibid.

wouldn't want your child to go to hell, would you? When I was younger I went to child evangelism club in the summer. It was usually held in someone's back yard. The teacher would show us the "Wordless Book" and she would ask: "Have you ever seen a book without words or pictures?" And then she would fan the pages to show the colors. I was spellbound.

She would say, "This book with pages of different colors tells a wonderful story from the Bible about the true and living God who made the world. I call my book the "Wordless Book." Each color reminds me of part of the story. Would you like to hear it?" Of course we would like to hear it, so we all shouted, "Yes!" There was actually something intriguing about this book of coloured pages with no words on them.

"Have you ever peeked at the last page of a book to see if the ending is happy or sad?" she would say. "I have! Let's look at the last page first. It tells us about a very exciting place. The gold page reminds me of heaven." And then she talked about heaven and the streets of gold. "But there is one thing that can never be in heaven." And she turned to the black page (the first page in the book). "That one thing is sin." And she told us that sin has to be punished and that because God loves us, he has made a way for our sins to be forgiven. Then she turned to the red page. "The red page shows the way," she said. And she talked about Jesus death on the cross and how he saves us from sin. "Red stands for the blood of Jesus. He died to save us from our sins." Moving on to the white page, the teacher explained that God can make us clean, "as white as snow," if we tell Jesus we are sorry for our sins and that we want God to forgive us. This booklet is still available today, with an on-line video coming to the website soon.[4]

There is another important booklet that explains how you can be saved. This one is meant for young people. It is called "The Four Spiritual Laws."

The booklet asks the question, "Have you heard of the four spiritual laws?" There are four laws, one to a page. Each law has verses from the New Testament to back it up:

1. God loves you and has a wonderful plan for your life (John 3:16, John 10:10).

2. Man [sic]is sinful and separated from God. Therefore, he [sic] cannot know and experience God's love and plan for his [sic] life (Rom 3:23, Rom 6:23).

4. "The Wordless Book," Erik Stuyck, Berean Computer Ministries, 2002, http://berean.org/bibleteacher/wb.html.

3. Jesus Christ is God's only provision for man's [*sic*] sin. Through Him you can know and experience God's love and plan for your life (Rom 5:8, 1 Cor 15:3–6, John 14:6).

4. We must individually receive Jesus Christ as Savior and <u>Lord</u>; then we can know and experience God's love and plan for our lives (John 1:12, Eph 2:8–9, John 3:18, Rev 3:20).[5]

By using this book in your witnessing, you can "lead someone to the Lord." This means that you explain the way of salvation to someone, ask them if they want to be saved, and then pray with them. If you do this, you have "led them to the Lord." Another way of expressing this is that you have "won a soul for Jesus" as the song says:

> Lord, lay some soul upon my heart
> And love that soul through me
> And may I humbly do my part
> To win that soul for Thee.

We are told that it is the soul of the person that needs to be saved, because it is the soul that lives on after we die. I can never get my head around what "soul" means. Where is it stored in a person's body? And what does it look like? Is it a "floaty" kind of thing that takes on a body after death? No one really knows. So if you "win souls" it means people are being saved for eternity, saved from hell. I am not a very good Christian, or maybe I'm not a Christian at all, because I never have won any souls for Jesus. We are supposed to have a passion to win souls and we sing about it:

> Jesus I long, I long to be winning men [*sic*] who are lost and constantly sinning,
> O may this hour be one of beginning the story of pardon to tell.

Not only had I not won any souls, I don't even have a passion to do it. In its place, I have guilt because the passion is not there.

"Outreach" is the word that refers to the efforts Christians make to tell others about Jesus; they "reach out" to others. This can be done by each individual or the church can decide to do it by having an "outreach program," an organized plan to bring people to Jesus and into the church.

---

5. "Four Spiritual Laws," New Life Publications, Campus Crusade for Christ, 2007, http://www.campuscrusade.com/fourlawseng.htm.

Closely related to the idea of outreach is missions. Missions refers to the work of the church to win souls. Some people are in it full time. They are called missionaries. Mission work can be done close to home, like in our own province or country. This is called home missions. An example of home missions is starting a new church somewhere in Canada. This is also called church planting.

Foreign missionaries are missionaries who go to other countries to tell people about Jesus. They go to places like South America, Africa, and India. When these missionaries are "on furlough," which means they come back to Canada for a number of months in order to report to the churches what they have done, they bring back interesting artefacts from foreign lands. They sometimes dress up like the "natives" (the people they are trying to reach for Jesus) and they show slides of their work. They talk about how many people have become Christians and how many new churches have been "planted."

Some missionaries are teachers, nurses, or medical doctors. But it is made very clear that, although they practice their professions on the mission field, their main goal is to lead people to Christ. Songs like this show the importance of mission work:

> We have heard the joyful sound, Jesus saves! Jesus saves!
> Spread the tidings all around, Jesus saves! Jesus saves!
> Bear the news to every land,
> Climb the steeps and cross the waves;
> Onward! 'tis our Lord's command: Jesus saves! Jesus saves!

There is a sense that God calls each person to some life work. If your walk with the Lord is a close one, you might actually hear God call you to some kind of Christian work, like being a missionary. And if God calls you to be a foreign missionary, it is the highest calling a Christian can have and you would be foolish not to follow the call. I have noticed that there are quite a few single female missionaries who come around to our church, talking about their work abroad. One of my fears is that God will call me to be a single missionary to some foreign land, when all I really want to do is find a guy and get married.

So that is what I thought when I was a teenager. Today, when I look back on it, I am struck by how narrow and clear-cut my beliefs were and how strongly they were enforced by the church and reinforced by singing the songs.

THE IMPACT OF FUNDAMENTALIST EVANGELICALISM ON CHILDREN

As I reflect on the impact of fundamentalist evangelicalism on children who are raised this way, I am conscious of a number of underlying messages children and youth receive when they are immersed in this system:

- The inspiration of the Bible, defined as God-breathed words, cannot be questioned. This is a given. It is foundational for the whole Christian faith. If you start to question this, you have begun to go down the slippery slope of unbelief. Your whole belief system may become unravelled, since every belief proceeds from the authority of the Bible.

- Every sin you commit needs to be forgiven. If the sin is against someone else, you must first apologize to that person, and then ask God's forgiveness. The underlying message is that you need to be perfect in order for God to accept you. The child who takes this seriously realizes that it is impossible to live without "sin" and that it is difficult to determine what sins you commit in any given day. And you would probably be labelled neurotic if in fact you did try to confess every sin, to both those whom you sinned against and to God.

- It is a challenge to feel good about yourself when you are told that you were born "bad," i.e., born in sin. Because you were born bad, God won't accept you until you are saved through the sacrifice of Jesus on the cross. This is a personal decision that only you can make. And even if you believe that your past sins have been forgiven at the time of conversion, the overall preoccupation with sin can lead to diminishment of self-worth.

Figure 2. That's All We're Interested In

- You are confused about the love of God. You are told on the one hand that God loves you and will forgive your sins, but on the other hand, that God judges you and can punish you for your sins when you die by sending you to hell. Most of the time it feels like God is more angry than loving. Part of the reason for this is that the impact of negative messages is very powerful and it takes many positives to override one negative.

- When you are converted, you should feel good inside and find it easy to live a good life. You have repented of your sin and you are a changed person. The Holy Spirit, who lives in you, helps you to do good works. If you don't have an emotionally charged conversion experience and if you don't feel like a changed person, it could be for one of three reasons: you didn't really mean the prayer of forgiveness, or you are not relying sufficiently on God to change your ways, or you went back to your old way of living after you asked God to save you. It can't be God's fault; there has to be something the matter with you.

- To doubt your experience of God is a sin. Jon Sweeney writes that "we held no real value for doubt in a spiritual life. It was something to be removed, a stain that could be cleaned up. Doubt was clearly a weakness."[6]

- A good Christian will want to tell others about Jesus. If you don't feel like doing this, there must have been something wrong with your conversion. Sweeney tells of a time when he took a Bible College course on evangelism in which students were told they had to witness to at least two people a week and write weekly reports as to their progress.[7] He recounts how he witnessed to many people over the course of that class, but he couldn't save a single soul.[8] He got a "B" in that class. *When I was in Bible School, I was part of a group that went into the big city every Saturday to witness to people on the street. This was very uncomfortable for me; it did not come naturally to me. So I thought I wasn't a true Christian.* If you don't win any souls for Jesus, you don't measure up. Winning souls gives you status in the world of fundamentalist evangelicalism and it is a sign that you are a good Christian.

- Jesus has to be number one in your life. If you think about dating boys more often than you think about pleasing Jesus, it means you haven't surrendered your "all" to him. "All to Jesus I Surrender" is a song that reinforces this.

- If you don't have devotions every day, you are not a very good Christian. Neither is it a good sign if you fall asleep during your bedtime prayers. It makes you feel guilty if you do. This is a sin of omission; you should have been able to stay awake to pray. You don't want to be like the disciples who fell asleep when Jesus had asked them to stay awake and pray. He said to them,

6. Sweeney, *born again and again*, 75.
7. Ibid., 82.
8. Ibid., 83.

"So, could you not stay awake with me one hour?" (Matt 26:40).

- It seems like you can never get ahead of the game. If talking back to parents and telling white lies means that you are not "right with God," it is difficult to think of yourself as a good Christian and you live with guilt and fear of hell.

- If you have any friends who are not Christian, they could lead you astray—lead you away from Christianity—and then you would be bound for hell for sure. So it is best to never have friendships outside the church, as Dave Tomlinson puts it, "The world, so I was told, was enemy territory, a place full of temptations and pitfalls for the Christian. . . . The clear policy was 'avoidance wherever possible.' Don't put yourself in situations of temptation, I was urged; avoid places like theatres; avoid friendships with unbelievers unless it is for evangelistic purposes."[9]

- If you hear God calling you to some vocation, you are truly close to God. If you can't hear God calling you, there must be some sin standing in the way.

- If you happen to die before you have been able to have all your sins forgiven, you will go to hell.

These messages were enforced and reinforced by Sunday School teachers, preachers, songs, and sometimes parents. *In my case, it was Sunday School teachers, preachers, and songs that impacted me.* Even though a child does not understand all the beliefs, she does understand that she had better believe them, because if she doesn't, she will go to hell. Incentive enough to believe!

From a young person's perspective then, that is what it feels like to live within the fundamentalist evangelical system. They do not know the definitions or even the words "fundamentalist" or "evangelical," but they know how it feels to be part of the only belief system that will get them into heaven.

9. Tomlinson, *The Post-Evangelical*, 123.

DEFINING EVANGELICALISM AND FUNDAMENTALISM

Both evangelicalism and fundamentalism are movements; they are not denominations or churches. They can describe a way of believing that can be present in any church or denomination.

Evangelicalism

The word "evangelical" has a long history. It comes from the Greek, *euaggelion*. *Eu* means "well" or "good" and *aggelion* is related to *aggellos* which means "angel" or "messenger." So *euaggelion* means a good message or a message of wellness. The New Testament translates it as "gospel" or "good news." One of its New Testament occurrences is in the first verse of the gospel of Mark, "The beginning of the good news (*euaggelion*) of Jesus Christ" (Mk 1:1).

While the idea of *euaggelion* was already evident in the first century CE, the evangelical movement as we know it today had its roots in the 1500s, the European Protestant Reformation, and in the spiritual Pietistic renewal that took place in Britain in the 1700s.[10] Baptist, Methodist, Presbyterian, and Congregational churches were all evangelical. Chapter 2 discusses the history of the evangelical movement in detail. Here I will refer only to some its defining characteristics.

Various authors have offered what they believe to be the primary tenets of an evangelical faith. David Bebbington identifies four primary evangelical beliefs that were evident in the mid 1800s: Biblicism, crucicentrism, conversionism, and activism.[11] The Bible held a central place for evangelicals in the 1800s, as did the crucifixion, thought of in terms of substitution, Christ taking the place of sinful humanity.[12] In order to become a Christian, one needed to experience a personal conversion from sin, which was deemed valid whether it was sudden or gradual.[13] By activism, Bebbington means that evangelical Christians felt compelled both to actively bring others to Christ and to work energetically at improving social conditions in the world.[14]

---

10. Noll, *The Rise of Evangelicalism*, 17.

11. Bebbington, *The Dominance of Evangelialism*, 23–39.

12. Ibid., 23–28.

13. Ibid., 31–36.

14. Ibid., 36–39.

Barry Hankins offers a useful summary of the beliefs of evangelical Protestantism when he writes that evangelicals are those "who affirm the authority of the Bible, insist on the necessity of a conversion experience made possible by the crucifixion and resurrection of Christ, and attempt to live a holy and active life of faith, sharing the gospel with others in an attempt to win them to the faith."[15]

James Barr identifies the following beliefs, which he believes all evangelicals hold:

1. The belief that all people have a sinful disposition. The substitutionary atonement of Christ's death is a sacrifice to remove sins. Christ can do this because he is God. People receive the gift of salvation by faith, accepting Jesus as their Savior. This results in a new relationship with God which has to be nurtured by studying the Bible, prayer and resisting temptation. The person must be sanctified by the Holy Spirit.

2. Belief in the priesthood of all believers. Anyone with a personal faith in Jesus Christ can talk about the gospel; scholarship is not as important as speaking from your heart, directed by the Holy Spirit.

3. The importance of prayer. Non-memorized prayers are the "real" prayers. Prayer must be personal. Intercessory prayer (prayer for others) makes a difference in people's lives.

4. An emphasis on evangelism. Every Christian must witness to the saving faith of Jesus. Friendship evangelism is one method of witnessing. This involves making friends with someone in order to win them to Jesus. Christians are expected to be persecuted and ridiculed for their faith.

5. An emphasis on foreign missions. All Christians should ask themselves whether God is calling them to be a foreign missionary.

6. Belief in heaven and hell and the second coming of Christ, when all will be judged. Because of Christ's second coming, there is an urgency to bring people to Christ while the opportunity still is there.

7. Belief that the Bible is the highest religious symbol.[16]

---

15. Hankins, *Evangelicalism and Fundamentalism*, 7.

16. Barr, *Fundamtentalism*, 28–31.

The Evangelical Fellowship of Canada (EFC), a Canadian association of evangelical churches founded in 1964, currently has forty affiliated member denominations, including Baptist, Brethren in Christ, Mennonite, Pentecostal, Church of God, Christian and Missionary Alliance, Evangelical Free Church, Foursquare Gospel, Salvation Army traditions, and others. Affiliate members agree on the following Statement of Faith:

- "The Holy Scriptures, as originally given by God, are divinely inspired, infallible, entirely trustworthy, and constitute the only supreme authority in all matters of faith and conduct.

- There is one God, eternally existent in three persons: Father, Son and Holy Spirit.

- The Lord Jesus Christ is God manifest in the flesh; members affirm his virgin birth, sinless humanity, divine miracles, vicarious and atoning death, bodily resurrection, ascension, ongoing mediatorial work, and personal return in power and glory.

- The salvation of lost and sinful humanity is possible only through the merits of the shed blood of the Lord Jesus Christ, received by faith apart from works, and is characterized by regeneration by the Holy Spirit.

- The Holy Spirit enables believers to live a holy life, to witness and work for the Lord Jesus Christ.

- The Church, the body of Christ, consists of all true believers.

- Ultimately God will judge the living and the dead, those who are saved unto the resurrection of life, those who are lost unto the resurrection of damnation."[17]

One might safely assume, then, that the forty member groups that consider themselves to be evangelical today agree with the above Statement of Faith.

When comparing the EFC Statement of Faith with the features of evangelicalism described by Bebbington, Hankin, and Barr, one can see some key similarities. All affirm that for evangelicals, the Bible is authoritative, that a personal conversion is possible because of Christ's

---

17. "Statement of Faith," The Evangelical Fellowship of Canada, last modified 2012, http://www.evangelicalfellowship.ca/page.aspx?pid=265.

crucifixion, and that Christians must be in the business of evangelizing—telling others about the Christ.

Outside of these beliefs, evangelical groups can be quite diverse. Mark Noll points out that evangelical denominations may tend to place more emphasis on some aspects of faith than on others: "Sometimes the experience of conversion takes precedence, at others the concentration on Scripture as ultimate religious authority and at still others the importance of missionary or social action. The evangelical traditions consistently maintain the major evangelical traits, but they have done so with a tremendously diverse array of emphases."[18]

An example of the emphasis placed by different Christian denominations is that of the Christian and Missionary Alliance Church. As the name suggests, this denomination gives missionary outreach a high priority. Another way of giving emphasis to a certain aspect of the faith is to have a Bible verse as a motto in large letters in the front of the church. In one Mennonite Brethren church, this motto was "Behold I come quickly" (Rev 3:11). This indicates that the second coming of Jesus was of particular importance to that congregation.

At the end of the 1800s and the early 1900s theories abounded about the "end times" and the second coming of Jesus. Some evangelical Christian groups were decisive as to exactly what would happen at Jesus' second coming, when events would take place, and who would be included or excluded from these events.

The influence of this kind of thinking was evident not only in North America at the end of the 1800s, but also in Europe among some evangelicals. *My own great-grandparents, along with about one hundred other families who lived in South Russia in the 1800s, went on a trek to Turkestan because a certain Claas Epp said Jesus would return there in 1889.*[19] *Some became disenchanted and left the group, my great-grandparents included.*

And now to fundamentalism.

18. Noll, *The Rise of Evangelicalism*, 20.
19. Block, "Family History," Unpublished manuscript, 2.

Fundamentalism

Fundamentalism is a movement that can be evident within any religion or ideology. It is generally not a word Christians like to use to describe themselves today. While some Christians do still call themselves fundamentalists, many evangelical Christians make a point of saying they are not fundamentalist since it is often associated with intolerance and violence, and Christians do not see themselves that way. But in the late 1800s and early 1900s Christians who called themselves fundamentalists saw themselves as those who upheld the fundamentals of Christian faith. They were proud to call themselves fundamentalists. According to them, others were being led astray by modernism, while they were upholding the true gospel. According to Joel Carpenter, "fundamentalism is a distinct religious movement which arose in the early twentieth century to defend traditional evangelical orthodoxy and to extend its evangelical thrust."[20]

Barr writes that in fundamentalism there is a concern to maintain the purity of the group.[21] This purity is maintained through control of thought and behaviour, as Stuart Sim states in *Fundamentalist World*: "religious fundamentalism, of pretty well all persuasions, seeks to exert control over our thought and behaviour."[22] One of the reasons control is so important is so that the purity of the doctrine can be retained. Sim sees this as "the true mark of the fundamentalist temperament" and the reason why monitoring of thought and behaviour are so important in the fundamentalist community.[23] And that is why in any fundamentalism there is a "lack of tolerance to perceived outsiders . . . The fundamentalist mind does not like difference, it does not like dissent. What it really likes is submission to the system, and uncritical adherence to the creed."[24] So in fundamentalism, boundaries are drawn to keep control of the community and keep it pure.

Randall Balmer writes that "fundamentalists have an aversion to modernity . . . when it represents a departure from orthodoxy."[25] Funda-

---

20. Carpenter, *Fundamentalism in American Religion*, 57.

21. Barr, *Fundamentalism*, 339–442.

22. Sim, *Fundamentalist World*, 100.

23. Ibid., 42, 100.

24. Ibid., 11–12.

25. Balmer, *Encyclopedia of Evangelicalism*, 232.

mentalist evangelicals militantly oppose modernism because they feel it is not consistent with the view that the highest authority is the Bible.

Fundamentalism often emerges in a time of uncertainty, either theologically or politically. What fundamentalism provides is certainty of belief and in an effort to maintain this certainty, adherents are "willing to do battle royal."[26] A militant stance is evident within fundamentalism, as exemplified in the writing of George Dollar, who was himself a fundamentalist. Dollar claims to have written the first "responsible and comprehensive history of fundamentalism," and in his *A History of Fundamentalism in America*, he asserts that fundamentalism is "the literal exposition of all the affirmations and attitudes of the Bible and the militant exposure of all non-Biblical affirmations and attitudes."[27]

In chapter 3 I will say more about the history and growth of the fundamentalist movement in the late 1800s and early 1900s.

But what do evangelicals and fundamentalist evangelicals have in common?

Evangelicals and Fundamentalists: Commonalities

For the most part Protestant fundamentalists hold the same beliefs as evangelicals. Both fundamentalists and evangelicals believe that the most important decision a person needs to make in life is to be "born again" and the earlier in life this decision is made the better.[28] While fundamentalists do it more militantly, both feel they must "defend the faith by defending the authority of the Bible."[29]

Both evangelicals and fundamentalists believe that God speaks personally through scripture, and that having devotions—daily private reading of the Bible and prayer—is very important for the Christian. They believe you can have a personal relationship with Christ, which is maintained through these "quiet times."

They both believe that God speaks to them (by the Holy Spirit) through the Bible, and they speak to God through prayer. The Holy Spirit ensures that they interpret the Bible correctly. Evangelicals often speak about being "struck" by certain verses in the Bible and about God

26. Ibid., 29.

27. Dollar, *A History of Fundamentalism*, vii and ix.

28. Sweeney, *born again and again*, 3–5.

29. Harris, *Fundamentalism and Evangelicals*, 20.

speaking to them through "God's Word." Both evangelicals and fundamentalists "feel that they allow scripture to speak for itself," and they feel that others "subject God's Word to human judgment and interpret it selectively to suit their particular sensibilities."[30]

What are the differences between fundamentalists and evangelicals who do not consider themselves to be fundamentalist?

Evangelicals and Fundamentalists: Differences

Richard Kyle views evangelicalism as a wider phenomenon than fundamentalism, with fundamentalism as a subgroup of evangelicalism, an extreme wing of the evangelical movement.[31]

Fundamentalists are more likely than evangelicals to keep themselves separate from other Christians and to believe that their way is the only right way to believe.

Sim sees the belief in the inerrancy of the Bible as one of the key differences between fundamentalists and evangelicals. Fundamentalists tend to emphasize literal interpretations of the Bible, with no exceptions, whereas evangelicals are more willing to interpret the Bible metaphorically. For fundamentalists, the Bible is "literal, revealed truth, the 'absolute transcript of God's mind' . . . it should not be questioned in any way."[32] Kyle says that evangelicals tend to be more likely to consider the circumstances around which biblical texts were written.[33]

Kyle writes that fundamentalists are prone to be anti-intellectual, whereas evangelicals are not.[34] Some evangelicals read more broadly and are open to consider other points of view than their own.

While both evangelicals and fundamentalists believe in the second coming of Christ, fundamentalists are more likely to design theories as to the timing of the event. They have a greater tendency toward dispensationalism (a biblical interpretation that proposes the division of human history into specific ages/dispensations).

So bringing fundamentalism and evangelicalism together, what did it look like in the late 1800s in North America?

30. Ibid., 180.
31. Kyle, *Evangelicalism*, 14.
32. Sim, *Fundamentalist World*, 13.
33. Kyle, *Evangelicalism*, 15.
34. Ibid. 15.

Fundamentalist Evangelicalism

Perceived threats to orthodoxy in the late 1800s resulted in a split within Protestantism in North America. Some Protestants accepted the theories arising from science and new biblical scholarship while others did not. Those who did not, shifted their emphasis and declared certain fundamentals necessary for admittance into the evangelical fold. They created boundary lines of belief, resulting in the fundamentalist evangelical movement. As a result, the differences between fundamentalism and evangelicalism became less pronounced.

The fundamentalist evangelicalism of the late 1800s and early 1900s had as its foundation the basic evangelical belief system, which was already in existence. It then added the strong need to militantly defend the Bible and uphold all fundamentals as non-negotiable. It emphasized the imminent return of Christ and judgment of all humankind, along with messages about salvation and the afterlife, especially hell. It was not open to hearing from those outside of their belief system, nor to discussing biblical interpretations different than those espoused by their own approved biblical scholars. It tended to see social and moral issues in "black and white" and was unwavering in the knowledge of the truth as they saw it.

In my quest to understand the origins of the fundamentalist evangelical movement, this chapter began with a reconstruction of the belief system of my teenage years, a personal history to set the stage for the discussion. I discovered that the messages children received in this movement were presented as a set of tightly intertwined concepts, starting with the all important and foundational belief in the authority of the Bible, inerrant and infallible. These concepts provided the believer with a complete approach to life, making it very difficult to incorporate new ideas and experiences. If there was something in the belief system that a person questioned, if it didn't seem to fit, then there was something wrong with the individual, not with the system. This system was the fundamentalist evangelical movement.

In order to better understand the origins of this movement, the next chapter will trace the history of the emergence of evangelicalism, since it was within evangelicalism that a fundamentalist approach to beliefs emerged.

2

History of the Evangelical Tradition

IN ORDER TO UNDERSTAND fundamentalist evangelicalism in North America, we must consider the evangelical tradition out of which it arose, the evangelicalism rooted in the Protestant Reformation in Europe and its emergence in North America at the time of the Great Awakenings. In this chapter we shall look at how these factors shaped the evangelicalism that dominated Protestantism in North America in the nineteenth and early twentieth centuries.

THE ROOTS OF EVANGELICALISM IN SIXTEENTH CENTURY EUROPE

The sixteenth century saw both scientific advancements in Europe, as well as religious unrest. Copernicus (1473–1543), a mathematician, astronomer, and upstanding member of the Roman Catholic Church, proposed that the earth and all the other planets revolved around the sun. It wasn't until after his death, when Galileo (1564–1642), also a mathematician and astronomer, tested the Copernican theory and found it to be valid, that the Roman Catholic Church took offense. So when Galileo was not compliant with the order not to spread the thesis that the sun was the centre of the universe, he was silenced by the Roman Inquisition, the Inquisition that had been set up by the Roman Catholic Church in 1542 to guard against heretical doctrines.

Martin Luther and the Protestant Reformation

Martin Luther, a Roman Catholic priest, was born in Germany in 1483. When he was twenty-one years old, he was hit by lightening. This frightened him so much that he became painfully aware of his own sin and feared going to hell. Desperately searching for personal assurance of salvation, he entered an Augustinian monastery. Being a conscientious student, he attained the standing of priest within one year. However, this did not rid him of his sense of sin and guilt. At age twenty-nine, as professor of theology at the University of Wittenberg, his preoccupation was, "how can I be saved from hell?" (This question has become a central theme of evangelicalism.) This informed all of his research.

As Luther was lecturing on the books of Romans and Galatians, he had an epiphany, based on Romans 1:17, "For in it [the gospel] the righteousness of God is revealed through faith for faith; as it is written, 'The one who is righteous will live by faith.'" The realization that he only needed to believe in order to be saved brought him inner peace.

In 1517 Luther posted his ninety-five theses (written in German so that all could read them) on the Wittenberg Castle church door. These theses were critiques of the Roman Catholic Church, one of them being a criticism of the selling of indulgences and another a critique of the belief that the bread and wine of the Eucharist actually becomes the body and blood of Christ. In January 1521, Pope Leo X excommunicated him from the Roman Catholic Church. Three months later he was called before Charles V, the Holy Roman emperor, and asked to recant his writings. Mark Noll believes that with Luther's words—"I am bound by the Scriptures I have quoted and my conscience is captive to the Word of God. I cannot and I will not retract anything"—Protestantism was born.[1]

Eight years later, at the First Diet of Speyer, it was decided that each German prince could determine for himself, whether his state would be Roman Catholic or Lutheran. At the Second Diet of Speyer, a compromise was made, which favoured Roman Catholics. It was decided that Roman Catholics living in Lutheran regions would be given religious freedom, but Lutherans living in Roman Catholic regions would not. Six Lutheran princes protested these arrangements and from then on they were called Protestants—protestors. It was not until 1555 with the

---

1. Noll, *Turning Points*, 154.

Peace of Augsburg that Lutherans and Roman Catholics were given equal rights in all regions of Germany.

Luther wrote thirty-seven hymns, *Ein feste Burg ist unser Gott* (A Mighty Fortress is Our God) written in 1527/28, is one of the most well known:

> A mighty fortress is our God, a bulwark never failing
> Our helper he amid the flood of mortal ills prevailing
> But still our ancient foe doth seek to work us woe
> His craft and power are great, and armed with cruel hate
> On earth is not his equal.
>
> Did we in our own strength confide, our striving would be losing
> Were not the right man on our side, the man of God's own choosing
> Dost ask who that may be? Christ Jesus, it is he!
> Lord Sabaoth his name, from age to age the same,
> And he must win the battle.
>
> And though this world with devils filled, should threaten
>   to undo us
> We will not fear, for God hath willed his truth to triumph
>   through us
> The prince of darkness grim, we tremble not for him
> His rage we can endure, for lo, his doom is sure
> One little word shall fell him.

The words of this hymn show Luther's confidence in his new-found belief and his unwavering commitment to it. He was convinced that "the right man" was on his side. This was God. Those who were formerly considered religious mentors were now deemed to be foes and devils. Luther was no longer afraid of "the prince of darkness"—"we tremble not for him, his rage we can endure, for lo, his doom is sure, one little word shall fell him."

In 1534 Luther translated and printed the Bible into the German language, which meant ordinary people in Germany now had access to the biblical text in their own language.

So with Luther the Protestant Reformation began. While he never intended to start a new denomination, Lutheranism emerged from his teachings. At first the new church was called the *Evangelische Kirche* (the Evangelical Church). Noll claims that while the word "evangelical" was not new in the 1500s, it became a word that was associated with the Protestant Reformation.[2] It was almost synonymous with Protestantism, with its beliefs in the doctrines of *sola gratia, sola fides, solus Christus* and *sola scriptura* (salvation by grace through faith in Christ, revealed in the Bible alone).[3]

Other European Reformers

Other European reformers included John Knox (1510–1572) in Scotland, Ulrich Zwingli (1483–1531) in Switzerland, and John Calvin (1509–1564) in France. Calvin had questions similar to Luther, but the answer that satisfied him was predestination (salvation dependent upon being elected by God) and the doctrine that once you received salvation, you were always saved. Out of Calvinism emerged other Christian denominations, including Presbyterian and Congregationalist.

An offshoot of the Protestant Reformation was the Radical Reformation or Anabaptism,[4] in keeping with the conviction that infant baptism was ineffectual for salvation and that a second baptism as an adult was necessary. In 1525, a number of people, including George Blaurock, Felix Manz and Conrad Grebel, left Zwingli because of the baptism issue. When Grebel re-baptized Blaurock, Anabaptism was born.[5]

Those of the Radical Reformation preached separation from the world, separation of church and state, non-resistance, the importance of living the faith, the belief in the Eucharist as only a memorial, voluntary church membership, belief in the final authority of the Bible, and the priesthood of all believers. As it spread, it reached the Netherlands and a priest by the name of Menno Simons joined the Anabaptists[6] and visited groups of people who were studying the Bible for themselves in their homes. Those who observed this phenomenon called the groups "Menists." Later, their name changed to Mennonists and then to Mennonites, which is what they are called today. A product of the Radical Reformation in Europe, Mennonites also have a link to the evangelicalism of the sixteenth century.

---

2. Noll, *The Rise of Evangelicalism*, 16.
3. Brown, *The Word in the World*, 2.
4. The word "Anabaptism" means to baptize again.
5. Estep, *The Anabaptist Story*, 34.
6. Ibid., 123.

The Radical Reformation saw the importance of social justice. Menno Simons believed that "true evangelical faith is of such a nature that it cannot lay dormant; but manifests itself in all righteousness and works of love; . . . clothes the naked; feeds the hungry; consoles the afflicted; shelters the miserable; aids and consoles all the oppressed; returns good for evil; . . . binds up that which is wounded; heals that which is diseased."[7] Simons's understanding of the word "evangelical" included social justice and caring for the needy. David Bebbington writes that "in its origins the social gospel movement was in large part a broadening expression of evangelicalism."[8] The concern for the poor, evident in the Radical Reformation, was also evident in the 1800s in North America among evangelical groups such as the Methodists, Congregationalists, and the Salvation Army. While the preaching of the gospel was considered primary, evangelicals believed that it was also important to pay attention to the physical needs of those they tried to reach for salvation. And they sought to make the world a better place by discouraging alcohol use and gambling.

Meanwhile, in England, the church in England broke away from the Roman Catholic Church when Parliament, under Henry VIII, passed the Act of Supremacy in 1534, which stated that taxes formerly paid to Rome would now go the Monarch. In his parliamentary address, the king proclaimed that "the King our Sovereign Lord shall be accepted and reputed the only supreme Head on earth of the Church of England, called *Anglicana Ecclesia*."[9]

During the reign of Queen Elizabeth I (1558–1603), the Puritans sought to purify the Church of England from within by trying to "wipe out vestiges of Roman Catholic worship and doctrine."[10] They encouraged pastors to preach from the Bible. They stressed the importance of experiential Christianity, and declared that Sunday should be a day reserved for worship. They emphasized that salvation depends on God alone; that the authority of the Bible must be upheld; and that church and state should be complementary. It was during this time that some Puritans went to New England in North America, where they established Plymouth Rock in the early 1600s.

7. Wenger, ed., *The Complete Writings of Menno Simons*, 246.

8. Bebbington, *The Dominance of Evangelicalism*, 248.

9. Bray, ed., *Documents of the English Reformation*, 114.

10. Noll, *A History of Christianity*, 32.

Influenced by the Puritans, the first Baptist church was established in England under John Smyth (1565–1612), who felt that he had to leave the Church of England in order to preserve true Christianity. Some Baptists were persecuted and imprisoned; others fled to Holland where they met Dutch Mennonite Anabaptists and were influenced by them to practice adult baptism, a baptism that they uphold to this day.

In the mid 1500s the Roman Catholic Church had their own Reformation, a Reformation that was intended to reform the Church, but was also meant to counter the doctrines of the Protestant Reformation. The Council of Trent met during three separate time periods in Italy between 1545 and 1563. Among other things, it reaffirmed seven sacraments, the doctrine of transubstantiation, and the equality of the Bible with tradition. It mandated specific training for priests and missionaries. It was also decreed that only prescribed music could be sung in the Church and that the Latin Vulgate was the only trustworthy translation of the Bible.

SEVENTEENTH CENTURY ANTECEDENTS TO EIGHTEENTH CENTURY EVANGELICALISM IN EUROPE AND NORTH AMERICA

During the seventeenth century there were more scientific advances, including the invention of the telescope, discovery of sunspots, the first map of the moon, a description of the landscape of Mars, a scientific explanation for the rainbow, discovery of the circulation of the blood, and drawing of a meteorological map. Sir Isaac Newton (1643–1727) explained the gravitational attraction of the sun, moon, and earth. In wanting to "purge Christianity of its mythical doctrines," he felt that his discovery actually helped to prove the existence of God.[11]

In the world of philosophy, the Copernican theory was considered a great threat to the Roman Catholic Church. Girodano Bruno (1548–1600), one of the supporters of the theory, was burned at the stake in 1600. And Johann Kepler's (1571–1630) book *The Epitome of the Copernican Astronomer* was banned by the Church.

René Descartes (1596–1650) believed that you could prove by reason that God exists and that through reason one could understand the world. Thomas Hobbes (1588–1679) claimed that governments are based on natural law and are not divinely sanctioned. Baruch Spinoza (1632–1677),

11. Armstrong, *The Battle for God*, 69.

a Jewish philosopher, said that God does not exist without the existence of the physical world. He was excommunicated by the Jewish authorities and the Catholic church put his books on their list of banned books. John Locke, in *The Reasonableness of Christianity,* wrote about tolerance and liberty; and believed human reason should inform belief.

The Dissenters

While Puritans generally tried to work for change from within, some, known as Dissenters, broke away from the legally constituted established church in Great Britain, the Church of England. Dissenting churches included Presbyterians, Quakers, Congregationalists, and Baptists.

John Bunyan (1628–1688), well known writer of *Pilgrim's Progress,* was a Puritan Dissenter. From 1660 to 1672 he was imprisoned for his convictions. Another of his books, *Grace Abounding to the Chief of Sinners*, spoke of his personal struggles with sin and the promise of forgiveness.[12] This kind of theology became central to the evangelical movement that emerged in the 1700s.

In seventeenth century Scotland, dissenters were persecuted for their evangelical tendencies. Within the space of one year (1660) three hundred men were removed from their offices as Presbyterian ministers.[13] Some dissenters were imprisoned and others were executed, the first executions taking place in 1666.[14] Persecution of the reformers tended to radicalize their religious beliefs and it was this radical belief system that influenced the character of evangelicalism.

We can gain insight into the mentality of Scottish Puritans through the life-writings of Scottish Presbyterian women who wrote of their faith experiences during this time. We learn from these writings the kind of faith experiences that were prevalent among these women.

There is evidence of women's consciousness of sin and their belief that God punishes sin through illness and hardship. Elizabeth Blackadder (1660–1732) wrote about her punishment, "there is a vast disproportion between my sin and my chastisement, for it is still the correction of a gracious father, who does it always for our profit."[15] Katherine Hamilton

12. Noll, *The Rise of Evangelicalism*, 57.
13. Mullan, *Women's Lifewriting in Early Modern Scotland*, 21.
14. Ibid., 3.
15. Ibid., 399.

(1662–1732) included in her 1698 New Year's prayer, a desire to leave behind, with the old year, "my old, sinful, crooked, worldly ways."[16]

Women wrote of their glorious experiences of salvation but also of their inability to maintain the emotional high it brought them. Their sense of sin returned and this led them to question the legitimacy of their initial experience. Near the end of her life, Blackadder wrote, "And this is my soul's grief, that I do not entirely trust the conduct of the glorious Joshua [Jesus] . . . I know his presence is salvation, and if he be with me I am sure I shall be safe, though he should in his sovereign justice (for my woeful unbelief) withhold his comforting presence . . ."[17]

Jean Collace found that she sometimes questioned everything, "Sometime I thought that the Lord by the word of his mouth would confirm to my soul that he loved me and that I was his. . . . At other times when I perceived my heart or practice unlike that which I heard the children of God were, I questioned all."[18] Collaces's comparison with "the children of God" shows a certain mimetic effect operative in these spiritual experiences. It was mimetic in that when women heard of each other's conversion stories, they wanted to experience the same thing in the same way.

Helen Alexander (1653–1729) wrote of her faith struggles, at one time experiencing the goodness of God and the next, feeling utterly sinful and plagued with doubts. She wrote, "I thought I saw the flames of hell, and wondered that the earth did not open its mouth and swallow me up; for I thought I did nothing but sin. O what soul-trouble I was under; for I thought it was needless for me to pray, for all my duties were defiled with sin. . . . and then, through the Lord's goodness, I found a great weight taken off me; but O, how sweet a time had I then. But afterwards . . . I fell in great fears and doubts, and thought all was delusion."[19]

Katharine Collace (1635–1697) spoke about this kind of experience as backsliding, "I was so filled with joy unspeakable, that the ordinances became like a little heaven to me; and I loathed all the vanities of this life as hell . . . but being ignorant of the life of faith . . . when the sense of the glory of God in the face of Jesus Christ was withdrawn, I turned less diligent in secret prayer, which was an inlet to backsliding."[20]

16. Ibid., 372.
17. Ibid., 409.
18. Ibid., 96.
19. Ibid., 192.
20. Ibid., 43.

Their concept of God was that God condescended to their lowly selves to help them, as Jean Collace writes, "I was sorely apprehensive of the Lord's displeasure with me because of sin, yet his condescendence was so great to my weakness that he keeped [kept] some glimpse of his infinite mercy in my sight."[21]

These women tended to take the Bible literally and were both convicted and consoled by verses they read. Blackadder wrote, "There was one day, when I was musing on (perhaps with too much of unbelief) my trouble, particularly my heavy charge of seven fatherless children, that scripture was brought to my mind, Exodus 2:2—it was the words of Pharaoh's daughter to Moses' mother—'Take this child to nurse it for me and I will give thee thy wages, so the child was her own and she got her reward for nursing.' This scripture, though it seems not so very applicable, yet the Lord my God was pleased to bless it as a means to quiet my troubled heart at that time."[22] From this verse in Exodus, Blackadder took courage in her mothering of seven children by herself. Just as Pharaoh's daughter felt rewarded for nursing a child that had been given to her, Blackadder, by reading this verse, realized her rewards as a mother.

These beliefs remained part of evangelicalism as it emerged in North America in the 1700s, including conviction of sin, the need for conversion, the use of the Bible for personal direction, the reality of hell, punishment for sin, and a literal interpretation of the Bible.

Pietism

Pietism can be seen as an antecedent to the evangelical movement of the 1700s. In the last half of the 1600s the Pietistic movement emerged in Germany under Philip Jakob Spener (1635–1705), a Lutheran minister who called for church renewal and believed that piety and faith should make a difference in daily life. Spener's *Pia Desideria* (Pious Wishes), written in 1675, had originally been the Preface to the publication of the sermons of Johann Arndt, a Lutheran minister in Germany.[23] In this lengthy Preface, Spener proposed what he thought to be true Christianity. This included a return to the Bible, an active

---

21. Ibid., 96.
22. Ibid., 397–98.
23. Spener, *Pia Desideria.*

role for laypeople, active godliness, and proper training for ministers.[24] Since this was a key document that shaped the evangelical movement in North America, the effects of which are still present today, we do well to discuss its contents.

From Spener's perspective, the Evangelical Lutheran Church in Germany had departed significantly from Luther's vision. His hope was that "through these pages other enlightened men [*sic*] . . . may be encouraged earnestly to undertake this most important work of advancing true godliness."[25] He pointed out what he considered to be the corrupt practices of congregations and preachers, and offered ways to bring reform. Focusing on the need for holy living, he wrote that there were those "who do not really understand and practice true Christianity"; . . . the clergy has "a worldly spirit, marked by carnal pleasure, lust of the eye, and arrogant behaviour."[26] He lamented the fact that there was so much disagreement over beliefs and he wished for more emphasis on piety. Writing about some people in the church, he referred to the "great mass of nominal Christians."[27] *What is interesting about this terminology is that three centuries later, evangelical Christians still were differentiating between "nominal" Christians and "real" Christians.* Believing there was power in the Eurcharistic bread and wine, he spoke disparagingly about those "evangelicals" who denied this power in the Eucharist. He made it clear that it was not enough to be baptized and to simply listen to the "Word of God."[28] It had to be acted upon.

In order to bring about reform, Spener felt the church must be pure. He advocated a strict discipline that excluded from the church those who had committed offenses and not shown evidence of reform. In his opinion, this exclusion would result in a church in which "the weeds will no longer cover the grain and make it unsightly, as is unfortunately often the case now, but the weeds will be covered by the grain and be made inconspicuous."[29] *This desire for a pure church, along with excommunication policies, was common in fundamentalist evangelical churches in North America into the twentieth century.*

24. Ibid., 39–122.
25. Ibid., 35.
26. Ibid., 45.
27. Ibid., 57.
28. Ibid., 63–64.
29. Ibid., 81.

Spener, along with August Hermann Francke (1663–1727), founded the University of Halle, from which were published religious writings and from which came the first Protestant missionaries.[30] This university was influential in the spread of Pietism to Denmark, the Netherlands, Scandinavia, Switzerland, Bohemia, Moravia, Salzburg, Silesia and later to North America and the Mennonite colonies in Russia. Its influence in Russia led to the reform of the Mennonite denomination and subsequent emergence of the Mennonite Brethren Church.

With Puritans active in Great Britain and Pietists in Germany, a movement was afoot to bring a more personal Christianity to the masses, both in Europe and North America.

THE EMERGENCE OF EVANGELICALISM

While the Protestant Reformation was in effect evangelical in nature, evangelicalism as a specific movement did not emerge until the 1700s. Noll suggests that "examples of more personal, more experiential, less formal, less hierarchical Christian faith had always been present in Christian history. But now [in the 1700s] in early modern Europe such examples were proliferating; they led directly to evangelicalism."[31]

Although the word "individualism" was not coined until the 1830s, with the coming of the Age of Reason in the 1700s, the phenomenon was already established. The door was open to question anything. Philosophers and scientists were thinking for themselves. They proposed their own theories, among them, Jean Jacques Rousseau (1712–1778) with his emphasis on spontaneity and spiritual freedom; David Hume (1711–1776) who challenged the rational arguments for the existence of God in *The Natural History of Religion*; and Immanuel Kant (1724–1804) who, in *The Critique of Pure Reason* suggested that "our age is, in especial degree, the age of criticism, and to criticism everything must submit. Religion through its sanctity and law-giving through its majesty, may seek to exempt themselves from it. But they then awaken just suspicion, and cannot claim the sincere respect which reason accords."[32] As a Lutheran Pietist, he believed that living a good

---

30. Ibid., 63.

31. Noll, *The Rise of Evangelicalism*, 53.

32. Kant, *The Critique of Reason*, 9.

life was what religion was all about. These theories often conflicted with the traditional orthodox teachings of the Roman Catholic Church.

And with more frequent travel to the New World, which held new economic opportunities, came a sense of freedom. Here, New England colonists had more space, both physically and psychologically, to think for themselves.

Considering the trend toward individualism, it is no surprise that the revivalist movement of the 1700s emphasized the experience of individual sin, guilt, and judgment, as well as individual personal conversion.

In this new evangelical era, important key people were instrumental in the growth of the movement. Allow me to introduce them.

Prominent Evangelical Leaders in the Eighteenth Century

John Wesley (1703–1791) and his brother Charles (1707–1788) belonged to the Church of England in Great Britain and were influenced by Puritanism, Pietism, and the Moravians. Both were students at Oxford University. George Whitefield (1714–1770), also of the Church of England, met the Wesleys at Oxford, where he also attended. Jonathan Edwards (1703–1758), a Calvinist theologian, was born in North America and followed in his father's footsteps as minister of a Congregationalist church in Northampton, Massachusetts. Noll wrote that "it is not excessive to claim that the early evangelicals created evangelicalism."[33] In these four men, all evangelicals in the Methodist tradition, we have one of the greatest preachers (Whitefield), a powerful theologian (Edwards), an organizer (John Wesley)[34] and a prolific hymn-writer (Charles Wesley). All played a role in the emergence of evangelicalism in North America.

Charles and John Wesley

In 1730, Charles and John Wesley started what was called the "Holy Club" at Oxford University in Great Britain, modelled after the *collegia pietatis* among German Pietists. (In Germany, meetings revolved around Bible study and Pietism.)

33. Noll, *The Rise of Evangelicalism*, 142.
34. Ibid., 141–142.

Six years later, Charles and John Wesley took a boat to Georgia in North America along with some Moravians. It was on this voyage that the Wesleys learned from the pietistic Moravians on board that one could enjoy assurance of salvation.[35] This was a huge discovery for John Wesley. He wrote, "I felt I did trust in Christ, Christ alone for salvation, and an assurance was given me that he had taken away *my* sins, even *mine,* and saved *me* from the law of sin and death."[36] Despite this assurance, however, John continued to be haunted by his own sense of sinfulness and the lack of assurance of forgiveness, as he wrote in 1766, thirty years later, "I do not love God. I never did. . . . Therefore I am only an honest heathen."[37] Noll remarks that "the Wesley whose preaching brought confident assurance to so many others would sometimes lack that assurance himself."[38]

While Charles was the primary hymn writer, John also wrote a few hymns. "We Lift Our Hearts to Thee" shows his struggle with his own sense of sin and his hope for assurance:

> We lift our hearts to Thee,
> O Day Star from on high!
> The sun itself is but Thy shade,
> Yet cheers both earth and sky.
>
> O let Thine orient beams
> The night of sin disperse,
> The mists of error and of vice
> Which shade the universe.
>
> How beauteous nature now:
> How dark and sad before!
> With joy we view the pleasing change,
> And nature's God adore.
>
> O may no gloomy crime
> Pollute the rising day;
> Or Jesus' blood, like evening dew,
> Wash all the stains away.

35. Catholic authorities had driven Moravians out of their country and a Saxon count, Nicholas Ludwig von Zinzendorf (1700–1760), became active in sheltering these refugees. In 1722, at his estate in Hernhut, Germany he established a place where those who had been exiled could safely settle. Here Zinzendorf encouraged a Pietistic revivalist faith.

36. Noll, *The Rise of Evangelicalism,* 97.

37. Ibid., 98.

38. Ibid.

May we this life improve,
To mourn for errors past;
And live this short, revolving day
As if it were our last.

In this song, references to a "night of sin," "mists of error," and "gloomy crime" are evidence of Wesley's despair. His hope was that all the stains would be washed away and that God's "orient beams" would get rid of sin, error, and vice.

Small groups gathered under the direction of the Wesleys but it was not until 1744 that they organized a conference, later regarded as the first Methodist conference. At this conference the following beliefs were affirmed:

1. Justification by faith.

2. Repentance and good works.

3. Assurance of salvation for every Christian, but varying degrees of this assurance.

4. Importance of holiness.[39]

It was not their intention to start a new church, but simply to rejuvenate the Church of England and Methodism was only established as a separate sect in 1808.[40]

Jonathan Edwards and the First Awakening

With Pietist and Puritan influence in the colonies, North America was ripe for revivalism. In the 1720s the Dutch Reformed churches of New Jersey and Scotch-Irish Presbyterians in Pennsylvania experienced revival.[41] The emphasis was on repentance and salvation.

Among the Congregationalists, a key event that signalled the beginning of a grand revival in North America in 1730 was what is called the First Great Awakening. Jonathan Edwards was one of its key figures. Edwards's grandfather, Solomon Stoddard had already been preaching in the 1720s about the need for conversion.[42] Edwards's father, Timothy

39. Ibid., 125–26.
40. Cusic, *The Sound of Light*, 33.
41. Hustad, *Jubilate!*, 147.
42. Hart et al., *The Legacy of Johathan Edwards*, 69.

Edwards, a preacher in a Congregational Church in Connecticut, was also concerned with conversion.[43] But it wasn't until 1734, with Jonathan Edwards as preacher in Northampton, Massachusetts, that large numbers of people became converted. That year, within the space of six months, three hundred people were converted in that region alone.

When news of Edwards's success reached his church in England, he was requested to record all the experiences of those converted. And two years later, he sent his report to England, entitled, "A Faithful Narrative of the Surprising Work of God." [44] (Edwards was thirty-three years old at the time.) From his lengthy report we can tell that Edwards was not the only preacher involved in "saving souls." Nor was Northampton the only city in which conversions took place. He wrote that "this remarkable pouring out in the Spirit of God, which thus extended from one end to the other of this county, was not confined to it, but many places in Connecticut have partaken in the same mercy."[45] He found these conversions extraordinary, both with regard to the number of people whose lives were being changed, as well as the broad spectrum of ages, from children to elderly persons. His report went on to describe what the conversions entailed. While he found that some were converted suddenly, for others it happened gradually. However, all of them were first convinced of "a sense of their miserable condition by nature," then were afraid they would be eternally lost and then realized what they needed to do in order to escape hell.[46] There was always the feeling that God was angry about their sin, that they didn't deserve to be saved and that they were too wicked for God to accept them. They believed God was just in condemning them and that they were worthy of condemnation. The last stage in their conversion process was the realization of the grace of God to forgive them. He wrote, "It was very wonderful to see how persons' affections were sometimes moved, when God did, as it were, suddenly open their eyes, and let into their minds a sense of the greatness of his grace, the fullness of Christ, and his readiness to save, after having been broken with apprehensions of divine wrath, and sunk

43. Ibid., 68.
44. Edwards, "A Faithful Narrative."
45. Ibid., 5.
46. Ibid., 8.

into an abyss, under a sense of guilt which they were ready to think was beyond the mercy of God."[47]

Near the end of his report Edwards noted that "the Spirit of God was gradually withdrawing from us, and after this time Satan seemed to be more let loose."[48] He initially came to this conclusion because someone had committed suicide, which Edwards attributed to Satan's influence. At the same time there seemed to be fewer conversions in comparison to the previous masses of people who had responded to his preaching.[49] This called for a stronger message. So five years after Edwards submitted his report, he preached a sermon in Enfield, Connecticut entitled, "Sinners in the Hands of an Angry God," a sermon that emphasized the extreme wickedness of every human being, the readiness of the devil to throw them into hell, and God's anger with human beings' wickedness.[50] Edwards wrote that, "the wrath of God burns against them . . . the pit is now prepared, the fire is made ready, the furnace is now hot, ready to receive them; the flames do now rage and glow. . . . The sovereign pleasure of God, for the present, stays his rough wind; otherwise it would come with fury, and your destruction would come like a whirlwind."[51]

Since the conversion rate was down, it is no wonder that Edwards began to preach this kind of sermon. It seems he was trying to scare them into heaven. It may have been Edwards who first coined the expression, "fire and brimstone," which appears in this classic sermon.

Edwards's sermons were always showered with quotations from the Bible, partly a reflection of his attitude toward the Enlightenment, which emphasized reason and the reasonableness of faith. Edwards took a different approach. He believed that while reason helped to understand certain things, revelation contained "the key to understanding the mysteries of religion. . . . Rather than use reason like others in the Enlightenment tradition, Edwards relied on Scripture."[52]

Edwards's life took a different turn when in 1750 he was dismissed as minister of the Northampton Church. His grandfather Stoddard had

---

47. Ibid., 15.
48 Ibid., 29.
49. Ibid., 30.
50. Edwards, "Sinners in the Hands of an Angry God."
51. Ibid., 2, 4.
52. Hart, *The Legacy of Jonathan Edwards*, 67.

had an open attitude towards the Eucharist, which they called Communion. Stoddard allowed all to take Communion in hopes it would bring people to Christ.[53] Edwards had a different opinion. He felt that Communion should be open only to those who were full members of the church.[54] With this conviction, expressed in his *An Humble Inquiry Concerning Communion,* he drew clear boundaries and narrowed the gap of those who could accept Communion.[55] This practice of exclusion carried over into the fundamentalist evangelical movement. *In the church I attended as a teenager, only those who were baptized by immersion could participate in Communion. All others had to physically leave the sanctuary during the taking of the bread and the wine. They were not even allowed to witness what was going on in the service. As a child, it seemed so mysterious to me. I wondered what was going on upstairs in the sanctuary while we who were not yet baptized waited in the basement.*

Meanwhile, back in England, George Whitefield joined the "Holy Club" at Oxford University and experienced a conversion in 1735.

George Whitefield

Besides preaching in various Church of England churches, Whitefield organized small groups of people who met for prayer and exhortation. In 1737, in the space of three months, he preached more than one hundred times, "He preached like no one Londoners had ever heard before. In the pulpit he simply exuded energy; his speech was to the highest degree dramatic; he offered breathtaking impersonations of biblical characters and needy sinners; he fired his listeners' imagination; he wept profusely, often and with stunning effect. When he was announced as the preacher, churches were jammed."[56]

In 1739 he travelled to North America, preaching in Georgia, and the next year he "addressed crowds of up to eight thousand people nearly every day for over a month."[57] When he preached, he was able to easily elicit an emotional response, as Sarah Pierrepont Edwards (Jonathan Edwards's wife) described, "It is wonderful to see what a spell he

53. Nichols, *Jonathan Edwards: A Guided Tour of His Life and Thought,* 128.

54. Ibid.

55. Ibid.

56. Noll, *The Rise of Evangelicalism,* 89.

57. Noll, *A History of Christianity,* 91.

casts over his audience by proclaiming the truths of the Bible. I have seen upwards of a thousand people hang on his words with breathless silence, broken only by an occasional half-suppressed sob."[58]

During that year he also preached in South Carolina, Pennsylvania, New York, Connecticut, Rhode Island, Massachusetts, New Hampshire, and Maine.

And he was not the only evangelist at the time. George A. Rawlyk writes that "for every Whitefield in the eighteenth century, there were hundreds of lesser known evangelists . . . who felt themselves to be the special conduits of the Holy Spirit bringing about the defining evangelical moment—the New Birth."[59] And some of these were in Canada. Evangelicalism in the form of the Calvinist New Lights, those who believed in an emotional, experiential faith, was brought to Nova Scotia by Henry Alline (1748–1784), who arrived there at a young age with his parents. Converted in 1775, he began preaching in the style of George Whitefield.[60]

NINETEENTH CENTURY EVANGELICALISM IN NORTH AMERICA

The Second Awakening, beginning in the late eighteenth century and continuing into the 1800s, was a time of great revival, with Charles Grandison Finney (1792–1875), a Presbyterian-Congregationalist, as one of its key figures. Finney was the primary evangelist in New York and the one to institute the "anxious bench," a bench placed at the front of the congregation where sinners could sit for special prayer during the service. (The "anxious bench" is the precursor to the altar call that came into existence later on.) Nancy Ammerman says that Finney was "the first to articulate the goal of revivalism as 'winning souls' and the first to set out a step-by-step method for achieving that goal and calculating its success."[61]

Finney, unlike some other evangelists, believed that moral reforms should be part of the new-found faith. Thus, evangelicals in New England encouraged abstinence from alcohol, established asylums, and worked against slavery. Some of the values of the movement was that it stressed the worth of each human being; it advocated penal and

58. Noll, *The Rise of Evangelicalism*, 106.

59. Rawlyk, *The Canada Fire*, xiii.

60. Noll, *A History of Christianity*, 128.

61. Ammerman, "North American Protestant Fundamentalism," 18.

education reform; and it stood for equality of race and class.[62] However, "changing the world was never as important for the early evangelicals as changing the self or as fashioning spiritual communities in which changed selves could grow in grace."[63]

Francis Asbury (1745–1816) was another influential leader in the Second Awakening. At twenty-six years old, he became a "circuit-rider," annually riding on horseback across North America to preach the gospel of salvation. When Asbury arrived in North America in 1771, there were about three hundred members in Methodist societies. Forty years later there were over three hundred thousand, due to a great extent to his preaching.[64]

During the Second Awakening, revivals in Kentucky and Tennessee took place at camp meetings. Thousands of pioneers would gather at a particular site for several days to listen to preachers, eat together, and sing. The most well known camp meeting took place in Cane Ridge, Kentucky in 1801 at which ten thousand to twenty-five thousand people assembled. Meetings lasted for several days and people were encouraged to spend the night at the site. Several preachers were brought in and participants experienced emotional transformations under their preaching, with accompanying jerking, falling, dancing, and laughing.[65] These camp meetings led to a growth of Presbyterian churches in the South.

This Awakening had a definite appeal to ordinary folk. At a time when people were dominated by a ruling highly educated elite and felt they had no voice, this personal, experiential kind of faith gave them a sense of being able to act. They could interpret the Bible for themselves. In addition, the movement brought "the revolutionary modern ideals of democracy, equality, freedom of speech and independence to the folk in an idiom that uneducated people could understand and make their own."[66]

In both the First and Second Awakenings there was a strong emphasis on personal salvation and a concern for renewal throughout the world. The difference between the two was that the First Awakening was led by Anglicans (George Whitefield), Congregationalists (Jonathan

---

62. Armstrong, *The Battle for God*, 92.

63. Noll, *The Rise of Evangelicalism*, 262.

64. Ibid., 190.

65. Finke, *The Churching of America 1776–2005*, 92–99.

66. Armstrong, *The Battle for God*, 89.

Edwards) and Presbyterians; and the Second Awakening was led by Methodists, Baptists, and Disciples. The First took place in urban areas, the second, in rural communities.

Due to these revivals, evangelicalism dominated the religious landscape in North America by the middle of the nineteenth century. Baptist and Methodist churches grew substantially and missionary societies were established to spread Christianity throughout North America and to other countries. The American Bible Society and the American Tract Society were formed in order to produce literature to convert Americans. Voluntary societies were organized to bring Christian education, through Sunday Schools and colleges, to Americans.[67]

There was a great impetus to revive the nation and to evangelize the entire world. Missionary training institutes were established and with the priority of missions, women became more involved. They had opportunities to preach and evangelize, in fact, already in 1837 Mary Lyon had opened a female seminary in Massachusetts to train missionary wives and single missionaries in liberal arts, domestic work, and ministry. Soon women's mission boards and mission societies were active in sending out female missionaries and supporting mission work.

Along with the Awakenings, divisions arose within evangelical churches and new denominations emerged. The Salvation Army started its work in the United States in 1880. In 1895, Charles Fox Parham (at age twenty-three) left the Methodist church to preach sanctification as a "second work of grace," as well as the "third blessing" (the baptism of the Holy Spirit).[68] These teachings were instrumental in the establishment of the Pentecostal movement.

The special emphasis on sanctification, which was evident in the Holiness movement in the early 1800s, led to the establishment of Holiness churches such as the Church of God and the Church of the Nazarene. Phoebe Palmer, who published *The Way of Holiness* in 1843, was one of the most well known Wesleyan Holiness speakers. While it was unusual for women to preach, there were some who did. Both Palmer and Catherine Booth (co-founder of the Salvation Army) advocated for female preaching.[69]

---

67. Noll, *A History of Christianity*, 227–30.

68. Balmer, *Encyclopedia of Evangelicalism*, 437.

69. Bebbington, *The Dominance of Evangelicalism*, 225.

Julia A.J. Foote (1823–1901) was "the first woman in the African Methodist Episcopal Zion Church to receive ordination as a deacon."[70] Like Finney, she was an itinerant preacher, travelling in Pennsylvania, New York, and Ohio, as well as preaching at camp meetings.[71] But this did not mean that churches approved of female preachers. In fact, her membership was withdrawn when she refused to stop preaching and it wasn't until much later, after she served as a missionary, that she was ordained as deacon.[72]

Dorothy Ripley (1767–1831) was another itinerant preacher, working as an evangelist to "enslaved Africans, slave owners, Native Americans, the imprisoned, infirm, and dying."[73] Her concern was not only for the salvation of these folk, but also for their well-being. Alongside her preaching ministry she had a passion for social justice.[74]

Nineteenth Century Evangelicalism in Canada

Noll states that in Canada, Christianity "was less fragmented, more culturally conservative, more closely tied to Europe, more respectful of tradition, more ecumenical, and less prone to separate evangelical theology. . . . But the greatest difference . . . Canada was not so much *a* Christian nation as *two* Christian nations, Catholic and Protestant."[75]

Lower Canada (Quebec) was predominantly Roman Catholic but Protestantism dominated Upper Canada (Ontario) religious culture, with Anglicans, Presbyterians, and Methodists being the primary Protestant groups. In 1842, the largest denomination in Upper Canada was the Anglican Church, which was later surpassed by Methodists and then Presbyterians. The Baptist church one of the smaller denominations.

After the War of 1812, when Upper and Lower Canada gained greater freedom from the influence of their southern neighbors, they tended to be more influenced by European movements than those of the United States. This meant they were more open to the theory of evolution and biblical criticism, yet holding to evangelical doctrine

70. Warner, *Saving Women*, 103.

71. Ibid., 132, 136.

72. Ibid., 133, 137.

73. Ibid., 17.

74. Ibid., 16–18.

75. Noll, *A History of Christianity*, 284.

and experience. Torontonian Nathaniel Burwash (1839–1910) was one of the leaders who held to evangelical beliefs such as original sin and new birth and yet was progressive in his openness to Darwin's theories and higher criticism. His work was instrumental in later uniting a large segment of Methodists, Congregationalists, and Presbyterians into the United Church of Canada in 1925.[76]

Thomas McCulloch (1776–1843), a Presbyterian minister, went to Nova Scotia from Scotland in the early 1800s and espoused a Protestantism that emphasized the authority of the Bible and the importance of a personal experience with Christ.[77]

The same kinds of religious movements that took place south of the border, such as the camp meeting phenomenon, were also evident in Canada. Methodist leader, Egerton Ryerson (1803–1882), was an itinerant preacher. Having experienced conversion himself, he preached the necessity of conversion and he believed that one of the best ways to do this was through the camp meeting. Another leader, John Strachan (1778–1867) of the Anglican tradition, emphasized a more orderly religion.[78]

With the completion of the Canadian-Pacific Railway in 1885, immigrants came to Canada from Europe, most of them settling in Ontario and the West. As a result, the number of Protestant denominations grew, with Lutherans, Mennonites, Greek Orthodox, and Ukranian Catholic arriving in significant numbers.[79]

Reasons for the Emergence of Evangelicalism

When we look for reasons why the evangelical movement emerged and grew, the answer is complex. We could look at it from the perspective of those within the evangelical system, those outside of the system but within Christianity, or those in this century looking back to the phenomenon from an outside perspective. According to those within the movement, from Martin Luther onward, evangelicalism was a work of God that brought Christians back to practicing Christianity as the early followers of Jesus did. They were convinced that the church had strayed from true Christian faith. The revivals of the 1700s were seen as

76. Ibid., 276–78.
77. Ibid., 263.
78. Ibid., 268–71.
79. Ibid., 284.

"the manifestation of the outpouring of the Holy Spirit."[80] The intent of eighteenth century evangelicals "was not to create new denominations but to found voluntary associations which might leaven the lump of existing churches, and charge them with fresh energy."[81] This was the intention of leaders like Whitefield, the Wesleys, and Jonathan Edwards, but what happened is that evangelicals started to use "the authority of personal religious experience and personal appropriation of Scripture to attack inherited religious authority."[82] And this resulted in schisms and the formation of new Protestant denominations.

According to those outside of evangelicalism (i.e., the Roman Catholic Church and the Church of England), the movement was perceived as heretical and thus evangelical Christians were sometimes imprisoned, tortured, and even killed. From their perspective, evangelicalism started with people who departed from orthodox Christianity, which was considered to be the true and only way.

Looking back with twenty-first century eyes we see that the Reformers (like Martin Luther, John Calvin, John Knox, and Menno Simons), by reacting to Roman Catholic doctrine, began a trajectory that resulted in an evangelical movement. This was spurred on by the Wesleys, Whitefield, and Edwards, all of them young, charismatic, powerful leaders who were highly influential in the emergence of the evangelical movement in North America. And in addition, the individualism that emerged in the 1700s had an impact on the formation of an evangelical Christianity in which individual salvation played a strong role.

Noll summarizes the roots of evangelicalism well when he says that, "evangelicalism grew out of earlier forms of heartfelt British Protestantism and was stimulated by contact with heartfelt Continental Pietism. It was grounded religiously in the innovative preaching of justifying faith. It was promoted and maintained by the effective exertions of capable spiritual leaders. . . . It represented a shift in religiosity away from the inherited established churches toward spiritual communities constructed by believers themselves."[83] This evangelicalism became the foundation for the fundamentalism that emerged in North America in the late nineteenth century.

80. Noll, *The Rise of Evangelicalism*, 139.

81. Ibid., 147–48.

82. Ibid., 220.

83. Ibid., 154.

3

Emergence and Growth of Fundamentalist Evangelicalism in North America

THE USE OF THE term "fundamentalist" to describe certain Protestant evangelical Christians was first proposed on the occasion of a Bible conference held in Buffalo, New York in 1920. It was at this meeting that Curtis Lee Lawes (1868–1946), a Baptist conference participant and editor of the Baptist periodical *The Watchman Examiner*, stood up and made the following motion, which was passed: "We here and now move that a new word be adopted to describe the men [*sic*] among us who insist that the landmarks shall not be removed. . . . We suggest that those who still cling to the great fundamentals and who mean to do battle royal for the fundamentals shall be called 'Fundamentalists.'"[1]

This chapter will look at the religious context within which fundamentalism developed in North America, the factors that led to its emergence among Protestant evangelical Christians and the reasons why these Christians felt it necessary to "do battle royal for the fundamentals." It will also discuss the growth of fundamentalist evangelicalism in the early 1900s.

Protestant Christianity in North America was essentially evangelical in the 1800s.[2] It was the emergence of fundamentalism that was instrumental in separating evangelical Christianity into conservative and liberal camps; there was a sense of us versus them. When the fundamentalist movement was named as such in the early 1900s, evangeli-

---

1. Harris, *Fundamentalism and Evangelicals*, 19.
2. Marsden, *Fundamentalism and American Culture*, 10, 12.

cal Christians who bought into the movement moved towards a literal interpretation of the Bible and those Christians who interacted with scholarly biblical criticism, which had recently reached North America from Germany, moved towards a more liberal, metaphorical approach. Within the literal approach a logical framework, namely, dispensationalism, was designed, within which apparent contradictions in the Bible could be explained.

RELIGIOUS CONTEXT FOR FUNDAMENTALIST EVANGELICALISM

Ernest R. Sandeen, who was Professor of History at Macalester College in Minnesota, was a National Book Award finalist for his book, *The Roots of Fundamentalism: British and American Millenarianism 1800–1970*.[3] He argued that fundamentalism had its origin in millenarianism, a movement that emphasized the doctrine of the second coming of Christ and accepted a literalist approach to the Bible. In the early 1800s millenarianism was brought to North America from Europe. By the 1840s dispensationalism dominated the millenarian movement in the United States and Canada.[4]

Millenarianism received its name from the thousand-year period of time referred to in Revelation 20:2–3, "He seized the dragon, that ancient serpent, who is the Devil and Satan, and bound him for a thousand years, and threw him into the pit . . . until the thousand years were ended. After that he must be let out for a little while." Interpreting the words of Revelation literally, some millenarians believed that Jesus would come back to earth before the thousand year period. These were the premillenialists. Those who believed Jesus would come back after the thousand year period were referred to as postmillennialists. Evangelicals took on premillenialism because they felt morality was in decline, a result of the social changes brought about through urbanization and industrialization in the 1800s. Believing that Jesus would return for them before the thousand years referred to in Revelation meant they would be out of this bad world sooner. And the particular type of premillenialism in which they believed was called dispensationalism.

---

3. Sandeen, *The Roots of Fundamentalism.*

4. Ibid., 55.

Theories of dispensationalism were discussed at prophetic Bible conferences and out of these conferences emerged lists of fundamental beliefs.

Dispensationalism

Dispensationalism was brought to North America by John Nelson Darby (1800–1882) of Britain. After practicing law in London, he became a minister in the Church of England at the age of twenty-five. Two years later he joined a small group that was studying the Bible on their own and in 1831 he became an important leader within the Plymouth Brethren, a group that had just been organized in England. It was within this Christian group that Darby developed an interpretation of the Bible that proposed the division of all human history into different ages/dispensations.[5] Dispensationalist thought varied as to the number of time periods envisioned and what exactly had happened or would happen in each period. One paradigm referred to seven time periods: Innocence (Garden of Eden), Conscience (Adam to Noah), Human Government (Noah to Abraham), Promise (Abraham to Moses), Law (Moses to Christ), Grace (Christ to the judgment of the world) and Kingdom or Millennium (during which the church becomes the bride of Christ and Israel gets the land).[6] Current history was believed to be in the period of Grace. Jesus would be returning soon to gather the "saved" ones to be with him (the final dispensation).

Between 1859 and 1874 Darby made several visits to North America, where men like Dwight Moody (1837–1899) and Cyrus Ingerson Scofield (1843–1921) were taken with his ideas. In fact, Scofield, a prominent dispensationalist and Congregationalist minister, published an annotated study Bible in 1909, called the Scofield Reference Bible. This particular Bible is the King James Version, complete with study notes heavily based on a literal-factual reading of the Bible, along with dispensationalist interpretation.[7] One example of his annotation on the biblical text is his interpretation of 1 Corinthians 15, which talks about the resurrection of Jesus and of those who have died. His notes,

---

5. Balmer, *Encyclopedia of Evangelicalism*, 171.

6. Sandeen, *The Origins of Fundamentalism*, 4.

7. Harris, *Fundamentalism and Evangelicals*, 84.

immediately following the pertinent verses in 1 Corninthians, explain the resurrections according to his own dispensationalist thought:

> The "first resurrection," that "unto life," will occur at the second coming of Christ (I Cor 15:23), the saints of the Old Testament and church ages meeting Him in the air (1Thess 4:16–17); while the martyrs of the tribulation, who also have part in the first resurrection (Rev 20:4), are raised at the end of the great tribulation. . . . The mysteries of the kingdom will be brought to an end by the "harvest" (Matt 13:39–43,49–50) at the return of the King in glory, the church having previously been caught up to meet Him in the air (1 Thess 4:14–17). Upon His return the King will restore the Davidic Monarchy in His own person, re-gather dispersed Israel, establish His power over all the earth, and reign one thousand years. . . . The kingdom-age constitutes the seventh Dispensation.[8]

Prior to the publication of the Scofield Bible, Scofield had offered courses of Bible study by correspondence.[9] These courses fed into the writing of his Reference Bible. This Bible became very popular in evangelical churches both in the United States and Canada and was one of the factors that led to the growth of the fundamentalist evangelical movement in North America. This same perspective was later evident in Hal Lindsey's *Late Great Planet Earth*[10] and the *Left Behind Series* and movies.[11]

What helped the initial spread of dispensationalism was a series of Bible conferences, called the Niagara Bible Conference.

Niagara Bible Conference

From 1868 to 1900 a small group of leaders, later called the Niagara Group, held summer conferences for one or two weeks each year, focusing on millenarian/dispensationalist ideas. From 1883 to 1898 these were held in Canada at Niagara-on-the-Lake. By 1890 this series of conferences came to be known as the Niagara Bible Conference. In attendance were representatives from various Protestant evangelical

8. Scofield, *Scofield Refernce Bible.*
9. Ibid.
10. Lindsey with Carlson, *Late Great Planet Earth.*
11. Jenkins and Lahaye, *Left Behind Series.*

Christian denominations, including Baptist, Presbyterian, Methodist, Congregationalist, and Lutheran.

International Prophetic Conferences were also being held, with the first one in New York City in 1878 and successive conferences in 1886, 1895, 1901, and 1914. While most of these conferences were fairly small events, those held in 1878 and 1886 were larger and were foundational for the emergence of early American fundamentalism.[12]

The purpose of prophetic conferences was to reinforce Christian teachings, especially with respect to the future of the world and the second coming of Christ. The particular dispensationalist viewpoint most accepted was the belief in a rapture of Christians, followed by the second coming of Christ, taken from a literal reading of verses in 1 Thessalonians, "For the Lord himself . . . will descend from heaven, and the dead in Christ will rise first. Then we who are alive, who are left, will be caught up in the clouds together with them to meet the Lord in the air" (1 Thess 4:16–17). It was believed that this rapture could happen at any moment, as a literal reading of the text in Matthew indicates, "Then two will be in the field; one will be taken and one will be left. . . . Keep awake therefore, for you do not know on what day your Lord is coming" (Matt 24:40,42).

The majority of those who attended the 1878 conference were from Baptist and Presbyterian denominations, mostly from the United States. Four Canadians were in attendance. However, this is not to say that Canadian influence in the fundamentalist movement was minimal. On the contrary, between 1870 and 1950 Canadians were also instrumental in shaping fundamentalist evangelicalism in North America.[13]

The Fundamentals

The Niagara Group produced fourteen articles, which they considered to be fundamental to the Christian faith. These articles, called "The 1878 Niagara Creed," were put forward and accepted at the 1878 conference. They were:

---

12. Dollar, *A History of Fundamentalism*, 43–48.
13. Rawlyk, *Amazing Grace*, 350.

1. Inspiration of Scripture,

2. Three persons of the Godhead,

3. The fall of humans from the state of being in the image of God,

4. The transmission of corruption of human nature to the entire race,

5. The necessity to be born again,

6. Redemption by the blood of Jesus,

7. Passing from death to life through accepting Jesus through faith,

8. Assurance of salvation,

9. All Scriptures centering on Jesus,

10. All who are baptized form the church, united by the Spirit,

11. The Holy Spirit sent to help and comfort Christians,

12. The holy calling to walk not according to the flesh but according to the Spirit,

13. Heaven and hell, and

14. The second coming of Christ to usher in the millennial age.[14]

Note that inspiration of the Bible was listed as the first article. It is important to understand that every other article, every other statement of belief flowed from this crucial fundamental.

What made the results of this conference important for the continued development of fundamentalism is the kind of media attention it received. The *New York Tribune* printed the conference presentations and fifty thousand copies were made. This enabled the spread of the ideas presented at the conference and since that time, many conservative Christian groups (including fundamentalist evangelicals) have adapted and incorporated elements of these fundamentals into their own system of beliefs.

In 1895, the International Prophetic Conference put forward a five-point statement of doctrine—inerrancy of the Bible, deity of Christ, virgin birth, substitutionary atonement of Christ, and the physical resurrection of Jesus and his bodily return to earth. Sandeen argues that it was the fourteen articles of the 1878 Niagara Creed that gave shape to the fundamentalist movement. Jerry Falwell, a leader in the movement

14. Sandeen, *The Roots of Fundamentalism*, 273–77.

since the 1980s, points out that the five-point statement has been at the heart of the movement since its inception.[15]

In 1910, the General Assembly of the Presbyterian Church accepted what they felt were the five basic beliefs of fundamentalism, which were very similar to those put forward at the 1895 Conference: inerrancy of Scripture, virgin birth, substitutionary atonement, physical resurrection, and the miracle working power of Christ.[16]

In 1919, R.A. Torrey (1856–1928) organized a world conference on Christian fundamentals in Philadelphia with over six thousand people attending.[17] The result was the establishment of the World's Christian Fundamentals Association. Their 1925 manifesto showed the desperate need of fundamentalists to separate themselves from what they called "modernism." It stated, "The time has come when Fundamentalists and Modernists should no longer remain in the same fold, for how can two walk together except they be agreed? Therefore we call upon all Fundamentalists of all denominations to possess their souls with holy boldness and challenge every false teacher, whether he [*sic*] be professor in a denominational school or state school; whether he [*sic*] be editor of a religious publication or the secretary of a denominational board; and whether he [*sic*] be pastor in a pulpit in the homeland or a missionary on the foreign field."[18]

It was at this conference that what had been called the millenarianist movement was changed to be called the fundamentalist movement.[19]

What is significant about this development is that the militant adherence to the succinctly expressed fundamentals resulted in a fork in the road for Protestant Christianity. It brought about a clear boundary between "liberals" and fundamentalists. Some veered toward a fundamentalist evangelicalism and others toward a more liberal Christianity that took into account philosophical thought, modern biblical scholarship, and scientific advances. This then led to ecclesiastical fighting and posturing for control of seminaries, publications, etc. It also led to a number of church divisions. To this day, "liberals" are demonized by the ideological grandchildren of fundamentalists, many of whom prefer to be called conservative or right wing Christians.

---

15. Falwell, *The Fundamentalist Phenomenon*, 7.

16. Sandeen, *The Origins of Fundamentalism*, 22.

17. Ammerman, North American Protestant Fundamentalism," 23–24.

18. In *Gospel Witness*, 18 June 1925 (quoted in Rawlyk, *The Canada Fire*, 360).

19. Sandeen, *The Roots of Fundamentalism*, 246.

The Fundamentalist Mindset

Fundamentalist evangelicals became immersed in a sub-culture that became their only and complete identity. Everything was informed by and related to their belief system—their social networks, their authority figures, their behaviour, their thinking, and their interpretation of the Bible as literal-factual truth. One of the aspects that set them apart from mainstream Christianity was that they held their beliefs in an exclusive way, feeling that they had the only right way to believe. They were convinced that they were the only ones who were preserving the true Christian faith, together with a set of beliefs they defined, a set of beliefs they believed had been there, with their definitions, since the beginning of Christianity. One of these beliefs was that a "true" Christian was one who had had a conversion experience. This further separated fundamentalist evangelicals from other Christians. And to ask the fundamentalist to modify their position was something they were unable to do.[20] They held fiercely to what they considered to be the fundamentals of Christian faith.

Fundamentalist views were expressed as doctrines, not theology. The only discussion around theology that took place was among like-minded people; they didn't know what other thinkers believed because they only studied what fundamentalists believed.[21] There was no openness to other points of view, especially views they considered as liberal approaches. Evidence of the need for an uncompromising position, as early as 1895 when fundamentalism was emerging, can be seen in Britton Tabor's book *Skepticism Assailed, or, The Stronghold of Infidelity Overturned*.[22] The Preface indicates that "there is no conceivable room for a compromise position" and that "the book will . . . prove a revelation to the very many who have been exceedingly anxious lest the foundations of their faith should be undermined."[23]

Another aspect that set them apart was the militancy with which they held these fundamentals. Writings of the time used this kind of language freely. Torrey wrote that opponents of the belief in the Bible's

---

20. Barr, *Fundamentalism*, 17.

21. Ibid., 160, 163–4.

22. Tabor, *Skepticism*.

23. Ibid., xiii.

divine origin were fond of *attacking* the book of Genesis.[24] One of the purposes of the *Sunday School Times* was "*warring* upon the evolutionary philosophy of life" and cartoons in the magazine pictured liberals as *enemies* of the Bible.[25] One of the articles in *World's Work* was entitled "The *War* in the Churches."[26] A book by Maynard Shipley, written in 1927, was called *The War on Modern Science*.[27] In 1981, Jerry Falwell, himself a proclaimed fundamentalist, wrote about the militancy of the movement when it began. He entitled chapter four "The *War* with Liberalism: 1900–1930," and he referred to "The History of the *War*," "a head-on *collision*," "*defense*," "*combat*," and "personalities of the *war*."[28]

Mainstream Protestantism, on the other hand, exhibited an openness to new ideas and continually sought to reinterpret the Bible in the light of new knowledge.

FACTORS THAT GAVE RISE TO THE FUNDAMENTALIST EVANGELICAL MOVEMENT

Emergence of Liberal Biblical Scholarship

One factor that gave rise to the divide between fundamentalist evangelicalism and mainstream Protestant Christianity was the emergence of liberal biblical scholarship that made its way from Germany to North America. Immanuel Kant (1724–1804), for instance, denied the doctrine of original sin and applied critical reason to the Bible. Kant, along with other philosophers, was critical of any kind of orthodoxy, including organized Christianity. Frederick Schleiermacher (1768–1834), who studied under Kant, saw God in humanity, nature, and history; and he downplayed doctrines and creeds. The academic, George William Frederick Hegel (1770–1831), took a philosophical approach to the Bible. According to him, "the world was to be explained as the working out of

---

24. Torrey, *Difficulties and Alleged Errors*, 29. Emphasis added.
25. Cole, *The History of Fundamentalism*, 241–42. Emphasis added.
26. Ibid., 244. Emphasis added.
27. Ibid., 344. Emphasis added.
28. Falwell, *The Fundamentalist Phenomenon*, 78–91. Emphasis added.

a rational principle, namely spirit or the Absolute Idea."[29] David Strauss (1808–1874) denied the existence of miracles and believed that Jesus was only human. F.C. Bauer (1792–1862) said the gospels were written after the first century and thus their reliability was in question. Albrecht Ritsch (1822–1889) focused on the love of God and ignored the idea of God's judgment. He did not believe people would suffer eternally for their sins. The cumulative effect of the work of these scholars was the tendency of many to understand the Bible rationally, as opposed to the fundamentalist evangelical literal understanding, which had a strong emotional base.

A huge threat to conservative Christianity came when Charles Darwin (1809–1882) wrote *The Origin of the Species*. Darwin amassed considerable evidence to show that complex species evolved from simpler forms of life. Even though he never intended this to be an attack on Christianity,[30] and even though some Christians positively engaged Darwin on his thesis, it was seen by much of conservative Protestantism as an attack on the supposed "factual" interpretation of the biblical origin of human life. Because this was seen as a threat to the "truth" of the Bible, conservative Protestants proclaimed biblical inerrancy as a core doctrine of Christianity, thus saving the Bible from Darwinism as well as from biblical higher criticism. Since they felt that Darwinism was a threat to the accuracy of the Bible, they held even more firmly to the belief in the creation of the world as interpreted literally in the Genesis account.

With the division of Protestantism into liberal and conservative camps, those on the conservative side distinguished themselves by holding fast to the literal reading of the Bible without relying on scholars for interpretation.[31] The more liberal understanding of the late 1800s was that the Bible is a history of how God works. It doesn't have to be historically or scientifically accurate. Beliefs were changed as new discoveries were made, as exemplified in a lecture presented at Harvard University in 1873, when the speaker suggested that the world is older than was previously thought.[32] Back in England, already in the mid 1800s, geologists Sir Charles Lyell and Dean Buckland had "established

29. Vidler, *The Church in an Age of Revolution*, 29.

30. Armstrong, *A Short History of Myth*, 130.

31. Marsden, *Understanding Fundamentalism and Evangelicalism*, 32.

32. Cole, *The History of Fundamentalism*, 21.

the geological succession of rocks and fossils, and showed the world to be much older than the accepted date for the Garden of Eden."[33] The conservative Protestant response was that "God had put misleading fossils into the rocks in order to test the faith of mankind [*sic*] or that the 'days' in Genesis One really meant long periods of time."[34] While the shift to liberalism in the 1800s came out of honest struggling with the facts and details of the Bible, conservative Christians saw this as an "attack on the Bible" and on the scriptural foundation of the church.[35]

Fundamentalist George Dollar wrote that after the Civil War in the United States "no large denomination escaped the ravages of Liberalism and radicalism."[36] He believed that before the civil war, the Bible was revered "with an attitude akin to veneration" but after the war, conservative Protestants felt there was a "war against the Word" and that the Bible needed to be defended; Christians needed to be "armed and active in the defence of Scriptural Truth."[37] Because of the perceived "attack" on the Bible by liberal scholars, people began to defend the trustworthiness of the Bible and to "preserve the faith once and for all delivered to the saints."[38] The goal of fundamentalism, then, was to defend the Bible, preserve the faith and maintain conservative Protestant beliefs, complete with the use of military language in defense of the Bible.

Discussions among fundamentalists on the topic of evolution peaked in 1925 in the Scopes Trial.[39] The prosecutor, the State of Tennessee, accused John Scopes of teaching evolution in school. The State won the trial and charged Scopes $100. Other Protestant denominations held similar heresy trials. In 1923/24 Charles Francis Potter, a Unitarian, challenged John Roach Straton, a New York Baptist pastor known as the "fundamentalist pope." These debates were on four specific topics: The Battle Over the Bible, Evolution Versus Creation, The Virgin Birth: Fact or Fiction?, and Was Christ both God and Man? The judge determined that Straton won.[40]

33. Vidler, *The Church in an Age of Revolution*, 114.

34. Dollar, *A History of Fundamentalism*, 115.

35. Ibid., 7.

36. Ibid., x.

37. Ibid., 1, vi.

38. Ibid., 2.

39. Harris, *Fundamentalism and Evangelicals*, 33.

40. Harris, *Fundamentalism and Evangelicals*, 31.

So out of this perceived threat to the Bible, the time was ripe for the fundamentalist movement to flourish so that orthodoxy, seen by the conservative Christian camp as the "true faith," could be defended. The rise of liberal biblical scholarship brought a certain amount of insecurity to the constancy of religious thinking that had previously been the norm. Stuart Sim notes that all fundamentalist thinking, whether religious, political, or economic, arises out of the need for certainty and security.[41] The Protestant fundamentalist movement offered just that, the certainty and stability that people wanted.

Secularization of Society

A second factor that contributed to the emergence of the fundamentalist movement was the secularization of society. The Enlightenment and the industrial revolution of the late 1700s brought with it intellectual, technological, and social changes in the 1800s. Science began to play a more prominent role in people's lives, for example, people realized that a good physician could heal the sick and that it didn't all depend on prayer. When people moved from rural communities to urban areas, and from self-employment to work in factories, life was not as simple as it once had been. The support and strictures of the rural community were gone.[42] Life became more secularized and the city held tempting pleasurable attractions. These factors were a huge threat to conservative Christianity.

Women's Roles

The effects of these changes were particularly noticed in women's roles, which were now expanding as women began to move from the private to the public sphere, finding work in factories or as secretaries, teachers, and nurses. Women also enrolled in post-secondary educational programs. They became involved in their communities, joining women's clubs, and becoming active in the suffragette movement. One of the largest clubs being the Women's Christian Temperance Union (WCTU), organized in 1873 in the United States and in 1874 in Canada. With

41. Sim, *Fundamentalist World*, 29.
42. DeBerg, *Ungodly Women*, 13.

more opportunities open to women, they felt they could have a greater role in determining domestic matters, including their desire for children. Women were marrying later in life and the birth rate was going down. As they became less economically dependent on men, divorce rates increased.

While women were gaining new opportunities in the public sphere, men's work was also changing. They were now working as employees in factories and corporations. They were no longer their own masters; they had to submit to their bosses in the workplace. And their role as masters of the home was threatened when their wives entered the public sphere: attending club meetings and suffragette rallies, working outside the home, and furthering their education. No longer were men able to exercise the same authority they once had in the home.[43] The male hegemony of the Victorian Age was breaking down.

As a result of these changes, conservative Christian denominations were concerned about the expanding roles for women and issues of morality, especially as it pertained to women. Karen Armstrong writes that fundamentalism was a religious system that "functioned . . . to support the gender roles and ideology of the Victorian era well into post-Victorian times" and that this ideology was evident in fundamentalist writings right through 1930.[44]

Leaders in conservative churches did not want Christian women imitating "worldly" women, so they used the written word (in church periodicals) and the spoken word (in sermons) to pressure women to adhere to modest dress standards and submit to their husbands. They made every effort to enforce the paradigm of the ideal virtuous woman who remained within the domestic sphere. They claimed that going back to the inerrant biblical text, as they called it, would restore order in the home, decrease divorces, foster good morals, and keep women in the home. Interpretation of particular biblical texts provided the needed authority to reinforce the sense that Christian women should not participate in worldly activities. One example of the use of biblical texts to keep women out of the public sphere was the equating of the "silly women" in 2 Timothy 3:6 with women in the suffragist movement.[45] Evangelist Dwight Moody indicated that not only was it immodest for

43. Ibid., 147.

44. Armstrong, *The Battle for God*, 148.

45. DeBerg, *Ungodly Women*, 126.

Christian women to emulate the "flapper girl"[46] but, beyond that, it could corrupt men.[47] Christian writers warned that the kinds of activities in which the "flapper girl" engaged could lead to immorality and prostitution. They also spoke against birth control and the suffragette movement, saying that women didn't even want the right to vote. They blamed the immorality and social decay of society on the fact that women were leaving the domestic sphere.

Evangelist Billy Sunday (1862–1935), preached that women could either be the most degraded beings or the purest and that it was women's responsibility to raise the morality of the country. Sunday believed that "all great women are satisfied with their common sphere in life and think it is enough to fill the lot God gave them in this world as wife and mother. . . . It remains with womanhood today to lift our social life to a higher plane. . . . The virtue of womanhood is the rampart wall of American civilization."[48]

At the same time, it must be noted that he preached against men's drunkenness and placed the blame of prostitution on men, "You hurl the burden on the head of the girl; and the double-dyed scoundrel that caused her ruin is received in society with open arms, while the girl is left to hang her head and spend her life in shame. . . . Rid the world of those despicable beasts who live off the earnings of the unfortunate girl who is merchandising herself for gain."[49]

But while there was an effort to keep women in the home, subservient to their husbands, evangelicalism did offer a certain religious freedom that women had not experienced before. Janette Hassey, in *No Time for Silence: Evangelical Women in Public Ministry Around the Turn of the Century*, argues the point that Protestant women in the late 1800s and early 1900s had considerable freedom to attend Christian educational institutions, pastor churches, become missionaries, and work as evangelists.[50] Hassey provides examples of women who were involved in these ways. She cites several reasons for women's greater church involvement at this time. First, evangelical theology promoted a certain

46. "Flapper girl" was the term used for a woman of the world who wore short skirts, had short bobbed hair, and went dancing and to movies.

47. DeBerg, *Ungodly Women*, 107–108.

48. Ellis, *"Billy" Sunday*, 129–130.

49. Ibid., 215.

50. Hassey, *No Time for Silence*, 123–25.

equality for women in Christian ministry. Second, social activism was encouraged among late nineteenth century evangelicals and this activity suited women's traditional roles. It was almost an extension of the women's caring role in the home. And third, men were beginning to recognize the spiritual leadership gifts of women.[51]

Betty DeBerg, in *Ungodly Women: Gender and the First Wave of American Fundamentalism*, argues that the opportunity for women to take on leadership roles in the church was only temporary, and was due to the femininization of religion at the end of the nineteenth century, at which time there were not enough men to fill leadership positions.[52] And for the most part, those women who did take on leadership positions remained in auxiliary positions as lay women. They were only granted roles as church pastors in rural churches where there was a shortage of male preachers and it was clear that they were not to have authority over men.[53] Hassey agrees that evangelicals/fundamentalists adhered to biblical texts that preclude authority over men.[54] She points out that it was Torrey, a teacher at the Bible Institute of Los Angeles, who may have been responsible for curbing women's role in the church, since in 1915 he indicated that the Bible prohibits women from taking a position of authority in the church.[55]

Hassey does recognize that the freedom, albeit somewhat limited, afforded to women in the late 1800s and early 1900s, was short-lived and that between the world wars women were again restricted in their roles. She offers four reasons for the change away from more freedom for women. First, the focus of the fundamentalist movement was directed away from social reform and more towards institutionalization within churches. And women had taken leadership roles in social reform. Second, institutionalization of the movement tended to squeeze women out of leadership roles as seminaries became more geared to professional church ministry for men. Third, church leadership focused on keeping women in the domestic sphere. This is the phenomenon to which DeBerg refers when she talks about the backlash due to "flapper"

51. Ibid., 125–36.

52. DeBerg, *Ungodly Women*, 75.

53. Ibid., 83.

54. Hassey, *No Time for Silence*, 26–29.

55. Ibid.

girl influences.[56] And finally, fundamentalists were re-examining biblical texts as they prepared fundamental principles to which followers should adhere, and among those principles were restricted roles for women.[57] This latter point exemplifies a hermeneutical methodology common in fundamentalism, namely that once a certain value or belief is established, Bible verses are found that support that value or belief. At the same time, they find ways to discredit any position that is not in support of that belief.

DEVELOPMENT OF FUNDAMENTALIST EVANGELICAL THOUGHT

There was a concerted effort on the part of conservative Protestant denominations to keep their people "in the fold" and keep them from being influenced by liberal theology and the effects of the secularization of society. According to Stewart Cole, this was accomplished through strong church leadership, professional evangelism, establishment of Bible schools and Christian associations, increased missionary activity, and literature distribution.[58]

Church Leadership

In the late 1800s and early 1900s key Christian leaders were instrumental in the shaping and growth of the fundamentalist evangelical movement, with the result that existing denominations and new emerging denominations developed a fundamentalist focus. Torrey and Scofield were two of the primary leaders in the movement at this time.

Albert Benjamin Simpson (1843–1919), originally a Presbyterian, shaped the Christian and Missionary Alliance,[59] a denomination that was fundamentalist in belief and practice. He organized branches of this denomination in the United States and Canada, with headquarters in Toronto, Ontario. Simpson spoke out against evolution, biblical criticism, and liberalism.

---

56. DeBerg, *Ungodly Women*, 99–117.

57. Hassey, *No Time for Silence*, 137–43.

58. Cole, *The History of Fundamentalism*, 31.

59. Rawlyk and Noll, *Amazing Grace*, 350–55.

Reverend T.T. Shields (1873–1955), minister of Jarvis Street Baptist Church in Toronto for thirty-five years, was president of the Baptist Bible Union of North America, " a group of militant fundamentalist Baptists whose object was to purge modernism from all Baptist churches, colleges, seminaries, and missionary organizations."[60] In 1948, Shields, together with Carl McIntye, a Presbyterian, formed the International Council of Churches, an organization intended to oppose the World Council of Churches, which was seen as too liberal.[61]

William Henry Griffith Thomas (1861–1924), an Anglican priest, taught at the Anglican Wycliff College in Toronto from 1910 to 1919. Becoming increasingly dispensationalist, he had to resign from this position and moved to Moody Bible Institute.[62] The skeptical attitude towards secular universities was a factor in the emergence of Christian colleges across the country in the early 1900s.

Peter Wiley Philpott (1865–1957), a Canadian preacher, formed networks among fundamentalist evangelicals, with links to the Salvation Army, Christian and Missionary Alliance, the Associated Gospel Churches (which he founded), the Church of the Open Door at the Bible Institute of Los Angeles, and the Moody Memorial Church which, after renovations, seated over four thousand people.[63] Evangelistic campaigns were held at the Moody Memorial Church by Torrey and Billy Sunday. Philpott, along with Shields and a few others, signed the manifesto of the World's Christian Fundamentals Association.

Aimee Semple McPherson (1890–1944), born in Ontario, was the founder of the International Church of the Foursquare Gospel in Los Angeles. Revered as the female Billy Sunday, she preached against modernism and intellectualism through the mediums of evangelistic meetings, radio, and drama.[64]

Oswald J. Smith (1889–1986), after graduating from the Toronto Bible College in 1912, became an evangelist, promoter of foreign missions, author, and hymn-writer.[65] He founded the Peoples Church in Toronto, a church that became a model for mega-churches that emerged

60. Ibid., 365.
61. Ibid., 368.
62. Ibid., 358.
63. Ibid., 359–60.
64. Ibid., 361–64.
65. Ibid., 369.

later, creating, what Rawlyk believes is "the shallowness of so much of late twentieth-century fundamentalism, which has favoured quantity over quality. Religious entertainment replaced worship, and the 'gospel' accordingly often lacked theological depth and a social emphasis."[66]

Professional Evangelism

Professional evangelism sought to bring and keep people within the fundamentalist evangelical faith. Between 1875 and 1900 there were large evangelistic campaigns with "countless thousands converted by the saving grace of God."[67] Cole claims that the majority of these evangelists were unschooled and that the substance of their preaching was ultra-conservative.[68] They emphasized a simple gospel, the authority of the Bible, the conversion experience, a personal relationship with Christ, and the need to bring others to the faith in the same way they had received it. These evangelists "sowed the seeds of doctrinal divisiveness and exclusive sectarianism, which later reaped a full harvest of reactionism against progressive religious culture."[69]

Evangelistic meetings had a particular form that included music—soloists, choirs, and songs sung by everyone—and short testimonies or personal narratives about the Christian experience. The culminating point was the evangelistic sermon, with the high point being the altar call, a time when those who wished to be "born again" or "rededicated to Christ" were invited to come forward for prayer.

One of the most well known evangelical preachers in North America in the 1800s was Dwight L. Moody (1837–1899), an evangelist who preached what he called the three Rs of the Bible: "*ruined* by the Fall, *redeemed* by the Blood and *regenerated* by the Spirit."[70] It was Moody who began Sunday School for children, in order to teach them the Christian faith. It was Moody as well who began the concept of the "inquiry room," a room where people could go for prayer after he had preached his evangelistic sermon and had issued a call for people

66. Ibid., 371.

67. Cole, *The History of Fundamentalism*, 71.

68. Ibid., 37, 40.

69. Ibid., 40.

70. George, *Mr. Moody and the Evangelical Traditions*, 5.

to come forward for counselling.[71] Music played a crucial role in his evangelistic meetings. Moody and Ira Sankey (1849–1908), his musical associate, made a powerful and successful team. Moody claimed that "audiences will forget what I say, but if they learn [the song] 'Jesus Lover of my Soul,' and sing it to themselves . . . they will get the Gospel along with it."[72] In fact it was Moody who popularized the genre of gospel songs within the evangelical world.[73] The Sunday School, evangelistic services with altar calls, and the singing of gospel songs at church services were practices that would continue to be primary vehicles to bring people to accept Jesus and indoctrinate them in fundamentalist evangelical beliefs. Chapter 4 is devoted to understanding the importance of music in the development of fundamentalist evangelicalism.

Another influential preacher was Billy Sunday, a former National League baseball player with Chicago, Pittsburgh, and Philadelphia teams. Sunday converted to Christianity at a rescue mission service. Once converted, he volunteered to help out with logistical matters in the campaigns run by evangelist John Wilbur Chapman (1858–1915).[74] After Chapman resigned from his ministry, Sunday became an evangelist himself. Since he had so much experience organizing meetings, assisting local committees and advertising, Sunday already knew how to conduct evangelistic campaigns.[75] He claimed that one of the secrets to his success was the practice of involving local churches prior to holding evangelistic meetings in a given community. In preparation for each set of evangelistic services in any given town or city, he organized a host of committees, including "a prayer-meeting committee, an entertainment committee, an usher committee, a dinner committee, a business women's committee, a building committee, a decorating committee, a shop-meetings committee . . . "[76] Prayer meetings would be set up across the city and it is said that people were already converted at these meetings, before the evangelistic services even began.[77] In addition, he

71. Ibid., 100–101.
72. Ibid., 108.
73. Ibid.
74. Ellis, *"Billy" Sunday*, 41.
75. Ibid., 56.
76. Ibid., 65.
77. Ibid., 63.

ensured that local newspapers carried news about the meetings, thus advertising them in advance.[78]

Everywhere Sunday went, he constructed large tabernacles in which to hold services, tabernacles with capacities up to twenty-five thousand people.[79] They were made of wood with sawdust aisles. *When I was a girl and attended evangelistic services, the term, "going down the sawdust trail" meant that you were walking down the church aisle when the altar call was given.* William Ellis explains that the term "hitting the sawdust trail" had its origins in the experience of lumbermen who lost their way in the woods. When they came across a trail of sawdust left by other lumbermen, they were able to find their way home. In the same way, claims Ellis, in Sunday's meetings it was the sawdust trail that "led the lost to salvation, the way home to the Father's house."[80]

Being athletic, Sunday's sermons tended to be entertaining; he seemed quite like an actor when preaching. And he was a man of the people, with little education, a point that he was not ashamed to admit, "I don't know any more about theology than a jack-rabbit does about ping-pong, but I'm on the way to glory."[81] While common people resonated with his words, politicians and wealthy people were also brought into the fold of fundamentalist evangelicalism through him.[82]

Ellis claims that the results of his preaching were seen in improved ethical behaviour. Employers treated their employees better, the rich gave to the poor, business practices became more honest, streets were safer, and there was less gossip in the community.[83] It was reported that when Sunday had completed his stint of services in a particular city, saloons would close down because so many people had been converted under him, "Fifteen hundred saloons were put out of business in a single day in Illinois, largely as the result of his work."[84]

It is evident that Sunday was quite aware of the influences of modern scholarship on Christianity. Ellis points out that Sunday was opposed to "modern" scholarship and that he used "an interpreted and

78. Ibid., 62.
79. Ibid., 66.
80. Ibid., 158.
81. Ibid., 121.
82. Ibid., 32.
83. Ibid., 170.
84. Ibid., 81.

annotated edition by one of the most conservative of Bible teachers."[85] This may in fact have been the Scofield Reference Bible, which was mentioned earlier. In one of his sermons, Sunday challenged the audience to go ask the philosopher to figure out "the problems and mysteries of life by the application of reason," the implication being that the philosopher is unable to do this and that reason is not the way to God.[86] And Ellis writes that "modernists" did not like what he was doing.[87]

In any given service, Sunday's primary message focused on the choice between being saved or lost: going to heaven or going to hell.[88] After the sermon he would call people to the front of the tabernacle to be converted. Here he would shake their hands and hand them a tract that told them what it meant to become a Christian and how to live a good Christian life. About this practice Ellis writes, "the unschooled American commoner, who could not pass the entrance examinations of any theological seminary in the land, has publicly grasped the hands of approximately a quarter of a million persons."[89] Behind the stage was a post office so that the names of each of the converted could be mailed to local churches that would follow up with those who made decisions to become Christians. It was reported that approximately three hundred thousand people were converted under Sunday in his twenty-five years of evangelistic ministry.[90]

Establishment of Bible Schools

Another method of keeping fundamentalist evangelical Christians in the fold was through the establishment of Bible schools. In the 1800s, many church-run colleges were established, and in the second quarter of the nineteenth century these theological institutions became more and more secularized. Liberalism became the norm in seminaries, and universities were now based on a scientific model.[91] Conservative Protestants, feeling threatened and feeling the need to reinforce the prin-

85. Ibid., 123.

86. Ibid., 406.

87. Ibid., 146.

88. Ibid., 140.

89. Ibid., 159.

90. Ibid., 17.

91. Marsden, *Understanding Fundamentalism*, 15.

ciple of biblical inerrancy,[92] and other fundamentals, established Bible schools. These operated from a defensive stance in order to preserve the gospel among young people, counter secularism, promote evangelism, and oppose liberal Christianity: "The entire program was a system of precepts supported by biblical proof-texts in order to combat popularly conceived enemies of God's word."[93] Courses had to do with biblical interpretation, doctrine, and theology. Mission work was emphasized and students were encouraged to spread Christianity throughout the world. Some institutions were inter-denominational, while others were denominationally based. By 1850 there were six thousand Protestant denominational Bible schools and colleges in the United States.[94]

To cite a few examples, Princeton Theological Seminary, founded in 1812, began with one professor, Archibald Alexander. Alexander asserted "that everything in the Bible was in accord with scientifically verifiable truth" and this stance pervaded the teaching in the Seminary.[95] The Moody Bible Insitute was founded in 1886 by Moody in Chicago, with the primary goal of training Christians to become evangelists. The Bible Institute of Los Angeles was founded by Torrey in 1908, with financial backing from the same men who funded the production of the twelve volumes of *The Fundamentals*. The Philadelphia School of the Bible was established by Scofield in 1914; and the Northwestern Bible and Missionary Training School in Minneapolis was founded in 1902 by William B. Riley, a fundamentalist leader.[96] In Illinois, Wheaton College, established in 1860, was one of the conservative Protestant colleges with a statement of faith that denied evolution and affirmed the second coming of Christ.[97] In Canada, the Herbert Bible School, a Mennonite Brethren school that taught dispensationalism, was founded in 1913 in Herbert, Saskatchewan. Prairie Bible Institute, an interdenominational school in Three Hills, Alberta, was organized in 1922. It stood for all the fundamentals of the fundamentalist evangelical movement.[98] These are just a few examples of Bible schools, colleges, and institutes that were

92. Ibid., 33–38.
93. Cole, *History of Fundamentalism*, 44.
94. Ibid., 8.
95. Ammerman, "North American Protestant Fundamentalism," 15.
96. Bender, *The Mennonite Encyclopedia*, 330.
97. Cole, *History of Fundamentalism*, 252.
98. Stackhouse, *Canadian Evangelicalism in the Twentieth Century*, 77.

established in order to keep young people within the fundamentalist evangelical faith.

Right after High School I attended the Mennonite Brethren Bible College, a liberal arts Bible college in Winnipeg, Manitoba, for a year. Then I went to Bethany Bible Institute in Hepburn, Saskatchewan. My reason for changing to the Bible Institute was that I was looking for something more personal, more spiritual and I thought Bethany would offer that. At that time, I still had the mindset described in chapter 1 of this book. Even though this was many years after the founding of Bible schools in North America, the reason for being and the courses taught were very similar. I recall taking a course entitled, "Personal Evangelism." One of the activities in which Bible school students were to participate at Bethany was in the area of outreach. This was to prepare students for mission work upon graduation. I decided to enrol in the street witnessing program which met for prayer on Saturday mornings and then travelled thirty miles to Saskatoon to actually do the witnessing. Each person was taken to a street corner in the city and left on his or her own to tell people about Jesus. I still remember my fear and dread thinking about talking to a stranger on the street about his or her soul. I was supposed to "lead them to the Lord."

Religious Associations

Christian associations were established in order to promote the growth of fundamentalism. The focus of the World's Christian Fundamentals Association was pre-millennialism. However, within three years its emphasis changed to working against evolution.[99] Active until 1930, its goal was to work against liberal thought.

In 1918/1919 the Christian Fundamentals League was formed in order to promote evangelical Bible conferences and distribute the Bible and other printed material that spoke against modernism.[100] The League had representatives from a number of countries, including Canada.

The Christian Endeavour Society was formed in 1881 "to promote earnest Christian life and to provide training for Christian service."[101] This society was formed in order to involve young people in the church.

99. Cole, *History of Fundamentalism*, 302.

100. Ibid., 238.

101. Marsden, *Understanding Fundamentalism*, 24.

There were weekly and monthly meetings for young people. The Society grew to 3.5 million members by 1910, with about two-thirds of them in the United States and Canada. *In Mennonite Brethren churches in Saskatchewan, particularly in town and rural churches, periodic Sunday evening meetings, called Christian Endeavour, were held. These were run by young people and were often seen as an opportunity to allow young boys to try out their preaching skills (an opportunity not open to young girls). In this way, church leaders would be able to tell which males might be budding preachers.*

Increased Missionary Activity

With the strong emphasis within the fundamentalist evangelical movement on evangelism—bringing the "lost" to Jesus—it is no surprise that in the late 1800s and early 1900s there was an increase in missionary work, both at home and abroad. And along with this the Sunday School movement was also seen as a way to evangelize children.

George Marsden writes that the period between 1890 and World War I was the time when missionary activity flourished in North America.[102] Nancy Ammerman suggests that the China Inland Mission was "the most famous extra-denominational mission agency."[103] Its goal was to bring the gospel to East Asia. Mission boards were organized in Protestant denominations, directed at both home and foreign missions. The particular mission board of the Mennonite Brethren Church of North America sent missionaries to India at the end of the nineteenth century. In 1898 Nikolai N. and Susie Wiebe-Hiebert were the first couple to be sent to India and in 1899, the first single woman, Elizabeth S. Neufeld, went to India and opened the first mission school in 1903.[104]

Women's church societies in all Protestant denominations were active during this time, with missions as a strong focus. In *The Work of Their Hands: Mennonite Women's Societies in Canada*, I show that Mennonite women, excluded from church leadership, exercised their primary role in the church within the separate church societies which they organized. These societies, not unlike those in other Protestant

102. Ibid., 23.

103. Ammerman, "North American Protestant Fundamentalism," 31.

104. Esau, *First Sixty Years of M.B. Missions*, 96–97.

denominations, contributed vast amounts of energy, time, and money to further the cause of missions and missionary activity overseas. This gave women an opportunity to participate in the mission work of the church on their own terms. Besides raising money for missions, these societies became a context in which women could speak, pray, and creatively give expression to their understanding of biblical texts.[105]

Writings

Another reason for the growth of the fundamentalist movement was the vast amount of printed material that was produced, the largest of which was the *The Fundamentals: A Testimony to the Truth*. Between 1910 and 1915 a huge literature distribution took place that involved the dissemination of over 2.5 million copies of this twelve volume set. This initiative was funded by two wealthy brothers from California, Lyman and Milton Stewart, who founded the Stewart Evangelistic Fund, which was used to spread Christian fundamentalism around the world.[106] The set was edited by A.C. Dixon, Louis Meyer, and Torrey, who had already written books in his own right, including *What the Bible Teaches* and *Difficulties and Alleged Errors and Contradictions in the Bible*. In these works Torrey wrote that we should not be surprised if finite beings have difficulty understanding parts of the Bible, because humans are "imperfect in intellectual development and consequently in knowledge. . . . When the finite tries to understand the infinite, there is bound to be difficulty. When the ignorant contemplate the utterances of one perfect in knowledge, there must be many things hard to be understood."[107] *This is exactly the reasoning I was provided in my youth when I asked questions about contradictions within the Bible. Finite human beings cannot understand an infinite God.*

The twelve volume set of fundamentals included such topics as the virgin birth of Christ, deity of Christ, proof of the living God, history of higher criticism, and personal testimony. They were sent to ministers throughout the United States and Great Britain, Sunday School

---

105. Redekop, *The Work of Their Hands*, 45–62.

106. Cole, *History of Fundamentalism*, 53–54.

107. Torrey, *Difficulties and Alleged Errors*, 9–10.

superintendents, overseas missionaries, and "others engaged in aggressive Christian work throughout the English speaking world."[108]

Proof that the first two volumes were widely read can be seen in the Foreword to the third volume, which stated that the Committee had received ten thousand letters of appreciation. They also received letters of criticism, which the Committee actually found encouraging because they felt it meant the books had been "read by some who need the truth they contain."[109]

Much written material upholding fundamentalist thought was written in the early 1900s, as fundamentalism emerged within Christian Protestant denominations. Evangelical denominations, as well as fundamentalist associations and institutions, had their own religious periodicals within which they could espouse their fundamentalist beliefs. Papers, magazines and journals included *The Truth, Bible Champion, Institute Tie* (a magazine produced by the Moody Bible Institute), *King's Business, The Spirit of Truth and the Spirit of Error, Christian Fundamentalist*, and *World's Work*, to name just a few. These spoke strongly against modernism and science.[110] Cole claimed that the Moody Bible Institute Colportage Association alone sold seventy-five thousand libraries of 125 texts each. He lists over seventy books written during this time, including *The Modernist-Fundamentalist Controversy, Why We Believe in the Virgin Birth of Christ, Modern Religious Liberalism, Modern Conflict Over the Bible, Is the Whole Bible Trustworthy?, The Menace of Modernism, What About Evolution?, The Fundamental Doctrines of the Christian Faith* and *Is the Higher Criticism Scholarly?*[111] Correspondence courses were also popular. Ammerman writes that "in 1937, the Moody Bible Institute enrolled nearly fifteen thousand people in its correspondence programs."[112]

I was fortunate enough to procure a few books that were written in the early 1900s by fundamentalist leaders. These books, used by Canadian and American fundamentalist evangelicals alike, are a sign of the spread of the fundamentalist movement. Scofield offered Bible classes by correspondence and wrote books that people could use for this

---

108. Torrey et al., *The Fundamentals: A Testimony to the Truth*, Preface.

109. Cole, *History of Fundamentalism*, 56.

110. Cole, *History of Fundamentalism*, 45–47, 345.

111. Ibid., 341–45.

112. Ammerman, "North American Protestant Fundamentalism," 33.

purpose, complete with test questions after each chapter. One of these books was the seventh edition of *Synthesis of Bible Truth*. Beginning with Lesson LXX, the book presents over sixty lessons on topics such as justification, redemption, salvation, conversion, forgiveness, etc.[113] Another book, entitled *Dr. C.I. Scofield's Question Box*, contains questions compiled by Ella Pohle, Scofield's assistant. The questions had been addressed to him from people who took his correspondence courses. The first section deals with what he calls "apparent contradictions" in the Bible. One of these refers to the number of Israelites mentioned in Numbers 1:39, which is contradicted elsewhere in the Bible. Scofield's answer is that it is "a mistranslation for which we cannot account.... It is well to remember that seeming contradictions are often due to mistranslations."[114] This was his way of accounting for this contradiction. Other questions have to do with Christian doctrine, and there is also a section on science, with questions and answers about creation and the flood.

Two other books, written by Torrey, were also made available to me. One of them is similar to Scofield's question and answer book, *Difficulties and Alleged Errors and Contradictions in the Bible*. In dealing with these difficulties, Torrey offers reasons for errors, including translation issues, subjective interpretations, defective knowledge, the finiteness of human minds, and "the dullness of our spiritual perceptions."[115] The assumption here is that the Bible is infallible, humans are not. Therefore humans cannot always fully understand what the Bible means. The other book by Torrey is *Personal Work: How to Work for Christ, A Compendium of Effective Methods*. As the title suggests, the book is a how-to guide to bring people to believe in Christ, including those who are not concerned about their souls, sceptics, those who lack assurance of salvation, backsliders, and those who want to put off their decision. He believed that "when the whole church of Jesus Christ shall rouse to its responsibility and privilege in this matter, and every individual Christian becomes a personal worker, the evangelization of the world will be close at hand."[116] This book was used as a textbook in the Moody Bible Institute.

---

113. Scofield, *Synthesis of Bible Truth*.
114. Pohle, *Scofield's Question Box*, 9.
115. Torrey, *Difficulties and Alleged Errors*, 17–25.
116. Torrey, *Personal Work*, 15.

Another book passed on to me, written by Daniel Kauffman, a Mennonite fundamentalist, is *The Conservative Viewpoint*. In it, Kauff- man admonishes Mennonites to hold to the conservative view, with a liberal viewpoint described as "one who chooses to put a flexible con- struction upon the teaching of the Bible as God's Word, holding the orthodox faith secondary in importance to the revelations of science or the demands of the present age."[117] This was a plea to Mennonites not to buy into the findings of science, but to remain true to the fundamentals of Christian faith.

So we can see that through the various forms of printed material, the tenets of fundamentalist evangelicalism spread throughout North America and beyond.

We began this chapter with a discussion on the origin of the term "fundamentalist" and the emergence of the movement out of the dis- pensational movement. We saw that there was a fork in the road in the late 1800s, when evangelicals either remained within mainstream Prot- estantism or opted for a more conservative, fundamentalist position. We also made reference to a unique characteristic of the fundamentalist evangelical movement, that of the militancy with which they held their beliefs.

Marsden sums it up well when he says that in the 1920s funda- mentalism was "militantly anti-modernist Protestant evangelicalism. Fundamentalists were evangelical Christians, close to the traditions of the dominant American revivalist establishment of the nineteenth cen- tury, who in the twentieth century militantly opposed both modernism in theology and the cultural changes that modernism endorsed. . . . Fundamentalism was a loose, diverse, and changing federation of co- belligerents united by their fierce opposition to modernist attempts to bring Christianity into line with modern thought."[118]

Being threatened by the rise of biblical scholarship and the theory of evolution in the mid-nineteenth century, some evangelical tradi- tions embraced the idea that certain fundamentals had to be believed and "fought for" in order to remain part of the true Christian church. Factors that were crucial for the growth of fundamentalist evangeli- calism in North America were strong church leadership, evangelism, establishment of Bible Schools, organization of religious associations,

117. Kauffman, *The Conservative Viewpoint*, 8.
118. Marsden, *Fundamentalism and American Culture,* 4.

missionary activity, and literature distribution. But music also played an important role. It is to this that we now turn.

4

The Role of Singing in Early Fundamentalist Evangelicalism

BY THE TIME THE fundamentalist movement was named in the early 1900s, the beliefs of fundamentalism had already spread through preaching and singing. A proliferation of gospel songs was written in the late 1800s and early 1900s, songs that were instrumental in spreading and reinforcing the fundamentals in evangelical churches. The goal of both evangelists and song leaders during this time was "to assure believers of the continuity of the ageless faith in a rapidly changing world,"[1] and to bring non-believers to conversion.

This chapter analyzes songs written in North America by men and women who wrote them between 1860 and 1920. These years saw tremendous growth in North America, with a population that grew from 31 million in 1860 to 106 million in 1920.[2] It was also a period of growth for Protestantism. Between 1860 and 1900 members in Protestant churches increased from 5 million to 16 million.[3]

In 1860 Abraham Lincoln became President of the United States and the Civil War followed from 1861 to 1865. Because of this unrest, North America was ripe for a message of religious security, and fundamentalism did just that. So when John Nelson Darby, a dispensationalist from London, made visits to North America between 1859 and 1874, some evangelicals were ready for his ideas. With the belief that history

1. Cusic, *The Sound of Light*, 56.
2. Ibid.
3. Ammerman, "North American Protestant Fundamentalism," 14.

was divided into dispensations, there was a greater emphasis on judgment and the afterlife.

In order to place the late nineteenth and early twentieth century song writing into a broader historical context, this chapter first examines the role of Christian music prior to this time. I will then analyze a collection of songs written during this time, all found within one hymnal. I will examine the content of these songs thematically; discuss the life situations of the songwriters and how this impacted their songs; and look at the usage of these songs during the emergence of the fundamentalist evangelical movement.

EARLY CHRISTIAN MUSIC

There is little information available as to the kind of singing that accompanied meetings of Christians in the first century. Biblical accounts talk about singing "psalms, hymns and spiritual songs to God" (Col 3:16). The psalms were likely a carryover from Jewish practice, using Hebrew melodies and responsive chanting.[4] The historian Pliny (governor of Bithynia ca. 111–113 CE) referred to Christians "meeting on a fixed day before daylight and reciting responsively among themselves a hymn to Christ as a god."[5]

At the time of the Council of Laodicea, held 363/364 CE, it was decreed that only appointed singers should be allowed to sing at Christian gatherings.[6] Psalms were sung by cantors and the congregation's participation was limited to responses at the end of each Psalm.[7]

As western Christianity developed, the Roman mass was celebrated as High Mass, Low Mass or the Sung Mass. In the Sung Mass, large sections of the Mass were sung, mostly by the choir. The *Schola Cantorum* (a school at which ecclesiastical chant was taught) was established by Pope Gregory the Great (ca. 540–604 CE) in order to standardize the official western chant to be used in the Roman church.[8]

---

4. Cusic, *The Sound of Light*, 7.

5. Hustad, *Jubilate!*, 96.

6. Cusic, *The Sound of Light*, 8.

7. Hustad, *Jubilate!*, 98.

8. Ibid., 105.

SINGING IN THE SIXTEENTH TO NINETEENTH CENTURIES

At the time of the Reformation in the 1500s, the kind of music sung in Reformation churches was dramatically different from the ecclesiastical chants of the Roman church. Luther put singing into the mouths of the congregation, replacing Latin songs with hymns sung in the language of the people (German) and often set to German folksong melodies. "Of the thirty-seven hymns he composed, twelve were translations from Latin hymns, four from German folk songs, and at least five were 'completely original hymns.'"[9] Although Luther provided the first hymnal to his congregation in 1524, it took a few years for his parish to actually sing these songs in church.[10]

The emergence of the Pietist movement in the late 1600s in Germany brought with it the writing of songs that portrayed an experiential subjective Christianity. One such song was *Jesu, meine Freude*, written by Johann Franck (1618–1677):

> *Jesu, meine Freude* (Jesus, my joy)
> *Meines Herzen's Weide* (My heart's longing)
> *Jesu, meine Zier* (Jesus, my beauty)
> *Ach, wie lang, ach lange* (Oh, how long, how long)
> *Is dem Herzen bange* (Is the heart's concern)
> *Und verlangt nach dir!* (And longing after you!)
> *Gottes Lamm, mein Braütigam* (Lamb of God, my bridegroom)
> *Ausser dir soll mir auf Erden* (May nothing on earth become dear)
> *Nichts sonst Liebers warden* (To me except you).[11]

In this song, Jesus is visualized as someone close to humans, even to the extent of calling Jesus one's bridegroom.

In eighteenth century Great Britain, Anglican songwriters, such as Isaac Watts (1674–1748), began to write hymns and anthems. His first collection of hymns, *Hymns and Spiritual Songs,* was published in 1707.[12] Some of his song writing was based on the Psalms, but more modernized, a departure from the practice of metrical Psalms that were

---

9. Cusic, *The Sound of Light*, 16.

10. Ibid.

11. Hustad, *Jubilate!*, 125.

12. Cusic, *The Sound of Light*, 27.

sung using the exact words of the Psalms. He also wrote hymns not related to the Psalms, "hymns of composure."[13] These were hymns reflecting his own theology and interpretation of the Christian life. One such song was "When I Survey The Wondrous Cross."

> When I survey the wondrous cross
> On which the Prince of Glory died,
> My richest gain I count but loss,
> And pour contempt on all my pride.

Watts's hymns were a reflection of Calvinist theology, which saw God as ruler and humans as sinful. They expressed the concept of election, which meant that certain people were predestined to be saved. For this reason, his songs did not contain an appeal to those who were not Christians.[14]

It was in Great Britain's Great Awakening of the mid-1700s that the precursor to evangelistic gospel songs emerged. These songs, reflecting Methodist theology, were about the need for the individual to make a choice to accept what was believed to be the sacrifice of Jesus for them. Songs now took on an evangelistic appeal, as the following hymn written by Charles Wesley in 1742:

> Arise my soul arise. Shake off thy guilty fears.
> The bleeding sacrifice in my behalf appears.
> Before the throne my surety stands,
> My name is written on his hands.
>
> Five bleeding wounds he bears, received on Calvary
> They pour effectual prayers; they strongly plead for me.
> "Forgive him, oh, forgive," they cry,
> "Nor let the ransomed sinner die."
>
> God is reconciled; his pard'ning voice I hear.
> He owns me for his child; I can no longer fear.
> With confidence I now draw nigh,
> And, "Father, Abba, Father," cry.

In this song, Jesus is seen as the sacrifice for sins, which was a ransom paid for sin, resulting in reconciliation with God. Because of this, people needed no longer be afraid. They became children of God, their Father. We will see that these same themes were also prevalent in the

13. Ibid.
14. Ibid., 28.

revivalist songs of the 1800s in North America, songs that undergirded the evolving fundamentalist evangelical movement.

Songs were starting to be written as a result of people's personal life experiences. In the late 1700s William Cowper tried to commit suicide but failed, following which he felt extremely guilty for having tried to take his life. He felt that in the eyes of God, this was a sin. Later he was convinced of the assurance that God forgave him and washed his guilt away. Following this experience, he wrote "There is a Fountain Filled With Blood":

> There is a fountain filled with blood,
> Drawn from Immanuel's veins
> And sinners plunged beneath that flood
> Lose all their guilty stains
> Lose all their guilty stains, lose all their guilty stains.
> And sinners, plunged beneath that flood,
> Lose all their guilty stains.
>
> The dying thief rejoiced to see that fountain in his day
> And there may I though vile as he, wash all my sins away.
> Wash all my sins away, wash all my sins away.
> And there may I though vile as he, wash all my sins away.

The writing of this song was a result of his strong belief that God forgave him and that he no longer needed to feel guilty. This song was used later in North America in camp revival meetings to bring people to salvation.

When immigrants from Great Britain arrived in North America, they of course brought their songs with them. Hymns in the New England colonies in the early 1700s were mostly psalm tunes, sung in a very slow tempo.

Even during the First Great Awakening under Jonathan Edwards, music at revival meetings continued to be primarily metrical Psalms. It was under George Whitefield, in the mid 1700s, that Watts's songs began to be sung in North America.[15]

As revival continued in North America into the 1800s, songs became more personal and experiential. Charles Finney, a Presbyterian revivalist preacher in the 1830s, together with music educator-composer, Thomas Hastings (1784–1872), published a songbook specifically targeted for revival meetings. This book contained a song for Finney's "altar call":

15. Hustad, *Jubilate*, 128.

Hearts of stone, relent, relent
Break, by Jesus' cross subdued;
See his body, mangled—rent,
Covered with a gore of blood.
Sinful soul, what hast thou done!
Murdered God's eternal Son.

Yes, our sins have done the deed,
Drove the nails that fixed him there,
Crowned with thorns his sacred head,
Pierced him with a soldier's spear;
Made his soul a sacrifice,
For a sinful world he dies.

Will you let him die in vain,
Still to death pursue your Lord;
Open tear his wounds again,
Trample on his precious blood?
No! With all my sins I'll part,
Savior, take my broken heart.[16]

In this song, all human beings are seen as guilty of murdering Jesus. They have done this because of their sins, for which Jesus has had to make the sacrifice of death. In return, they are urged to give their hearts to the "Savior" and sin no more.

Hustad believes that Finney's use of music in revival meetings was "the beginning of a clearly defined evangelistic music ministry."[17] Broughton says that at this time "dreary psalms were being replaced by soul-stirring . . . songs, more closely expressing the simple faith . . . of the people."[18]

The use of the term "gospel song" was the product of revivalism. With the emergence of the "camp meeting" in the early nineteenth century, songs that could be sung by memory, songs that were repetitive and songs that had refrains were used to accompany passionate preaching. These songs were generally referred to as gospel songs.

It was in 1859 that the first of these songs was mass-produced under the title *Devotional Melodies*.[19] Erik Routley points out that

16. Hustad, *Jubilate!*, 130.

17. Ibid.,151.

18. Broughton, *Too Close to Heaven*, 24.

19. Routley, *The Music of Christian Hymns*, 138.

they began to be called "gospel songs" when Philip Bliss, a songwriter, compiled a collection of them in 1874 under the title *Gospel Songs*.[20] The following year, Ira Sankey, singer for Dwight L. Moody's revival meetings, produced a book of songs called *Gospel Hymns and Sacred Songs*. And from then on, this particular genre of evangelical songs was called "gospel songs." Unlike the hymns of Charles Wesley and Watts in the previous century, what characterized these songs was a simple catchy melody and harmony; a lively rhythm; and most always a refrain. In the songs I will examine in this chapter, over 80 percent have refrains, refrains which tend to emphasize the main theological points of the song.

Gospel songs were generally "confined to three chords, the tonic, the subdominant and the dominant."[21] This made them easy to sing. For example, there are the only three chords in the song "There's Not a Friend like the Lowly Jesus." This song is written in the Key of G and begins with the tonic chord, which is the G chord. In the second measure it moves briefly to the C chord (the subdominant) and then back to the G chord. In the third and fourth measures the music alternates between G chord and D chord (the dominant). The pattern of these four measures is repeated in the rest of the song. Since there are only three chords in this song, it makes it easy to play on the piano and easy to sing. The tenor line has only four different notes to sing, as does the bass. Songs arranged with only three chords resulted in a stronger melody and less complicated harmonies.

There are ways in which the structure of the music of gospel songs helps to enforce the message of the words.[22] First, there is the melody line. In "All to Jesus I Surrender" the descending melody line is simply "I surrender all" and is repeated three times in the refrain. Each time it is a descending line. As the melody line moves down the scale, one has the sense of going down as well, surrendering "all to thee my blessed Savior, I surrender all."

In another song, "Savior 'Tis a Full Surrender," the last line of the refrain, "all I have I bring to Jesus, I surrender all," unravels the complete scale of D, from high D to an octave lower—the low D—as if the melody is surrendering to the lowest tonic possible.

20. Ibid., 136–37.

21. Ibid., 137.

22. I am indebted to Quinn Redekop, for insight on the relevance of the musical structure of gospel songs.

A descending line can also mean sadness, as in "Does Jesus Care?" The last line of each verse moves down from B flat to D along with the words, "and the way grows weary and long" in verse one; "does he care enough to be near?" in verse two; "tho' my tears flow all the night long?" in verse three; and "is it aught to him? Does he see?" in verse four.

An ascending line, on the other hand, can point to optimism and something positive. In "Jesus May Come Today" the refrain, beginning with the words, "Glad day, glad day," starts on high D, then moves up to E flat and finally further up to F for the final "Glad Day" and the "crown" in "crowning day." And the high F is usually sung loudly, thus giving the sense of great jubilation.

In addition to the function of the melody line, a second element is the key in which the song is written. Songs written in sharps are brighter than those in flats. "There's a Peace in My Heart," written in two sharps, speaks of abiding in Jesus and never being left lonely because "Jesus is mine." It's an upbeat song. Singing it leaves one feeling good. On the other hand, "I Must Tell Jesus All of My Trials," written in three flats, talks about the trials, troubles, temptations, and burdens of life. While the song does indicate that Jesus cares and will help the individual, it does have a deep and soulful feel to it, both because of the words and the key in which it is written.

Thirdly, repetition within the songs made it easier for people to learn and remember them. In the song previously mentioned, "There's Not a Friend like the Lowly Jesus" the phrase "No, not one! No not one!" is repeated at the end of each line in the verse, as well as in the refrain. This means that if one were to sing the entire song of five verses, this phrase would be repeated fifteen times. Routley suggests that the songs were themselves a type of preaching, "with a minimal rational and maximal emotional content."[23]

What started to happen in the later nineteenth century was that the use of songs in evangelism became systemized and these songs were deliberately used for certain effects and results. This was particularly exemplified in the evangelistic services under Moody and Billy Sunday. Moody knew that music, paired with preaching, was a powerful combination to bring people to salvation.

During the Second Awakening in North America, preacher and soloist worked in tandem. This was a formula for success. Sometimes

---

23. Routley, *The Music of Christian Hymns*, 137.

they were so much in tune with each other that when the preacher felt the mood of the meeting called for a song, he could ask the soloist to sing at a moment's notice.

Moody had a music partner in Ira Sankey, to whom he could turn for a song at any time before, after, or even during his preaching. With Sankey at his side and a choir of singers situated directly behind Moody, preaching and music went hand in hand to enforce the need for salvation. Songs sung at Moody's revival meetings tended to focus on the sinful human condition and salvation through Jesus. On one occasion, after he preached a sermon on "Jesus the Good Shepherd" he called unexpectedly on Sankey for a song. At first, not knowing what to sing, Sankey remembered that he had in his pocket a poem he had read in the newspaper. He took it out and on the spot composed music for "The Ninety and Nine," which he sang immediately:

> There were ninety and nine that safely lay
> In the shelter of the fold.
> But one was out on the hills away,
> Far off from the gates of gold.
> Away on the mountains wild and bare.
> Away from the tender Shepherd's care.
> Away from the tender Shepherd's care.
>
> "Lord, Thou hast here Thy ninety and nine;
> Are they not enough for Thee"?
> But the Shepherd made answer: "This of Mine
> Has wandered away from Me;
> And although the road be rough and steep,
> I go to the desert to find My sheep,
> I go to the desert to find My sheep."
>
> But none of the ransomed ever knew
> How deep were the waters crossed;
> Nor how dark was the night the Lord passed through
> Ere He found His sheep that was lost.
> Out in the desert He heard its cry,
> Sick and helpless and ready to die;
> Sick and helpless and ready to die.
>
> "Lord, whence are those blood drops all the way
> That mark out the mountain's track"?
> "They were shed for one who had gone astray

Ere the Shepherd could bring him back."
"Lord, whence are Thy hands so rent and torn"?
"They are pierced tonight by many a thorn;
They are pierced tonight by many a thorn."

And all through the mountains, thunder riven
And up from the rocky steep,
There arose a glad cry to the gate of Heaven,
"Rejoice! I have found My sheep!"
And the angels echoed around the throne,
"Rejoice, for the Lord brings back His own!
Rejoice, for the Lord brings back His own!"[24]

In this song, Jesus is seen as the shepherd, the ninety-nine sheep are those who have already been converted, and the one lost sheep stands for those who have not yet accepted Jesus' sacrifice for their sins, Jesus' blood "shed for one who had gone astray."

With the establishment of the Moody Bible Institute in 1886, many preachers and songwriters were trained. Students and teachers of the Institute were among those who wrote gospel songs in the late nineteenth and early twentieth centuries.

After Moody, other evangelists followed, each with their own music partner. Both R.A. Torrey and John Wilbur Chapman had Charles Alexander (1867–1920) as their song leader. Fred Fischer and Homer Rodeheaver (1880–1955) were soloist-choir leaders for Billy Sunday. With the concept of the soloist-song leader, songs were sung, not only by the soloist, but also by the congregation. Everyone was singing the creed, so to speak.

William Ellis, writing about the music in Billy Sunday's services, referred to the emotional effect of singing the gospel songs. He writes of an occasion when Rodeheaver conducted the mass choir in the song "Almost Persuaded,"[25] followed by the invitation for people to respond. Ellis writes that "all this is psychological; it fosters the mood which the sermon has created. Music mellows as many hearts as spoken words."[26]

Sunday was known to start his services with an hour or so of music prior to the service. This was done intentionally to work up a receptivity

24. George, *Mr. Moody and the Evangelical Tradition*, 110.

25. "Almost persuaded, harvest is past! Almost persuaded. Doom comes at last! Almost cannot avail; almost is but to fail! Sad, sad, that bitter wail, almost, but lost!"

26. Ellis, *"Billy" Sunday*, 164.

to the message.[27] He knew that if emotions were high, aided by the kinds of songs that were sung, people would respond to the invitation to accept Jesus, "The Tabernacle music in itself is enough to draw the great throngs which nightly crowd the building. . . . Without his choirs Sunday could scarcely conduct his great campaigns."[28] Another technique he used was to have the choir sing a line of a song that asked a question and then have the back rows of the audience sing the response line.[29] With the response coming from the back of the tabernacle, those sitting in the rows closer to the front would hear the answer from behind. It was thought this would urge them to respond to the message of the song.

The pattern of a music/evangelist team continued with Billy Graham in the 1940s, who had George Beverley Shea as soloist and Cliff Barrows as song leader and choir conductor of the mass choirs that were an integral part of the evangelist service.

And now to the gospel songs that reinforced the fundamentalist doctrines of the fundamentalist evangelical movement of the early 1900s. The time period between 1860 and 1920 was a time when the fundamentals of evangelicalism were developing and culminating, as we have seen, in the publication and distribution of a series of booklets published between 1910 and 1915, booklets that explained the fundamentals that were thought to be crucial for fundamentalist evangelicals in the late nineteenth and early twentieth centuries. As songs were written and set to music, they mimicked the fundamentalist evangelical doctrine and played a crucial role in defining people's identity. These songs, reflecting the accepted beliefs of the time, were repeated over and over again, as people attended church services and revival meetings. And with the invention of the phonograph in 1877 and radio in 1895, gospel songs could be heard again and again in the privacy of one's own home.[30]

When I was a teenager, I took piano lessons. Soon I was able to play these gospel songs on the piano and sing along. And since music speaks to people at an emotional level, it was a way to cement the beliefs in my mind and feel their emotional impact in my body. I would sing these songs over and over. I thought I needed to believe the songs exactly as they were

27. Ibid., 264.
28. Ibid., 262–63.
29. Ibid., 264.
30. Cusic, *The Sound of Light*, 77–78.

written. And the songs said the same thing the preachers were saying. No one ever told me that these songs were only metaphors and that they didn't express every truth in the Bible. I believed the songs expressed the most important truths of sin, salvation, holy living, and heaven and that all of life could be understood in these terms. These beliefs became a lens through which I understood life.

By hearing and singing the songs repeatedly, the fundamentals of faith became deeply engrained in both children and adults. They helped to set in motion a religious cultural identity that extended well into the 1900s in some evangelical denominations.

ANALYSIS OF A COLLECTION OF GOSPEL SONGS WRITTEN BETWEEN 1860 AND 1920

The songs I have chosen to analyze are a subset of a much larger number of gospel songs written between 1860 and 1920, numbering in the thousands, with Fanny Crosby alone writing eight thousand of them. The challenge for me was to select a smaller sampling of songs to examine.

While in my brother's home, I came across a Mennonite Brethren Church Hymnal, a navy, hardcover book with gold lettering. It was published in 1953, in time for the one-hundredth anniversary of the Mennonite Brethren Conference of North America, celebrated in 1960.[31] Since it served as the Mennonite Brethren hymnal until a new one was published in 1971, this was the Hymnal from which I sang from the age of seven through my early twenties.

As I paged through the book, I noticed a good number of songs written in the latter half of the nineteenth century, most of them, gospel songs. Using these songs for my analysis would serve two purposes: it would give me a manageable sample of songs to examine, and it would tell me which songs survived long enough to be included in a hymn book in circulation more than fifty years after the naming of the fundamentalist evangelical movement.

In addition to the songs in this hymnbook, there were other gospel songs that were popular within the movement and were used in inter-church evangelical gatherings. There were also special Sunday School and youth song books. Many of these songs ended up in several

---

31 Richert et al., eds. *Mennonite Brethren Church Hymnal,* v, vi.

evangelical denominational hymnbooks. For example, fifty-nine percent of the songs I examined also appear in the 1956 Baptist Hymnal.[32] The usage of the same songs by several denominations laid the groundwork for something that became trans-denominational. You could easily recognize an evangelical soul mate by their kind of religious discourse and the songs they sang.

Upon examining the songs in the Mennonite Brethren Church Hymnal more closely, I discovered that 196 (39 percent) of its 501 songs were written in North America between 1860 and 1920. (See Appendix A for a list of these song titles and Appendix B for the names of the songwriters.) I will examine the lyrics of 184 of these songs, determining how they relate to common fundamentalist evangelical themes of the time.[33] In my analysis, I will discuss people's experience in the third person, but the excerpts from songs, woven into the text, will be in the second person, as they appear in the songs. When I quote phrases from these songs, I will simply refer to the songs with the number assigned to them in Appendix A.

Themes of the Songs

As noted in chapter 3, the first fundamental in the 1878 Niagara Creed was "Inspiration of Scripture." Everything that was sung about was based on this fundamental. Two songs in our sample refer to the importance of the Bible as the Word of God: "Break Thou the Bread of Life, Dear Lord, to me," and "Thy Word is a Lamp to My Feet."

> Break Thou the Bread of Life, Dear Lord, to me,
> As Thou didst break the loaves beside the sea;
> Beyond the sacred page I seek Thee, Lord;
> My spirit pants for Thee, O living Word.

> Thy Word is a lamp to my feet,
> A light to my path alway,
> To guide and to save me from sin,
> And show me the heav'nly way.

---

32. Sims, *Baptist Hymnal.*

33. The twelve songs that I will not analyze focus on adoration, creation, patriotism, Christmas, and Easter.

Refrain: Thy Word have I hid in my heart,
That I might not sin against Thee;
That I might not sin, that I might not sin,
That I might not sin against. Thee.

Forever, O Lord, is Thy Word established and fixed on high;
Thy faithfulness unto all men [*sic*] abideth forever nigh.

The literal-factual interpretation of the Bible as God's inspired Word was a given in the evangelical community. And from this interpretation of the Bible flowed all other fundamentalist evangelical beliefs.

The themes of the remaining 182 songs can be divided into five major categories: sin, the process of salvation, benefits of salvation, experiences of the "saved" individual, and heaven.

Fifty-three songs deal with aspects of sin and salvation, ninety-one songs address the experiences of the life of the person once they are "saved," and fourteen deal with heaven. In addition, there are twenty-four songs for which the full gamut of beliefs is covered in each song (I am sinful; Jesus died on the cross to save me; I need only to accept his love and forgiveness; if I do this I will be happy and be able to live a holy life; and I will go to heaven when I die.) First we will examine the songs that have within them all five major categories.

Songs That Include All Five Themes

The songs that include all five themes usually start off with a verse that indicates that people are sinners and thus need to be saved from sin. The first verse is usually about this, as in "Come, Every Soul by Sin Oppressed": "Come, every soul by sin oppressed, there's mercy with the Lord." The second verse in these kinds of songs talks about the way out of sin through Jesus' death on the cross. This is the process of salvation. For example, in "One Day When Heaven Was Filled With His Praises," the second verse says,

One day they led Him up Calvary's mountain
One day they nailed Him to die on the tree
Suffering anguish, despised and rejected
Bearing our sins, my Redeemer is He!

After the song tells about the way to be free from sin, other verses or the refrain describe the benefits of salvation, for example, in "I Wandered in the Shades of Night," the refrain talks about the happiness of the saved individual:

> Sunlight, sunlight, in my soul today
> Sunlight, sunlight all along the way,
> Since the Savior found me, took away my sin,
> I have had the sunlight of his love within.

These songs also refer to the experiences the person will have after they are saved. They will tell others about Jesus, " I cross the wide extended fields, I journey o'er the plain, and in the sunlight of his love I reap the golden grain" (#67). The grain they reap refers to "souls" to whom they are bringing the message of Jesus.

They will also have Jesus as a friend:

> If friends, once trusted, have proven untrue
> Let Jesus come into your heart.
> Find what Friend He will be unto you,
> Let Jesus come into your heart.

The songs usually end with a verse about the afterlife, as in "The Whole World Was Lost":

> No need of the sunlight in heaven, we're told,
> The Light of the world is Jesus
> The Lamb is the Light in the City of Gold
> The Light of the world is Jesus.

Songs About Sin

Now to the theme of sin. What I found astounding is that so many songs refer to some aspect of sin and salvation. From what do people need to be saved? What do the songs say about the state of the individual before salvation? What terminology is used to denote the act of being saved? What metaphors are used? What do these songs say about the individual's self-identity, their self-designation as a sinner?

The songs speak about the unhappy life people have prior to being forgiven of their sins. They talk about being "tired of the load of your sin" (#99), being unclean, wayward, lost, sick, wounded, broken hearted, weak, oppressed, and stained by sin. Their "inbred sin" (#39) is seen as the result of Adam and Eve's sin; they are "ruined by the fall" (#39). It's like there are fetters holding them down. They have sunk and cannot rise. Their soul is "in sad exile out on life's sea" (#160). They feel shame and guilt. They are "vile and helpless" (#43). Sin has ruled them and because of sin, they are condemned, they are cursed, they are "bruised by the fall" (#34). Their life is "wrecked by sin and strife" (#173), they are filled with discord, despair, and darkness. They are full of doubts and fear, they can't see where they are going, they are weary, they have fallen so much that they feel faint, life is worthless, they cannot even come near to God, their friends can no longer be trusted, they feel a void, they find no good within themselves, they are filled with sorrow, they experience failure and loss, they are arrogant and proud, they don't have rest, they dread death, they are unworthy, they are threatened with "infinite loss" (#104), they have "sin-blinded eyes" (#161), their sin has caused them misery, they've "wandered far away from God," (#83), and they have the feeling that they have "wasted many precious years" (#83).

Several metaphors are used in these songs to depict the experience of sinfulness. It is seen as carrying a heavy load and shadows on a path. The pre-salvation state is as a tempest that cannot be stilled, a storm that one is caught up in, a feeling of despair while drowning in "angry waves" (#102). The sinful state is compared to music that is discordant and played on broken strings. It is a lost feeling like that of a sheep that has gone astray. It feels like they cannot see anymore. They are in a room with "grim curtains of night" (#4) always drawn. One verse of the song, "Marvelous Grace of Our Loving Lord" tells of the stain of sin that they cannot hide:

> Dark is the stain that we cannot hide,
> What can avail to wash it away?
> Look! there is flowing a crimson tide,
> Whiter than snow you may be today.

We can see that what is said about sin in these songs mimics the evolving fundamentalist doctrine of the sinful self.

For the person singing these songs regularly, what image of self do they have? What is their identity in the pre-salvation state? They realize that apart from Jesus they are nothing. The words paint a pitiful picture of humanity as completely disempowered. They are unacceptable the way they are. They are bad. There is nothing they can do on their own to take them out of their guilt. Relationships are not good; people cannot be trusted. They are defined solely by their lostness. They are deficient in all their human needs. See figure 3 below.

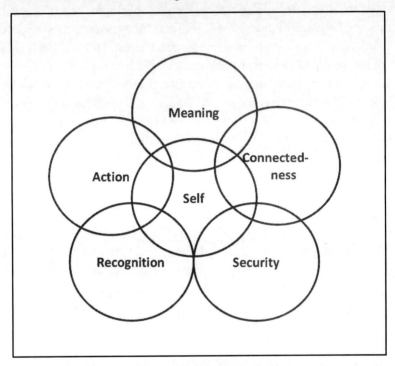

Figure 3. Human Identity Needs

They lack *security* because they are not good enough, they can't take meaningful *action*, they are not *recognized* for any good thing, they lack *meaning* in their lives because they are so sinful, and they feel *unconnected* because they cannot embrace those who are not "saved" and they themselves are not yet "saved," so they don't feel connected to those who have accepted salvation. And in addition, they are bound for an eternal life without God, an afterlife in hell. They don't feel connected to God.

Songs About the Process of Salvation

According to these songs, salvation is possible because of Jesus' death on the cross. Jesus loved sinners so much that he died for them. It was love that brought him "from above" (#9). "I was lost, but Jesus found me, found the sheep that went astray, threw his loving arms around me, drew me back into his way" (#69). Through his death, sins are carried far away—"buried, he carried my sins far away" (#125). He "bore our sorrows" and "for our sins he suffered and bled and died" (#131). This was all done because of Jesus' love, "love paid the ransom for me" (#156).

There is a lot said in these songs about Jesus' death. He was led "up Calvary's mountain" where they "nailed him to die on the tree" (#125). He suffered, in anguish, despised, rejected, afflicted, homeless, poor, and "writhing in anguish and pain" (#156). He wore thorns on his head, his blood was spilled/outpoured, salvation achieved "at highest cost" (#39). He took the burden for "my sins and sorrows" and "made them his very own," bearing them to the cross, where his sweat was "sweatdrops of blood" (#65).

Jesus is seen as the Redeemer. The songs speak of the efficacy of the blood of Jesus to take sins away, "there's pow'r in the blood . . . wonderworking pow'r . . . in the precious blood of the Lamb" (#169). He offers his blood in which sinners can be cleansed, "plunge now into the crimson flood that washes white as snow" (#16). The blood is applied to one's heart, "There to my heart was the blood applied" (#27). Many songs talk about Jesus' death as atonement for sin, a death that pays the price of cleansing from sin, "I am bought, but not with gold; bought with a price, the blood of Jesus, precious price of love untold" (#116). The debt the individual owes to God has now been paid, "my debt by his death was all paid" (#165). A number of songs speak about this "purchase of God" (#9), this debt/ransom paid on one's behalf. The "blood of the cross" is seen as the only foundation, "the blood of the cross is my only foundation, the death of my Savior now maketh me whole" (#116). Once saved, they are "born of his Spirit" (#9) and have been forgiven, "He hath granted me forgiveness, I am his and he is mine" (#92).

One of the songs refers to the story in the Hebrew Bible in which the Israelites put blood on their doors so that when the angel of death would come killing the oldest sons, the angel would see the blood on their doors and pass over them and their sons would not be taken. This song is "Christ our Redeemer died on the cross, died for the sinner, paid all his due; sprinkle your soul with the blood of the Lamb, and I will pass, will pass over you" (#14). In this song the point is made that when individuals avail themselves of the saving blood of Jesus, God will save them from destruction.

Jesus' role is seen as the model, the sacrifice, the one who loves and gives his life for humanity. There is very little of the human Jesus in these songs. The overall picture you get is of the bloody Jesus washing people clean with an infinite amount of blood, enough blood to wash everyone clean.

With Jesus' sacrifice for sin as a given, the songs tell people how to get out of the darkness and guilt that they feel. What do they need to do to feel complete in themselves again? To have their identity needs met? They need to be saved, but how exactly does one become "saved"? The songs say that it all starts with the Bible, "by trusting in his Word" (#16) because Jesus is revealed in the Bible. Jesus is calling and pleading for people to come to him. He is "tenderly calling thee home" (#87). According to the lyrics in these songs, people need to "list to the loving call" (#193). There is a lot said about the need to make the advance to Jesus, "will you come, will you come" (#191), "look to the Lamb of God" (#101), "I hear Thy welcome voice that calls me Lord to Thee" (#59), "listen to the blessed invitation" (#100). And this is done through prayer, prayers to God to "hear my humble cry" (#130) and prayers that tell God that "I'm coming home" (#83).

When people do come to Jesus, he will not cast them out. The song, "Down at the Cross where My Savior Died," asks the singer to "come to this fountain (of blood) so rich and sweet; cast thy poor soul at the Savior's feet; plunge in today and be made complete" (#27). The call is to "come," "cast," and "plunge." So the first step in the process of salvation is to look to Jesus, listen to the invitation, and come to him. It is spoken of as a choice one must make, "let us freely make him our choice" (#18). One song talks about giving up oneself before being washed clean, "I give up myself and whatever I know, now wash me and I shall be whiter than snow" (#189). Another talks about the importance of submission, "perfect submission, perfect delight" (#9) and "counting all but dross" (#55).

Next, the individual needs to repent and "believe in his mercy" (#124), trust in God's "marvellous grace" (#104), trust in the words of the Bible, respond to the Spirit who is "convicting men [*sic*] of sin" (#61), have faith in Jesus, believe in "grace that will pardon and cleanse within" (#104), by faith claim Jesus as theirs, "come to the light" (#161) and ask Jesus to take away their sins. God's favour is obtained by faith.

Several metaphors are used to explain the process of salvation. Individuals must ask Jesus into their hearts and open the door for him, "swing the heart's door widely open" (#46). They can get washed in the fountain of blood, "there's a fountain flowing for the soul unclean, O be washed in the blood of the Lamb" (#7). They can hide "in the saving soul-cleansing blood" (#46) And there is a water fountain in which they can bury their burden "deep in its waters" (#19). Metaphors relating to the sea are also used; through salvation their souls can be anchored "in the haven of rest" (#160). If they do this, they are safe in Jesus forever, even though "the tempest may sweep o'er the wild stormy deep" (#160).

Songs About the Benefits of Salvation

Once salvation has been bought, what do the songs say about the benefits of salvation? Individuals have received "wonderful words of Life" (#193), they now have "mercy and pardon" (#145), and they are sanctified (made holy) forever. They are made complete. Their soul is reconciled to God; their pardon is sealed. God "reigns and rules" in their hearts (#183). They now live "in his presence daily" (#66), and they experience true pleasure. They have received Jesus' Spirit. Jesus has lifted them "out of the night into glorious light" (#85). They can begin a new life; they are pure and cleansed. They have experienced the healing touch of Jesus. They are no longer condemned. They are free from sin, their burdens have fallen off, and they feel relieved. Their "hearts are pure and free" (#18). Their doubts are gone. They have the assurance that Jesus belongs to them, "blessed assurance, Jesus is mine" (#9). They are redeemed "once for all" (#34). They will not perish. They are safe. Their lives are now hidden "in the depths of his love" (#48).

When difficult times come, in "each trying hour," they can "triumph" (#183). They can be assured that "when sorrows like sea billows roll . . . it is well with my soul" (#80). Jesus is their "guide and keeper" (#92). Even if their way has some difficult moments they will be able to "see His footprints all the way" (#6). They are safely led by Jesus' hand.

They can "join the glad songs of the blest" (#99). They can now walk every day "by the Savior's side" (#7). They have a feeling of rest and "are perfectly blest" (#79). They are love struck, " lost in his love" (#9).

Jesus smiles upon them continually and watches over them. They have freedom, gladness, light, joy, health, hope, strength, comfort, shelter, a balm for sorrow, and they live in Jesus' love and in "the peace of thy sheltering fold" (#129). They have Jesus' goodness and sunlight within them. Jesus completely satisfies them and gives them joy. Before they were stained and ruined, now they are "whiter than snow" (#189). They press on "with holy vigor and leave the world behind" (#67). They now possess "overcoming power" (#183) and they have "victo'ry o'er Satan's power" (#39). They are not afraid anymore.

Jesus' love will cheer them and "fill your heart with song" (#101). They are singing a melody in their hearts, which is the voice of Jesus who "whispers sweet and low, fear not I am with thee, peace, be still, in all of life's ebb and flow" (#173). Every longing has been filled and this keeps them singing. From now on they have a wonderful song to sing. Jesus guards their footsteps and gives them "songs in the night" (#133).

They can conquer all their foes. They feel triumphant, even at the moment of death. The light has dawned upon them and they don't experience darkness anymore. The light of Jesus' presence is with them continually. Every day gets brighter since they are now in a "heavenly union" (#167). They are God's children forever. They have a sense of "glorious fullness" (#39) and they are so full of joy that they have on earth a foretaste of the life in heaven, a life they are sure to obtain since they have a "pledge of endless life above" (#154). They now have victory even over hell.

And what happens to those strings that were broken? Well, they are fixed, because "Jesus swept across the broken strings, stirred the slumbering chords again" (#173). And what happens to all that darkness which the poor sinner experienced? It is dissipated by "the light of the world" (#161), which is Jesus. They "wandered in the shades of night till Jesus came to me, and with the sunlight of his love bid all my darkness flee" (#67). Their sin is gone, "My sin, not in part, but the whole is nailed to the cross and I bear it no more" (#80).

Since Jesus did all this for them, what can the saved individual do in return? They can "do service for Jesus your King" (#169). Songs speak of bearing one's own cross daily for Jesus, even to the extent of sharing his "cup of grief" (#95), the reason being that Jesus did exactly that for them, so they should be willing to do the same for Jesus. There is the sense that the saved individual owes everything to Jesus, "Jesus paid it all, all to him I owe" (#89).

What a picture this is of a perfectly happy peaceful life, free of fear and guilt!

Going back to the discussion on the identity needs that were not met while they were sinners, we can surmise that if individuals believe and appropriate Jesus' death for them, their primary identity needs will be fully met. They have the *security* they lacked before they were saved from their sinful selves. Their fears are gone. Security is possible because "He (Jesus) is able to keep that which I've committed unto Him against that day (the day of judgment)" (#61). Their need for *connection* is now met since they are connected with Jesus; in fact Jesus is within them. They are part of a heavenly union. Before they couldn't trust their friends, but now they have a friend (Jesus) they can trust. They are also connected with everyone else who has bought into the same salvation. They have new *meaning* in their lives because they have begun a new life with Jesus. They have *recognition* within the community of those who believe the same as they. Others recognize their experience as authentic, just like theirs. And they can take *action* when they bring other people into the peace they have found. We will see this action more fully in our discussion of what the songs say about the saved individual's responsibility to tell others of the good news of salvation.

Songs About the Experiences of the "Saved"

This broad category can be divided into six sub-categories: the inner life/prayer (twenty songs), surrender (nine songs), consolation/comfort (twenty-one songs), guidance (nine songs), courage/conquering foes (eight songs) and evangelizing/witnessing (twenty-four songs). I will analyze the lyrics in the gospel songs according to each of the six sub-categories.

Songs about the inner life and prayer

First, the theme of the inner life of the person who has been "saved." These songs emphasize the need to be close to Jesus, to be like Jesus, to trust Jesus, to live in an upright way, and to pray.

BEING CLOSE TO JESUS

"I Need Thee Every Hour" is a song that reads like a prayer. It acknowledges one's need for Jesus and asks Jesus to stay close by so that the individual is not tempted to sin, "temptations lose their pow'r when Thou art nigh" (#63). The song asks Jesus to show the individual what Jesus' will is for them, fulfill Jesus' promises in them, and bless them:

> I need Thee every hour, teach me Thy will
> And Thy rich promises in me fulfill.
> I need Thee, O I need Thee, Every hour I need Thee;
> O bless me now, my Savior, I come to Thee.

"I Am Thine, O Lord, I Have Heard Thy Voice" is also a prayer song. It is a prayer to be drawn closer to Jesus, a prayer to be consecrated to service for Jesus and a prayer for one's will to be lost in Jesus' will. The song extols the value of prayer, saying, that "when I kneel in prayer, and with Thee, my God, I commune as friend with friend" (#57).

The songs also talk about staying close, not only to Jesus, but to Jesus' cross. "Jesus Keep Me Near the Cross" is also in the form of a prayer, a prayer that the individual will "walk from day to day with its shadows o'er me." They want to stay close to the cross because they see it as "a precious fountain" from which a "healing stream" flows (#112). Referring to Jesus as "the bright and morning star" (#112), the song says that the cross sheds the beams of Jesus around the individual. In the song, "Nearer the Cross," there is the desire to come nearer "the fountain's crimson tide, nearer my Savior's wounded side" so that they can become stronger in faith and see Jesus more clearly. They want their love to grow deeper and in the end, they want to be nearer the joy they will have in heaven and nearer the crown they will wear there.

In "My Song Shall Be of Jesus" Fanny Crosby lists all the reasons why she wants to sing about Jesus: "his mercy crowns my days, he fills my cup with blessings and tunes my heart to praise," "who gave himself my ransom and bought me with his blood," and "I'll sing the grace that saves me and keeps me at his side."

There are two songs that focus on the actual name of Jesus, but what they actually seem to mean is the person of Jesus, "Take the Name of Jesus With You" and "The Name of Jesus is So Sweet." The reason to take the name of Jesus with them is that it gives joy and comfort; and it is a shield from temptations. All they have to do is say the name of Jesus when they are tempted to sin. The reason that "the name of Jesus is so sweet" is because "it makes my joys full and complete" (#162). Jesus knows their "griefs and bears a part . . . bids all anxious fears depart" (#162). The name cheers them and "dries the falling tear" (#162).

BEING LIKE JESUS

In order to be like Jesus, nothing can come between the individual and Jesus, especially sin, "nothing between my soul and the Savior, naught of this world's delusive dream; I have renounced all sinful pleasure, Jesus is mine; there's nothing between" (#118). Songs list several things that could come between the saved individual and Jesus: habits of life that seem harmless on the surface, pride, status, the self, and friends, "Nothing preventing the least of his favour. Keep the way clear! Let nothing between" (#118). And when there is nothing between the individual and Jesus, "there's sunshine in my soul . . . for when the Lord is near, the dove of peace sings in my heart, the flowers of grace appear" (#150).

Their goal is to be like Jesus and learn from him.

> More like the Master I would ever be,
> More of His meekness, more humility;
> More zeal to labor, more courage to be true,
> More consecration for work He bids me do.
>
> More like the Master is my daily prayer;
> More strength to carry crosses I must bear;
> More earnest effort to bring His kingdom in;
> More of His Spirit, the wanderer to win.
>
> More like the Master I would live and grow;
> More of His love to others I would show;
> More self denial, like His in Galilee,
> More like the Master I long to ever be.

Jesus is their mimetic model. They want to be like him in meekness, humility, courage and consecration. They want strength to carry their own crosses. They want to bring in Jesus' kingdom. They want to deny themselves and show love to others.

Not only do they want to be more like Jesus, they also want to learn more about him and his way of being in the world:

More about Jesus would I know,
More of His grace to others show;
More of His saving fullness see,
More of His love who died for me.

More about Jesus let me learn,
More of His holy will discern;
Spirit of God, my teacher be,
Showing the things of Christ to me.

More about Jesus; in His Word,
Holding communion with my Lord;
Hearing His voice in every line,
Making each faithful saying mine.

More about Jesus; on His throne,
Riches in glory all His own;
More of His kingdom's sure increase;
More of His coming, Prince of Peace.

To be like Jesus, that is their desire, "Be like Jesus, this my song, in the home and in the throng; be like Jesus all day long! I would be like Jesus" (#70).

TRUSTING JESUS

Trusting Jesus is seen as the way to get through life, especially the difficult spots, "trusting through a stormy way; even when my faith is small, trusting Jesus, that is all" (#142). If they trust Jesus, they won't fall and they will be safe from danger. Trusting and obeying is the only way "to be happy in Jesus" (#187).

LIVING UPRIGHTLY

The song, "I Would Be True," speaks of the ways in which saved individuals aspire to upright living. They desire to be true, pure, strong, brave, generous, and humble. *So you can see there's lots of room for guilt if you don't measure up.* They want to be learning "the lessons my Heavenly Father gives me in his word" and they want to be "prompt and glad to do the things I've heard" (#71). There is the sense that there is always more they can do to live a good Christian life, expressed in "I'm Pressing On the Upward Way." This song talks about the aim of being on higher ground." They want to "live above the world" and "scale the utmost height." The refrain says, "Lord, lift me up and let me stand, by faith, on Heaven's table land, a higher plane than I have found; Lord, plant my feet on higher ground" (#73).

PRAYER

Another part of the emphasis on the inner life is the matter of prayer. There is a sense that the experience of prayer is wonderful: "what a balm for the weary! O how sweet to be there! Blessed hour of prayer" (#177). When they pray, Jesus comes near to them and listens to their prayers. They can "cast at his feet every care" (#177). When they are "tempted and tried" (#177) they can come to Jesus in prayer. They believe that in prayer they will "lose every care" (#177). When they pray, they believe they are "near to the heart of God" (#166). This is a "place of quiet rest . . . comfort sweet . . . full release . . . joy and peace" (#166). *And if you don't get joy and peace when you're praying there is something wrong with your prayer.* In this place sin "cannot molest" (#166). Here they meet Jesus. They pray for "showers of blessing" (#170) that will bring revival. In "There Shall Be Showers of Blessing," the actions of God are likened to precipitation. They want not only rain, but "abundance of rain" and "seasons refreshing" (#170). These are the showers. Currently there are only "mercy drops" (#170) falling. What they want is showers, lots and lots of whatever blessing they are asking for; they want it in abundance.

Songs about surrender

Giving everything to Jesus means surrendering all one's thoughts, words, actions, days, and hours to Jesus. When they have given "all for Jesus" they can see only him, "since my eyes were fixed on Jesus I've lost sight of all beside; so enchained my spirit's vision, looking at the crucified" (#1).

There is the sense that everything has to be placed "on the altar of sacrifice" (#79) in order to live a life filled with peace, contentment and faith. One's body and soul must be fully controlled by Jesus, "Is your all on the altar of sacrifice laid? Your heart, does the spirit control? You can only be blest and have peace and sweet rest, as you yield him your body and soul" (#79). This surrender must be a "full surrender" (#138) in which everything is left behind to follow Jesus. They have to come in "deep contrition" and "full confession," leaving behind all pleasures and riches (#138). The refrain of "Savior, 'Tis a Full Surrender" says, "I surrender all, I surrender all! All I have I bring to Jesus, I surrender all!" The song, "I Surrender All" is similar. Everything is given freely to Jesus as the person lives daily in Jesus' presence. They have forsaken "worldly pleasures" and they feel "the sacred flame" (#66). (The flame may refer to the Holy Spirit.)

The feeling of surrender is that of yielding to Jesus' way. This is expressed in the song, "Have Thine Own Way, Lord" (#45) and "Is Your All on the Altar?" (#79):

> Is your all on the altar of sacrifice laid?
> Your heart, does the Spirit control?
> You can only be blest and have peace and sweet rest,
> As you yield Him your body and soul.

This is all consuming. Absolutely no room for anything in your life but Jesus.

In the song "Would You Live for Jesus," all the good things about the Christian life hinge on people letting Jesus "have his way":

> Would you live for Jesus, and be always pure and good?
> Would you walk with Him within the narrow road?
> Would you have Him bear your burden, carry all your load?
> Let Him have His way with thee.
>
> Refrain: His power can make you what you ought to be;
> His blood can cleanse your heart and make you free;
> His love can fill your soul, and you will see
> 'Twas best for Him to have His way with thee.
>
> Would you have Him make you free, and follow at His call?
> Would you know the peace that comes by giving all?
> Would you have Him save you, so that you can never fall?
> Let Him have His way with thee.
>
> Would you in His kingdom find a place of constant rest?
> Would you prove Him true in providential test?
> Would you in His service labor always at your best?
> Let Him have His way with thee.

This song says that when Jesus has his way with individuals, they will be pure and good. They will be who they were meant to be; they will be free. They will have peace and will give their absolute best for Jesus.

The song, "When We Walk With the Lord," also tells about all the good things that come to Christians when they surrender to Jesus, when they "trust and obey" (#187). Jesus' smile will drive away the shadows and clouds. They won't have any more doubts, fears, sighs or tears. Even though they do have burdens and sorrows, Jesus repays them somehow. When they have surrendered, they do what Jesus says and go where he sends them.

In the song, "Open My Eyes, That I May See," the songwriter is praying for "glimpses of truth" and "voices of truth" (#128). She is praying to have her heart opened so that she can share Jesus' love with others. She awaits illumination, "silently now I wait for Thee, ready, my God, Thy will to see; Open my eyes, illumine me, Spirit divine" (#128).

Another aspect of surrender is going where Jesus leads them and in the song, "I Can Hear My Savior Calling" the songwriter envisions going with Jesus into the garden of Gethsemane where Jesus prayed prior to his death and then to the judgment hall where his crucifixion was decided. The thought is that the Christian should follow Jesus to the cross.

So the inner life of individuals after salvation begins by getting closer to Jesus so that they can become like Jesus. Through prayer, as they become more and more like Jesus and fully surrender to him, they will actually come to know what Jesus wants of them. They will renounce all worldly pursuits and aspire only to know Jesus and follow him. Jesus has become their mimetic model and their entire way of being is Jesus oriented.

Songs about consolation and comfort

The lyrics of these songs offer assurance that "there's one who can comfort when all else fails" (#84). This comfort comes to individuals who experience dreary days, burdens, heavy crosses, ill health, taunts from enemies, danger, creeping up of old age, doubts, fear, temptations, trials, sorrow, grief, loneliness, discouragement, and anxiety about the future. When these things come upon Christians, they can count on help from Jesus, who is seen as their friend, "there's not a friend like the lowly Jesus, No, not one! No not one!" (#115). It is Jesus who "knows all about our struggles" (#115). They can tell everything to him. There is a sense that his arm is around them, he "watches o'er me day and night"

(#86). Jesus is always near, "never forsaking . . . ready to help me, ready to cheer" (#94). He answers their call.

He provides a song. "a song of deliverance, of courage of strength" (#168). God will take care of them. They can rest "sweetly in Jesus' control" (#31). Jesus knows their pain and "will make a way for you and will lead you safely through" (#98). They can abide in Jesus because Jesus belongs to them, "Constantly abiding, Jesus is mine . . . he never leaves me lonely, whispers, oh so kind: I will never leave thee, Jesus is mine" (#21).

Several metaphors are used to express the consolation that is available through Jesus. People can rest "in the shadow of his wings" (#76). Jesus is seen as a bird that has wings of love and it is under those wings they can stay, "beneath his wings of love abide, God will take care of you" (#42). They can feel safe there; no evil will harm them there; they are sheltered and protected.

Another metaphor used is that of a rock, a "rock of ages" (#52). It is in the cleft (opening) of the rock that they can hide. Their security is also compared to the cables attached to an anchor, this anchor "is safely moored . . . for 'tis well secured by the Savior's hand; and the cables, passed from his heart to mine, can defy the blast, thru strength divine" (#182). In times of fear, they also have access to rest on Jesus' bosom, "let thy bosom be my pillow" (#51).

Songs about guidance

Closely related to consolation and comfort is the aspect of guidance. Lyrics portray Jesus and God anthropomorphically with hands, arms, a mouth, eyes, and feet. God will lead them with his hand, "by his own hand he leadeth me" (#50). God will lead them through gloomy times and even through death. They need only to trust "the arm that is strong to defend us" (#149) and lean "on the everlasting arms" (#97).

Jesus will feed them "with the living bread" (#2). God has promised to guide them with God's eye, "Precious promise God hath given to the weary passerby, on the way from earth to Heaven, 'I will guide thee with mine eye'" (#132). God's eye will keep them from succumbing to temptations and will guide them through death.

Christians walk with Jesus on a "pilgrim journey" (#15). Through "each winding path" (#2) Jesus leads them. As they walk with Jesus, they try to walk in his steps, "trying to walk in the steps of the Savior," and to walk as closely as they can to him, "pressing more closely to him who is leading" (#149). They follow their guide, their example, because "he the great example is, and pattern for me" (#151).

Jesus is also seen as a pilot of a ship that guides them "over life's tempestuous sea" (#91). There are "unknown waves" and "hiding rock," but Jesus has the "chart and compass" to avoid these and bring them safely to shore (heaven) (#91). The song, "Upon a Wide and Stormy Sea" encourages people to "sail on, sail on, the storms will soon be past" (#181). Even though the sky is overcast, the canvas of the ship is torn, comrades are trembling, and the waves are threatening to sink the ship, "thy great Admiral orders thee: Sail on! Sail on! Sail on!"[34]

Songs about conquering the foe

The idea of a faith that can conquer foes is another aspect of the life of the "saved" individual. Songs with battle language were written after the American Civil War (1861–1865) and two of them were written by Major Daniel Webster Whittle, who became an evangelist after the War ("Be Ye Strong in the Lord" and "The Banner of the Cross"). In these songs, the use of battle language offers a comparison between conquering sin and conquering an enemy in battle. God "shall lead you safely through the thickest of the fight, you shall conquer in the name of the Lord" (#8). They are "satisfied to know that with Jesus here below . . . (they can) conquer every foe" (#158).

There is reference to Christian soldiers who are "encamped along the hills of light" (#29). "The day of march has come" (#96). In fields of conquest, they are to "fight manfully onward; dark passions subdue" (#196). They don't fight with real swords; their sword is the Word of God and "deeds of love and mercy" (#96).

The "soldiers of the King" (#157) have a royal banner. (Their banner is a gospel banner; it is love.) It is a crimson color (the blood of Jesus). They lift it up and march on to crown Jesus King "beneath the banner of the cross" (#157). They use all their strength to fight against

---

34. In the late 1800s a lot of people travelled to North America from England, so they will have had personal experience of transatlantic travel and the journey will have been perilous. The metaphor of a pilot in this circumstance was powerful for them and the fear was substantial.

the foe, who is "on every hand . . . drawn up in dread array" (#29). Even though the foe rages and there are many of them, they never turn away from the foe. The foe advances, "clad in brilliant array" (#20). But they wear salvation as helmets and "vanquish all the hosts of night in Jesus' conquering name" (#29). God will lead them because they are "battling for the right" (#8). The King is "leading the host of all the faithful into the midst of the fight" (#20). And when the standard (flag) is displayed the foe is conquered.

> Conquering now and still to conquer,
>   who is this wonderful King?
> Whence are the armies which He leadeth,
>   while of His glory they sing?
> He is our Lord and Redeemer, Savior and Monarch divine;
> They are the stars that forever bright
>   in His kingdom will shine.
> Not to the strong is the battle,
>   not to the swift is the race,
> Yet to the true and the faithful victory
>   is promised through grace.

They sing the battle song and go "on to victory at the King's command," because "he'll hold thee while battling for the right" (#8). They are sure to win the battle, since "faith is the victory that overcomes the world" (#29). The King eternal leads them and the armies God is leading are "faithful and true to the last" (#20). If they engage in this fight, they will "find in mansions eternal, rest, when their warfare is past" (#20).

Songs about witnessing and evangelism

Another experience of the "saved" individual is that of witnessing and evangelism, the act of telling others of Jesus. This task is seen as something they love to do, "I am happy in the service of the King . . . I have peace and joy that nothing else can bring" (#56). They are pleased to do "one more day's work for Jesus, one less of life for me" (#126). The lyrics indicate what is wrong with those who haven't been "saved" by Jesus and the songs are clear about what to tell them. If Christians go and tell others, they will be rewarded.

Songs ask them to go and spread the word about Jesus. Some songs indicate this by questions of invitation while others express it as an imperative. "Have You Sought for the Sheep?" is full of questions: "have you sought . . . have you been . . . have you knelt . . . have you gone . . . have you carried . . . have you stood . . . have you followed . . . have you pointed . . . have you asked . . . have you told?" (#47). Questions in other songs include:

- "Who'll go and help this shepherd kind, help him the wandering ones to find?" (#11)

- "Who'll bring the lost ones to the fold?" (#11)

- "Why do you tarry, why linger so long? See he [sic] is sinking, oh, hasten today" (#175).

- "To their cry of pity dare we heedless be?" (#178)

- "Who will go and work today?" (#44)

- "Who will bear the sheaves away?" (#44)

- "Who, who will go, salvation's story telling?" (#32)

In some songs the call to go and save "the lost" comes as an imperative because "duty demands it" (#134):

- "Heed the call that he gives today" (#75).

- "Throw out the life-line" (#175).

- "Gather them in" (#35).

- "Go forth, go forth, with a loving heart and gather the wanderers in" (#35).

- "Gather now the sheaves of gold" (#30).

- "Go and seek their rescue ere it is too late" (#178).

- "Give of your best to the Master; give him first place in your service; give him your loyal devotion; give him the best that you have" (#36).

- "To the work! To the work! We are servants of God" (#179).

The Christian answers the call willingly, "Here am I, send me, send me" (#44). It is a pleasure to work for Jesus, "I'll answer, dear Lord, with my hand in thine, I'll go where you want me to go" (#72). Since the call comes as a "message from God above" (#35), the Christian is eager to "follow the steps of Jesus where-e'r they go" (#152) for "tis joy, not duty, to speak his beauty" (#126). And they are not afraid, because "if Jesus goes with me, I'll go anywhere" (#82). They can go safely if Jesus is with them.

So what is wrong with the people to whom God is sending them and what message are they to bring these folk? The people living "far, far away," those in "foreign" lands, are referred to as "heathen" (#32). These "millions of souls" (#32) are seen as forever lost. There are "souls to rescue . . . souls to save" (#140). They live in lands "which are in gloom and night" (#179). They live in darkness and sin. They are "crushed by the tempter" (#134). They have fallen. They are in the wrong, "the erring ones" (#134). They are weary, weak, wayward, and hungry. They are "sinking in anguish" (#175). They are drifting away; they have wandered. Like sheep, they have gone astray. Their souls are dying. They are drifting "to eternity's shore" (#175). That is why there's a rush to save them.

The message to bring to these sinful people is, of course, a message of salvation "full and free" (#90). They are to tell of Jesus' love for them, the "story of pardon" (#37). They are to "gather them into the fold of grace, and the arms of the Savior's love" (#35). With loving words, they are to rescue them, snatch them, plead with them, lift them up, preach the word, "carry the blessed word of life" (#82). What they are to say and do is to stand by the "trembling captive" (#47), tell them of salvation, urge them to believe and tell them about everlasting life. There is no ambiguity here; they are lost and they need to be saved.

Several metaphors are used in these lyrics to describe the act of winning the lost to Jesus. These include planting and reaping metaphors, battle images, and comparisons with light, sheep, and water.

There is the sense that Christians are going out into a harvest field, and by winning souls they are making sheaves of the grain that is ready to harvest, "far and near the fields are teeming with the waves of ripened grain" (#30). There is a lot of work to do in this harvest field, "for the grain is ripe and the reapers few" (#75). By "sowing in the morning, sowing seeds of kindness, sowing in the noontide . . . sowing in the shadows . . . sowing for the Master," they will be "bringing in the sheaves" (#12). The prayer is that God will send reapers into the harvest field "ere the harvest time pass by" (#30). There is an urgency to the task, so workers are needed.

Battle images are used in a few of the songs that speak of telling others about Jesus. As "soldiers of Christ" (#32), they are to "sing above the battle strife" and go onward with the song of victory, "Jesus saves! Jesus saves!" (#90). "Clad in salvation's full armor," with forces united, they are fighting in a "battle for truth" in their service to Jesus (#36). They need to be ready to spread the word about Jesus because they may be needed "at the battle's front" (#72).

The news they are spreading to the "lost" is seen as light, gospel light, "To the millions living o'er the deep, deep sea, speed the light . . . the blessed gospel light" (#178). This is because souls are "in gloom and night" (#178). They are being asked to "send the light, the blessed gospel light, let it shine from shore to shore" (#140).

Those who have not been "saved" are seen as sheep who have gone astray. They are not "sheltered from the cold" (#11), so Christians need to go and find them and bring them back to the fold, "bring them in, bring them in, bring the wandering ones to Jesus" (#11).

Those who are "lost" are pictured as being in an ocean drowning in the waves. They need a lifeline and Christians are called to give them one, "throw out the life line across the dark wave, there is a brother [*sic*] whom someone should save . . . someone is sinking today" (#175). Christians may be called by God to go "beyond the billow's foam" (#82) to tell others of Jesus.

It should be noted that these images can be linked both to biblical texts and to people's experiences. The Bible talks of conquering enemies and wearing a helmet of salvation. It also tells the story of a shepherd looking for one lost sheep among ninety-nine others. Jesus is seen as the light of the world. In terms of their experiences, as noted before, they undoubtedly experienced frightening times on the sea and they had just come out of a civil war, so these images were used by songwriters to compare their experiences with people's spiritual state.

If they follow the call to bring the gospel to others, there is a reward, "Heavenward then at evening wending, thou shalt come with joy untold" (#30). They are to "keep the bright reward in view" (#75). Songs tell about that reward. The "harvest home in the realms above" will be achieved by everyone who "has toiled and strove" (#75). If they have gathered "the sheaves of gold" (#30), they will be extremely joyful when they get to heaven. Their reward will include "a robe and a crown" (#179) because they have been faithful. In their act of bringing others to Jesus they are gathering "jewels for a crown above" (#140). In heaven they will be welcomed and greeted with the words, "Inasmuch as 'twas done for my brethren [*sic*], even so it was done unto me" (#47).

"Have You Sought For the Sheep" is a song that includes all the aspects of the witnessing/evangelism theme:

> Have you sought for the sheep that have wandered far away on
> the dark mountains cold?
> Have you gone like the tender shepherd to bring them again to
> the fold?
> Have you followed their weary footsteps and the wild desert
> waste have you crossed?
> Nor lingered till safe home returning, you have gathered the
> sheep that were lost.
>
> Have you been to the sad and the lonely whose burdens are
> heavy to bear?
> Have you carried the name of Jesus and tenderly breathed it in
> prayer?
> Have you told of the great salvation he died on the cross to
> secure?
> Have you asked them to trust in the Savior whose love shall
> forever endure?
>
> Have you knelt by the sick and the dying, the message of mercy
> to tell?
> Have you stood by the trembling captive alone in his dark
> prison cell?
> Have you pointed the lost to Jesus and urged them on Him to
> believe?
> Have you told of the life everlasting that all, if they will, may
> receive?
>
> If to Jesus you answer these questions and to Him have been
> faithful and true,
> Then behold in the mansions yonder are crowns of rejoicing
> for you;
> And there from the King eternal your welcome and greeting
> shall be,
> "Inasmuch as 'twas done for my brethren, even so it was done
> unto me."

The questions in this song imply the imperative of witnessing to others. Those who do not know Jesus are portrayed as sad and lonely with heavy burdens. They are like lost sheep who need to be brought back to the fold. It is up to Christians to point these lost ones to Jesus and as a result to everlasting life. If they do this, they will be welcomed into heaven by the King eternal.

Songs about Heaven

The last heading under which I will examine the lyrics of these selected songs is that of heaven. While the idea of heaven is seen in many of the songs, there are fourteen songs that focus almost exclusively on the concept of heaven.

Not much is said about judgment and hell. Just one song, "Nor Silver Nor Gold" talks about the judgment, "judgment is coming, all will be there, each one receiving justly his [*sic*] due" #116).

The songs say that the way into heaven is through redemption, which has been purchased for them, "nor silver nor gold hath obtained my redemption, the way into heaven could not thus be bought" (#116). The refrain of this song goes on to say, "I am redeemed, but not with silver; I am bought, but not with gold; bought with a price, the blood of Jesus, precious price of love untold."

The song, "Will Jesus Find Us Watching" tells us who is ready for heaven:

> Have we been true to the trust He left us?
> Do we seek to do our best?
> If in our heart there is naught condemns us,
> We shall have a glorious rest.
>
> O can we say we are ready, brother?
> Ready for the soul's bright home?
> Say, will He find you and me still watching,
> Waiting, waiting when the Lord shall come?

One song speaks of a roll call that will take place in heaven, "when the roll is called up yonder, I'll be there" (#186).

They believe Jesus will return to earth someday. When this happens, those Christians who have died will rise from the dead, "the dead in Christ shall rise" (#186). Those who are still alive at this time will be "caught up through the clouds with our Lord into glory" (#81). They will fly to "worlds unknown" and they will "wing my flight to worlds unknown" (#173). This will be announced by a trumpet, which "will sound for his coming" and "the skies with his glories will shine" (#125). They don't know exactly how or when this will occur, whether they will "meet him in the air" (which means they will be alive at the coming of Jesus to earth) or whether they will "walk the vale with Him" (which means they will die before Jesus returns) (#61). What they do know is that Jesus is "wooing" them to heaven, "sinner, list to the loving call, wonderful words of life. All so freely given, wooing us to heaven" (#193).

Where is this heaven? It is "over the fields of glory, over the jasper sea" (#135). It is "on the golden shore" (#135) and "in the better land" (#64). It is at a river "that flows by the throne of God" (#141). At the same time it is "far beyond the starry sky" (#28). One songwriter talks of it as a "mansion in the sky" (#185) that will be entered through "gates of light" (#164). It is a "celestial land" (#16) and a "home beyond the skies . . . up yonder" (#186). Jesus waits for them "at the open door" (#164). The "pearly gates will open" and "we shall tread the streets of gold" (#144).

In heaven, the "city of God" (#161), their souls will be at rest and "at home with God" (#164). They will be "free from the blight of sorrow, free from my doubts and fears" (#135). They will be "safe in the arms of Jesus, safe on his gentle breast . . . safe from corroding care, safe from the world's temptations" (#135). They will no longer be susceptible to sin. They will have immortal joy and "endless delight" (#108). There will be great rejoicing.

They will sing a "melody of peace" (#141). They will sing with the other saints as they gather by the "crystal sea" (#69). The themes of their songs will be Jesus' love for them and "how he ransomed me" (#64). "Stirring anthems" will fill the earth and sky as the "grand, victorious army (lifts) its banner up on high" (#25).

They will wear "glittering crowns" (#108) and a "robe of spotless white" (#185). Their garments will be glorious and shining, "blood washed garments pure and white" (#25). The reason their garments are spotless is because they are part of the "glorious church without spot or wrinkle, washed in the blood of the Lamb" (#25).

Jesus is pictured as a lamb and the light of heaven (there will be no night there), "the Lamb is the Light in the City of Gold" (#161). They will see Jesus' glorious face and they will know who he is "by the print of the nails in his hand" (#185). They will worship and adore Jesus, the bridegroom who has come for his bride. They will reign with him. They will share Jesus' glory and they will actually be like him.

When they get to heaven, they will understand the meaning of experiences they didn't understand while they were living on earth, as indicated in the song, "Sometime We'll Understand":

> Not now, but in the coming years,
> It may be in the better land,
> We'll read the meaning of our tears,
> And there, some time, we'll understand.
>
> We'll catch the broken thread again,
> And finish what we here began;
> Heav'n will the mysteries explain,
> And then, ah then, we'll understand.
>
> We'll know why clouds instead of sun
> Were over many a cherished plan;
> Why song has ceased when scarce begun;
> 'Tis there, some time, we'll understand.
>
> God knows the way, He holds the key,
> He guides us with unerring hand;
> Some time with tearless eyes we'll see;
> Yes, there, up there, we'll understand.

There is the conviction that when Christians die, they will meet other Christians in Heaven, "till we meet at Jesus' feet . . . God be with you till we meet again" (#38). In heaven they will meet other "chosen ones" who are already there, "then he'll bear me safely over where the loved ones I shall meet" (#69). One songwriter says that "friends will be there I have loved long ago" (#123). Those who are already in heaven are seen as "glorified saints" (#81). Another songwriter talks about how "the dear ones in glory" (#185) are beckoning her to come there as well. These "dear ones" will welcome her home when she gets to heaven.

So we can see that, according to the lyrics of the songs about heaven, it is envisioned as a real place being prepared for Christians, a place that is likely in the sky (sometimes spoken of as a land), a well-nigh perfect place where happiness and singing will abound, where Christians will see Jesus, look like him and reign with him.

SUMMARY OF THEMES

What strikes one in the lyrics of these songs are the extremes. Individuals are extremely sinful and then they get extremely happy through salvation. Everything is black and white; there is no room for ambiguity or questioning. The flow goes like this: humanity is sinful, Jesus died to redeem humanity from sin, people need only to accept Jesus as Savior. Then they are saved. Once saved, they are called to witness of Jesus to others. And as they surrender everything to Jesus, they are given guidance and comfort in this life. With Jesus they can conquer any hardship they might experience. And when they die, they will go to a glorious heaven where all is wonderful. Through these songs they enter a world where their experience is validated and metaphors are lived concretely. This becomes the paradigm by which all of life is viewed.

The Songwriters

Of the 115 songwriters represented in the songs I analyzed, twenty-eight were female (24 percent) and eighty-seven were male (76 percent). It was in this era that there was a substantial increase in female songwriters, which could be due to the belief within evangelicalism of the priesthood of all believers. This gave a certain freedom for women to become actors within evangelicalism, especially in the area of song writing. The most prolific female songwriter was Fanny Crosby. Twenty-eight of her songs are among those I examined.

In order to get an idea of who these songwriters were, I will examine where they lived, their religious affiliation, their occupations, and their roles in the church. I will also look at some of the life situations of a few of the writers to see how their experiences in the New World of North America shaped the lyrics of the gospel songs they wrote.

Where the Songwriters Lived

Information about where the songwriters lived is available for 105 of them. It is interesting to note that most of them spent a lot of their time in the Northern United States and it was the North that won the Civil War. And what we saw from the themes of the gospel songs, battle and victory metaphors were used in the songs to talk about victory gained through Jesus. A number of writers moved from place to place; for example, Herbert George Tovey lived in Illinois, California, Washington and Colorado; Civilla Martin moved from Nova Scotia to Georgia; and Joseph Henry Gilmore moved from Massachusetts to New York to Pennsylvania to New Hampshire. Writers lived in Maryland, Philadelphia, Ohio, New York, Massachusetts, Illinois, Michigan, Iowa, Indiana, Colorado, New Hampshire, New Jersey, Maine, Connecticut, Washington DC, Delaware, Missouri, Wisconsin, Minnesota, and Vermont. In the South, writers lived in Florida, Georgia, North Carolina, Kentucky, Louisiana, Texas, and Oklahoma. In the West, they were in Washington, California, Kansas, South Dakota, and Oregon. And the few writers who were Canadian were from Nova Scotia, Ontario, and Quebec.

Religious Affiliation of the Songwriters

Religious affiliation is known for seventy-four out of the 115 writers. Forty-five percent were Methodist. By 1844, the largest Protestant denomination in North America was Methodist and at that time they had approximately four thousand circuit riders who rode on horseback, preaching salvation to large crowds of people.[35] So it is understandable that such a large percentage of songwriters were of the Methodist tradition. The next highest religious affiliation was Baptist (20 percent) and then Presbyterian (19 percent). The remaining were Congregational, Salvation Army, Unitarian, Quaker, and Church of the Nazarene. This shows how much the songs of the fundamentalist movement penetrated numerous Christian denominations with an evangelical mindset.

Songwriters' Occupations and Roles in the Church

Those who wrote gospel songs tended to have leadership roles in the church or in church-related institutions. Women's occupations and roles in the church are known for eighteen (64 percent) of the twenty-eight female songwriters. A number of them held supportive roles in the church and worked with children in Sunday School. Four were ministers' wives and five were Sunday School teachers. A few women had leadership experience within the Sunday School. A few worked in the

35. Addison, "How the West Was Won," 6.

literary field. They were poets, writers, and editors. One of these wrote for the Women's Temperance Movement. A few were school teachers and others were in the music field.

Men's occupations and roles in the church are known for seventy-four (85 percent) of the eighty-seven male songwriters. Forty-eight (65 percent) of male songwriters were ministers or evangelists. Twenty (27 percent) were in the music field: song leaders, choir directors, music directors, music editors, music professors, musicians, or composers. Several of these worked with evangelists as singers and song leaders. Eight of them had a connection with Moody Bible Institute, either having attended the school or having taught there. One of these was first Rector, later Dean and then President of the Institute. Only one of the male songwriters taught in a Sunday School. Careers unrelated to the church were held by some of these men. A few were engaged in the army, others were poets, editors, and teachers. Some worked in the medical field and others were employed in publishing companies.

Life Circumstances of the Songwriters

A good number of songs were written in response to difficult life circumstances. Life was not easy for many of the songwriters. People lost relatives at sea. Everyone probably knew someone who was killed in the Civil War or World War I. Besides the deaths that accompanied war, the war brought insecurity and fear.

In this era, the infant mortality rate was high and many died young. Where there were chronic health concerns, these often were untreatable, so people just had to live with them. Three of the women were either ill or disabled for some or all of their lives. This experience impacted the lyrics of their songs.

In order to examine more closely how life circumstances influenced the songs that were written, I will look closely at six female songwriters and seven male.[36]

JESSIE BROWN POUNDS (1861–1921)

Of the six female songwriters, four had health issues. Jessie Brown Pounds was in poor health right from childhood. She started to write

36. Information on the life circumstances of the songwriters is taken from the *The Cyber Hymnal*™ database at www.hymntime.com/tch/.

poetry and submitted articles to religious publications. After an editor told her that her poems would make good songs, she began writing gospel songs. One of her songs is "Anywhere With Jesus":

> Anywhere with Jesus I am not alone;
> Other friends may fail me He is still my own;
> Though his hand may lead me over dreary ways,
> Anywhere with Jesus is a house of praise.
>
> Anywhere with Jesus I can go to sleep,
> When the dark'ning shadows round about me creep;
> Knowing I shall waken never more to roam,
> Anywhere with Jesus will be home, sweet home.

THIS SONG EXPRESSES HER loneliness and the comfort Jesus gave her, even in tough times, which for her included the discouragement of being ill. She wrote over four hundred songs.

CIVILLA DURFEE MARTIN (1866–1948)

When Civilla D. Martin was sick in bed, and her husband was off preaching, she wrote "God Will Take Care of You":

> Be not dismayed whate'er betide, God will take care of you;
> Beneath His wings of love abide, God will take care of you.
>
> Through days of toil when heart doth fail, God will take care
>   of you;
> When dangers fierce your path assail, God will take care of you;
>
> All you may need he will provide, God will take care of you;
> Nothing you ask will be denied, God will take care of you.
>
> No matter what may be the test, God will take care of you;
> Lean, weary one, upon his breast, God will take care of you.

Martin's comfort was that God would take care of her, no matter what the test, the emphasis shown by the repetition of "God will take care of you." She clung to this hope. The song could have functioned almost as a mantra for her.

ELIZA EDMUNDS HEWITT (1851–1920)

Eliza Edmund Hewitt was a teacher, but she didn't teach very long before she developed a spinal problem. This resulted in being an invalid for most of her life. She wrote over seventy songs, among them, "Stepping in the Light":

> Pressing more closely to Him who is leading
> When we are tempted to turn from the way
> Trusting the arm that is strong to defend us
> Happy, how happy our praises each day.
>
> Refrain: How beautiful to walk in the steps of the Savior,
> Stepping in the light, stepping in the light,
> How beautiful to walk in the steps of the Savior,
> Led in paths of light!

It is interesting that she used walking metaphors, since she likely had difficulty walking. In the song, she imagines that in the spiritual world, she does walk and that this is a beautiful experience for her.

Hewitt also wrote about the prospect of going to heaven, a future that would surpass the pain of her illness. In "Sing the Wondrous Love of Jesus," she wrote of the "day of rejoicing" to occur "when we all get to heaven." The second verse speaks of her experience in life compared with her anticipated life in heaven:

> While we walk the pilgrim pathway,
> Clouds will overspread the sky;
> But when trav'ling days are over,
> Not a shadow, not a sigh.
>
> Refrain: When we all get to heaven,
> What a day of rejoicing that will be!
> When we all see Jesus,
> We'll sing and shout the victory
> —Fanny Crosby (1820–1915)

The most prolific female songwriter, Fanny Crosby, was blinded by an incompetent doctor at six years of age. Crosby saw her visual impairment as a gift that enabled her to experience God through music. Her songs talk about her close relationship with God, "He Hideth My Soul," "Safe in the Arms of Jesus," "Close to Thee," "All the Way My Savior Leads Me," "Redeemed How I Love to Proclaim It," and "My Song Shall Be of Jesus." Her song, "Tis the Blessed Hour of Prayer" expresses the sweetness of her prayer time:

> 'Tis the blessed hour of prayer,
> When our hearts lowly bend,

And we gather to Jesus, our Savior and friend;
If we come to Him in faith, His protection to share;

Crosby wrote under ninety-eight pseudonyms, fourteen of which were male names and many simply initials. One of the reasons she wrote with so many pseudonyms is so that it would not appear that the majority of songs in particular hymnbooks had been written by her.[37]

Eliza Hewitt offered the following poem, which was read at Crosby's funeral:

Away to the country of sunshine and song,
Our songbird has taken her flight,
And she who has sung in the darkness so long
Now sings in the beautiful light;
The harp-strings here broken are sweetly restrung
To ring in a chorus sublime;
The hymns that on earth she so trustfully sung
Keep tune with eternity's chime!

What heart can conceive of the rapture she knows
Awakened to glories so bright,
Where radiant splendor unceasingly glows,
Where cometh no shadows of night!
Her '*life-work is ended*,' and over the tide,
'*Redeemed*' in His presence to stand,
She knows her Redeemer, for her crucified,
'*By the print of the nails in His hand*.'

'*Blessed Assurance*'—the lamp in her soul
That made earthly midnight as naught!
A 'New Song' of joy shall unceasingly roll
To Him who her ransom had bought.
To '*Rescue the Perishing*,' her greatest delight,
What bliss, in the Homeland, to meet
With those she has told of the Lord's saving might,
Together, to bow at His feet.

Good-bye, dearest Fanny, goodbye for a while,
You walk in the shadows no more;
Around you, the sunbeams of glory will smile;
The Lamb is the Light of that Shore!

37. "Fanny Crosby," *Christian History*, August 8, 2008, http://www.christianity today.com/ch/131christians/poets/crosby.html.

> Someday we will meet in the City above;
> Together, we'll look on His face;
> Safe, *'Safe in the Arms'* of the Jesus we love;
> Together we'll sing, *'Saved by Grace!'*

(Words in italics above are either titles of songs Crosby wrote or lyrics from those songs.) The poem is all about the life in heaven, so firmly believed by fundamentalist evangelicals.

ANNE MAY SEBRING MURPHY (1878–1942)

Anne May Sebring Murphy, another female songwriter, was widowed early and because of this became very poor. Her song, "Constantly Abiding," talks about the security she found in Jesus.

> There's a peace in my heart that the world never gave,
> A peace it cannot take away;
> Tho' the trials of life may surround like a cloud,
> I've a peace that has come there to stay!
>
> Refrain: Constantly abiding, Jesus is mine;
> Constantly abiding, rapture divine;
> He never leaves me lonely, whispers, O so kind:
> "I will never leave thee," Jesus is mine.
>
> All the world seemed to sing of a Savior and King,
> When peace sweetly came to my heart;
> Troubles all fled away and my night turned to day,
> Blessed Jesus, how glorious thou art!

ADELAIDE ADDISON POLLARD (1862–1934)

Adelaide Addison Pollard, writer of over one hundred songs, attended Moody Bible Institute and taught at the Christian and Missionary Alliance Training School in New York. She felt that God was calling her to go to Africa as a missionary, but was unable to raise enough funds to go. This was very distressing to her, but at a prayer meeting, she heard a woman pray, "It doesn't matter what you bring into our lives, just have your own way with us." This got Pollard thinking and that night she wrote, "Have Thine Own Way, Lord":

> Have Thine own way, Lord! Have Thine own way!
> Thou art the potter, I am the clay.
> Mould me and make me after Thy will,

While I am waiting, yielded and still.

Have Thine own way, Lord! Have Thine own way!
Hold o'er my being absolute sway!
Fill with Thy spirit 'till all shall see
Christ only, always, living in me.

The song was a prayer to God that showed she had accepted what she felt was God's way, even though it was not what she wanted.

HORATIO GATES SPAFFORD (1828–1888)

And now, turning to male songwriters, Horatio G. Spafford, a businessman, wrote "It Is Well With My Soul" after two major personal traumas. The first was the Chicago fire in 1871 that brought him to financial ruin. The second was the death of all his four daughters at sea. At a later date when Spafford's ship passed the spot where his daughters died, he wrote the song:

When peace, like a river attendeth my way,
When sorrows like sea billows roll,
Whatever my lot, thou hast taught me to say,
It is well, it is well with my soul.

When Satan should buffet, tho' trials should come,
Let this blest assurance control
That Christ has regarded my helpless estate
And hath shed His own blood for my soul.

Although in grief about the loss of his daughters, he took comfort in the assurance of Jesus giving his "blood for my soul."

DANIEL WEBSTER WHITTLE (1840–1901)

Daniel Webster Whittle lost his right arm in the Civil War and was interned as a prisoner of war. It was then he began reading the Bible. One day an orderly told him there was a young boy in the prison hospital who was dying and wanted someone to pray with him. Since the orderly had seen the Major reading the Bible, the orderly asked the Major if he would be willing to go pray with the boy. Hesitant at first, the Major did go to the boy's bed, but as he knelt beside it, the Major himself became a Christian. When he got up from his prayer, the boy was dead. The Major believed that it was through this dying boy that he came to Jesus. One of the songs he wrote was "I Know Whom I Have Believed":

I know not why God's wondrous grace

To me he hath made known,
Nor why unworthy Christ in love redeemed me for His own.

Refrain: But I know whom I have believed
And am persuaded that He is able
To keep that which I've committed unto Him against that day.

Another of Whittle's songs reflects his military background and shows the comparison with his spiritual experience:

There's a royal banner given for display
To the soldiers of the King;
As an ensign fair we lift it up today
While as ransomed ones we sing.

Refrain: Marching on, marching on,
For Christ count everything but loss!
And to crown Him King, toil and sing
'Neath the banner of the cross!

Though the foe may rage and gather as the flood,
Let the standard be displayed;
And beneath its folds as soldiers of the Lord,
For the truth be not dismayed!

Military references are plentiful in this song: royal banner, soldiers, crown, King, foe, standard, and folds (of the flag). In the same way that enemies were fought in the Civil War, Whittle felt the spiritual foes of the gospel needed to be fought.

ROBERT LOWRY (1826–1899)

One very hot day in July 1864, Robert Lowry, a professor of literature and Baptist minister, was exhausted from the heat. In his state of physical exhaustion, he imagined a future heaven with a river, clear as crystal. Out of his imagination came the song, "Shall We Gather at the River?"

Shall we gather at the river where bright angel feet have trod,
With its crystal tide forever flowing by the throne of God?

Refrain: Yes, we'll gather at the river,
The beautiful, the beautiful river
Gather with the saints at the river
That flows by the throne of God.

On the margin of the river, washing up its silver spray
We will walk and worship ever all the happy, golden day.

This song contains images from the book of Revelation, which talks about the throne of God, a crystal river, worship of God, and the gathering of saints on that "happy, golden day."

JOSEPH HENRY GILMORE (1834–1918)

During the Civil War, Joseph Henry Gilmore preached on Psalm 23 at the First Baptist Church in Philadelphia. When he came to the words in the Psalm, "He leadeth me," his mind turned to the reality of the Civil War. He decided right then that whatever the outcome of the war would be, the important thing for him was that God was leading. Out of this personal realization, he wrote the song "He Leadeth Me":

> He leadeth me; O blessed th't!
> O words with heav'nly comfort fraught!
> Whate'er I do, where'er I be,
> Still 'tis God's hand that leadeth me.
>
> Sometimes 'mid scenes of deepest gloom
> Sometimes where Eden's bowers bloom,
> By waters calm, o'er troubled sea;
> Still tis His hand that leadeth me.
>
> Lord, I would clasp thy hand in mine,
> Or ever murmur nor repine,
> Content whatever lot I see,
> Since 'tis my God that leadeth me.

JUDSON WHEELER VAN DEVENTER

Judson Van DeVenter taught art in a school in Pennsylvania. While at a meeting in the home of a certain George Sebring he found himself struggling as to whether he should have a career as an artist or enter the field of evangelism. His act of surrendering to God and his decision to become an evangelist was the catalyst for writing the song, "All to Jesus I Surrender:"

> All to Jesus, I surrender;
> All to Him I freely give;
> I will ever love and trust Him,
> In His presence daily live.
>
> Refrain:
> I surrender all, I surrender all,
> All to Thee, my blessed Savior,
> I surrender all.

All to Jesus I surrender;
Humbly at His feet I bow,
Worldly pleasures all forsaken;
Take me, Jesus, take me now.

WILLIAM ORCUTT CUSHING (1823–1902)

William Orcutt Cushing was a minister who began writing songs after his wife died and after his own health declined. His song, "Under His Wings," reveals his deep sorrow, his health challenges, and his trust in sheltered protection while resting in Jesus:

Under His wings I am safely abiding,
Though the night deepens and tempests are wild,
Still I can trust Him; I know He will keep me,
He has redeemed me, and I am His child.

Refrain: Under His wings, under His wings,
Who from His love can sever?
Under His wings my soul shall abide,
Safely abide forever.

Under His wings, what a refuge in sorrow!
How the heart yearningly turns to His rest!
Often when earth has no balm for my healing,
There I find comfort, and there I am blessed.

Under His wings, oh, what precious enjoyment!
There will I hide till life's trials are o'er;
Sheltered, protected, no evil can harm me,
Resting in Jesus, I'm safe evermore.

CHARLES ALBERT TINDLEY (1851–1933)

Charles Albert Tindley, a son of slaves, taught himself to read and write. He obtained his Divinity Degree while a janitor of a Methodist Episcopal Church in Philadelphia. Later he became minister in that church. The struggles he had as an African American, both to get a good education and to succeed in becoming a minister, are evident in one of the songs he wrote, "If the World From You Withhold":

If the world from you withhold of its silver and its gold,
And you have to get along with meager fare,

Just remember, in His Word, how He feeds the little bird;
Take your burden to the Lord and leave it there.

Refrain: Leave it there, leave it there,
Take your burden to the Lord and leave it there.
If you trust and never doubt,
He will surely bring you out.
Take your burden to the Lord and leave it there.

If your body suffers pain and your health you can't regain,
And your soul is almost sinking in despair,
Jesus knows the pain you feel, He can save and He can heal;
Take your burden to the Lord and leave it there.

When your enemies assail and your heart begins to fail,
Don't forget that God in Heaven answers prayer;
He will make a way for you and will lead you safely through.
Take your burden to the Lord and leave it there.

When your youthful days are gone and old age is stealing on,
And your body bends beneath the weight of care;
He will never leave you then, He'll go with you to the end.
Take your burden to the Lord and leave it there.

As a janitor, he had "to get along with meagre fare," but he took his "burden to the Lord." Even though he was "almost sinking in despair" he trusted in God's healing and guidance.

These songwriters wrote out of their own experiences, many of which were difficult to bear. And as some began to write songs, others did so as well. There was a mimetic effect in the writing of songs, in that songwriters expressed their experiences and beliefs with the same style of music, the same themes, and the same musical patterns.

Usage of the Songs

Singing was crucial to the success of the fundamentalist evangelical movement. The songs that people wrote, often flowing from their own personal experiences, were successful in reinforcing the firmly held beliefs of the fundamentalist evangelical movement. Gospel songs spoke to the heart; they had a certain emotional pull that brought people to make decisions to accept Jesus. And since these songs were sung again and again, people became attached to the music and the words, so much so that they would sing them wherever they were, not just at religious services.

Even though it has been many years since I sang these songs, I still remember all the verses of most of the songs mentioned in this chapter. And after I worked through a few drafts, I found myself drawn to the piano and I played and sang some of my old favourites, which brought me back to the time when I passionately believed every word of every song.

A large number of songs were written specifically for camp meetings, revival services or Sunday Schools. One of these writers was Philip Paul Bliss (1838–1876), who was persuaded by Moody to go into a full-time gospel music career. Major Whittle was one of the evangelists with whom Bliss worked. Bliss's song, "Almost Persuaded Now to Believe" was inspired by the words of Reverend Brundage, who at the end of his sermon said, "He [*sic*] who is almost persuaded is almost saved, and to be almost saved is to be entirely lost." So Bliss wrote:

> Almost persuaded now to believe,
> Almost persuaded Christ to receive;
> Seems now some soul to say, "go, Spirit, go thy way,
> Some more convenient day on Thee I'll call."

> Almost persuaded, come, come today,
> Almost persuaded, turn not away;
> Jesus invites you here, angels are ling'ring near,
> Prayers rise from hearts so dear, O wanderer come.

> Almost persuaded, harvest is past!
> Almost persuaded, doom comes at last!
> Almost cannot avail, almost is but to fail!
> Sad, sad that bitter wail, almost but lost!

This sung was sung to bring people to accept salvation. There was no ambiguity here. You were either persuaded and received Christ or you were lost.

Another writer who wrote songs for evangelistic usage was Herbert George Tovey. Tovey studied at Moody Bible Institute and taught at a number of Bible institutes, including the Bible Institute of Los Angeles. He was also a Baptist minister. His song, "Give Me a Passion for Souls Dear Lord," shows how much he was convinced that people needed to be saved:

Give me a passion for souls, dear Lord,
A passion to save the lost;
O that Thy love were by all adored,
And welcomed at any cost.

Refrain: Jesus, I long, I long to be winning
Men [*sic*] who are lost, and constantly sinning;
O may this hour be one of beginning
The story of pardon to tell.

Though there are dangers untold and stern
Confronting me in the way,
Willingly still would I go, nor turn,
But trust Thee for grace each day.

How shall this passion for souls be mine?
Lord, make Thou the answer clear;
Help me to throw out the old lifeline
To those who are struggling near.

The song shows his strong desire for a "passion to save the lost."

During an evangelistic meeting when a preacher talked about "new birth" using the biblical text about Jesus telling Nicodemus that he must be "born again" in order to be "saved," musician George Stebbins had the idea to put those words to music, so he approached William True Sleeper to write a song. What resulted was:

A ruler once came to Jesus by night
To ask Him the way of salvation and light;
The Master made answer in words true and plain,
"Ye must be born again."

Refrain: "Ye must be born again,
Ye must be born again,
I verily, verily, say unto thee,
Ye must be born again."

Ye children of men [*sic*], attend to the Word,
So solemnly uttered by Jesus the Lord;
And let not this message to you be in vain,
"Ye must be born again."

O ye who would enter that glorious rest,
And sing with the ransomed the song of the blest,

> The life everlasting if ye would obtain,
> "Ye must be born again."
>
> A dear one in Heaven thy heart yearns to see,
> At the beautiful gate may be watching for thee,
> Then list to the note of this solemn refrain,
> "Ye must be born again."

This song, inspired by a sermon, was suitable for use at evangelistic services. The "born again" metaphor became a dominant way of talking about salvation.

Relationship of the Songs to the Fundamentalist Evangelical Belief System

The content of gospel songs mimicked the fundamentalist evangelical theological beliefs of the late nineteenth century. During this time, various checklists of beliefs were formulated at the prophetic conferences and by specific denominations, but all of them included a belief in the sinfulness of human nature; the necessity of conversion; redemption through Jesus' blood; living a holy life; belief in heaven and hell; and Jesus' bodily return to earth. All of these beliefs are evident in the songs I examined. The songs reflected the dearly held evangelical beliefs and played a primary role in strengthening the emerging fundamentalist evangelical movement.

The songs present a formula for salvation that was dependent on a sacrificial view of Jesus' death. First people live in chaos; they feel sinful, bad, unworthy, isolated, and condemned. Next, all of this is put onto Jesus who, according to the lyrics, died a violent, sacrificial death. Through faith in Jesus "blood" all the terrible sinners are transformed and united. There is order, togetherness, relief, and an end to chaos. After this, Jesus is deified and an eternal happy life in heaven is possible for believers.

Fundamentalism presents Jesus' death as a sacrificial ritual and these songs mimic that belief. When people sing these songs again and again, they are repeatedly drawn into the sacrificial myth as they retell the story in a stylized fashion, a way that gets them hooked into thinking of salvation only in terms of the sacrifice of Jesus. Singing these songs becomes a ritualized way of telling the story of their salvation again and again. They sing in an uncritical and personal way, that "Jesus died for me." While the songs are sung in the community, everyone individually has gone through the experience of salvation and collectively they have this in common, that "Jesus died for our sins and we are made whole."

The system works well as long as everyone believes the fundamentals. A problem arises when the ritual doesn't work for people anymore. When this happens, there is a crisis, both for individuals and for fundamentalism. Several books have been written, telling the stories of people for whom the story as told in these songs doesn't hold true anymore. These stories form the basis for the third section of this book, a section analyzing the personal experiences of former fundamentalist evangelicals. But before we look at these stories, I will discuss in the next section, methods of interpretation of the Bible, since it is one's approach to the biblical text that informs one's belief system. And in fundamentalism this is especially important because it was the higher critical approach to biblical interpretation that was threatening, and formed the basis of the rift with liberalism.

PART II

Engaging the Fundamentalist Evangelical Interpretation of the Bible

WHEN FUNDAMENTALIST EVANGELICALISM EMERGED, there were several lists of fundamentals drawn up. The Niagara Creed, developed at the 1878 prophetic conference in Niagara-on-the-Lake, contained fourteen separate articles. These focussed on the inspiration of the Bible, the sinfulness of human nature, the necessity to be born again, redemption through Jesus' death, and the belief in heaven and hell. Of these, two functioned as anchor points, strands of belief that were tied together in a tight web that linked every text in the Bible together, to form a worldview that informed the fundamentalist evangelical mindset. These were a belief in the authority and infallibility of the Bible, and a belief in hell as the destination for those who would not embrace the message of the Bible as derived through the hermeneutical lens of the fundamentalist framework.

These two strands of belief form the substance of Part II, in which I engage the fundamentalist evangelical approach to the interpretation of the Bible by offering a perspective that reveals the human dimensions in the writing of the Bible, including its subsequent translations and versions. I show how biblical exegesis functions when matters of language and content are combined with a hermeneutics of suspicion that dares to look for meaning other than that exemplified within fundamentalist evangelical orthodoxy. I propose an alternate approach to biblical interpretation through an intra-biblical case study of a 1 Timothy text that was used to justify forbidding women to preach. Using my own translation from the Greek, I show how the traditional way of interpreting this text is not true to either the words of the text or to the cultural context within which it was written. And finally, I combine a study of the concept of hell in ancient times and in a number of religious traditions, together with biblical exegesis of New Testament texts that speak about the afterlife.

5

Authority of the Bible:
A Primary Fundamental

FOR THE FUNDAMENTALIST EVANGELICAL, the whole Bible is read through the lens of the fundamentals, all of which are claimed to have been derived from the Bible. Since the Bible is understood as a unified book, with a singular author (God), where everything has been predetermined in order to get the message of salvation across, the entire Bible has authority and each individual verse is there for a purpose. It is all mutually reinforced. In the Bible one finds the fundamentals that need to be absolute. The reason they need to be absolute is because they deal with ultimate truth. The need for ultimate truth results in the need for absolute authority. The Bible itself is then read for evidence that is absolutely infallible. Verses are found to support this; the circle is closed and it becomes a complete thought system.

THE FUNDAMENTALIST EVANGELICAL APPROACH TO THE BIBLE

For fundamentalist evangelicals the Bible holds the authority it does because they believe it comes directly from God. It is believed that in the Bible is found everything a person needs to know about God, salvation, Jesus, what to believe, how to live, and what happens after death. It is seen as the inspired and infallible Word of God. One text that is often quoted is 2 Timothy 3:16, "All scripture is given by inspiration of God, and is profitable for doctrine, for reproof, for correction, for instruction in righteousness" (King James Version). It is important to realize that by "scripture," first century Christians meant the Hebrew Bible (Old Testament). That is the scripture they possessed and referred to in their writings. Yet in the centuries that followed, this verse was taken to mean that the whole Bible was God's inspired words to humans. The fundamentalist evangelical rationale for this point of view was that when God directed that particular verse to be included in 2 Timothy, God already had in mind that the New Testament would eventually be written, and when written, it too would be included in "all scripture." But if we look at the context of that verse within 2 Timothy, we observe that the author's concern in the Pastoral letters (1 and 2 Timothy and Titus) was to promote sound teaching and to fight off what he considered to be heretical teaching. There is reference to "fruitless discussion" (1 Tim 1:6), "making assertions about the law without proper understanding" (1 Tim 1:7), "worldly fables" (1 Tim 4:7), "controversial questions and disputes about words, abusive language, different teachings" (1 Tim 6:4), and "worldly and empty chatter and opposing arguments of what is falsely called knowledge" (1 Tim. 6:20–21). So it makes sense that the author would want to reinforce to his readers that scripture, as they understood it, was "given by inspiration of God," and that they should not follow other teachings, referred to as heretical or false teachings.

The other thing to note about this verse is that the Greek word for "inspiration of God," (*theoneustos*) does not appear anywhere else in the New Testament. So there is no point of comparison to help determine its context and meaning.

Inerrancy of the Bible

As a result of the reaction to science and liberal biblical scholarship, the belief in the inerrancy of the Bible was prominent among fundamentalist evangelicals in the early 1900s. This view of the inerrancy of the Bible has persisted among fundamentalist evangelicals into the later 1900s. In 1978, for instance, evangelical leaders met in Chicago to launch the International Council on Inerrancy to defend the Bible against liberal approaches. The Council prepared a statement on biblical inerrancy, which was signed by three hundred evangelical scholars. It stated that "the written Word in its entirety is revelation given by God . . . that inspiration is the work in which God by His Spirit, through human writers, gave us His Word . . . that Scripture, having been given by divine inspiration, is infallible . . . that Scripture in its entirety is inerrant, being free from all falsehood, fraud, or deceit . . . that a confession of the full authority, infallibility, and inerrancy of Scripture is vital to a sound understanding of the whole of the Christian faith."[1] In more recent times, not all evangelicals have held to the infallibility of the Bible in this same narrow way.

A Literal-Factual Reading

When it makes sense to do so, fundamentalist evangelicals read the Bible in a literal-factual way. It should be noted that some verses and contexts are not taken literally, for example, when Jesus says that people are the salt of the earth (Matt 5:13), it is understood that people are not really made of salt. However, anything presented in a historical narrative genre is taken to be literal historical fact, to the point where, in the biblical story of the creation of the first man and the first woman, Adam and Eve are understood to have been the first human beings on earth. David Tomlinson notes that "if the Bible says that God gets angry or rejoices, or if it tells us that God is a father or a king, then that is fairly much the way it is."[2] When the Bible says there was a flood over the whole earth, it is taken as history, "The waters swelled so mightily on the earth that all the high mountains under the whole heaven were covered" (Gen 7:19). And when it says all living things were "blotted out from the earth" (Gen 7:23) then they really were blotted out. And when the Bible says that Jonah was in the belly of a large fish for three days, that's where he was, "Jonah was in the belly of the fish three days and three nights" and then the fish "spewed Jonah out upon the dry land" (Jon 1:17; 2:10). *As a child this was puzzling to me. I could believe that a fish could eat a person, but how could the person be spit up on shore in one piece? Don't fish usually eat what they swallow? Yet, because I was taught that every word in the Bible was true, I believed it. God can do anything and I shouldn't worry about the logistics of it.*

Moses was in the wilderness for forty years. Jesus was in the desert forty days. There were twelve tribes of Israel. Jesus had twelve disciples.

---

1. International Council on Inerrancy, http://www.kulikovskyonline.net/herme neutics/csbe.htm, 1978.

2. Tomlinson, *The Post-Evangelical*, 96.

There was no thought in fundamentalist evangelicalism that these numbers might not actually refer to forty days, twelve tribes, and twelve disciples, and that the numbers have been used in a symbolic sense.

When advances in science made belief of certain biblical texts difficult, fundamentalist evangelicals could easily explain them. For example, if science showed that the earth was not created in six days, as indicated in Genesis 1, some believed science was wrong. But others found biblical texts to explain it. They quoted 2 Pet 3:8, "with the Lord one day is like a thousand years," and they said that six days may not have meant six literal days as we know them today, since God thinks of time differently than we do.

When apparent contradictions or inconsistencies in the Bible were pointed out, these could usually be explained by fundamentalist evangelicals. In cases where they were unable to explain them, the reason given was that humans are finite. No need to worry about the details. Anything not understood now, would become clear by and by in the life hereafter. This rationale was reinforced by songs such as "We'll Understand it Better By and By."

A Selective/Adaptive Literal Reading

What is interesting is that not all texts are interpreted literally. There is a practice of selective literal reading of texts. When it says in 1 Timothy 2:8 that men should "pray, lifting up holy hands" and that women should not braid their hair (1 Tim 2:9), fundamentalist evangelicals explain that this text was specific to the first century and not meant for today. So today men don't have to lift hands when they pray and women are allowed to braid their hair. If this is so easily done for some texts, it seems inconsistent that they cannot do the same for other texts, texts for instance that are used to keep women from taking on certain roles in the church or texts quoted to support their belief that homosexuality is sin. There is a selective literal-factual reading only of those biblical texts that support their already firmly held fundamentalist beliefs.

Closely related to the selective literal reading of the Bible is what Steve Miller calls adaptive reading, which he defines as "twisting the meaning of a text to say something quite different from what was intended."[3] An example of this is 1 Timothy 2:11 where the versions of the Bible that

3. Miller, "Inerrancy and Authority," 4.

were deemed to be accurate translated the text as "let women be silent in the church." But as my own exegesis of the Timothy text shows (see chapter 6), this is not at all what was meant by the Greek text.

Proof-Texting

Another kind of reading of biblical texts is called "proof-texting." Proof texting involves taking biblical texts out of context and using them to make certain points. The texts are used without reference to who wrote them, when they wrote them, why they wrote them, the cultural context, nor the context of the texts within the larger piece of literature (such as preceding and succeeding chapters and books).

Verses from here and there in the Bible are sometimes strung together to prove the validity of a particular dearly held belief. Sermons are dotted with biblical quotations from all over the Bible in order to make certain points. *When I was in my early twenties I got a new Revised Standard Bible. This particular Bible had a few empty pages in the front and in the back. I used these pages to record key points of sermons given by our pastor. It turned out that our pastor at that time was very keen on dispensationalism. It was on one of these empty pages that I recorded the main points of a sermon called "What We Believe About Hell." And it is an excellent example of using several verses to make certain points: proof texting. His first point was "After death comes the judgment" and texts to support it included Heb 9:27, Matt 5:22 and 2 Pet 2:9. For his second point—"This judgment comes in the form of eternal retribution"—he used Matt 25:41 and 46. For his third and final point—"This Place is Hell"—he referred to Sheol in the Old Testament and Gehenna in the New Testament, mentioning that it is "a gaping mouth which asks for more souls." He didn't tell us that Sheol was an underground place for all who die and that Gehenna was a real place in the real world, a nuisance ground just outside of Jerusalem.*

The doctrine of sin and salvation is based on verses that are lifted out of their literary and historical contexts and used to prove the point that all have sinned and need to be saved by Jesus. The story goes like this: Since a verse in the Bible says, "All have sinned and fall short of the glory of God" (Rom 3:23), this is taken to mean that all humankind are sinners and there is no way God will accept people with all that sin. This became a universal principle. But all may be saved, because "God so loved the world that he gave his only Son, so that everyone who believes in him, may not perish but may have eternal life" (John 3:16). It's simple. If you believe in God's Son, you will not "perish" (burn in hell). And how does Jesus' death save you from hell? It was a sacrifice for everyone's sins, as it says in the book of Hebrews: "And it is by God's will that we have been sanctified through the offering of the body of Jesus Christ once for all. . . . But when Christ had offered for all time a single sacrifice for sins, he sat down at the right hand of God" (Heb 10:10, 12). Jesus' death paid for our sins. And when one accepts Jesus, the news of salvation is too good to be kept to oneself. The Bible tells readers they are to spread the good word: "Go therefore and make disciples of all nations" (Matt 11:19). And those who are "saved" will be in heaven with Jesus: "For since we believe that Jesus died and rose again, even so, through Jesus, God will bring with him those who have died. . . . And so we will be with the Lord forever" (1 Thess 4:14, 17).

So there it is in a nutshell: the primary fundamentals proven with a few verses from the Bible and of course, reinforced by many other verses with the same message. All of this is done without reference to the particular contexts of the books that contain these verses. And any other verses that have to do with sin, salvation, Jesus' death, Jesus' resurrection, heaven, and hell are read through this lens, which is reinforced by songs and preaching.

HOW THE BIBLE CAME TO US

In an effort to understand the Bible in a non-fundamentalist way, we can ask how the Bible came to be written. The human side of the Bible comes through in the writing of the text, translating the text, choosing the books that will be accepted into the biblical canon, producing versions of the Bible, and deciding how to interpret it.

The Writing of the Bible

Those who wrote the texts we now have in the Bible reflected on events and experiences, interpreted them, and wrote about them. They wrote in a particular language (Hebrew, Aramaic or Greek) and in a particular genre (narrative, poem, song, letter, reporting of events). How did they know what to write? Some wrote about what they had heard and seen, some copied what other writers had written, and others wrote to get information across to people they had met. They wrote letters that are now included in the New Testament. Some had a certain point they wanted to make. In the letter by Jude, for example, the argument Jude is making is to persuade readers to keep the faith as he taught it, "I find it necessary to write and appeal to you to contend for the faith that was once for all entrusted to the saints. For certain intruders have stolen in among you . . . who pervert the grace of our God into licentiousness" (Jude 3, 4).

What influenced their writings? They wrote using their own cultural lens and their own perception of events and experiences. They were influenced by what others had already written. They may have been aware of concurrent similar writings, for example, while the Jewish people were exiled in Babylonia, they will have heard about the Babylonian creation story, which has a striking resemblance to the Genesis creation account. Writers were also influenced by their audience, whether it was to an individual they were writing (like Paul to Timothy) or to a community (like the book of Romans, written to facilitate reconciliation between Jewish and Gentile communities).

The books of the Hebrew Bible were already written and compiled by the time of Jesus. In the third century BCE, as Egypt became Hellenized, the Hebrew Bible was translated into Greek. This was called the Septuaginta and was done by seventy-two translators, six elders from each of the twelve tribes of Israel[4]. Translations into Aramaic, called the Targums, were written for the Jews who lived further north and spoke Aramaic.[5]

We do not have any originals of the Bible. The oldest copies of New Testament texts date from the second century or later. These are the closest we have to the original text.

The first biblical manuscripts were written on papyrus, a plant that stood twelve to fifteen feet high and six inches across. It was cut into foot long sections and split open lengthwise. Then the pith was cut into thin strips. A layer of these was placed perpendicular to another layer and pressed together. Papyri were rolled together to form a scroll or *biblos*. By the second century, pages were laid on top of each other and tied with string. This was called a *biblion* (the origin of our word, Bible).

4. The Jewish Publication Society, *Tanakh*, xv.
5. Ibid.

Papyrus was used for writing up to 300 CE. All papyrus manuscripts found of the New Testaments are fragments, the oldest fragment being of John 18:31–33, which is dated to approximately 150 CE.[6]

From 300 CE to the medieval era, texts were written and copied on parchment (the skin of cattle, sheep or goats). Some of these were uncials (written in capital letters) and others miniscules (in cursive script).

Several kinds of documents were examined in order to decide on the most reliable text of the Greek New Testament. There were papyri and parchment. There were commentaries by the church fathers—leaders in the early church after the apostles died—(written between 200–900 CE), Greek lectionaries (800–1400 CE), and ancient versions of the Greek text translated into Latin, Coptic, Gothic, Armenian, Ethiopic, Georgian, and Syriac (300–1400 CE).[7] *When I was in seminary studying New Testament Greek, I saw firsthand at the bottom of each page of the Greek New Testament, the names of all the existent variant readings of the texts.* These were the texts that went into the making of the Greek New Testament text. Decisions needed to be made along the way as to which of the manuscripts (since there were no originals) were most accurate and thus deserved to be included in the New Testament.

The New Testament Canon

Since there were thousands of manuscripts, how was it decided which ones should be included in the New Testament? Scholars refer to this process as the development of a canon. The word "canon" is a Greek word meaning "a reed used for measurement," so the word started to signify "the norm" or "the standard." The canon would eventually include all books that were accepted as authentic and authoritative, but by whose standards?

It is interesting to note that there are more than four gospels in existence. In fact, there were at least fifty gospels, some known only by their title.[8] To name a few, there is a second gospel of Matthew, the Infancy Gospel of Thomas, the Gospel According to Hebrews, the Gospel of Mary, the Gospel of Peter, the Gospel of Nicodemus, and the Gospel

6. Bruce, *The Books and the Parchments*, 181.

7. Aland, et al., *The Greek New Testament*, xiii–xl.

8. Notes from the class, "Introduction to Biblical Studies," taught by Professor David Ewert, Mennonite Brethren Biblical Seminary, Fresno CA, Fall 1980.

of the Ebionites. And there are other epistles (letters), including the Epistle to the Laodiceans, and Letters of Christ and Abgar (correspondence between Abgar and Jesus). One reason for the inclusion of only four gospels in our New Testament may have arisen because Irenaeus, bishop of Lyons (ca. 130–202 CE) said that since there are four quarters of the world and four winds, and since the church is scattered, it should have four pillars, thus the four gospels. Or from Jerome (347–420 CE), biblical scholar and church father, who argued that there should be four gospels because there were four corners of the ark and four creatures in Ezekiel.[9]

In the later first century and early second century, church leaders identified the names of particular writings that had become popular both as written works and in church liturgy. Around 100 BCE a grouping of epistles (letters) appeared in the writings of the church fathers Clement of Rome (ca. 35–101CE), Ignatius of Antioch (35–110 CE), and Polycarp of Smyrna (69–155 CE). In 140 CE Marcion of Rome rejected the Old Testament books and proposed that only Luke and some letters by Paul should be included in the canon. In reaction to this rejection of so many books, the Muratorian canon was put forward in 200 CE; it contained twenty-two books and included the four gospels. It was Origin (185–254 CE), a theologian from Alexandria, who was the first to make reference to all twenty-seven books of the New Testament.

In 325 CE the Roman emperor Constantine summoned a council of bishops at Nicaea to settle questions of Jesus' status with respect to God. For Constantine, this was a political decision to heal the religious strife within the Empire.[10] The Presbyter Arius did not want Jesus to be equated with God; Bishop Athanasius did. (Both men were from Alexandria.) With over two hundred bishops present at the council, Athanasius's side won and the words in the creed read then, and still read today, that Jesus is "very God of very God."[11] Forty-two years later, in 367 CE, Bishop Athanasius listed all twenty-seven New Testament books as we have them today.[12] A church council in Hippo, North Africa in 393 CE also listed the twenty-seven books and the Synod of Carthage confirmed this list in 397 CE, decreeing that "in these alone is proclaimed the doctrine of godliness. Let no man [*sic*] add to these,

9. Ibid.

10. Noll, *Turning Points*, 51.

11. Ibid., 57.

12. Ibid., 37.

neither let him [*sic*] take aught from these."[13] Then in 400 CE Jerome translated these books from Greek into Latin and the Hebrew Bible from Hebrew into Latin. This was called the Vulgate.

So we see that it took until almost 400 CE to establish which books would be included in the New Testament, the criteria for canonicity being that the book had to be attributed to an apostle or the disciple of an apostle; it had to have orthodox doctrine; and it needed to have been widely used in church liturgies.[14]

The fundamentalist evangelical response to this human recounting of how the canon of the Bible was decided is that God willed it that way. God made sure that the "inspired" books were included, the books that God wanted to be part of the Bible.[15] Yet it is clear that the history of the development of the New Testament canon is quite fraught with human intervention, which doesn't take away from the value of the New Testament as a significant text for Christians. It simply means that it raises questions about the New Testament as the "inerrant Word of God."

Translations and Versions of the Bible

Moving on from the translation of the Bible into Latin in 400 CE, it wasn't until the 1300s that John Wycliff, an Oxford theologian, translated the Vulgate into English. This was the first English translation of the entire Bible from Latin. The first printed Hebrew Bible appeared in 1488 and the first printed Greek New Testament in 1514[16]. With the invention of the printing press in the mid 1400s, Bibles could be printed for the masses. Luther's German translation in 1534 was based on the Latin Vulgate, as well as Hebrew and Greek manuscripts. His German Bible was followed by Dutch, French, and additional English translations.

In England, when William Tyndale, a theologian and scholar, published the first translation of the Greek New Testament into English in 1525, thousands of copies were burned and he was burned at

13. Ibid.

14. Ibid., 38.

15. The Roman Catholic Bible includes additional apocryphal books in their canon.

16. Bruce, *The Books and the Parchments*, 222.

the stake. In the following years, two other Bibles were published, the Coverdale Bible in 1535 (translated from the Latin Bible, Luther's Bible, and Tyndales' version) and Matthew's Bible in 1537 (based on a variety of versions, including those of Coverdale and Tyndale).[17] Then in 1539 the Great Bible was published, a revision of Matthew's Bible, "of which a copy was placed in every church in England in accordance with Henry VIII's injunction."[18]

In 1560, two years after Elizabeth I began her reign, the Geneva Bible was published, a version translated directly from Hebrew and Greek. Because of its superiority to the Great Bible, English bishops, not to be outdone, ordered a revision of the Great Bible, resulting in the Bishop's Bible in 1568.

In 1604, King James called a conference to discuss the rivalry that had occurred among those who used the Geneva Bible, and those who used the Bishop's Bible. This version, authorized by the King, was published in 1611, the King James Version (KJV). While it was a revision of the Bishop's Bible, translators also used other English versions as well as the Hebrew and Greek versions that existed.[19]

I remember the great debate over whether we should use any version other than the King James Version, which was thought to be closest to the original text. What I found out later was that the King James Version was actually a revision of the Bishop's Bible, which was considered inferior to the Geneva Bible.

The Revised Standard Version (RSV), published in 1946, claims in the Preface that "the King James Version of the New Testament was based upon a Greek text that was marred by mistakes, containing the accumulated errors of fourteen centuries of manuscript copying. . . . We now possess many more ancient manuscripts of the New Testament, and are far better equipped to seek to recover the original wording of the Greek text."[20] Table 1 below shows the publication details of Bible translations and versions from the 1300s to 1611:

17. Ibid., 224.
18. Ibid.
19. Ibid., 229.
20. *RSV Bible*, v.

TABLE 1. PUBLICATION OF BIBLE TRANSLATIONS AND VERSIONS

Date of Translation/ Version	Name of Bible or Translator	Sources Used for Translation
1300s	John Wycliffe	Latin Vulgate into English
1525	William Tyndale	Greek New Testament into English
1534	Martin Luther	Latin Vulgate into German
1535	Coverdale's Bible	Latin Vulgate, Luther's Bible and Tyndale into English
1537	Matthew's Bible	Coverdale and Tyndale into English
1539	Great Bible	Matthew's Bible (a revision) into English
1560	Geneva Bible	Hebrew Bible and Greek New Testament into English
1568	Bishop's Bible	Great Bible (a revision) into English
1611	King James Bible	Bishop's Bible along with other manuscripts consulted, into English,

It is interesting that the KJV is the version some fundamentalist evangelicals continue to prefer, believing it to be the most accurate biblical text. One could think of several reasons why this is so. First, it was an English Bible authorized by the King of England. The fact that it was authorized seems to carry some weight. Second, the continued use of the KJV may have been partially due to the fact that fundamentalist evangelicals had become used to this version. Their concept of God may have become so firmly linked to the language of the KJV that when the Revised Standard Version came along in 1946 (New Testament only at that time) they were not willing to give up the version they had so much associated with God. For some, the KJV almost seemed to be God's language. And third, since fundamentalist evangelicals held suspect any higher biblical scholarship; they were reluctant to accept the Revised Standard Version, which had been prepared by liberal scholars.

For whatever reason, there are still fundamentalist evangelicals today who believe that the King James Version is closest to the original words of the Bible and that it is the most reliable text.

Besides the Revised Standard Version, the twentieth and twenty-first centuries have seen numerous other translations and paraphrases, including the New Revised Standard, New American Standard, New International, Jerusalem Bible, New English Bible, The Inclusive Bible, Living Bible, Good News Bible, Phillips Modern English, and The Message.

THE DEVELOPMENT OF BIBLICAL INTERPRETATION

Now that we had the Bible in its numerous languages and versions, it had to be interpreted. Considering what we know about how the Bible was produced, how do we best interpret it almost two thousand years later?

My exposure to methods of biblical interpretation that were not based on inerrancy began in the early 1980s when I attended the Mennonite Brethren Seminary in Fresno, California. Professors of biblical studies were decidedly not fundamentalist in orientation. At times they even cautioned us against sharing with people in the pews the scholarly insights they presented. One of the most striking realizations I had in my first year of seminary was in the Biblical Backgrounds course, taught by Professor Allen Guenther. I discovered that the Genesis creation story was not the only one; there was a Babylonian creation story as well. The fact that there was another creation story opened my eyes to a broader interpretation of the Bible than I had previously known.

Interpretation is what we all do when we try to make sense of any book. And we all have personal convictions, perceptions, and viewpoints that color how we interpret what we read. When we interpret the Bible, we can see it as God's words to humans, i.e., what God wants humans to know; or we can see it as a human response to God, the product of ancient communities, an ancient peoples' experience of God. The fundamentalist evangelical is likely to see the Bible as God's words to humans. Whether one approaches the Bible as God's words to humans or human's ideas about God, it can become a sacred text for the reader.

The Bible can be interpreted at either a pre-critical or critical level. The word "critical" comes from *krinō*, the Greek word for "to distinguish," "to judge," "to determine the truth of the matter," and "to discern."[21] When one speaks of criticism of a particular text, it means that one is making judgments about its origins and composition, its meaning, and its importance.[22] It does not mean that one is criticizing the text.

At the pre-critical level we simply hear the stories of the Bible as true stories that really happened. For example, when we hear the Christmas story, we believe that the star stood still over the place where Jesus was born. We don't question it. Somehow, it just happened that way. When it says that Jesus rose from the dead, we believe that's exactly what happened, he physically rose from the dead. And when it says he ascended into heaven, that's what he did, he went straight up into the sky. In a pre-critical model, one believes the Bible word for word as literally true in every way. At the critical level of thinking, a level of thinking that usually begins to develop in early adolescence, we ask questions: How could one star point to the place Jesus was born? Stars don't point. And how could it stand still over one place? When you look at the stars, you can't tell what house (or inn) is directly beneath it." And we might ask, "How could Jesus have gone straight up to heaven? In the sky, there is just more sky; there's a whole universe out there."

So how and when did the field of biblical criticism develop? For this discussion I am indebted to John Sandys-Wunsch, a research fellow at the University of Victoria. His book, *What Have They Done to the Bible? A History of Modern Biblical Interpretation*, provides an excellent review of the development of biblical interpretation from the Renaissance to the 1800s. His work is a result of thirty years of research, during which time he made an effort to read cited authors in the original languages.[23] Sandys-Wunsch holds a doctorate in Old Testament Studies and has taught for many years in Canadian universities.

At the time of the Renaissance (1450–1600), when the first English New Testament was translated from the Greek, scholars laid the foundation for the discipline of textual criticism.[24] Textual criticism is the examination of texts in order to establish the wording closest to the original. It involves looking at the handwritten manuscripts that are copies of copies of copies, and deciding which ones might be closest to

21. Arndt and Gingrich, *A Greek-English Lexicon of the New Testament*, 451.

22. Sandys-Wunsch, *What Have They Done to the Bible?*, xiii.

23. Ibid., xvii, xix.

24. Ibid., 74.

the original. Ancient biblical manuscripts are studied in order to determine the correct reading, in hopes of discovering the original author's own words. Scholars use certain criteria to do this. The more reliable text is one that is:

1. The earlier date of the manuscript,

2. The more difficult reading,

3. The shorter reading, and

4. The closest to the style, vocabulary, and context
   of the rest of the book.[25]

In the Baroque Period (1600–1660) languages came to be better understood and grammatical and philological studies (the study of linguistics) were more heavily based on concrete evidence.[26] While scholars did not have a modern understanding of the origins of the Bible, they were starting to observe textual and grammatical problems in the biblical text.

The early Enlightenment (1660–1700) brought increased skepticism about the infallibility of the Bible. Benedict Spinoza (1632–1677) pointed out inconsistencies within the Bible and uncertain translations. Yet he believed that the Bible "contained" the Word of God.[27] Another scholar, Jean le Clerc (1657–1736), tackled the question of biblical inerrancy by trying to interpret the Bible rationally.[28] The Bible began to be seen as "a book whose origins took place within human history."[29]

In the 1700s, with the discovery of thousands of additional manuscripts, translators came to realize that translation was not straightforward. So they established guidelines for translation, such as, the more difficult text is likely the most reliable. This was an important guideline because it was believed that scribes who copied manuscripts would be more likely to correct texts they deemed to be difficult.

Increasingly the Bible came to be studied as literature. This did not mean that people appreciated the Bible any less. Johann Wolfgang Goethe, for example, loved to read the Bible, but for him, "the Bible had become not a source of doctrine but a literary work that inspired him

25. Metzger, *The Text of the New Testament*, 209–10.
26. Sandys-Wunsch, *What Have They Done to the Bible?*, 117.
27. Ibid., 150–51.
28. Ibid., 167–68.
29. Ibid., 169.

with its images and its poetry."[30] In studying the Bible as literature (literary criticism), scholars evaluated the language of the text, the meanings of the Hebrew and Greek words, the structure of the text, and the style of writing.

In realizing that biblical texts originated in different eras and cultures, scholars began to study the Bible within its historical and cultural contexts. In the 1700s and 1800s the Bible started to be seen more and more as not a book that fell from heaven but a book that told of events that took place within human history. Jean Alphonse (1671–1737) summarized this mentality well when he said, "One must put oneself into the times and into the surroundings in which biblical authors wrote, and one must see what concepts could arise in the souls of those who lived at that time."[31] In what is called historical criticism, scholars determine the circumstances in which the book was written, the culture out of which it arose, the time of composition, the author, and the audience. Considering the plethora of circumstances, it was not surprising to find differences in perception within biblical texts and it made sense that there were contradictions and inconsistencies.

With the emergence of science (especially Charles Darwin's *Origin of Species* in 1859), anthropology, and sociology in the 1800s, the conservative understanding of the Bible continued to be challenged. The Bible was no longer seen as the authority in matters of science, ancient history, geography, and other disciplines.

In the 1800s Moses' authorship of the first five books of the Bible was questioned. Biblical scholars saw the differences in style of writing and more than one name for God within the five books, which then pointed to parallel stories and to different themes that accompanied the different names for God. This observation led them to believe that different sources were used in the construction of these books; scholars call this source criticism.

Source criticism examines the sources behind the text: what did the authors use to write their work? In the 1800s the four-source theory was proposed for the Pentateuch (first five books of the Old Testament). Biblical scholars said these five books were not written by Moses, as was originally thought, but that they were a combination of four different documents: J (getting its name from the name Yahweh used for God),

30. Ibid., 223.
31. Krentz, *The Historical-Critical Method.*

E (from the name *Elohim* for God), D (for Deuteronomy, a book of laws) and P (a document concerned with priestly matters). This theory was not accepted by Protestant conservatives and as late as 1964, when *The New Chain-Reference Bible* was published, it was still believed that Moses wrote the first five books of the Bible.[32]

A two-source theory was proposed for the synoptic gospels.[33] In this theory, the book of Mark is seen to have been the first gospel. Matthew's gospel is thought to contain 90 percent of the book of Mark, and Luke, approximately half of the book of Mark. There was an additional source called "Q," named after the German word for "source," *quelle*. This document emerged between 40 and 70 CE, a document that contains sayings of Jesus and his teachings. It contained the material Matthew and Luke had in common; since this material was not in Mark it indicates that Matthew and Luke each had two sources (see table 2).

TABLE 2. TWO-SOURCE THEORY

	Mark as Source	Q (*quelle*) as Source
Matthew	Used 90 percent of Mark	Used 10 percent of Q
Luke	Used 50 percent of Mark	Used 50 percent of Q

The four-source theory proposes that, in addition to the two sources, Matthew and Luke each added their own material (see table 3).

TABLE 3. FOUR-SOURCE THEORY

	Mark as Source	Q (quelle) as Source	Matthew's Own Material	Luke's Own Material
Matthew	Used some of Mark	Used some of Q that is not in Mark	Used author's own material	
Luke	Used some of Mark	Used some of Q that is not in Mark		Used author's own material

32. Thompson, *The New Chain-Reference Bible*, 188–90.

33. Krentz, *The Historical-Critical Method*, 27.

To illustrate how the four-source theory works, we will examine the texts from Matthew, Mark and Luke below, each text referring to the same event.

TABLE 4. ILLUSTRATION OF THE FOUR-SOURCE THEORY

Matthew 10:1	Mark 6:7	Luke 9:1–2
And he called to him his **twelve** *disciples* and **gave them authority over unclean spirits,** *to cast them out,* and <u>to heal</u> every <u>disease</u> *and every infirmity.*	**And he called** to him the **twelve**, and began **to send them out** two by two, and **gave them authority over the unclean spirits.**	**And he called** the **twelve** together and **gave them** power and **authority** *over all demons and to cure* <u>diseases,</u> and he **sent them out** *to preach the kingdom of God* and <u>to heal</u>.

According to the four-source theory, Matthew and Luke borrowed the following phrases from Mark: "and he called twelve," and "gave them authority." Matthew took "over unclean spirits" from Mark, and Luke took "send them out" from Mark. "To cure/heal diseases," found only in Matthew and Luke could very well be taken from the Q source. "And every infirmity" might well be Matthew's own material and "to preach the kingdom of God" could be Luke's own material.

As I grew up I thought that Matthew wrote the book of Matthew, Mark wrote the book of Mark and so on. But in seminary I discovered that there were no titles given to these books when they were written. Titles were added later and the names that were provided as titles were not necessarily the names of those who wrote the books. I learned that the variety of literary styles in the book of John, for example, is evidence that the book was written by more than one person; scholars suggest that the Gospel of John was written by the Johannine community. It could have been written in Ephesus where tradition tells us that Mary went to live with John after Jesus' death. This would explain why Mary's experience is prominent in the book of John, for example, her role at the wedding at Cana in John 2.

Sandys-Wunsch says that "the final collapse of the structure [the orthodox view of biblical interpretation] did not take place in the mind of the general public until the nineteenth century, and even today there are people working in the ruins to reconstruct some semblance of the old edifice."[34] The old edifice of the literal-factual interpretation of the Bible is alive today, and not only in churches that are considered to be fundamentalist. You could walk into almost any Christian church and hear a biblical text read without any explanation that perhaps it should not be taken literally. Take for example, all the readings of the birth narratives at Christmas and the resurrection stories at Easter. There is no indication that these should be taken anything but literally when they are read. If a non-literal view is to be taken, parishioners have to do the reframing in their own minds because few pastors will do it for them. John Shelby Spong suggests that "the biblical scholarship of the past two hundred years has simply not been made available to the man or the woman in the pew."[35] This is indeed unfortunate.

34. Sandys-Wunsch, *What Have They Done to the Bible?*, 117.

35. Spong, *Rescuing the Bible from Fundamentalism*, 14.

6

A Case Study of an Alternative Approach to Biblical Interpretation

MY MASTERS DEGREE WAS *in the area of biblical studies, specifically the New Testament. When I started my PhD program, my intention was to conduct research on what the Bible says about women's roles. In the end, my research topic changed, but along the way I decided to do my own translation and exegesis of a text that was used at the time to prevent women from taking leadership roles in evangelical churches, particularly the role of minister. This was in the late 1980s and at that time I still held a belief in the literal text of the Bible, but I believed it was likely mistranslated in places. I believed so strongly in the Bible that I approached I Timothy 2:8–15 with fear and trepidation. What if the text really did say that women should remain silent in the church? What would I do then? It wasn't until several years later that I dared to conduct my own translation and interpretation of the Timothy text that was used to prevent women from taking leadership positions in the church. Why did I wait so long? Because my emotional attachment to the fundamentalist position of the authority of the Bible, literally understood, was still strong. However, once I conducted my own exegesis of I Timothy 2:8–15, I could not believe what it actually said. This chapter is the result of that research.*

What follows is a revision of the article I wrote for *Studies in Religion/Sciences Religieuses* in 1990.[1] Interspersed within the article are my current thoughts about what I wrote and any further insights I have. These interjections are easily recognized because they are in italics.

---

1. Redekop, "Let the women learn."

John G. Stackhouse observed that restrictions on women in church leadership result from a "traditional regard for the unique authority of Scripture, for literal exegesis and for straightforward application of text to faith and practice."[2] 1 Timothy 2:8–15 is among the texts that have been literally interpreted and straightforwardly applied. *It is interesting that, while new interpretations have arisen for many biblical texts, the translation of this text has remained the same. The RSV translates 1 Timothy 2: 11–12, "Let a woman learn in silence with all submissiveness. I permit no woman to teach or to have authority over men; she is to keep silent." Even the most modern translations have translated the key verses with the same intent. Even the Inclusive Bible, claiming to be the first egalitarian translation, published in 2007, translates these verses in a similar way, "Women are to be quiet and completely submissive during religious instruction. I don't permit a woman to teach or to have authority over a man. She must remain silent." One of the reasons why this translation may have remained the same as in other versions is that it was written by a Roman Catholic group, Priests for Equality. And in the Roman Catholic tradition, women still are not permitted to become priests*

In 1981 the Mennonite Brethren Church accepted a resolution on the ministry of women in the church which stated that "we do not hold that the passages in the New Testament (such as 1 Corinthians 14 and 1 Timothy 2), which put restrictions on the Christian woman, have become irrelevant . . . we do not believe that the Mennonite Brethren Church should ordain women to pastoral leadership."[3] *Today, although Mennonite Brethren women are permitted to take positions as pastors, they may not be ordained. This is not so, however, in Mennonite Church Canada and Mennonite Church USA. In these denominations women may be ordained.* This phenomenon was not limited to Protestant denominations; in 1976 the "Declaration on the Question of the Admission of Women to the Ministerial Priesthood" from the Sacred Congregation for the Doctrine of the Faith of the Roman Catholic Church declared that 1 Timothy 2:12 is a normative text in which "the prohibition concerns the official function of teaching in the Christian assembly."[4]

2. Stackhouse, "Women in Public Ministry," 141.

3. General Conference of Mennonite Brethren Churches, "Resolution on the Ministry of Women in the Church."

4. "Declaration on the Question of the Admission of Women."

It is my contention that faulty conclusions have been drawn from the Timothy text because of a biased translation and a failure to take into account the primary concerns of the pastor who wrote the letters. I will argue for an alternate translation from the Greek text on the basis of the author's agenda, studies of key words, and a verse-by-verse exegesis of the text. *My issues in 1990 were solely with the text itself. Because I felt I had to believe the text, I needed to know what it said. I asked myself, was it mistranslated? Was it in line with the agenda of the author? What was the role of cultural belief and practice in the text?*

THEMES OF THE PASTORAL LETTERS

The Pastoral Letters (1 and 2 Timothy and Titus) address such issues as the organization of the church, Christian conduct, and the importance of guarding sound teaching.[5] Church leaders are admonished to fight off heresy and remain within the parameters of the Pauline tradition.[6]

In the discussion of the agenda of the Pastorals several scholars have referred to the dominant-submissive pattern of the patriarchal household as a model for the church community.[7] As David C. Verner points out, however, the Pastorals nowhere describe the relationship between the offices of the church nor do they "expressly set forth a hierarchy of office."[8] The functions and position of deacons and elders are not mentioned, "it thus appears that the Pastorals' author is not interested in describing and defending a particular ecclesiastical structure."[9] Therefore one should not assume that this text is meant to define the generic role of all women in the church or to set out the positions to which they can be appointed. This assumption concerning the agenda of the text has continued to inform the interpretations of 1 Timothy 2:8–15 to such an extent that the conclusion is reached that women should "learn in silence, learn in subjection, a posture that reflects their subordinate station in relation to men."[10] The paradigm of the church

5. Koester, *History and Literature of Early Christianity*, 297.

6. Hanson, *The Pastoral Epistles*, 11.

7. Fiorenza, "The Study of Women in Early Christianity," 48–49 and Verner, *The Household of God*, 127–69.

8. Verner, *The Household of God*, 147.

9. Ibid., 150.

10. Ibid., 169.

as the patriarchal household of God, patterned after the patriarchal household in society, has skewed the exegesis of the text.

The problem of false teachers is clearly evident in the Pastorals. Since this will help to shed light on the interpretation of 1 Timothy 2:8–15 it is important to clarify as much as possible the characteristics of these heretics.

At times it appears that the false teachers are a reference to a Jewish-Christian group. They are referred to as "teachers of the law" (1 Tim 1:7) and they preach "Jewish myths" (Tit 1:14).[11] At the same time heretical teaching seems to have been influenced by Gnosticism, which included a demand for abstinence from certain foods and prohibition of marriage (1 Tim 4:3); the claim that the resurrection had already taken place (2 Tim 2:18); and "empty chatter and the opposing arguments of what is falsely called knowledge" (1 Tim 6:20). Since it is difficult to identify one specific type of false teaching, I agree with Helmut Koester that various heretical groups could have been seen as a threat to the purity of the faith handed down.[12]

As we look more closely at the actual accusations made by the author toward these false teachers we notice that much of it centers around speaking and teaching. The author warns against "fruitless discussion" (1 Tim 1:6), "making assertions about the law without proper understanding" (1 Tim 1:7), "worldly fables" (I Tim 4:7), "controversial questions and disputes about words" (1 Tim 6:4), "worldly and empty chatter and opposing arguments of what is falsely called knowledge" (1 Tim 6:20–21), "not to wrangle about words" (2 Tim 2:14), "empty talkers and deceivers" (Tit 1:10), and "foolish controversies and genealogies and strife and disputes about the Law" (Tit 3:9).

While on the one hand the author cautions the readers against disputes and heresy, on the other hand he emphasizes the necessity for good judgment and sound teaching, "you will be . . . nourished on the words of the faith and of the sound doctrine" (1 Tim 4:6), "pay close attention to yourself and to your teaching" (1 Tim 4:16), "retain the standard of sound words" (2 Tim 1:13), "the Lord's bondservant must be . . . able to teach" (2 Tim 2:24), "preach the word . . . for the time will come when they will not endure sound doctrine" (2 Tim 4:2–3),

11. Quotations from the New Testament in this chapter are from the New American Standard Bible, unless indicated otherwise.

12. Koester, *History and Literature of Early Christianity*, 10.

"holding fast the faithful word which is in accordance with the teaching, … to exhort in sound doctrine and refute those who contradict" (Tit 1:9), and "speak the things which are fitting for sound doctrine" (Tit 2:1). The point is also made that the preparation for sound teaching is careful study (2 Tim 2:15).

Thus, 1 Timothy 2:8–15 must be interpreted within the context of the concern for guarding the "knowledge of the truth," a phrase which occurs four times in the letters (1 Tim 2:4; 2 Tim 2:25; 3:7; Tit 1:1).

IMMEDIATE CONTEXT OF 1 TIMOTHY 2:8–15

The second chapter of 1Timothy is about attitude during worship and prayer. Verses 8–15 contain instructions to both men and women.[13] The lengthier section addressed to the women simply signifies that, for some reason, the author was more concerned about women's attitude in worship.

VERSE-BY-VERSE EXEGESIS OF 1 TIMOTHY 2:8–15

In my exegesis of the text I will first provide the translation from the New American Standard Bible (NASB) and then follow that with my own translation. I will examine each key word, determining its meaning in the light of its other occurrences in the New Testament. The implications of the context will be considered for each verse.

> Verse 8
> NASB: Therefore, I want the men in every place to pray,
> Lifting up holy hands, without wrath and dissension.
>
> My translation: Therefore, I want the men in every place to pray,
> raising holy hands without anger and dispute.

The instruction to men is to pray in the usual Jewish posture for prayer, "without anger and dispute." Considering the many references in the Pastorals to controversies and disputes that were prevalent among false teachers who were threatening the church, it is understandable

---

13. Padgett, "Wealthy Women at Ephesus," 22 and Howard, "Neither Male nor Female," 40.

that the pastor of 1 Timothy would ask men to clear themselves of "anger and dispute" when they come to prayer.

> Verses 9 and 10
> NASB: Likewise, I want women to adorn themselves with proper clothing, modestly and discreetly,
> not with braided hair and gold or pearls or costly garments;
> but rather by means of good works,
> as befits women making a claim to godliness.

> My translation: Similarly I want women to make themselves attractive
> in respectable inner and outer demeanour
> with reverence and good mental judgment
> not with anything braided and gold
> or with pearls or costly clothing (to show off their wealth),
> but women, by means of good works,
> should do what is necessary
> in order to proclaim a godly religion with conviction.

Since a great deal hinges on these verses, I will examine nine key words, testing their usage within the New Testament. I will also attempt to determine which women the pastor is addressing.

1. "Make attractive," *kosmein*, appears ten times in the New Testament. It can mean "to put a house in order," "to trim the lamps," or "to decorate an object." It is used in the sense of making something attractive in order to prepare it for an important event, such as a bride getting ready for the bridegroom (Rev 21:2). Titus 2:10 refers to "making attractive the doctrine of God." The only other instance where this word refers to women is in 1 Peter 3:5 where it signifies an attractive inner spirit. In 1 Timothy 2:9 our English versions commonly translate it "adorn." Since "adorn" carries the connotation of putting on clothing, and since we cannot assume that meaning here, "make attractive" is a more accurate translation.

2. "Demeanour," *katastolē*, occurs nowhere else in the New Testament. Since it is thus a *hapax legomenon*[14] it is difficult to

---

14. When a word is referred to as a *Hapax legomenon*, it means that word appears only once in that particular piece of literature, and thus, it is very difficult to determine its meaning within the context of the rest of the book.

be certain of its meaning. It can refer to either inner or outer demeanour or both. Most English versions assume that this word refers only to outer clothing. Along with Alan Padgett I have chosen both meanings, since later in verse 10 the pastor refers to both inner deportment and outer clothing.[15]

3. *Kosmios* is usually translated "modest," "suitable," "proper," or "becoming" in 1 Timothy 2:9, all referring to a type of outer clothing. Since its only other use in the New Testament is in 1 Timothy 3:2, where a bishop is to be "respectable," the reference to outer clothing cannot be assumed in our text. Because of this, I have chosen the translation "respectable," in keeping with its meaning in 1 Timothy 3:2.

4. *Meta aidous*, "with reverence," occurs twice in the New Testament, here and in Heb 12:28 where it refers to the attitude with which one is to render acceptable service to God. In 1 Timothy 2:9, translators have translated it as "modestly," "decently," or "shamefacedly." These words do not refer to a particular attitude, so in keeping with its use in Hebrews and in order to be able to use the word to describe both inner and outer demeanour, I have chosen the translation "with reverence."

5. *Sōphrosynē* together with its derivatives appears sixteen times in the New Testament. Ten of these occurrences are in the Pastorals. In all ten instances the reference is to "mental soundness," "reasonableness," or "good judgment," yet in 1 Timothy 2, when it refers to women, most translate it "discretely," "decently," or "with propriety." The King James Version and the Revised Standard Version do hint at mental soundness in their translations, "with sobriety" and "sensibly." However, since in these versions the word modifies the verb "adorn," the association with clothing remains.

6. *Himatismos*, translated "clothing" or "apparel," appears sixty-nine times in the New Testament and means "outer clothing" in every instance. That outer clothing is in view here seems unmistakable.

15. Padgett, "Wealthy Women at Ephesus," 22.

7. *Prepei* occurs seven times in the New Testament in the sense of "proper," "fitting," or "necessary." Three times it refers to the proper thing to do. For example, in Ephesians 5:3 the writer says that immorality must not be evident among the readers because it is not "proper among saints." In the other instances it refers to something that is necessary to do in order to reach a particular end: "in this way it is fitting for us to fulfil righteousness" (Matt 3:15), "the things which are fitting for sound doctrine," (Tit 2:1) and "fitting . . . to perfect the author of their salvation through sufferings" (Heb 2:10). In our text, the end to be reached is the proclamation of a godly religion.

8. *Epaggelō*, "proclaim with conviction," can refer to a promise of something to someone, or a profession in which one makes oneself out to be an expert in a particular area. Of its fifteen usages in the New Testament it means "promise" all but two times, here and in 1 Timothy 6:21, where it is used of those who proclaim "what is falsely called knowledge." The prefix *epi* gives added emphasis to the verb; therefore my translation reads "proclaim with conviction."[16]

9. The particular word for "religion," *theosebeia*, occurs only here in 1 Timothy 2:10. The word most commonly used in the Pastorals is *eusebeia*. The only difference between the two is that *theosebeia* specifies more clearly that the object of religion is *theos*, "God." In 3 Corinthians 3:10, a pseudepigraphic writing, *theosebeia* implies a religion "without images, sacrifices or elaborate ceremonies."[17]

So who were the women to whom this part of the letter was addressed? The reference to "anything braided or gold or with pearls or costly clothing" in verse 9 indicates that these women were wealthy. So it makes sense that he would focus on wealthy women's attire. The problem of wealth in the community was of concern to the pastor. In chapter six of the same letter to Timothy, the pastor writes, "But those who want to get rich fall into temptation . . . for the love of money is a root of all sorts of evil, and some by longing for it have wandered away

---

16. Dana and Mantey, *A Manual Grammar*, 106.
17. Arndt and Gingrich, *A Greek-English Lexicon*, 358.

from the faith. . . . Instruct those who are rich in this present world not to be conceited or to fix their hope on the uncertainty of riches, but on God" (1 Tim 6:9, 10, 17).

False teachers, designated as "lovers of money" (2 Tim 3:2), were considered a bad influence on the women who had admitted them into their homes and had become captivated by them (2 Tim 3:6).[18] As far as the pastor was concerned, this was especially threatening to sound teaching within the church because churches met in the homes of wealthy women, the practice being that whoever owned the home would be the leader of the church. It appears that these wealthy women, tutored by false teachers, were teaching what they had learned. Thus they were "always learning and never able to come to the knowledge of the truth" (2 Tim 3:7). This situation forms the basis for the author's concern expressed in 1 Timothy 2.[19]

Therefore verses 9 and 10 are addressed to these wealthy women who are proclaiming their godly religion with conviction. The author instructs them to "make themselves attractive" inwardly with "reverence and good mental judgment." Then they will be able "to proclaim a godly religion with conviction" (verse 10).

> Verse 11
> NASB: Let a woman quietly receive instruction
> with entire submissiveness.
>
> My translation: Let a woman learn, ·
> in an atmosphere of peace, harmony, and reverence
> with all submission (to the teachers who are teaching the sound
> doctrine).

We will examine three key words in this verse.

1. "Learn," *manthanetō*, includes learning both through instruction and practical experience. Six of its twenty-five instances in the New Testament appear in the Pastoral letters. In 1 Timothy 5:4 the reference is to learning by experience, "learn to practice piety." The occurrences in 2 Timothy 3:7 and 14, on the other hand, refer to learning through formal instruction, "learning and never coming to the knowledge of the truth,"

18. Padgett, "Wealthy Women at Ephesus," 23.
19. Ibid.

"continue in the things you have learned and become convinced of." Verse 11 of our text could conceivably encompass both senses of the word. Verse 10 refers to proclaiming a religion "by means of good works," learning through experience. On the other hand, women were also learning from "false" teachers in a formal way, thus learning through instruction.

2. A crucial word in this verse, *hēsychia*, is commonly translated "silent." The Timothy text, as well as 1 Corinthians 14:34, "let the women keep silent in the churches," has led to silencing of women in various Christian contexts. Initially, it is important to note that the word for "silent" in 1 Timothy is not the same word as in 1 Corinthians 14:34, where *sigatōsan* means "stop speaking." (Versions of the English Bible translate both *sigaō* and *hēsychia* with "silence," "keep quiet," "quietness," and "not to speak"; a separate study would be necessary in order to determine the meaning of the word in the Corinthian letter.) The word in our text, commonly translated "silence," is used together with its derivatives twelve times in the New Testament. In all instances the reference is to "peace," "harmony," "rest," or "reverence." In several texts the reference is to harmonious and orderly living (1 Thess 4:11; 2 Thess 3:11–12; 1 Tim 2:2). In 1 Peter 3:11 it refers to the inner spirit of women. Thus, this verse is an admonition for women to learn in an atmosphere of peace, harmony, and reverence, in contrast to the atmosphere of disputation and anger so prevalent in the community.

3. "Submission," *hypotagē*, appears only four times in the New Testament and is derived from the verb, *hypotassō*, meaning "to submit," "be subjected," or "obey." An object of submission is "to your confession of the gospel of Christ." The object of submission in Galatians 2:5 is "false brethren." 1 Timothy 3:4 is addressed to overseers who are required to keep their children "in submission." In our text the object of submission is not specified. Submission of women to either husbands or male leaders in the church has been assumed.[20] J. Keir Howard suggests that the submission in mind here is submission to

---

20. Hanson, *The Pastoral Epistles*, 72.

Christ.[21] However, since there is evidence in the Pastorals that women had been submitting to false teachers, the admonition to learn "with all submission" seems to imply a learning from the women's true teachers. I concur with Padgett, that submission in 1 Timothy 2 is to the teachers, i.e., Timothy and Paul.[22]

> Verse 12
> NASB: But I do not allow a woman to teach
> or exercise authority over a man,
> But to remain quiet.
>
> My translation: And I do not permit a woman to teach,
> neither to have authority over a man,
> (until she has learned the true teaching)
> but she is to be in (an atmosphere of) peace, harmony, and reverence.

The only key word in this verse which has not been examined thus far is *authentein*, "have authority." In his analysis of extra-biblical literature of the time, George Knight has shown that the word does not have the connotation of "domineer."[23] Even though this is its only occurrence in the New Testament, this word has been used by both scholars and church bodies to support the belief that we have here a permanent instruction to women, prohibiting them from teaching when men are present.[24]

In order to gain insight into the meaning of this instruction, we may find help in an examination of the verbs in our text. This is the third instance, in 1 Timothy 2, of a first-person singular verb. 1 Timothy 2:8 began with the first person, "I want the men in every place to pray." The same verb is implied in verse 9 where the author addresses the women, "(I want) women to make themselves attractive." And in verse 12 we have another first person verb, "I do not permit." In the Greek language there are nine different uses of the present tense,[25] and the first-person present tense of the verb can be used to indicate a temporary restriction.[26] With that sense of the verb, a time restriction comes into play.

---

21. Howard, "Neither Male nor Female," 40.

22. Padgett, "Wealthy Women at Ephesus," 24.

23. Knight, "*Authentein* in Reference to Women," 143–55.

24. Bernard, *The Pastoral Letters*, and Howard, "Neither Male nor Female," 40–41.

25. Dana and Mantey, *A Manual Grammar*, 181–86.

26. Payne, "Libertarian Women at Ephesus," 169–70.

Until women have learned what they need in order to get a full grasp of the true teaching, they are not to teach or have authority over men. There is no reason why these women might not later be free to teach with authority (like Phoebe, Prisca, and Junia) if they will first learn the true teaching, submitting to Timothy for instruction.[27]

> Verses 13 and 14
> NASB: For it was Adam who was first created, and then Eve.
> And it was not Adam who was deceived,
> but the woman being quite deceived,
> fell into transgression.
>
> My translation: For Adam was formed first, then Eve;
> (men were the teachers first)
> and Adam was not led astray,
> but Eve was completely led astray
> (wealthy women were led astray by false teachers)
> and became and continue to be
> in the transgression (of the law).

This verse contains two words for "lead astray." The first, used with reference to Adam, is *apataō*, and means to "deceive," "cheat," or "mislead." The only other instances in the New Testament have to do with deceptive speech (Eph 5:6; James 1:26). Thus, we can infer that this sentence refers to Adam's deception by Eve's words regarding the tasting of the fruit.

The second word for "lead astray" is *exapataō*, and is used in our text for Eve's deception. Of the six times it appears in the New Testament, four times it has the sense of being led astray from something good (from the law in Rom 7:11; from good teaching in Rom 16:18; from wisdom in 1 Cor 3:18; and from the purity of Christ in 2 Cor 11:3). The prefix *ex* gives this word a particular emphasis, and thus the translation, "completely led astray." Eve was "completely led astray" from something good.

This verse has given rise to some issues in the understanding of 1 Timothy 2. The reference to creation has led some to believe that the prohibition is permanent and normative.[28] Before we concur with that conclusion, however, it is important to consider the various ways in

---

27. Padgett, "Wealthy Women at Ephesus," 25.

28. "Declaration on the Question of the Admission of Women," 10, and Bernard, *The Pastoral Letters*, 48.

which the Jews of the first century interpreted Scripture. What kind of exegesis was the author of 1 Timothy using here?

Some interpretive approaches of the day included *targum, midrash, pesher, halakah, haggadah*, and typology. [29] If, along with Daniel Patte and Padgett, one understands the approach of 1 Timothy 2 to be typological, then Eve serves as a type for those women whom the author of 1 Timothy addresses.[30] The typological interpretation would sound like this: wealthy women of 1 Timothy 2 have listened to "the snake," i.e., the false teachers. They have been "completely led astray" from the good, sound teaching. Men, who were teachers first, i.e., "formed first," serve as a type of Adam. Therefore, the reference to Adam and Eve serves as a warning to the women of what might happen if they continue to be led astray by the false teachers.

> Verse 15
> NASB: But women shall be preserved through the bearing of children
> if they continue in faith and love and sanctity with self-restraint.
>
> My translation: But she (Eve) shall be saved through the bearing of children,
> if they (the female teachers) remain in faith and love and holiness with good mental judgment.

Teknogonia, "bearing of children," is used only here in 1 Timothy 2, in no other instance in the New Testament. Thus, being a *hapax legomenon*, it is not easy to determine its meaning within the context of the Bible. The word for "good mental judgment" is the same as in verse 9, where it refers to "mental soundness" and "reasonableness." Verse 15 has been understood in a variety of ways, ranging from a reference to salvation by the birth of Mary's son to a declaration that woman's place is in the home. According to Padgett, J.H. Bernard, and Anthony Tyrrell Hanson, verse 15 indicates that women should primarily be confined to the role of bearing children.[31] Although Padgett sees nothing in the text which excludes women from the teaching ministry, in the same breath he interprets the text to say that women should "return to their role

29. Patte, *Early Jewish Hermeneutic in Palestine*.

30. Ibid., 315–24, and Padgett, "Wealthy Women at Ephesus," 26.

31. Padgett, "Wealthy Women at Ephesus," 30; Bernard, *The Pastoral Letters*, 49; and Hanson, *The Pastoral Epistles*, 74.

as givers of life."[32] Hanson concludes that "the neutral interpretation is that woman, a weak, gullible creature, should find her natural vocation in a life of domesticity in subordination to her husband."[33]

Looking at the context of verse 15, we see that it is the Genesis creation story, with a reference to Genesis 3:16 in particular, "I will greatly multiply your pain in childbirth." Thus, it makes sense that the interpretation of verse 15 is continuous with the Adam and Eve typology of verse 14.

The change in verse 15 from "she" to "they" has led to various explanations. According to Hanson, the subject changes to "they" simply because the author is quoting directly from a source document.[34] Bernard assumes that both verbs refer to Christian women in general.[35] Martin Dibelius and Hans Conzelmann allow for the possibility of the second verb, "they remain," to refer to children which the women bear. In this case, the verse would mean that women will be saved if their biological children remain "in faith and love and holiness."[36] However, if this verse is a continuation of the author's typological use of an Old Testament scripture, the first verb, "she shall be saved," would refer to Eve and the second verb, "if they remain," to the women whom the author of 1 Timothy is addressing. Thus, verses 13 and 14 serve as a type of deception and verse 15, a type of salvation. As a cautionary type, the warning is that the women of 1 Timothy must not be deceived by false teachers as Eve was deceived by the snake. As a type of salvation (verse 15), Eve, the beginning of the line of covenant seed, was saved from the snake by her seed, that is, God's promise was fulfilled through the process of childbirth. The women in 1Timothy will be saved if they learn the true teachings before they themselves teach others,[37] and "if they (the women of 1 Timothy) remain in faith and love and holiness with good mental judgment" (verse 15b).

Another consideration in the interpretation of this verse is the extent to which false teachers were influenced by the teachings of Gnosticism, in particular the teaching of forbidding marriage (1 Tim

32. Padgett, "Wealthy Women at Ephesus," 30.
33. Hanson, *The Pastoral Epistles*, 74.
34. Ibid.
35. Bernard, *The Pastoral Letters*, 49.
36. Dibelius and Conzelmann, *The Pastoral Epistles*, 48.
37. Padgett, "Wealthy Women at Ephesus," 27–29.

4:3). Thus, the writer may have wished to emphasize that childbirth was a positive experience and part of salvation history. This conclusion, however, removes the verse from the continuity of the typology. Thus, the more likely meaning is the one that continues the comparison of Eve and the women of 1 Timothy.

Paying attention to the language, context, and structure of 1 Timothy 2:8–15, we can conclude that the pastor's concern is that those women who teach in the church must first learn the "sound teaching." Then they may "proclaim a religion with conviction."

This kind of in-depth exegesis is important for the understanding of biblical texts, especially if texts are used to formulate doctrines and implement church policies.

7

What Do We Know About Hell?

In *The Hell Jesus Never Intended*, Keith Wright writes that "the fires of hell have captured the terror, imagination, and passion of Christians across two millennia, and those fires continue to rage today."[1]

As I was working on this chapter, my junk mail included what was called "a gift to hang in your home." On one side of the 8 ½ by 11 inch poster was a print out of John 3:16 in the King James Version, "For God so loved the world that He gave His only begotten Son that whosoever believeth in Him should not perish but have everlasting life." On the other side was the interpretation of each phrase in that verse as well as a pictorial description of "The Two Roads and The Two Destinies."

This colorful picture started with two roads, a broad road and a narrow road. You can enter the narrow way through a particular door. If you are on the broad road, your soul goes to hell when your body dies. The door to heaven is closed to you from then on. Later you are judged and go to "the lake of fire." If, on the other hand, you choose the narrow road, your soul goes go to heaven when you die. Your body is raised, and you are judged. Just prior to the emergence of the new heavens and the new earth, the picture shows a tribulation and a millennium. Each of these aspects in the picture has a verse from the New Testament to support it, for example, John 10:9 is the verse indicated to support the idea of a door by which you must enter to get to the narrow road. That verse reads, "I am the door. By me if any man [sic] enters in, he [sic] shall be saved" (King James version). Saved from what? It doesn't say. It assumes that this

---

1. Wright, *The Hell Jesus Never Intended*, 9.

means *"saved from hell."* In each case, these verses are taken out of their textual context and their first century cultural meanings. It is selective proof texting. But the scare tactics work. And if you've heard this message since childhood, it can easily become truth for you. Any time you read those verses, the whole system of hell for sinners, heaven for the saved is conjured up in your mind.

Back to the poster, I asked myself, who sent this out? It turns out it was distributed by the Seed Sowers of Portage la Prairie, Manitoba and Cedar Rapids, Iowa. But why were they putting it in my mailbox? I looked further into the plastic bag in which it came and there was a small brochure that invited me to come to the River Road Gospel Hall in Ottawa for nightly services from September 20 to 30. Ah! That's why it was in my mailbox. Now I understood. Evangelistic services were to be held at the Gospel Hall and I was invited—a flashback to the meetings I attended as a youth. The brochure assured me that they didn't know my name and address and they didn't want my money. Why? Because they were concerned about my soul. They wanted to be sure I'd get to heaven. They genuinely were concerned about my spiritual condition and didn't want me to have to go to hell when I die. The little self addressed card (complete with stamp) asked me only two question: "Do you have everlasting life and KNOW that you are going to heaven?" and "Would you like to receive a free booklet 'Ultimate Questions'?" Years ago, I would have said "no" to the first and "yes" to the second and then hoped, after receiving the booklet, that I would finally be sure I wasn't going to hell.

Fundamentalist evangelical Christians today still believe there is a literal hell for all unbelievers when they die. The way to avoid hell is to accept Jesus' sacrifice on the cross for one's sins. Many seem confident that this will keep them out of hell, but there are those who know they have fulfilled all the requirements to stay out of hell, yet have nagging doubts that they may not quite have believed everything necessary in order to escape hell.[2] That was me.

My idea of hell was fairly straightforward when I was a child. I believed that those who were born again would go to heaven and those who were not, would go to hell. If you asked Jesus to forgive your sins, you wouldn't go to hell when you died.

The sermons I heard about hell when I was young were coined "fire and brimstone" sermons. "If you were to die tonight, do you know where

2. Ibid., 27.

you'd be going?" was the question often asked at evangelistic services. Each evening of the one to two week evening services ended with one form or another of this question. That was what it came down to. That was the bottom line.

I didn't know exactly where hell was—under the ground some-where—but it was hot and flaming. I was convinced it was real but I had no way of knowing for sure whether I would escape the eternal fire after I died.

On the other hand, there was heaven, that glorious place for all the redeemed. We sang:

> When we all get to heaven
> What a day of rejoicing that will be
> When we all see Jesus
> We'll sing and shout the victory.

There were a lot of songs about that wonderful place, like "Mansion Over the Hilltop:"

> I'm satisfied with just a cottage below,
> A little silver and a little gold;
> But in that city were the ransomed will shine,
> I want a gold one that's silver lined.
>
> Don't think me poor or deserted or lonely,
> I'm not discouraged, I'm heavenbound;
> I'm just a pilgrim in search of a city,
> I want a mansion, a harp and a crown.
>
> Refrain: I've got a mansion just over the hilltop,
> In that bright land where we'll never grow old;
> And some day yonder we will never more wander,
> But walk the streets that are purest gold.

And there was "Sweet By and By":

> There's a land that is fairer than day,
> And by faith we can see it afar;
> For the Father waits over the way,
> To prepare us a dwelling place there.
>
> Refrain: In the sweet by and by,
> We shall meet on that beautiful shore.

Considering the painstaking steps I took to believe, I should have known I was on my way to heaven, but I was never sure, never sure I would end up in that beautiful place.

Many who no longer believe in the reality of hell are still haunted by this "threat of a place of eternal torment."[3] This is understandable for those who are former fundamentalist evangelicals, considering the aggressive preaching they have had on the subject of the need to be saved from the fires of hell.

In this chapter I want to unpack the meaning of the underworld (hell) as understood in ancient times. Where did the idea of a hell, complete with fire, judgment, and eternal punishment, originate? As we compare these ideas and see how universal were the understandings, it raises the question, "In what ways does it appear that New Testament writers may have been influenced by beliefs about the underworld that were already out there?"

We will then look at New Testament texts that speak of the underworld, examining the various words used in the New Testament for the underworld and the meaning of those Greek words within their context. We will consider the agenda of New Testament writers in determining how best to interpret these texts and what purpose was served by these New Testament teachings.

THE CONCEPT OF HELL AND JUDGMENT IN ANCIENT TIMES

Historian Alan Bernstein argues that when we try to understand biblical texts that speak of the underworld, we need to keep in mind that "neither the evangelists, those earliest biographers of Jesus, nor his later defenders . . . lived in a cultural vacuum. They knew the Jewish Scriptures, Greek philosophy and mythology (however indirectly), and the practices of the Roman state, its official religion, and the paganism of their neighbors around the Mediterranean. . . . No correct understanding of hell is possible, therefore, without taking into account the conceptual background of the ancient world prior to Christianity."[4]

Going back four thousand years ago in Mesopotamia we realize that the underworld was not always visualized as a place of torture where

3. Ibid., 29.

4. Berstein, *The Formation of Hell*, 2.

sinners belonged and it didn't always last forever.[5] Moving through the centuries to the current era, we see that there have been different names given to the underworld. It has been visualized in various ways by different religions and cultures. The following discussion on the history of the concept of hell will refer to the names for the underworld, where it was believed to be located, what it looked like, who was in charge, who went there, the relationship of the underworld to justice, what happened to the people who went there, and how long they stayed in the underworld.

Names For the Underworld

First then, the names for the underworld. Names have included the Sumerian Kurnugia (also known as the Land of No Return or Great Below), Duat (Ancient Egyptian), Jigoku (Japanese Buddhist), Niflheim (of the Vikings), Kuzimu (Swahili hell), Xibalba (Mayan), Sheol/Hades/Valley of Hinnom/Gehinnom (Jewish), Tartarus (Greek), and Jahannam (the Islamic hell). These names together take in a large geographical area from Sub-Saharan Africa to southern and northern Europe, to Mesopotamia, to Japan, and to Central America. This suggests an almost ancient universal consensus about some form of underworld as a place of the dead.

Location of the Underworld

Where did people visualize the underworld to be? With the exception of Gehinnom (Gehenna in the New Testament), which was actually a valley just outside Jerusalem, the underworld was seen to be beneath the earth, where the body was buried. The Hebrew Bible, assembled between 900 and 165 BCE.[6], mentions Sheol sixty-five times. It refers to the grave, a place that was the farthest removed from God, "For

---

5. This discussion on the ancient underworld makes use of Chuck Crisafulli and Kyra Thompson, *Go to Hell: A Heated History of the Underworld*; Alice K. Turner, *The History of Hell*; Alan E. Bernstein, *The Formation of Hell: Death and Retribution in the Ancient and Early Christian Worlds*; Sharon L. Baker, *Razing Hell: Everything You've Been Taught about God's Wrath and Judgment*; and Keith Wright, *The Hell Jesus Never Intended*.

6. Bernstein, *The Formation of Hell*, 133.

in death there is no remembrance of you; in Sheol who can give you praise?" (Ps 6:5). In Numbers 16, it is recorded that Korah, Dathan, and Abiram incited 250 people against Moses and Aaron. The result was that "the ground under them was split apart. The earth opened its mouth and swallowed them up . . . So they with all that belonged to them went down alive into Sheol; the earth closed over them. . . . And fire came out from the Lord and consumed the 250 men offering the incense" (Num 16:31–35). This story places Sheol under the earth and associates it with fire.

The Egyptian underworld (Duat) was thought to be far beneath the ground with gates to pass through to lower levels of the underworld, and deeper levels reserved for the worst sinners. In the 600s and 700s CE the Kuzimu-Swahili hell descended through seven levels. The Mayan Xibalba had nine levels with Mitnal at the lowest level. The Zoroastrian underworld (late 500s to the 300s BCE) had a bridge leading to either heaven or hell. The lowest level of Hades in the Greek underworld was Tartarus, which was referred to as a bottomless pit.

Appearance of the Underworld

What did the underworld look like? In ancient cultures there were terrifying strange creatures, monsters, deserts, hurricanes, pits, demons, avalanches, caverns, scrubland, bridges, rivers, important trees, gateways, and water that must be crossed. Sheol was a dusty, gloomy shadowy place of oblivion. In Zorastrianism there was eternal punishment with flames of fire. But not all underworlds were fiery. Besides eight fiery hells, the Japanese Jigoku had eight icy hells. Niflheim had no fire and Kuzimu was extremely cold.

Rulers of the Underworld

In most accounts of the underworld where were rulers in charge. These included Queen Ereshkigal in Kurnugia, Mara in some Buddhist sects, Emmo-O-Great Judge of hell in Jigoku, Angra Mainyu (Lord of Lies) in Zorastianism, Hel (the Viking goddess of death) in Niflheim, Ah Puch (a death god) in Xibalba, and Hades in Hades. In corresponding fashion, Christianity presented Satan/Lucifer as the ruler of hell, depicted poignantly as such by Augustine.

People in the Underworld

Who went to the underworld? Here we see a progression through time from the idea that everyone who died went to the underworld to only sinners going there. In the Mesopotamian underworld of 2000 BCE there was no concept of punishment after death. There was no judgment in the Babylonian Kurnugia. The first sense of judgment after death was seen in Egyptian thought in 1500 BCE. Alan Bernstein calls this the "moral" death, "the dead are judged by the standard of known criteria and then rewarded or punished."[7] It was believed that the heart was placed on a scale and weighed against a feather; if the heart failed the test it was devoured by a monster.[8] While there are signs of post-mortem suffering in the *Book of the Dead,* this suffering was not eternal.

In the Hebrew Bible there is evidence that both the wicked and righteous were thought to go to Sheol upon their death. "Sheol does not divide the good from the bad or the wicked from the righteous (Eccl 9:2–6, 10). No judgment of character of deeds takes place at all."[9]

The Underworld and Justice

Some writers in the Hebrew Bible raise the point that sending both the righteous and the wicked to the same place (Sheol) is not just. In Psalm 73 the author looks at the prosperity of the wicked and sees that they are healthy and well to do. But they oppress others and seem to be getting along just fine in this world. The author feels that his righteous behavior has been to no avail, "All in vain I have kept my heart clean and washed my hands in innocence" (Ps 73:13). The writer of Ecclesiastes offers the same thought when he says, "There is a vanity that takes place on earth, that there are righteous people who are treated according to the conduct of the wicked, and there are wicked people who are treated according to the conduct of the righteous. . . . the same fate comes to all, to the righteous and the wicked. . . . This is an evil in all that happens under the sun, that the same fate comes to everyone (Eccl 8:14–9:3).

The writer believes that all experience the same thing after death, but he is calling for a differentiation. Job has the same complaint as the

7. Ibid., 3.

8. Ibid., 13.

9. Baker, *Razing Hell*, 128.

Psalmist and the writer of Ecclesiastes, "One dies in full prosperity, being wholly at ease and secure . . . another dies in bitterness of soul, never having tasted of good. They lie down alike in the dust" (Job 21: 23–26). It is in Ezekiel (dated between 593 and 571 BCE) that there is a distinction in the afterlife.[10] There is a differentiation between the righteous and the wicked, those "who spread terror in the land of the living" have their places in Sheol, "Assyria is there, and all its company, their graves all around it. . . . Their graves are set in the uttermost parts of the Pit" (Ez 32:22–23). The author then proceeds to name other nations who have spread terror and go to the Pit as well. They are Elam, Meshech, Tubal, Edom, the princes of the North, and Pharaoh, all sent to the same compartment of the Pit. Bernstein indicates that the mapping of Sheol is similar to that of the separate regions of the Egyptian Duat.[11]

A differentiation is also seen in Isaiah 14 (written in the 700s BCE) in the railing against the King of Babylon. About Babylon, the writer says, "But you are brought down to Sheol, to the depths of the Pit. . . . All the kings of the nations lie in glory, each in his own tomb; but you are cast out, away from your grave . . . clothed with the dead, those pierced by the sword. . . . You will not be joined with them in burial, because you have destroyed your land, you have killed your people" (Is 14:15–20).

Here Babylon is in "the depths of the Pit" away from the kings who are buried "in glory each in his own tomb." Bernstein sees this as one of the earliest expressions in the Hebrew Bible of belief in differentiation after death.[12]

In the book of Daniel, probably written around 165 BCE, there is evidence of a belief in judgment of both the living and dead. Daniel has a vision of a court of judgment and that "many of those who sleep in the dust of the earth shall awake, some to everlasting life, and some to shame and everlasting contempt" (Dan 7:26; 12:2). Bernstein says that in Daniel, "the wicked and the righteous are both raised from the dead, separated, and given over to fates that last forever."[13]

Socrates (ca. 469–399 BCE) believed that people's souls survived death and that "the fate in the next world depends on how well one

10. Bernstein, *The Formation of Hell*, 162.
11. Ibid., 165.
12. Ibid., 167.
13. Ibid., 175.

has prepared it in this world. . . . If souls such as those of philosophers indicate a life devoted to 'piety and truth,' he [the judge] sends them to the Isles of the Blessed."[14]

The Book of Enoch is a Jewish religious work that dates between 300 BCE and the first century BCE. Some verses in Enoch have this to say about judgment,

> Woe to you, ye sinners, when ye have died. If ye die in the wealth of your sins, those who are like you say regarding you: "Blessed are the sinners: they have seen all their days. And how they have died in prosperity and in wealth, and have not seen tribulation or murder in their life; and they have died in honour, and judgment has not been executed on them during their life." Know ye, that their souls will be made to descend into Sheol and they shall be wretched in their great tribulation. And into darkness and chains and a burning flame where there is grievous judgment shall your spirits enter; and the great judgment shall be for all the generations of the world. Woe to you, for ye shall have no peace (Enoch 103: 5–8).

There is the thought that there will be justice at the end of life. Deeds will be judged and those who seemed to have lived a joyous and prosperous life, even though they were murderers, will be judged for their evil deeds after death.

The Psalms of Solomon, possibly written between 70 and 45 BCE, comprise eighteen psalms. They also discuss the fate of the wicked, "Sinners and transgressors, who love (the brief) day (spent) in companionship with their sin; their delight is in fleeting corruption, and they remember not God. For the ways of men [*sic*] are known before Him at all times, and He knoweth the secrets of the heart before they come to pass. Therefore their inheritance is Sheol and darkness and destruction" (Ps of Sol 14:6–9).

Moving ahead to the first century CE, philosophical views of the afterlife, stemming from Platonism, held that there was a body and soul. The two were separated upon death, and there was a differentiation as to destination, "the fate after death is different for different souls."[15]

While first century Jewish beliefs about the afterlife differed as to the type of retribution after death, what was consistent, for those who

---

14. Ibid., 56.

15. Lehtipuu, *The Afterlife Imagery*, 87.

believed in an afterlife, was the belief that the fate of the dead was either in the form of rewards or punishment.[16]

So we see that since the second millennium BCE the line of thinking has been that in the afterlife those who had done good deeds were separated from those who had done evil deeds. It didn't seem fair to award both with the same afterlife.

Type of Existence in the Underworld

When souls or bodies got to the underworld, what did they do? Those in Sheol existed as ghosts and had no knowledge, memory or feeling. In Kurnugia the dead had to procure their own clothing and food. Many of them sat in dust and darkness in bird costumes. In Niflheim souls were hungry and sat in cold darkness. The only thing they seemed to be able to do was to gaze at Hel, the goddess of death.

In Tibetan Buddhism, the *Tibetan Book of the Dead* was said to prepare the living person for their time in the underworld. However, in the Egyptian Duat, the *Book of the Dead* was to be consulted after you had died. It was believed to help a person through the underworld and assist them in the judgment that was to take place after death.[17]

For Virgil, a Roman poet (70–19 BCE), the underworld had a fork in the road and souls were bound for either Elysium or Tartarus, freedom and joy to the right and punishment to the left.[18]

Length of Time in the Underworld

How long did the dead stay in the underworld? In Tibetan Buddhism, the soul remained in the underworld forty-nine days and then was reincarnated or went to paradise. In Zoroastrianism, it was believed that hell would cease to exist when the god of light, Ahura Mazda, would triumph over Angra Mainyu, god of lies. When this would happen, all souls would go to heaven. In the Greek Hades, souls were busy trying to find their way to heaven.

16. Ibid., 158.
17. Clark-Soles, *Death and the Afterlife*, 30.
18. Bernstein, *The Formation of Hell*, 68.

Plato (ca. 469–347 BCE) distinguished between those who were curable and those incurable; the incurable were punished eternally, "Justice therefore, demands the immortality of the soul; and the immortality of the soul makes eternal punishment possible. . . . Plato is the earliest author to state categorically that the fate of the extremely wicked is eternal punishment."[19]

Virgil wrote about an afterlife that was based on one's earthly life. Only a few stayed in the Elysian fields (heaven); the rest stayed in the underworld for one thousand years and then were reborn on earth.[20]

To summarize, we have seen that the ancient concept of hell, called by a variety of names in different cultural contexts, was primarily thought to be under the earth, sometimes several levels deep. The ancient underworld was often depicted as a dark place, sometimes fiery, sometimes icy, but usually with barriers to overcome, gates to go through, or bridges to cross. There was always someone in charge. The Egyptian Duat appears to be the first with differentiation for the righteous and sinners. In the Hebrew Bible, some authors asked the question of justice with regard to the afterlife, thinking there should be a differentiation at death, dependent on a person's deeds. In the first century, some believed justice would be realized after death, when people would be punished or rewarded for their deeds. In contexts where there was a differentiation between the righteous and the wicked, there was a sense that people would not stay in the underworld (hell) forever, except for Plato's "incurables," who would be punished forever.

COMPARISON OF THE ANCIENT UNDERWORLDS WITH NEW TESTAMENT REFERENCES

We can notice some similarities between ancient concepts of the underworld and those found in the New Testament.

Like the ancient idea of separation of good and evil after death, the New Testament also refers to differentiation between the righteous and the wicked after death. Matthew records Jesus talking about the judgment of nations "when the Son of Man comes in his glory" (Matt 25:31). At this time, "he will separate people one from another as a shepherd separates the sheep from the goats, and he will put the sheep at his right hand and

19. Ibid., 57, 61.
20. Lehtipuu, *The Afterlife Imagery*, 83.

the goats at the left (Matt 25:32–33). And it turns out that the sheep are the righteous, those who have fed the hungry, clothed the naked and visited those in prison (Matt 25:37–40). The goats are those who have not done this; their destination is eternal punishment (Matt 25:41–46).

The writer of Revelation mentions dragons, strange creatures, earthquakes, rivers, a desert, and darkness. In this vision of an afterlife, the writer uses images that had previously been used in earlier ancient conceptions of the underworld. There is also mention of the bottomless pit (nine times in Revelation), the term used for the Greek Tartarus.

The New Testament speaks of deeds recorded in a ledger. The writer of Revelation talks of those "who are written in the Lamb's book of life. And I saw the dead, great and small, standing before the throne, and books were opened . . . and the dead were judged according to their works as recorded in the books" (Rev 21:27; 20:12). In Zoroastrianism, there is also a ledger to record one's deeds.

Since the Hebrew Bible was Scripture for the early Christians, the most logical context for the New Testament idea of hell was that of Sheol. Gehenna and Sheol are terms used by writers of the New Testament. Other than the influence of the Hebrew Sheol, it is difficult to say exactly how Jesus and the New Testament writers would have been influenced by ancient and first century ideas of the afterlife and judgment. But it makes sense that they would be.

NEW TESTAMENT TEXTS ON HELL

Fundamentalist evangelical teaching on hell has traditionally focused on New Testament texts that refer to Hades, Gehenna, or fire (often with "and brimstone" thrown in), so these are the concepts we will discuss.

Hades

The Greek word *hadēs* means what is unseen and in the New Testament refers to the underworld. The word appears eleven times in the New Testament, once in 1 Corinthians, twice in Acts, twice in Matthew, four times in Revelation, and twice in Luke.

In 1 Corinthians, which was written before Acts, Matthew, Revelation, and Luke, it is clearly the Sheol of the Old Testament, a place for disembodied souls, the place of the dead. It means simply the grave.

In the context of Paul's teaching on the resurrection of Christ and the resurrection of others who have died, he proclaims, "Oh death where is thy sting? Oh grave [*hadēs*], where is thy victory?" (1 Cor 15:55– KJV), which is a quote from the Hebrew Bible, "O death, where are your plagues? O Sheol, where is your destruction?" (Hos 13:14). Paul wrote that because of Jesus' resurrection, the grave is not victorious.

In the book of Acts, Peter quoted the Hebrew Bible when he referred to Hades. In his address to a crowd he tried to show that God raised Jesus from death. He quoted Psalm16:10 and applied it to Jesus, "For you will not abandon my soul to Hades or let your Holy One experience corruption" (Acts 2:27). He said that "he [Jesus] was not abandoned to Hades, nor did his flesh experience corruption" (Acts 2:31). This is a reference to Psalm 16:10, which says, "For you do not give me up to Sheol or let your faithful one see the Pit." In Acts, as in I Corinthians, Hades seems to simply mean death, since the writer of Acts is using the quotation from Psalm 16 to make his point that Jesus was not left to die.

The word Hades is used in the book of Matthew when Jesus tells Peter that he is the rock upon which the church will be built. So sure of this was Jesus that he proclaimed, "the gates of Hades will not prevail against it" (Mt 16:18). Not even death would prevent this from happening. Again, Hades refers to death.

Both Matthew 11:23 and Luke 10:15 contain the same saying of Jesus—his reproach to those who were unrepentant—"And you, Capernaum, will you be exalted to heaven? No, you will be brought down to Hades." Again, this text calls to mind a section of the Hebrew Bible. In Isaiah 14, the haughtiness of the King of Babylon will bring him down to Sheol, down to the Pit. Babylon is accused of saying that they will "ascend to heaven" and raise their throne "above the stars of God" (Is 14:13). They want to make themselves like God (Is 14:14). By saying that they will be brought down to Sheol, the prophet means that they will be brought low and humbled. The leaders of the other nations will say to Babylon, "You too have become as weak as we! You have become like us!" (Is 14:10). This is the text quoted by Matthew and Luke in their reference to Capernaum being brought down to Hades. And why did Jesus quote Isaiah here? Because in Capernaum he had displayed "his deeds of power" but "they did not repent" (Matt 11:20). So Jesus' prediction was that Capernaum would be humiliated; it would be brought low.

In the book of Revelation (Rev 1:18; 6:8; 20:13–14), a highly symbolic apocalyptic book, each of the four times Hades is used it accompanies the word for death and seems to mean "the grave." In Revelation 20, both death and Hades are thrown into the lake of fire, which would seem to suggest that both death and the grave vanish.

In the story of the rich man and Lazarus, Luke perceives Hades as a place of torment with flames, a place where one has unquenchable thirst (Lk 16:19–31). The visual image this story elicits is full of details. Paintings have portrayed the agony of the rich man in Hades. The story features a wealthy man who did not share his food with a poor sick man named Lazarus. It is clear that the rich man was Jewish, since he addressed Abraham as Father Abraham. They both died and were buried. Lazarus reclined on Abraham's chest. The rich man could see Abraham from where he was buried, but he was tormented, thirsty, and "in agony in these flames" (Lk 16:24). He begged for some water but Abraham pointed out that the rich man was receiving the consequence of his stinginess and that there was a large chasm between them, so they were unable to bring him water. And when he asked if he could go back to earth to warn his family about "this place of torment," he was told that it wouldn't do any good to warn them, since they have the writings of Moses and prophets, and if they don't apply those, it wouldn't do any good for someone to come back from the dead to tell them (Lk 16: 27–31).

There are a number of details in the Luke story that are comparable to the philosophical and literary thought of the time. These include the following:

- When Lazarus dies, angels take him to his afterlife (Lk 16:22). In the *Odyssey*, Hermes escorts the dead to the underworld.[21]

- There is a fixed chasm between Lazarus and the rich man (Lk 16:26). Other underworld descriptions also have chasms and other barriers.[22]

- It is to Abraham that Lazarus goes when he dies (Lk 16:22). In the Jewish tradition, patriarchs such as Abraham are said to receive the dead.[23]

- In this story there is fire and thirst. These too are common themes

21. Lehtipuu, *The Afterlife Imagery*, 233.
22. Ibid., 234.
23. Ibid., 233.

in both Jewish and Greek thoughts of the underworld.[24]

Let us examine this story more closely. The immediate context within the gospel of Luke is that the story is situated among parables told by Jesus (the parable of the dinner to which the poor and lame were invited, the parable of the lost sheep, the parable of the lost coin, the parable of the prodigal son, and the parable of the manager who was dishonest about the amount of goods owed). And Luke indicates that the Pharisees were "lovers of money" (Lk 16:14). All these parables make the point that Jesus was concerned for the lost ones, those who were poor and sick and alone. This is consistent with other stories of Jesus as healer and as one who reached out to those who were perceived as the outcasts of society. And it is consistent with Luke's agenda of paying attention to those less fortunate.

In my growing up years the story of the rich man and Lazarus was used to scare people about hell, a place of torment complete with flames of fire and unquenchable thirst. A place where, once you get there, there is no going back to change your life choices. And you can't go back to tell your friends and relatives what to do to escape hell. "So decide today to accept Jesus as your Lord and Savior so that you can be sure you won't end up in hell."

Plutarch (ca. 46–120 CE), a Greek historian, believed that upright behavior could be encouraged through a belief in punishment after death.[25] The same goal of morality was seen in the belief in judgment after death in first century mystery religions. The belief in rewards and punishment after death was also prevalent in first century Jewish beliefs.[26] And with this story, Jesus is making the same point that one should look after the poor in society. If the hearers share their wealth with the poor, they will be treated well in the afterlife. Similar lessons can be drawn from the other parables that are placed alongside this story.

Thus, in Luke's story, the idea of a division of souls to a place of goodness (where Abraham is) or torment (where the rich man is) is consistent with both Greek and Jewish first century beliefs in the differentiation of the destiny of the dead to a place of either reward or punishment. Its function is to inspire those living to lead moral lives. The idea of differentiation after death was inherent in the general

---

24. Ibid.

25. Clark-Soles, *Death and the Afterlife*, 33.

26. Lehtipuu, *The Afterlife Imagery*, 158.

world view of the time. Given the prevalent belief that there was a differentiation between the fate of the upright and the wicked after death, it makes sense that Jesus used that belief to tell a story that had as its moral the idea that people who are rich should think twice about their value system. It was a story of justice. The point of the story was a this-worldly point about riches. It was not meant to set out for all time the nature of hell.

Gehenna

Gehenna is another word used for hell in the New Testament. This word appears twelve times: seven times in Matthew, three times in Mark, once in Luke, and once in James. Since some of these references occur in more than one gospel, I will only discuss the seven unique uses of the word in Matthew.

The instances in Matthew when Jesus is reportedly to have said that his hearers were liable to Gehenna are the following:

- If you say "you fool" to a sister or brother, you are liable to the Gehenna of fire (Matt 5:22).

- If your right eye has caused you to sin, you are to cut it out and throw it away. Better this than having your whole body thrown into Gehenna (Matt 5:29).

- If your right hand has caused you to sin and you don't cut it off and throw it away, your whole body will be thrown into Gehenna (Matt 5:30).

- The "Father in heaven" has the ability to throw both body and soul into Gehenna, so fear him instead of being afraid of the persecutors (Matt 10:28).

- If you eye causes you to stumble, you should tear it out and throw it away, rather than be thrown into the Gehenna of fire (Matt 18:9).

- In denouncing the scribes and Pharisees, Jesus calls them children of Gehenna and accuses them of making their converts the same (Matt 23:15).

- Again, in denouncing the scribes and Pharisees as hypocrites, Jesus calls them snakes and a brood of vipers and says they cannot escape "being sentenced to Gehenna" (Matt 23:32).

To what does Gehenna refer? It is literally a valley just southwest of Jerusalem, called the Valley of Hinnom or Geh ben Hinnom. At the time of Jesus it was a garbage dump, which was always on fire. Looking back into the history of the Valley, when Manasseh was King of Judah from 687 to 642 BCE, "he made his son pass through fire in the valley of the son of Hinnom, practiced soothsaying and augury and sorcery, and dealt with mediums and with wizards. He did much evil in the sight of the Lord, provoking him to anger" (2 Chr 33:6). We can see here that the Valley of Hinnom is associated with evil. Sacrifice of children seems to have been a practice of the Israelites (Lev 18:21), but King Josiah, king from 640 to 609 BCE, put a stop to it, "he defiled Topheth, which is in the valley of Ben-hinnom, so that no one would make a son or a daughter pass through fire as an offering to Molech" (2 Kgs 23:10).

Isadore Singer and George Barton say that "in the last days of the kingdom human sacrifices were offered to YHWH as King or Counselor of the nation and that the Prophets disapproved of it and denounced it because it was introduced from outside as an imitation of a heathen cult and because of its barbarity."[27] Jeremiah was one of the prophets in the 600s BCE who spoke against this practice, saying that God said, "And they go on building the high place of Topheth, which is in the valley of the son of Hinnom, to burn their sons and their daughters in the fire, which I did not command, nor did it come into my mind. Therefore, the days are surely coming . . . when it will no more be called Topheth, or the valley of the son of Hinnom, but the valley of Slaughter: for they will bury in Topheth until there is no more room" (Jer 7:31–32).

To whom were these child offerings made and why was the practice followed? Jeremiah indicates that these child offerings were to the god Baal (Jer 19:5). And Micah, prophet in Judah in the early 700s BCE, revealed the purpose for these offerings, "Shall I give my firstborn for my transgression the fruit of my body for the sin of my soul?" (Mi 6:7). There is strong evidence that the practice was introduced by the Phoenicieans.[28]

So we see that the references to Gehenna in the New Testament do not refer to a flame-burning hell under the ground where people go when they die. The other thing to mention is that Jesus was prone to use stories, metaphors and hyperbole to get his listeners to pay attention to his

27. Singer and Barton, "Moloch (Molech)," www.jewishencyclopedia.com.
28. Ibid.

teaching.[29] Jesus' use of exaggeration was not meant to be taken literally. This can be illustrated in his instruction to a would-be follower of his to "follow me, and let the dead bury their own dead" (Matt 8:22). This is an impossible request but it appears that Jesus responded in this way to impress upon the disciple what it would take for him or her to follow Jesus. He did not actually mean that those who were already dead should take up the task to bury others who were dead. Similarly, when he said it would be better that people cut out their eyes than that their whole body go to Gehenna, he did not mean they should literally cut out their eyes or that they would actually end up in the garbage dump outside Jerusalem. He used the reference to Gehenna to show his strong displeasure with certain behaviors and as a metaphor for a place that "would have indicated a life far removed from the laws of Yahweh."[30]

Since the concept of Gehenna is used more often by Matthew than by Mark and Luke, it is useful to look at the cultural context of the Matthean community. What was Matthew's agenda? What was his community facing?

Because of Matthew's dependence on Mark and the fact that the writer of Matthew makes reference to the fall of Jerusalem, the book was most likely written between 80 and 100 CE. Stephen was a Jewish Christian living in Jerusalem in the first century. After Stephen's martyrdom by a Jewish contingent (Acts 7), increased persecution of Jewish Christians prompted many of them to flee to the Judean countryside and northward to Samaria, Phoenicia, Cyprus, and Antioch in Syria. (Antioch in Syria was likely the location of the Matthean community.[31])

Matthew's Jewish Christian community suffered severe persecution at the hands of both Jews and Gentiles. A step back in history will shed some light on the reasons for the persecution. Since 63 BCE Palestine had been subject to Roman rule. When Herod the Great (37–4 BCE) ruled the area, he sought to bring Greco-Roman religion and culture to the region. Jews who were not loyal were punished. When he died, his son, Herod Antipas, was appointed ruler. Palestine was under his rule at the time of Jesus.

Between 6 and 66 CE, there was a succession of fourteen procurators in Judea who tried to bring the region under Roman rule. Violent

29. Baker, *Razing Hell*, 132–35.

30. Turner, *The History of Hell*, 41.

31. Court, *The New Testament World*, 217.

acts were committed against the Jewish people and their religion. The last procurator, Florus (64–66 CE), plundered the temple treasury. When Jewish people protested, he had many of them crucified. By 66 CE an organized revolt against Rome resulted in what has been called the Jewish War of 66 CE. Rome won the war and the temple in Jerusalem was destroyed.

Now to the Matthean community in Antioch. How were they affected by the war of 66 CE? There would have been several synagogues in Antioch, a city in which Jewish communities had existed since 300 BCE when Antioch was founded.[32] Even though Antioch was north of Jerusalem, the Jews living there were not spared violence at the hands of the Gentiles. At the end of the Jewish War, they were accused of setting fire to parts of the city. In spite of the fact that the Roman governor declared their innocence, relations between these ethnic groups remained strained. This is confirmed by the fact that on two different occasions, Titus (Roman emperor from 79–81 CE) was asked by the city of Antioch to expel Jews from Antioch, a request he did not grant.[33]

It seems probable that even though the Matthean community was Jewish Christian, they suffered the same fate as other Jews at the hands of the Gentiles. Soon after the Jewish War, when a coalition of Pharisees and scribes worked towards imposing uniformity of religious thought, Jewish Christians had to leave the Antiochene synagogue. It is unclear exactly when the split between Jewish Christians and Pharisaic Jews occurred. If Matthew's community was still part of the Jewish synagogue at the time of the writing of the book of Matthew, as John and Kathleen Court suggest,[34] then it is understandable that these Jewish Christians would have received the same treatment as other Jews in Antioch. Even if they had already broken with the synagogue, "it is unlikely that a bloodthirsty crowd, intent on harming all Jews, would not have known or cared about the finer details of a theological (and Christological) dispute between traditional synagogue Jews and their Jewish Christian opponents."[35]

In addition to the persecution by the Gentiles, there were clashes between the Jewish Christians and the Jews. Jewish Christians were

---

32. Ibid., 216.
33. Sim, "The Gospel of Matthew and the Gentiles," 36.
34. Court, *The New Testament World*, 196.
35. Sim, "The Gospel of Matthew and the Gentiles," 38.

ostracized by the Jews because they had accepted Christianity. Thus the Matthean community appears to have suffered persecution at the hands of both Jews and Gentiles around the time of the writing of the gospel. Matthew's community was a victimized community, victims of both Jewish and Gentile persecution. Their Christian status made them susceptible to Jewish persecution; their Jewish status made them candidates for violence from Gentiles.

Besides the historical evidence of Gentile persecution of the Matthean community, the text of Matthew itself gives us an indication that the community for which the book was written was persecuted by Gentiles. This is seen in references to the Gentiles, which occurred exclusively in Matthew. For example, in Matthew 10, Jesus warns the disciples of coming persecution, when "they will hand you over to councils and flog you in their synagogues; and you will be dragged before governors and kings because of me, as a testimony to them and the Gentiles" (Matt 10: 17–18). Here Matthew singles out the Gentiles as a group who will persecute them. In Mark's parallel text, the reference to the Gentiles is absent. Matthew 5:46–47, a text that deals with love of enemies, asks the question, "And if you greet only your brothers and sisters, what more are you doing than others? Do not even the Gentiles do the same?" The parallel Lucan text says, "even sinners do the same" (Lk 6:32–33). In Matthew, Gentiles are seen as those doing the bare minimum. Matthew's readers are admonished to do better than Gentiles. In the introduction to the "Our Father" prayer, Matthew advises readers not to "heap up empty phrases as the Gentiles do" (Matt 6:7). This assumes that the prayers of the Gentiles lacked meaning. In the well-known text on not worrying about what to eat, drink, or wear, the Matthew version says, "Therefore, do not worry . . . for it is the Gentiles who strive for all these things" (Matt 6:31–32). The Lucan parallel says, "for it is the nations of the world that strive after all these things" (Lk 12:30). Here again, in Matthew Gentiles are specified as those who worry about things they should not worry about.

In Matthew 10, when Jesus sends out the disciples to cast out unclean spirits and cure diseases, he gives instructions to "go nowhere among the Gentiles, and enter no town of the Samaritans, but go rather to the lost sheep of the house of Israel" (Matt 10:5–6). Neither Mark nor Luke include this instruction. It is unique to Matthew, signifying perhaps the animosity between Jews and Gentiles in Matthew's community.

Finally, in the text that outlines the procedure to be taken if one person has a complaint against another, Matthew instructs readers that "if the offender refuses to listen even to the church, let such a one be to you as a Gentile and a tax collector" (Matt 18:17). This text, in which Gentiles are portrayed as those who are shunned by the readers, is unique to the book of Matthew. Therefore, both the historical context and internal evidence point to the fact that there were problems between the Matthean community and the Gentiles. Gentiles were viewed as outsiders who were to be shunned. These texts "reflect a very negative attitude toward the Gentiles. They affirm that the Gentile world is filled with irreligious people who provide anti-role models and with whom contact should be minimal."[36]

Realizing the persecution of the Matthean community by both Jews and Gentiles helps us understand the agenda of the writer of the gospel of Matthew. He wrote to a community that was in danger for their lives. So it makes sense that in the teaching about the afterlife there would be a differentiation. Hence, the numerous references to Gehenna in Matthew, associating it with the persecutors, vindicated the Jewish Christians and gave them the hope that justice would eventually be served.

We have looked at the concepts of Hades and Gehenna in the New Testament. Now to the idea of fire, at times associated with the afterlife and sometimes accompanied by brimstone. Before examining the New Testament texts that speak to this, we will look at the uses of the word "fire" in the Hebrew Bible.

Fire

Fire was very important to ancient people. It was used to cook, shape tools and weapons, make dishes, and also for light. Because fire was hard to produce, every village had a fire that never went out, from which people could come and get their own fire. At the temple of Vesta in Rome, Vestal virgins devoted their lives to attending the fire. Fire was regarded as a gift of the gods, and thus sacred.

Although there are four Hebrew words for "fire," the one used almost exclusively in the Hebrew Bible is *ʾēsh*, which means burning,

36. Ibid.

fiery, flaming, or, simply, hot. Most frequently, this word is used when setting fire to something, such as in animal sacrifices (Lev 3:5); when roasting food to eat (Ex 12:8); or when explaining what happens during a thunderstorm with lightening. This latter meaning is expressed in the phrase "fire from heaven" and is often accompanied by "sulphur" (brimstone), which likely refers to a volcanic eruption in which sulphur dioxide is released. This is seen in the reference to the destruction of the cities of Sodom and Gomorrah when "the Lord rained sulphur and fire out of heaven" (Gen 19:24). Ezekiel 38 talks about what will happen to Gog, Prince of Meshech, and Tubal, "I will summon the sword against Gog . . . and I will pour down torrential rain and hailstones, fire and sulphur, upon him and his troops" (Ezek 38:22). So the word "fire" in the Hebrew Bible was used both for good (food) and for destruction.

We recall that ancient hells were often associated with fire. In the Egyptian *Book Am-Tuat,* (literally, that which is in the underworld), there are references to pits of fire and goddesses who spew fire from their mouths.[37]

In the New Testament, *'esh* is translated as *pur*, and means fire.

It is in Matthew that we hear the most about the fires of Gehenna:

- "Every tree therefore that does not bear good fruit is cut down and thrown into the fire" (Matt 3:10). This is part of John the Baptist's criticism of the Pharisees and Sadducees.

- "He [Jesus] will baptize you with the Holy Spirit and with fire. . . . The chaff he will burn with unquenchable fire" (Matt 3:12). This is John's prediction as to what Jesus will do.

- "If you say 'you fool,' you will be liable to the Gehenna of fire (Matt 5:22). Jesus is extending the commandment, "you shall not murder," to include not even becoming angry with one another.

- "Just as the weeds are collected and burned up with fire, so will it be at the end of the age" (Matt 13:40). In Jesus' explanation of the parable of the sower, the weeds refer to "the children of the evil one" (Matt 13:38).

- "The Son of Man will send his angels, and they will collect out of his kingdom all causes of sin and all evildoers, and they will throw them into the furnace of fire, where there will be weeping

37. Bernstein, *The Formation of Hell*, 18.

and gnashing of teeth" (Matt 13:42). Also part of the explanation of the parable of the sower, Jesus now includes a broader sweep of evil, "all causes of sin and all evildoers."

- "The angels will come out and separate the evil from the righteous and throw them into the furnace of fire, where there will be weeping and gnashing of teeth" (Matt 13:49–50). This is said after likening the kingdom of heaven to a net of fish; the good fish are kept and the bad are thrown out.

- "Then he will say to those at his left hand, 'You that are accursed, depart from me into the eternal fire prepared for the devil and his angels' . . . and these will go away into eternal punishment, but the righteous into eternal life" (Matt 25:41, 46). After the parables of the ten bridesmaids and of the talents, Jesus says that "when the Son of Man comes in his glory" the sheep will be separated from the goats. The sheep are those who have fed the poor, welcomed strangers, clothed those who had no clothing, took care of the sick, and visited those in prison. The goats are those who have not done these things (Matt 25:31–46).

The Matthew texts are reminiscent of Isaiah 66:24, "And they shall go out and look at the dead bodies of the people who have rebelled against me; for their worm shall not die, their fire shall not be quenched." The fire in the Isaiah text is the fire burning in the Valley of Hinnom. The point made here by Isaiah is that those in Judah, those faithful to Yahweh, will see the corpses of those who rebelled against him.[38] A kind of justice, I suppose, to see your enemies burning forever.

Sharon Baker proposes an alternative meaning of fire when it is associated with the afterlife. She sees fire in terms of purification. Rather than the idea that individuals are punished by burning in flames forever, she understands the purpose of the fire metaphor as burning off evil, thus leaving individuals pure.[39] We recall that John the Baptist predicted that Jesus would baptize people with the Holy Spirit and fire. In this instance, fire could have a positive connotation, especially since later on the day of Pentecost, there is the story of people having "tongues, as of fire" resting on each person (Acts 2:3).

38. Bernstein, *The Formation of Hell*, 171–72.
39. Baker, *Razing Hell*, 142–44

In Matthew 3 it is recorded that Jesus will "gather his wheat into the granary; but the chaff he will burn with unquenchable fire" (Matt 3:11,12). And what is left when the chaff is burned off? The pure wheat. And with respect to the reference to the lake of fire in Revelation, Baker says that, "the people reading about the lake of fire would interpret it as a lake of divine purification, a lake of cleansing so that the purified object (a person) can be dedicated and restored to God."[40]

Weeping and Gnashing of Teeth

In sermons that were given about hell there was sometimes a reference to "weeping and gnashing of teeth" and we were told that it was going to be so terrible in hell that people would be doing just that—weeping and gnashing their teeth. This fact added to the fearfulness of the prospect of going to hell.

The phrase "weeping and gnashing of teeth" appears primarily in the book of Matthew where the writer indicates that evildoers will be thrown into darkness "where there will be weeping and gnashing of teeth." In fundamentalist evangelical circles this is commonly understood to refer to the afterlife in hell.

This phrase appears six times in Matthew and once in Luke. In order to help us understand its meaning in the New Testament, we will first examine the concept in the Hebrew Bible. The Hebrew word, *châraq*, literally means "to grate the teeth." Of the five times it appears, it is used once for what the wicked do when they see that the righteous are prospering, once for what God is doing, and three times for the wicked mocking the righteous in their misfortunes.

In Psalm 112, the writer recounts the wellbeing and prosperity of the righteous. At the end of the chapter, he observes that when the "wicked" see how well the righteous are doing, "they gnash their teeth and melt away" (Ps 112:10). Here gnashing of teeth arises out of envy of those who are prosperous. It may denote frustration and anger towards those who are doing well.

Job, who believes he is suffering innocently, has a lot to say, both to God and to the friends who have come to supposedly comfort him. At one point, when speaking to God, Job says, "surely now God has worn

40. Ibid., 144.

me out; . . . he has shriveled me up . . . he has torn me in his wrath, and hated me; he has gnashed his teeth at me" (Job 16:7–9). In this instance Job assumes that God must be angry with him and thus, God gnashes God's teeth in anger.

The writer of Lamentations, grieving the destruction of the temple in 586 BCE, says that Israel's enemies, when seeing the destruction, "hiss, they gnash their teeth, they cry: 'We have devoured her! Ah, this is the day we longed for; at last we have seen it' " (Lam 2:16). Similarly, in Psalm 35 and 37, the writer talks about his enemies gloating over his misfortunes, "But at my stumbling they gathered in glee, they gathered together against me; . . . they impiously mocked more and more, gnashing at me with their teeth" (Ps 35:15, 16); "the wicked plot against the righteous, and gnash their teeth at them" (Ps 37:12). In all these instances, Israel's enemies are gnashing their teeth at those whose suffering they have caused. It is a grating of teeth, a gloating, perhaps accompanied by laughter, as if to say, "ha, ha, look at you now, look what we've done to you."

So we can see that the phrase "weeping and gnashing of teeth" in the Hebrew Bible has nothing to do with the afterlife. Instead, it is a grating of teeth by one who looks upon the prosperity or misfortune of another. It's about what happens in this world, not in the next.

And now to the New Testament texts that refer to "weeping and gnashing of teeth." These are often accompanied by throwing the offending persons into darkness. In all but one case this phrase appears within one of Jesus' parables, stories told by Jesus to make a certain point.

In the particular case in which it is not a parable, a non-Jewish person asks Jesus to heal his servant. He believes that Jesus can do this on the spot, without even seeing the servant. Seeing the faith of this person, Jesus exclaims that many "will eat with Abraham and Isaac and Jacob in the kingdom of heaven, while the heirs of the kingdom will be thrown into the outer darkness, where there will be weeping and gnashing of teeth" (Matt 8: 11–12). In this case, Jesus' own people, those who are legitimate heirs, are told that non-Jews are the true heirs. So they weep and gnash their teeth; they are angry that they didn't achieve the status they felt was due them.

The parables where this phrase is used are the following:

- In the explanation of the parable of the sower, "the Son of Man will send his angels, and they will collect out of his kingdom all causes of sin and all evildoers, and they will throw them into the furnace of fire, where there will be weeping and gnashing of teeth" (Matt 13:41–42). This is contrasted with the righteous, who "will shine like the sun in the kingdom of their Father" (Matt 13:43).

- In the parable of the net that catches good fish and bad fish. Jesus likens the separation of good and bad fish to the separation of the evil from the righteous. The evil ones will be thrown "into the furnace of fire, where there will be weeping and gnashing of teeth" (Matt 13:47–50).

- In the parable of the wedding banquet those who were invited "made light of it . . . and seized his slaves, mistreated them, and killed them." So the king had these invitees killed and he burned their city. Then he sent his slaves to invite the people on the streets, both good and bad, to come to the banquet. But it turned out that one of the invitees was not wearing the proper attire, so the king ordered him to be bound and thrown "into the outer darkness, where there will be weeping and gnashing of teeth" (Matt 22:1–13). Jesus ends his parable with the words, "for many are called, but few are chosen" (Matt 22:14). Again, there is a differentiation between the good and bad, those who are selected to stay at the banquet and the one who was sent away.

- Matthew recounts a parable in which a slave was put in charge of the master's household when the master went away. The slave will be commended if the master finds him working hard when he returns. However, if that slave mistreats the other slaves and "eats and drinks with drunkards," the master will not be pleased when he returns, "he will cut him in pieces and put him with the hypocrites, where there will be weeping and gnashing of teeth" (Matt 24:45–51). Again, there is contrast between the anticipated behavior of a good slave and a bad slave.

- In the parable of the talents (money), various amounts of money were given to the master's slaves. Most of them invested the money, but the person who only got one talent, hid it. When the master came back, he commended those who had invested their money. They were told they were trustworthy. The master was pleased and put them in charge of even more. But the one who hid the money said to the master, "I knew that you were a harsh man, reaping where you did not sow, gathering where you did not scatter seed; so I was afraid, and I went and hid your talent in the ground. Here you have what is yours" (Matt 25:24–25). This did not please the master, who called him "wicked and lazy." The command was given to throw "this worthless slave . . . into the outer darkness, where there will be weeping and gnashing of teeth" (Matt 25:14–50). The parable's lesson: "For to all those who have, more will be given, and they will have an abundance; but from those who have nothing, even what they have will be taken away" (Matt 25:49).

- In Luke 13, Jesus says that when the owner of the house closes the door, it is too late to enter. Those wanting to come in will claim to know Jesus, but Jesus calls them evildoers and sends them away, "there will be weeping and gnashing of teeth when you see Abraham and Isaac and Jacob and all the prophets in the kingdom of God, and you yourselves thrown out" (Lk 13:28). Jesus then exclaims that people will "eat in the kingdom of God. Indeed, some are last who will be first, and some are first who will be last" (Lk 13: 29–30).

In each of these cases there is a differentiation in the fates of the righteous and evildoers. There is no indication as to what or where the "outer darkness" is (fundamentalist evangelicals have assumed this is hell) nor how long they weep and gnash their teeth.

In the Hebrew Bible "weeping and gnashing of teeth" symbolizes a feeling towards others, either jealous of others' well being or gloating over others' misfortune. In the occurrences in the New Testament, the feeling is towards oneself, grating one's own teeth because one has not invested the master's money, or because one has missed the banquet, or because one has not invested the master's money. There is profound regret.

Thus we can assume that "weeping and gnashing of teeth" is what an individual does to express a sentiment, either frustration, gloating, or regret. The context of the use of the term is one in which Jesus wants to motivate people to change behavior and to reflect on how they might feel in the long run about what they do. The parables are meant to take people out of their primal existence and view their lives objectively with a new frame of reference. They become the means of achieving another level of consciousness (see chapter 9). To associate the phrase with the concept of hell, complete with flames, does not appear to be supported either in the Hebrew Bible or in the New Testament.

NEW TESTAMENT TEXTS ON JUDGMENT

Besides the references in the New Testament to "weeping and gnashing of teeth" and to hell, expressed by the three Greek words we have examined, there is reference to judgment. Just as the idea of hell is not unique to the writings of the Bible, neither is the concept of judgment. The concept of a day of judgment was not new. It did not start with the New Testament, nor with the Christian God.

The Pre-Christian Idea of Judgment

In Zoroastrianism (500s BCE) there was separation of good and evil after death; one's deeds were recorded in a ledger and credited or debited at the Day of Judgment. If the evil outweighed the good, the soul crossed the bridge into hell.[41]

In the Sibylline Oracles, pseudoepigraphal literature that originated ca. 150 BCE–300 CE, there is reference to judgment of the wicked:

> But when the final judgment of the world
> And mortals comes, which God himself shall bring,
> Judging at once the impious and the just,
> The ungodly under darkness he will send,
> And they shall know what wickedness they wrought.
> (Sibylline Oracles IV: 49, 50).

In order to understand the background for judgment in the New Testament, it is important to look at the concept of judgment both within the Hebrew Bible and in first century thought.

Judgment in the Hebrew Bible

The words used for judgment in the Hebrew Bible stem from *shâphat*, meaning to "judge," "vindicate," "govern," or "discriminate between

---

41. Crisafulli and Thompson, *Go to Hell*, 39.

persons."[42] In the Hebrew Bible, God was seen as the judge, "This belief may well go back to tribal religion in which God was regarded as both legislator and legal partner. His judging consisted in watching over the social relationship of the tribe and in intervening for it in war."[43] The judgment of God was also expressed in executing justice for a suffering people who had no rights, "Therefore the Lord waits to be gracious to you; therefore he will rise up to show mercy to you. For the Lord is a God of justice" (Is 30:18). The word for "justice" here is also *shâphat*.

The Idea of Judgment in First Century Thought

Plutarch believed in an "orderly system of justice and punishment with an eye to encouraging moral behavior in the living."[44] He believed that punishment after death was dependent on a person's deeds during their life, "the gods are not malevolent but use punishments in order to execute justice."[45] After death there were two potential destinies for the soul, one for the person who was righteous and the other for the one who was not righteous.

First century mystery religions, religions that focused on secret rites and mystical experiences in order to achieve unity with the deity, also had a belief in judgment. This served the purpose of encouraging better morals in the living, but also was a comfort to the living "by assuring them that the good earthly reputation enjoyed by the dead would attend and assist them in the underworld."[46]

In the time of Jesus, Pharisees (there were different kinds of Pharisees and both Jesus and Paul were Pharisees) believed in the resurrection of the dead and that all would be judged.

In the New Testament, the Greek word for the verb, to judge, is *krinō*, and can mean to "separate, distinguish, select, prefer," . . . "judge, think, consider," . . . "reach a decision, propose, intend."[47] It is used as a legal term for court proceedings. When used of God or Jesus, it can mean to administer justice, "where the judgment of God is spoken of,

42. Brown, *Hebrew and English Lexicon*, 1,047.

43. Herntrich, "*krino*," 924.

44. Clark-Soles, *Death and the Afterlife*, 33.

45. Lehtipuu, *The Afterlife Imagery*, 96.

46. Clark-Soles, *Death and the Afterlife*, 59.

47. Arndt and Gingrich, *A Greek-English Lexicon*, 451.

resulting in the vindication of the innocent and the punishment of the guilty."[48]

It is interesting that Mark, the first gospel to be written, does not speak of the day of judgment and the perspective in the book of John is that judgment occurs in the present life, "those who believe in him are not condemned [judged]; but those who do not believe are condemned already" (Jn 3:18). Judgment happens in the here and now.

In the New Testament we find references to the day of judgment, judgment after death, and the judgment seat of Christ. These are found in Matthew, Paul's writings, 2 Peter, Jude, and Revelation.

Judgment in Matthew

In Matthew chapters 10 to 12, the author mentions the day of judgment six times (three of these same references are also in Luke). This should not surprise us, considering the emphasis he gave to the concept of Gehenna, seen earlier in this chapter, and considering the victim mentality of his audience. What victims want to know is that their perpetrators will be held accountable for their actions. But let's take a closer look at these three chapters in Matthew. What is happening here?

In Matthew chapter 10, Jesus appoints twelve men to go to "the lost sheep of the house of Israel" (Matt 10:6), specifically instructing them not to go to Gentile regions. He warns them that they will be rejected by many and says that he is sending them out "like sheep among wolves" (Matt 10:16). He expects that they will be brought to court and maybe even killed, but assures them that they are more precious to God than sparrows. In chapter 11, Jesus is clearly upset that villages where he performs healings do not respond to his teachings. Chapter 12 is about Jesus' encounter with the Pharisees when they catch Jesus' disciples eating heads of grain on the Sabbath and when Jesus is observed to be healing on the Sabbath. Jesus ends up calling them a "brood of vipers . . . how can you speak good things when you are evil?" (Matt 12:34). Jesus makes the point that it is fine to do good on the Sabbath. So we see that in chapters 10 to 12 there is a lot of resistance and anticipation of resistance, both to Jesus' teaching and to his disciples' teaching.

48. Ibid., 452.

Among these happenings are the six references to the day of judgment. Jesus indicates that it will be more tolerable for Sodom and Gomorrah on the day of judgment than for the villages that reject his followers. It was to Sodom that Lot went when he and his uncle Abraham went different ways and Gensis13:13 says that "the people of Sodom were wicked, great sinners against the Lord." In fact, as the story has it, one day when Lot had overnight male guests, some men who lived in Sodom came to the house and demanded to have sex with his guests (Gen 19:1–5). Sodom and Gomorrah were destroyed by fire in the Genesis story (Gen 19:24). Sodom came to symbolize the epitome of evil. So Jesus, referring to the Sodom story, says that on the day of judgment, people who did not accept Jesus' disciples will be no better off than Sodom, where people were "great sinners." The judgment is on cities that do not receive Jesus' disciples.

The same idea is expressed in chapter 11 where cities in which Jesus performs healings do not repent, "Woe to you, Chorazin! Woe to you, Bethsaida! For if the deeds of power done in you had been done in Tyre and Sidon, they would have repented long ago in sackcloth and ashes" (Matt 11:20–22). Jesus gives the same reproach to Capernaum, saying that if he had performed the same "deeds of power" in Sodom as he did in Capernaum, Sodom would not have been destroyed. And then Jesus says that "on the day of judgment it will be more tolerable for the land of Sodom than for you" (Matt 11:24).

There is another reference to the day of judgment when Pharisees accuse Jesus of healing a blind and mute man by demonic power. Jesus makes a comparison with healthy and unhealthy trees, bearing either good or bad fruit (Matt 12:22–37). This is to show that his power to heal can only come from a good source, not an evil source, just like you can't get good fruit from a bad tree. And he closes the discourse with, "I tell you, on the day of judgment you will have to give an account for every careless word you utter; for by your words you will be justified, and by your words you will be condemned." (Matt 12:36–37). It was the accusation made by the Pharisees that upset Jesus. It upset him because, in his own mind, Jesus felt very close to God, so how COULD they accuse him of getting his power from demons? He wants them to know that they will be held accountable for their accusing words.

Jesus also refers to the day of judgment with respect to the people of Nineveh who left their evil ways when Jonah preached to them (Matt

12:41). Jesus says that the people of Nineveh, who repented when Jonah preached to them, will condemn Jesus' generation at the day of judgment, because Jesus is greater than Jonah. The people of Nineveh listened to Jonah but the scribes and Pharisees do not accept Jesus' teaching (Matt 12:41). And since Jesus claims to be greater than Jonah, the fact that they don't believe Jesus is even more serious in Jesus' estimation.

Another reference to judgment is with respect to the "queen of the South," the queen of Sheba. Scholars have suggested that Sheba could refer to present-day Yemen, Eritrea, or Ethiopia. In any case, this queen had heard of the wisdom of Solomon, so she took a trip to Jerusalem to see him (1 Kings 10). Being very impressed, both with his accomplishments and his wisdom, she said, "Blessed be the Lord your God . . . he has made you king to execute justice and righteousness" (1 Kgs 10:9). With this story, Jesus makes the same point he made with the story of Jonah, that at the day of judgment, the queen of Sheba will condemn Jesus' generation because Jesus is greater than Solomon and is not being recognized even to the degree to which Solomon was praised (1Kgs 10:6).

In these instances, it was Jesus who experienced injustice. He could not understand why people did not accept him; he believed he had important things to say. His self-understanding was that his teachings came from God. His power to heal came from God. So in his frustration he told his enemies that they would be judged for their rejection of him and his disciples.

What we learned from sermons in fundamentalist evangelical churches was that if we didn't receive Jesus, it would be worse for us at the day of judgment than for the worst sinners you could imagine. Sinners would be devoured in flames because God could not tolerate the atrocities of their sin. That thought was pretty scary and the logical question to ask was, how can I escape that kind of judgment? The answer: only by believing in Jesus, and in the fundamental beliefs of the church.

In Matthew there is no indication as to the process of judgment, nor to the time and place. We can assume that the readers knew what the author had in mind when referring to the day of judgment, a concept, as we have seen, that was well known at that time. The belief in a day of judgment helped people make sense of the injustice they were experiencing in their world. It was a way for the author of Matthew to console the Jewish Christian community that even though they were being treated unjustly, they would be vindicated in the end.

We can see in the Gospel of Matthew a dual context. There was the context of Jesus, in which he provided teachings that were recounted and passed on through oral history, some of them written down. And then there was the context of the writer who framed these teachings to address another context, that of people suffering great injustices. Just as Jesus suffered rejection in the first context, his followers were persecuted in the second context. With this double contextual meaning, it becomes clear that the images of judgment, Gehenna (the garbage dump), and experiences of deep regret (symbolized in the "weeping and gnashing of teeth") on the part of the persecutors, vindicated the victims and reassured them in their beliefs. To take these literally as absolute authority, applying them to every age and context, can happen only when the Bible is objectified as a literal authority.

Judgment in Paul's Writings

It is believed that Paul's writings are the earliest New Testament texts. Bernstein argues that Paul's primary teaching is about the future of the righteous, which explains why he says nothing about the concept of eternal punishment for the wicked.[49] Paul does talk about judgment according to one's deeds, but he does not say there will be eternal punishment for the wicked. He says that God "will repay according to each one's deeds: to those who by patiently doing good seek for glory and honor and immortality, he will give eternal life; while for those who are self-seeking and who obey not the truth but wickedness, there will be wrath and fury" (Rom 2:6–8). The fate of the wicked is not expressed in terms of consequences that are eternal, rather, they are judged and then annihilated, "All he tells of the fate of those who chose wrongly, however, is that they will not inherit the kingdom of God. This fate is not said to be . . . eternal. Simple exclusion is all that is mentioned."[50] Even in the classic verse used to convince people to be "born again," the consequence for sin is simply death; no mention is made of an eternal punishment: "For the wages of sin is death, but the free gift of God is eternal life in Christ Jesus our Lord" (Rom 6:23).

49. Bernstein, *The Formation of Hell*, 207–27.
50. Ibid., 217.

In Acts we have the story of Paul in the city of Athens. Seeing all the religious shrines and altars in the town square, he argues that God does not live in those shrines. Paul points this out to his Athenian audience that God is within, "for in him we live and move and have our being, as even some of your own poets have said." (Acts 17:28). He goes on to say that God commands "all people everywhere to repent, because he has fixed a day on which he will have the world judged in righteousness by a man whom he has appointed, and of this he has given assurance to all by raising him from the dead" (Acts 17:30–31).

In the book of Romans, the author says readers should not judge others, because if they do, they will not escape the judgment of God (Rom 2:2–3). The context of this chapter in Romans is that those to whom the author is writing (Jewish and Gentile factions) were not accepting of each other; they were judging each other. Paul is trying to help them understand that just having the law on their side (the Jewish faction) is not enough. Those who live according to the Jewish law (and these could also be Gentile folk) will be justified.

In 2 Corinthians Paul says, "For all of us must appear before the judgment seat of Christ, so that each may receive recompense for what has been done in the body, whether good or evil" (2 Cor 5:10). In this letter, written in the mid 50s CE, Paul defends his authority and his ministry. He recounts his episodes of persecution for the sake of the gospel, asserts that he belongs to Christ just as much as his readers do, talks about his own visions, and claims that his confidence comes from God. Within this context Paul makes the point that all will be judged for what they have done. Perhaps he thinks this may lessen the judgment his readers have of him. As in Matthew, but with less hyperbole, the language of judgment is used to vindicate the writer.

Judgment in the Book of Hebrews

The book of Hebrews was written to increase the faith of those who were wavering. It talks about judgment after death, "it is appointed for mortals to die once, and after that the judgment . . . if we willfully persist in sin after having received the knowledge of the truth, there no longer remains a sacrifice for sins, but a fearful prospect of judgment, and a fury of fire that will consume the adversaries" (Heb 9:27; 10:26–27).

George Wesley Buchanan, writer of the Anchor Bible commentary on the book of Hebrews, claims that Hebrews, written in the latter part of the first century or early second century CE, is actually a homiletic midrash on Psalm 110.[51] In Psalm 110, the Israelites were chafing under tyrannical rule; they wanted to know that God would hold the tyrants accountable. The Psalm speaks of assurance of victory under a priest/king, "according to the order of Melchizedek." It says that God will use this priest/king to "shatter kings on the day of his wrath. He will execute judgment among the nations" (Ps 110:4–6). The writer to the Hebrews compares this priest/king with Jesus, who has "become a high priest forever according to the order of Melchizedek" (Heb 6:20).

It is important to note that the scholars who wrote *midrashim* "were primarily dogmatic theologians who used the scripture to prove points they wanted to defend."[52] And in this case, the writer to the Hebrews wants to prove that Jesus is the great high priest (Hebrews 4). To do so, the author shows that his statements about judgments (Heb 9:27; 10:26–27), quoted above, are in line with current Rabbinic thought, i.e., that after death every person under covenant will appear before God's tribunal, at which time they will be judged according to their deeds. Rabbi Eliezer b. Jacob said that a person who performed just one good deed acquired one defense attorney and the one who performed just one transgression acquired one accusing attorney.[53] These attorneys would then argue the individual's case after death.

The statement about the "fury of fire that will consume the adversaries" (Heb 10:27) comes from Isaiah 26 where the writer calls upon God to deal with those who "do not learn righteousness . . . let them see your zeal for your people, and be ashamed. Let the fire for your adversaries consume them" (Is 26: 10–11). The same sentiment is expressed in 2 Baruch, written in the early second century, where the writer says, "Because of this, a fire will devour their plans, and in flame the concerns of their hearts will be tested; for the Judge will come and will not delay" (2 Bar. 48:33–39).

The end of the first century and early second was a time of harsh Roman persecution against Christians. As in other contexts, the idea of

---

51. Buchanan, *To the Hebrews*, xxi. Homilectic *midrashim* are sermons based on Hebrew Bible texts.

52. Ibid., xxi.

53. Ibid., 155.

a final judgment against the persecutors provided a reassuring sense of justice.

Judgment in 2 Peter and Jude

The epistles of Peter also refer to a judgment of the dead, "they will have to give an accounting to him who stands ready to judge the living and the dead . . . for if God did not spare the angels when they sinned, but cast them into hell [*Tartaros*] and committed them to chains [pits] of deepest darkness to be kept until the judgment . . . then the Lord knows how to rescue the godly from trial, and to keep the unrighteous under punishment until the day of judgment" (1 Pet. 4:5; 2 Pet. 2:4–9). The same thought is expressed in Jude, where the author indicates that fallen angels are in chains until "the judgment of the great day" (Jude 6). Jude, after condemning heretics, quotes from the book of Enoch, saying, "It was also about these that Enoch . . . prophesied, saying, 'See, the Lord is coming . . . to execute judgment on all, and to convict everyone of all the deeds of ungodliness that they have committed in such an ungodly way, and of all the harsh things that ungodly sinners have spoken against him.' " (Jude 14–15).

What is significant about the word used for hell in 2 Peter is that the Greek word is *Tartaros*, which refers to the Greek Tartarus, the place mentioned earlier in this chapter that refers to the lowest part of the Greek underworld. This usage of the word shows that the writer of 2 Peter was familiar with the Greek ideas of the underworld and was influenced by them. The writers of 2 Peter and Jude, written in a time of persecution, sought to comfort their readers and encourage them to keep the faith, "You therefore, beloved, since you are forewarned, beware that you are not carried away with the error of the lawless and lose your own stability. But grow in the grace and knowledge of our Lord and Savior Jesus Christ" (2 Pet. 3:17–18). The reference to angels being cast into *Tartaros* is meant to assure them that they will be rescued from the present persecution (2 Pet 2:9). Thus, in 1 and 2 Peter and in Jude, we also see the assumption that judgment will occur, a thought prevalent in the first century. It was not a new concept originating within Christian thought. As we saw earlier in our discussion of the history of hell, there was a belief in judgment after death in Egyptian thought as early as the 1500s BCE. It was a way to believe that eventually perpetrators would be held accountable for their actions.

Judgment in the Book of Revelation

In the book of Revelation, there is the scene of the great white throne at which all the dead are judged, "the sea gave up the dead that were in it, Death and Hades gave up the dead that were in them, and all were judged according to what they had done . . . and anyone whose name was not found written in the book of life was thrown into the lake of fire" (Rev 20:11–15).

The title of the book of Revelation is *Apokalupsis Ioannou*, the Apocalypse of John. The word, apocalypse, hints at the type of literature it is, apocalyptic literature. Apocalyptic writing was common between 200 BCE and 100 CE, a kind of writing that flourished in periods of persecution. The Greek word *apokalupsis* refers to the disclosure of secret truths that have been hidden. In *apocalyptic* writing, these truths had to do with the eventual triumph of good over evil, God over Satan. It was a way to explain why the righteous suffered and why God's intervention seemed delayed. This way of envisioning the future gave hope to a suffering people. Apocalyptic literature was written in code to protect those being persecuted. It was highly symbolic and often spoke of dreams, visions, monsters, and catastrophes.

People interpret the book of Revelation in a number of different ways. If its meaning is understood with reference to events that took place only within the first few centuries CE, the primary message is that God has final victory over the suffering of the early Christians. They will be vindicated. In this view, predictions in the book are seen to have been fulfilled either by the time of the fall of Jerusalem in 70 CE or the fall of Rome in 476 CE. It is seen as symbolic and only the intended readers really know what it means. Another viewpoint is that the events in the book are a forecast of events that will take place from the time of writing right up to one's own time. In a third view, the whole book is seen as belonging to a future time period, events that will occur sometime in the future. In these last two perspectives, the book is taken quite literally. Dispensationalists find within it a description of all the ages since the beginning of time until some future time when, as they believe, Jesus will return to earth. There is a fourth way to understand this book, the timeless symbolic view. In this view the book is seen to describe basic principles on which God acts and will continue to act throughout history.

And now to the scene of the "great white throne" (Rev 20). In the view that the book of Revelation refers to actual events that will take place, the throne would be seen as a literal throne with someone sitting on it. The scene is reminiscent of Daniel 7, "As I watched, thrones were set in place, and an Ancient One took his throne . . . the court sat in judgment and the books were opened . . . and as I watched, the beast was put to death, and its body destroyed and given over to be burned with fire" (Dan 7:9–11). There was also a similar belief in Zoroastrianism where there was thought to be a future " final cosmic battle between Good and Evil and Evil will be conquered forever . . . penitent sinners will be forgiven; and there will be a universal resurrection of the body, which will reunite with the soul. Hell will be destroyed—burned clean by molten metal—and the kingdom of God on earth will begin."[54]

In the Revelation 20 scene, two books are opened, one of them called the book of life. These books seem to be a record of the deeds of all the dead. All are judged according to what they have done in life. Death and Hades itself and all those whose names are not found in the book of life are thrown into the lake of fire. And as Baker suggests, the lake of fire is a purifying fire that destroys both death and Hades.[55] What follows this account is the very positive description of the new heaven and the new earth, "and I saw the holy city, the new Jerusalem, coming down out of heaven from God, prepared as a bride adorned for her husband" (Rev 21:2). Seen within the first century context this is comfort for the persecuted ones; they have a sense that justice will be done. Their oppressors will not taste the good life, in fact, they will be judged for their evil deeds; and the oppressed will enjoy a time when "God himself will be with them; he will wipe every tear from their eyes. Death will be no more; mourning and crying and pain will be no more, for the first things have passed away" (Rev 21:3–4). In their present sorry state, this is what they can anticipate.

So what we notice in the New Testament texts about judgment is that first of all, the idea of judgment in the afterlife was something quite familiar to first century Christians. A coming day of judgment

54. Turner, *The History of Hell*, 18.
55. Baker, *Razing Hell*, 144.

was assumed. They knew about it from their philosophers, Judaism, Greek mythology, and mystery religions. Belief in eventual judgment was a way that enabled them to deal with injustices they saw in society and the persecution they were experiencing. A belief in their own vindication gave them a sense of hope.

INTERPRETATION OF TEACHINGS ON HELL AFTER THE FIRST CENTURY

Moving ahead to the centuries after Jesus, let's look at how early Christians interpreted teachings about the underworld.

Clement, bishop of Rome in the late first century, wrote two epistles to the Corinthians. In the second epistle he warns against "wicked lusts" and writes that "the day of judgment is already approaching as a burning oven" (2 Clement XVI:3).

Bernstein says that the *Apocalypse of Peter* (ca. 135 CE) was the "first major Christian account of postmortem punishment outside the New Testament," complete with great detail.[56] He shows how this punishment was envisioned as the result of sins, and consequences meted out for various wrongdoings: blasphemers hanging by their tongues, male adulterers suspended by their thighs, and those who were disobedient walking across a narrow bridge with fire below.[57] Bernstein argues that the references to slime and filth could be "extensions of such stinking heaps or pools as were known in the ancient world: the privy, the slaughterhouse, the bathhouse . . ."[58] Sin is given much more emphasis in the *Apocalypse of Peter* than faith and "torments that are summed up in one word in the New Testament are elaborated here in dramatic detail."[59]

The strong language used in the *Apocalypse of Peter* was later mitigated in the fourth century writing of the *Apocalypse of Paul*.[60] In this writing Paul is taken on a tour of the afterlife, both heaven and hell. He is shown the involved court system where souls are judged and he sees

---

56. Bernstein, *The Formation of Hell*, 282.

57. Ibid., 285–87.

58. Ibid., 289.

59. Ibid., 288.

60. Ibid., 291.

that God gives extra chances to enable people to pass the judgment.[61] The shift to legal approaches to deal with sin can be an "indication of more clearly defined procedures within the church as an institution by the fourth century."[62] Paul sees that in hell, there are regions both of fire and of icy cold (reminiscent of the Japanese Jigoku underworld) and in even the worst level of hell, punishments are moderated.[63]

Origen (ca. 185–254 CE) took the view that punishment really meant restoration and that "all would eventually by restored to God."[64]

Augustine (354–430 CE), influenced by Virgil's detailed description of hell, played a major role in the development of the Christian idea of hell, which differed dramatically from Origin's view. Augustine believed in eternal damnation with real fire, to which the wicked would be subjected after the resurrection of their bodies and after the last judgment.[65] Thus, both soul and body of the wicked would burn in hell. *That this view greatly influenced the development of fundamentalist evangelical thought is evidenced by the fact that this belief is what I, along with other fundamentalist evangelicals, was raised to believe, that is, after death our bodies will be raised and we will be judged. And depending on the verdict, we may suffer in hell, soul and body, forever.* After Augustine, there was the thought that the Christian underworld contained a place called limbo, just below heaven, for those who weren't quite good enough for heaven. Here they would stay until the judgment, when they would be taken to heaven.[66]

The idea of purgatory developed in medieval times. This was thought to be a place where souls, not worthy of heaven, were purified by fire.[67] At this time, preachers emphasized the literal view of hell and linked it to the sinfulness of humanity, "hell was their great weapon, for only they were authorized to administer the rites of baptism and absolution that could save a soul. . . . They could send a soul to hell."[68] When Johannes Scotus Erigena (ca. 815–877 CE) voiced his disbelief

61. Ibid., 294.

62. Ibid., 300.

63. Ibid., 303.

64. Ibid., 307.

65. Ibid., 329.

66. Crisafulli and Thompson, *Go to Hell*, 136.

67. Ibid., 140.

68. Turner, *The History of Hell*, 90, 112.

in a literal hell, he was killed for this "heretical" belief.[69] Later Dante Alighieri (1265–1321 CE), in his *Inferno*, imagined nine circles of hell beneath the earth. Alice Turner argues that "by making it possible to think about it in fictional or allegorical terms . . . he [Dante] made it easier for intellectuals of the Renaissance and the Enlightenment to reject its reality."[70]

In the Reformation of the 1500s, Luther went back to Augustine's real and eternal hell and preached that people are only saved from it by grace. At the same time, Roman Catholicism affirmed the reality of hell, along with eternal punishment. Even in the Royal Society of London for the Improvement of Natural Knowledge, an organization of scholars established in the late 1600s, there was discussion about the details of hell. In 1714, Tobiz Swinden published *An Enquiry into the Nature and Place of Hell*, which held that hell is located on the sun, because "only the sun was big enough, fiery enough, and eternal enough to hold the enormous number of damned souls, past and future[71]." In 1740 William Whiston, in *The Eternity of Hell Torments Considered,* wrote that all souls are held in Hades, under the earth, until the judgment, at which time the good and the wicked are separated, the good rising to spiritual bodies and the wicked sent to the fire.[72]

As indicated in chapter 3, when revival swept across the eastern colonies in North America in the 1700s, along with it came preaching about hell, as found, for example in Jonathan Edwards's sermon entitled, "Sinners in the Hands of an Angry God." In this sermon Edwards says, "O sinner! Consider the fearful danger you are in: it is a great furnace of wrath, a wide and bottomless pit, full of the fire of wrath, that you are held over in the hand of God, whose wrath is provoked and incensed as much against you, as against many of the damned in hell. You hang by a slender thread, with the flames of divine wrath flashing about it, and ready every moment to singe it, and burn it asunder."[73]

In the Roman Catholic world, Pope Leo XIII issued a bull in 1879 "affirming an eternal hell and the existence of the Devil."[74]

69. Ibid., 89.
70. Ibid., 143.
71. Ibid., 194–5.
72. Ibid., 196.
73. Edwards, "Sinners in the Hands of an Angry God," 4–5.
74. Turner, *The History of Hell*, 235.

In 2004, biblical theologian Keith Wright argued that "hell, as a place of eternal punishment, does not fit with God's struggle to enable human beings to be what God intends for them to be" and "it does not square with the unfolding drama of the Bible in which God works patiently with people and nations to bring about redemptive changes."[75] Referring to the New Testament story of the prodigal son, Wright points out that the son who left home with his inheritance endured a hell of hunger and deprivation (Matt 15:14–19). He believes that hell is not a futuristic concept, but something we create for ourselves here and now.[76] The hell that has been taught by fundamentalist evangelicalism is not what Jesus intended.

So what do we know about hell? We have explored two levels of meaning through which we have tried to understand the concept of hell. The first was the comparison of the belief in hell through time. We looked at how it had been conceptualized in ancient times in various traditions. We discovered that the idea of hell evolved to serve a particular purpose, a primary reason being to come to terms with the injustice in the world. It was also a way to motivate people to live moral lives.

A second level of meaning was to examine biblical texts that speak of Gehenna, Hades, and fire and look at their context intra-biblically. We found that the texts that have traditionally been quoted for a fundamentalist evangelical understanding of hell actually do not refer to a burning place of fire where all who have not accepted Jesus as Savior end up after death. What happened is that fundamentalist evangelicalism seized upon the concept of hell and made it into a literal entity, the primary purpose of which was to establish a need for salvation through Jesus. Having done this, they took every reference to hell or Gehenna or lake of fire as a literal corroboration of hell as they understood it. They linked their version of hell to the Fall in the garden of Eden and original sin, which made hell the default destination for humankind. They then reinforced the need for salvation through selective, literally understood biblical texts.

If we compare ancient cosmologies with what we know of the universe today, we realize that the concept of hell emerged at a time when the earth was believed to be flat and people had seen hot molten

75. Wright, *The Hell Jesus Never Intended,* 30–31.
76. Ibid., 91.

lava coming out from the earth. Given this reality, they could easily imagine a burning hell under the earth. With our current knowledge of the universe, does it not make more sense to approach the concept of hell as something that arose at a given time and place and that our conception of reality calls for new discourse around our understanding of the afterlife?

Dismantling the idea of a literal hell also calls into question the fundamentalist evangelical concept of salvation and, more basically, the human condition. What we can take from all of this, however, is that humans are very sensitive to injustices and go to great lengths to devise interpretive systems and institutions that will give them a sense of justice being done. The fundamentalist evangelical movement can be seen as one of these attempts.

We will now look at the narratives of those who struggled with and eventually extricated themselves from fundamentalist evangelicalism.

PART III

Engaging the Fundamentalist Evangelical Experience

WE HAVE SEEN THAT for people who embrace the fundamentalist evangelical belief system it is absolutely essential to believe a certain way. This belief system forms their entire identity, both socially and religiously. Socially, they associate only with others who believe as they do. Religiously, they restrict themselves to hear and read only fundamentalist evangelical viewpoints. They live in a safe cocoon of secure belief, with assurances of prayer answered, guidance in decision-making, and an afterlife in heaven. The Bible is the absolute authority for all decisions in their lives, and Jesus is their personal friend. Since fundamentalist evangelicalism is so central to their world of meaning, it is not surprising that it can have a tremendous hold on them emotionally.

A few decades ago, religious authority figures within fundamentalist evangelicalism used to discourage young people from going to university because it was thought this might destroy their faith. And indeed it did for many. Learning from sources and people outside of the fundamentalist evangelical movement meant that, for some, they saw cracks in their belief system. Young people raised questions about the absolute nature of the inerrancy of the Bible, about evolution, and about the exclusiveness of their belief system. Since the church was unable to engage them in their doubting, some left the church. Others became depressed and even contemplated suicide.

Part III looks at the experiences of seventy-three former fundamentalist evangelicals, examining the process of leaving fundamentalist evangelicalism and their reasons for leaving. It discusses these experiences in relation to stages of faith, levels of consciousness, and stages of death and dying, in this case, the death of the belief system. Finally, Part III looks at the possibility of fundamentalist evangelicalism as an addictive system, and discusses ways in which ex-fundamentalist evangelicals have faced the trauma of leaving.

8

Personal Experiences of Former Fundamentalist Evangelicals

THE PROCESS OF LEAVING fundamentalist evangelicalism is in some ways similar to giving up the belief in Santa Claus. At first, it is really exciting for children to have Santa Claus bring them exactly what they ask for, year after year. It means there really is a Santa Claus. In the same way, in fundamentalist evangelicalism, there are a myriad of indicators reinforcing the absolute truth of the fundamentals. There are answers to prayer, testimonies of people whose lives have been transformed, emotionally charged songs, and convincing assurances from high profile people. But in the same way that there are stages of doubt and questioning in children's belief in Santa Claus as they grow older, people's departure from fundamentalist evangelicalism often happens in stages. They seldom walk away from it suddenly. As they come into contact with people who hold other perspectives and people of other religions, and as they read more broadly, they sometimes start to doubt the existence of the fundamentalist God and the belief system in which they so fervently believed. It is a process that does, in some instances, take many years..

In order to understand what people experience when they leave the fundamentalist evangelical movement, I read and analyzed the stories of the faith journeys of seventy individuals and conducted three interviews as case studies. The body of literature that recounts people's stories of leaving fundamentalism contains both monographs and edited collections of stories. I will first discuss the monographs and then look at the case studies and collections of stories found in edited books. I will then look at the process of leaving fundamentalism that is evident in these stories, and discuss commonalities regarding such issues as questions and doubts, the process of leaving, the sense of loss, and possible end points.

MONOGRAPHS ABOUT PEOPLE LEAVING FUNDAMENTALIST EVANGELICALISM

Of the sixteen monographs I reviewed, six were faith stories of women. Seven people had been ministers, evangelists or missionaries in evangelical denominations. Their stories show the emotional and spiritual struggles resulting from the process of leaving fundamentalist evangelicalism.

In *My Fundamentalist Education: A Memoir of a Divine Girlhood,* Christine Rosen tells of her experience in Keswick Christian School, a fundamentalist school she attended as a child. The school was in St. Petersburg, Florida, where Rosen's family lived. In fact, the school is still operative today with its mission, "Responding to the biblical command that families raise their children in the knowledge and admonition of the Lord, Keswick Christian School provides a Christ-centered education that permanently instils and reinforces Christian thought, belief and practice in all areas of life. . . . Children are sinners who need to be redeemed and then submit to the authority of God in all areas of life."[1]

In her book, Rosen investigates a number of statements of faith that were important in the school and writes of her reaction to them.

By the time she was six years old, Rosen "had learned who God was . . . how the world began and how it would end . . . what I had to do to get to heaven and what might send me to hell."[2] *By six years old, I also knew these things. God was a God of love, but only if you had asked Jesus to forgive your sin. Otherwise he (and God was definitely male) was a God of judgment. I knew I had to be saved from sin in order to get to heaven and if I died without having confessed my sin, I would go to hell, a place of fire, and stay there forever and ever.*

1. Keswick Christian School. "Mission and Philosophy," 2010. No pages. Online: http://keswickchristian.org/mission-and-philosophy/.

2. Rosen, *My Fundamentalist Education,* 30.

By the third grade, not having "converted a single living soul," Rosen began to have doubts about the story of salvation as it was taught to her.[3] Later, when she became curious about the theory of evolution, the school allowed her to read only Christian books on the topic. This frustrated her.[4] She learned that there were questions she should not ask.

Another area of questioning for Rosen was with regard to gender. She noticed that girls who were assertive were more likely to get punished than boys, "after all, the very fact that there were so many words for bad women—harlots, whores . . . —suggested a history of trouble. And I wasn't sure what that history had to do with my future."[5] By the eighth grade she realized that her enemy was not Satan, but the whole fundamentalist culture within which she was immersed, "The longer I spent inside this closed world, the more eager I was to see what was on the other side of that wall."[6]

In giving up fundamentalism, she could no longer read the Bible in a literal way. Now she no longer turns to the Bible for answers; she learns from other religions, science, and history.[7] However, she does see her experience at the school as "comfortable swaddling—it protected me from all that was cold and harsh while I was still vulnerable," but she adds, "Eventually, when you begin to crawl, you must leave your swaddling behind."[8] The last Bible verse she memorized at Keswick— John 8:32: "and ye shall know the truth, and the truth shall make you free"—has been fulfilled for her; she says that she is now free, free from fundamentalism.[9]

Virginia Ramey Mollenkott in *Sensuous Spirituality: Out From Fundamentalism* tells how, as a child, she memorized a lot of Scripture. She cites one verse in particular that, among other texts, led her to believe that she was "totally depraved": "The heart is deceitful above all things and desperately wicked" (Jeremiah 17:9).[10] As a lesbian woman, her journey out of fundamentalism meant that she needed to accept

3. Ibid., 89.
4. Ibid., 105.
5. Ibid., 204.
6. Ibid., 205.
7. Ibid., 221.
8. Ibid., 227.
9. Ibid., 229.
10. Mollenkott, *Sensuous Spirituality*, 15.

herself as she was created.[11] She remained within the Christian tradition; her freedom came as she discovered biblical texts that empowered women and honoured diversity. So for Mollenkott, the issue prompting her to leave fundamentalism had to do with the teaching of depravity and sin, especially with regard to sexuality; she was forced to leave because of her gender and her sexual orientation.[12] If she had remained a fundamentalist, she would have had to believe that she was not okay the way she was. Fundamentalism judged her at the very core of her identity, which was her female body. When she was able to find in biblical texts an affirmation of diversity and respect for herself as she was, she was able to leave fundamentalism yet retain a Christian faith.

Skip Porteous in *Jesus Doesn't Live Here Anymore: From Fundamentalist to Freedom Writer* tells how, as a fundamentalist Pentecostal minister, his worldview unravelled when he was divorced and consequently was asked to leave his position as pastor of a church. He had been very involved in the evangelistic movement and had heard many of the big name evangelists, including Vernon McGee of the Church of the Open Door and Billy Graham. He was convinced about the importance of witnessing and "winning lost souls" and had been active doing so wherever he went. When his marriage fell apart and the church asked him to step down as pastor, "for the first time in many years I allowed myself to take an honest look at the faith I blindly embraced for so long."[13] When he began to understand that a massive number of different manuscripts were used in the writing of the Bible, he wondered how one could be assured of what the original said. Even as a child he had been puzzled by the contradictions he saw in the Bible. As he started to record his story, he realized that the "two building blocks of fundamentalist Christianity" that troubled him most were guilt and fear.[14] Eventually he stopped praying. He stopped believing in the concept of sin and it set him free. [15] When he had no more guilt and fear, he could honestly say that Jesus did not live in his heart anymore. Thus the title of his book.

11. Ibid., 16.
12. Ibid., 168.
13. Porteous, *Jesus Doesn't Live Here Anymore*, 158.
14. Ibid., 175.
15. Ibid., 179.

Marlene Winell's book, *Leaving the Fold: A Guide for Former Fundamentalists and Others Leaving Their Religion*, is a self-help resource intended to enable survivors of fundamentalism to understand their experiences and arrive at a healthier spirituality. It offers exercises readers can use to assist them to come to terms with their fundamentalist experience and move towards healing and growth. In one of her chapters, Winell tells her own story. As a daughter of missionary parents with Assemblies of God, she spent a large part of her childhood in Asia. The message she repeatedly got was that she was sinful.[16] When there was conflict in her family of origin, she felt at fault.[17] As a Christian, she thought God should empower her to be a better Christian in her home setting. And as she thought about her own "faults" with respect to family relationships, she began to realize that, rather than thinking of these as faults and sins, these experiences "could be the result of environmental conditioning rather than sin."[18] Later on she realized that what her family needed was better communication skills.

When her family moved to North America and she went to college, she began to study other philosophies and meet people who were not Christian fundamentalists. And it seemed to her that some people of other faiths were more "Christian-like" than certain Christians she knew.

Winell was frustrated with the patriarchy of the church and hearing sermons about the need for women to be submissive.[19] She left the fundamentalist movement gradually and reluctantly.

In *Farewell to God: My Reasons for Rejecting the Christian Faith*, Charles Templeton discusses the reasons why he considers himself an agnostic. He defines the agnostic as someone who "cannot" know there is a God, someone who has tried to determine if there is a God and has found out that you cannot know if there is one.[20]

After attending Princeton Seminary, Templeton became an evangelist under the National Council of Churches in the United States and spent several years going on "preaching missions."[21] His approach as an

16. Winell, *Leaving the Fold*, 221.
17. Ibid., 32.
18. Ibid., 35.
19. Ibid., 36–37.
20. Templeton, *Farewell To God*, 18.
21. Ibid., 11.

evangelist was different from the hell-fire and brimstone methods; he used an "attractive, persuasive approach that presents religion as a commodity necessary to life . . . he set a new standard for mass evangelism."[22] However, his struggles with believing the fundamentals reached a level where his health was in jeopardy. After leaving the field of evangelism, he took other positions in the evangelical world, but increasingly felt uncomfortable identifying as a Christian.

Templeton's questions of faith centered around his realization that sacred books, such as the Bible, while having valuable insights, are "not the revealed word of a deity but the conclusions and insights of men and women who, across the centuries, have sought to understand and explain the mysteries of existence."[23] He found that he could no longer believe in a literal reading of the Bible as expressed by fundamentalist evangelicalism, and that the Old Testament reveals "an all-too-human deity" who is "biased, . . . vindictive, and jealous . . . a primitive tribal god."[24] In his discussion of Jesus, Templeton points to contradictions and inconsistencies with respect to the birth and resurrection stories.[25] He also concludes that the Jesus of the Bible would not be comfortable with the churches of today and that the church has "become removed from the spirit and teaching of their founder."[26]

At the end of his book, Templeton articulates what he does believe. This includes the following:

1. There is no higher being with human attributes.
2. There is the Presence of "a Life Force, a First Cause, a Primal Energy, a Life Essence,"[27] not a being that can love.
3. No one hears our prayers, but meditation can serve as a form of prayer.
4. We can make the world a better place by making good choices.
5. The greatest motivator is love.

---

22. Ibid.
23. Ibid., 20.
24. Ibid., 71.
25. Ibid., 124.
26. Ibid., 169.
27. Ibid., 232.

6. When we die we cease to exist.
7. Life is a gift and should be celebrated.[28]

Jon M. Sweeney in *born again and again: surprising gifts of a fundamentalist childhood* writes of both the negative and positive affects that fundamentalism had on him. Raised in a fundamentalist community, he remembers when he believed "that heaven and hell were as sure as death. In fact, we had greater confidence in the afterlife than we did in death because we expected that at any time Jesus could come in the air to save us from death."[29] *The belief in heaven and hell and the off chance that we might meet Jesus in the air were very real to me as well, in fact, so real that it scared me, since I wasn't sure I would go to heaven.*

When Sweeney was unsuccessful "saving souls," he was told he should listen more carefully to God's voice and if he did, he would be directed to the right people to whom he should witness. He tried this, "but God was very quiet."[30] *When I was in Bible School, a close friend said that when she prayed to God, God came so close to her that if she were to stretch out her arm, she thought she would be able to touch God. This was the experience I wanted. So I would spend up to three hours in the prayer room in order to bring God closer. And as in Sweeney's experience, God was quiet.*

After Bible College, Sweeney went to the Philippines under the Conservative Baptist Foreign Missionary Society to convert those in the Roman Catholic tradition to the Baptist tradition. This experience was a crucial factor in his rejection of fundamentalism:

> By the time that my summer was over, I was convinced that what we were doing was wrong in its disregard for the life, community, culture, and the faith of the people that we had come to help. I came face to face with a series of real, human examples of how the faith of my childhood might hurt others. Was the kingdom of God really so divisive? Were the sheep and goats really the Baptists and the Catholics, as I had grown up thinking? I didn't think so. My missionary experience became for me a case study of how truth is not as simple as I had been told it was.[31]

28. Ibid., 232–33.
29. Sweeney, *born again and again*, 67.
30. Ibid., 84.
31. Ibid., 94.

His college and missionary experiences changed Sweeney's spiritual identity. He writes that "souls before me no longer looked so desperate. I was no longer convinced that they were in fact dying. I was no longer faced with a sea of souls needing the stamp of right faith . . . I began to understand that I had a spiritual identity, that it was nuanced, unique, and that everyone else had one, too."[32]

After more study of the Bible, Sweeney began to question the doctrines of original sin and the atonement. And he became convinced that everyone needs to be saved again and again, saved from the vices that consume us every day, "the formula was not as simple as I was led to believe."[33] He eventually joined the Episcopal Church.

Of the things Sweeney still values about fundamentalism is that it taught him "the certainty of God's presence in our hearts and lives . . . that we are all of us born again and again"[34] and it taught him to take his faith seriously, "I learned to imagine God at work in the world, and to imagine my own essential role in the divine plan."[35] But now his faith is much broader and inclusive. He believes that Christians and Jews have "an equal claim on truth," and that, even though he calls himself a Christian, he considers Muslims to be his "first cousins in faith."[36]

Patton Dodd, in his book, *my faith so far*, writes that he was raised a Southern Baptist; at age eighteen he joined a charismatic mega-church, only to leave it two years later.[37] As a fundamentalist evangelical he was serious about giving up drugs, attending church, listening to Christian music, and having a daily quiet time in which he prayed and read the Bible, along with devotional literature. He loved to sing and dance in worship. He considered himself a "Protestant Evangelical Charismatic Pentecostal Christian."[38] During this time Dodd identified his beliefs as "eternal salvation through faith in Jesus; the Bible's perfection, authority, and utter reliability; God's discernible action and presence in the world, especially through the gifts of the Holy Spirit such as speaking in

---

32. Ibid., 97, 103.

33. Ibid., 105.

34. Ibid., 165, 169.

35. Ibid., 28.

36. Ibid., 70.

37. Dodd, *my faith so far*, 49.

38. Ibid.

tongues and prophecy; and my responsibility to be a part of the ongoing effort to share these ideas with everyone on the face of the planet."[39]

Certain events and experiences along the way caused him to question his new-found faith. He was losing arguments with non-Christians on contentious topics such as homosexuality.[40] He questioned whether he would be responsible for non-Christians going to hell if he didn't tell them about Jesus and he struggled with his own sin and lack of faith.[41] Thinking that attending Oral Roberts University would bring him closer to God, he enrolled. But he continued to have faith questions: "The Question gives rise to the Suspicion gives rise to the Critique gives rise to the Cynicism. The seed of Doubt gets planted in the new and fertile soil and germinates and grows into the biggest plant in the garden and if not carefully tended it can choke all the tender stalks, both good and bad. No matter how much you fight off the Critique it won't leave you alone. The Critique becomes the glasses you wear during each church service."[42]

Dodd spent hours praying and seeking God. He hoped that "the guilt will fall off and the doubt will break away . . . I'll be back—back to innocence. . . . The Bible will make sense again. . . . God will fix me in a moment if only I seek Him hard enough."[43] But Dodd found that God did not fix him. The bottom fell out and left him in the middle, "not rejecting completely, not embracing uncritically, but deliberating. Working on my doubt from a position of faith."[44]

Dan Barker, a former fundamentalist, tells of his deconversion in *godless: How an Evangelical Preacher Became One of America's Leading Atheists.* After receiving "the call" to become a minister, he was an evangelical preacher for nineteen years. His questions about fundamentalist evangelical beliefs came gradually, the first being when he was invited to speak in a Baptist church.[45] The Baptist pastor informed him that some in the congregation did not believe that Adam and Eve were historical people. While this did shock Barker, it led him to see that not all Christians needed to necessarily think alike and not everything was as

39. Ibid., 51.
40. Ibid., 68.
41. Ibid., 69, 71.
42. Ibid., 118.
43. Ibid., 144.
44. Ibid., 172.
45. Barker, *godless*, 33.

black and white as he thought.[46] This realization prompted him to read books that were not based on fundamentalist premises; he delved into philosophy, psychology, science, and liberal theology, and he writes: "I went through an intense inner conflict. On the one hand I was happy with the direction and fulfillment of my Christian life; on the other hand, my intellectual doubts were sprouting all over. Faith and reason began a war within me. And it kept escalating. I would cry out to God for answers, and none would come. Like the lonely heart who keeps waiting for the phone to ring, I kept trusting that God would someday come through. He never did."[47]

For Barker, there was no specific turning point, but in the end, he ceased to believe in God.

Frank Schaeffer, in *Crazy for God*, tells the story of his experiences at L'Abri in Switzerland, a place of evangelical study founded and directed by his parents, Francis and Edith Schaeffer.[48] This was a place where people could come for a time and discuss their questions about the Christian faith. Francis and Edith were quite open-minded and many interesting discussions took place on topics such as art, philosophy, and religion.

Schaeffer's questions about faith first began when he got polio as a child and was treated with a serum from chimpanzees. He concluded that, since the chimpanzee serum made him better, "it proves the atheists are right . . . it looks like my treatment proves evolution . . . this means that Darwin is right . . . And I think Dad should change what he teaches about creation."[49] When he was sent to school in Great Britain, he observed that people could have faith and still seem quite ordinary; he had been led to believe that people of faith had to be different from the world.[50] When Schaeffer married Genie, whose family was not part of the evangelical culture, he saw that her family was a good family, even though they were not evangelical.[51] Realizing that goodness was not exclusive to evangelicals was another step along the way that led to his exit from fundamentalist evangelicalism.

46. Ibid., 34.
47. Ibid., 39.
48. Schaeffer, *Crazy for God*, 36.
49. Ibid., 36.
50. Ibid., 181.
51. Ibid., 250.

When Schaeffer directed the film *How Should We Then Live?*, one of the shots in the film was near Michelangelo's David. But when Gospel Films saw that David's genitals were showing in the shot Frank directed, they demanded stock footage be used that did not reveal David's private parts. This did not make sense to Schaeffer. Why could Christian films include the breast of Mary, but not the genitals of David?[52] This was a contributing factor to his decision to leave the evangelical fold.

When Schaeffer joined the pro-life movement, both he and his father denounced the sinfulness of North America and went on speaking tours to preach about it.[53] Later, when he, together with his wife and their children, moved to North America, Schaeffer realized that America was not as sinful as he had assumed. This was another step in the direction away from fundamentalist evangelicalism. He says, "I began to get the feeling that maybe I was on the wrong side."[54]

One thing that kept Schaeffer within Christianity was the behaviour of his brother-in-law John, who, while working at L'Abri during Francis Schaeffer's more conservative era, refused to sign a statement written by his father-in-law, Francis Schaeffer, regarding the inerrancy of the Bible. As a result, John was banned from teaching there, but he stayed at L'Abri to look after chores that were necessary to keep the physical complex operative. His selfless behaviour and ability to return good for evil impressed Frank Schaeffer and these actions contributed to his remaining in the faith.[55]

Schaeffer converted to the Greek Orthodox tradition for several reasons: the beauty of the liturgy, the mystery of worship, the "slow journey to God, wherein no one is altogether instantly 'saved' or 'lost' and nothing is completely resolved."[56] Faith for Schaeffer is the struggle for truth, and the longing for meaning, forgiveness, and reconciliation. He experienced this forgiveness when his daughter, Jessica, gave him her newborn baby to hold. And Schaeffer writes, "This new love was the strongest I'd ever felt. . . . The peace that 'passes understanding' seeped from Amanda to me. Jessica watched us both and let us be. . . . So maybe there is a God who forgives, who loves, who knows. I hope so.

52. Ibid., 270.
53. Ibid., 289.
54. Ibid., 315.
55. Ibid., 311.
56. Ibid., 388–90.

Anything is possible in a world where a daughter forgives her father, for ignorance, for anger, for failure, and places her daughter in his arms."[57]

Kenneth Daniels, son of missionary parents and a former evangelical missionary with Wycliffe Bible Translators, tells his story of deconversion in *Why I Believed: Reflections of a Former Missionary*. His move away from Christianity to humanism was a long, painful process, taking more than ten years. He describes it in terms of six crises points, which we could call his stages of leaving faith:

1. In his junior year in college he had difficulty with contradictory Old Testament texts and texts that revealed bad ethics.

2. Finding errors in the Bible, he determined it was not divinely inspired.

3. Coming to believe in evolution, he began to doubt the existence of God.

4. He doubted that the Bible was the word of God.

5. After reading books written from other than Christian perspectives, he found objections to the New Testament, including discrepancies within the text and the belief in hell.

6. He gave up the idea of a personal God who intervenes in the lives of humans. During this stage he seemed desperate to believe and asked for God's intervention in his life, but nothing happened.[58]

Daniels found it difficult to leave his evangelical faith because his faith had given him a sense of purpose; he was part of a nice evangelical family and community; and he was haunted by the "what if" phenomenon: what if it's all true after all and I end up in hell.[59] While all of his stages of crisis contributed to his loss of faith, the final contributing factor was his belief that a superhuman intellect was not responsible for the natural world.[60]

Daniels writes that during the years of doubting, "I desperately wanted to believe, so I focused my attention on things that bolstered my faith. This approach worked for many years, but ultimately I could

57. Ibid., 406.
58. Daniels, *Why I Believed*, 21–56.
59. Ibid., 86.
60. Ibid., 117.

not sustain it."[61] After giving up his evangelical faith, he had a sense of freedom because he had followed his search for truth, but he admitted that he still sometimes felt "the sting of knowing my life lacks the cosmic significance I once thought it had."[62]

In *Dating Jesus: A Story of Fundamentalism, Feminism and the American Girl,* Susan Campbell, a former fundamentalist, writes of her love/fear relationship with Jesus, "I love Jesus, yes, but I also fear him. I fear his return for Judgment Day, when he will come like a thief in the night, when I most likely will be found not ready, and I will shoot straight to hell."[63] Her first questions about fundamentalist religion began when her brother was asked to preach at age twelve and she realized that she wasn't asked because she was a girl.[64] The gender inequality that she perceived as a young girl continued with her into adult life, when she was branded a feminist. In one instance, she was asked to teach religion to girls but not to boys because that would be "usurping authority over a man."[65] Her reading of feminist theologians like Mary Daly and Elisabeth Schüssler Fiorenza made her realize that the Jesus community had not initially been misogynist.

Campbell believes that people are longing to return to the original Christianity where people shared what they had and that it was the wrong Jesus whom she had dated; the real Jesus believed in equality, loved "mouthy" women, and was not hung up on rules.[66]

Having left the religion of her childhood and youth, Campbell calls herself a floater, but she misses the community she once had, "I miss that feeling of belonging to something."[67] Sometimes she still finds herself enjoying those old gospel songs, "When I'm home alone, I'm usually singing. It is my guilty pleasure, to harmonize at the top of my lungs, to gospel tunes. . . . Forgive me for that. You can run at full speed from your fundamentalist upbringing, but it's going to catch up with you, regardless."[68]

61. Ibid., 326.

62. Ibid., 317.

63. Campbell, *Dating Jesus*, 9.

64. Ibid., 17–18.

65. Ibid., 105.

66. Ibid., 166, 204–5.

67. Ibid., 199.

68. Ibid., 203.

Christine Wicker talks about her struggles with the Christian faith in her book, *God Knows My Heart: Finding a Faith that Fits*. Wicker, a former Southern Baptist, talks about her journey to faith after losing the beliefs she had been taught. She first doubted her church's beliefs about the role of women when, in a youth Sunday School class, the leader talked about women keeping silent in the church.[69] In her second marriage she gained a new appreciation for God. Her husband, Philip, so totally accepted her, despite her behavior, that she wondered if God would do less.[70] This realization started her journey back to faith.

Throughout her faith journey Wicker struggled with how to connect with God. In her job as religious reporter she was exposed to many religious perspectives and her communication with Hare Krishnas, Buddhists, evangelical Christians, Muslims, and Jews helped her to develop her own understanding of faith. Proceeding with an open mind and determining not to judge, she saw that people in other religions had valid and meaningful religious experiences and beliefs. This reinforced her idea "that God is so abundant, anyone can reach Him in a multitude of ways . . . faith might be radically different for different people and . . . what we need from God might be different according to our individual natures."[71]

Wicker's reason to remain within Christianity was that "Christianity is deeply embedded in my heart. . . . One of the old hymns we used to sing in church has a line about standing on the promises of God. I like Buddhism. I still meditate. I think its wisdom is greater in many ways than the Christianity I knew as a child. But if I have to stand somewhere, I'm reluctant to move from the promises that my family has stood on."[72]

While she has left the fundamentalist faith of her childhood, she has come to believe that as one seeks to know one's own authentic self, one will know God as well. She believes in the abundance of God and grace—the kind of grace she experienced in her husband's unconditional acceptance of her—"I'm more hopeful. . . . I'm at least a little bit more confident in the idea that there is something else out there besides an empty void. I'm a little easier on myself . . . I'm more confident that

69. Wicker, *God Knows My Heart*, 6.
70. Ibid., 28.
71. Ibid., 111.
72. Ibid., 133.

I can follow my own way to God."[73] And she sees herself continuing to refine what she believes.

Howard Teeple, a Protestant fundamentalist by the time he was in Grade Eight, began to doubt his faith when he took a university course on Bible history and as a result, realized that some fundamentalist doctrines were erroneous.[74] In his book *I Started to be a Minister: From Fundamentalism to a Religion of Ethics*, he recounts a course he took on the life of Jesus, which launched his investigation into what Jesus actually did and said, and how Christianity began.[75] Subsequently, he travelled across the United States, visiting university libraries and reading whatever he could find on Christian origins. After completing his PhD he accepted an offer to work on the International Greek New Testament Project in Atlanta.[76] In this project, he discovered a list of variant readings in ninety-nine manuscripts of the Greek text of Luke alone.[77] This realization led him to believe that translation of the biblical text was not as straightforward as he had once believed.

Teeple's research on biblical texts caused him to realize that churches were unaware of what scholars were learning in seminaries and universities. In his desire to make the historical knowledge of Christian origins available to the public, Teeple founded the Religion and Ethics Institute, which had as its purpose "to promote the discovery and distribution of sound historical and scientific knowledge in the fields of religion and ethics."[78] Through this institute Teeple published works such as *The Noah's Ark Nonsense* and *The Historical Approach to the Bible*.

Teeple's studies led him to reject a fundamentalist approach to Christianity. He adopted a Christianity based on truth and ethics, claiming that the gospels reveal a Jesus who emphasized both.[79]

Ruth Tucker, a seminary professor, tells her faith story in *Walking Away from Faith: Unraveling the Mystery of Belief and Unbelief*. Converted at the age of seven, she very soon began to have questions about

---

73. Ibid., 198–9, 205.

74. Teeple, *I Started to Be a Minister*, ix.

75. Ibid., 4.

76. Ibid., 129.

77. Ibid., 138.

78. Ibid., 219–20.

79. Ibid., 247–50.

how the existence of dinosaurs could be reconciled with the biblical story of creation.[80] At age thirteen, she committed herself to become a missionary, even though she was still plagued by doubts. In college, while taking a course on the Bible, she started to wonder about the biblical canon and "who decided which books would be in the canon."[81] This seemed to her to have been a human decision and thus there was room for error. After her mother's sudden death in an accident, she decided to put God on trial, and what she found was a silent God, "my problem was God's silence. . . . I simply cannot connect with God."[82] She writes that the only time she feels any connection is when she is singing, "It is here where sometimes I think I hear the voice of God and I sense the presence of God."[83] *This resonates with my own experience. I have always found it difficult to connect with God. When I sit down at the piano and sing is the closest I come to sensing a sacred connection.*

Tucker has given her unbelief to God. She has not abandoned faith, even though she still wonders if God exists.[84] In moments of doubt, she asks herself why she still is a seminary professor: "They'd fire me if they only knew."[85]

Besides telling her own story of belief and unbelief, Tucker discusses some of the reasons why people walk away from their faith. These include the challenges of science, philosophy, biblical criticism, psychology, and disappointment with God and other Christians. She challenges ex-believers to reconsider their decision but also challenges Christians to seek to better understand those who have walked away from faith, realizing that for them the process of leaving has been difficult.[86]

John W. Loftus tells his story in *Why I Became an Atheist: A Former Preacher Rejects Christianity*. Loftus became a fundamentalist Christian in his youth. His crisis of faith came while he was a minister. Because he had a different perspective of the Christian faith, others were threatened

80. Tucker, *Walking Away From Faith*, 18.
81. Ibid., 19.
82. Ibid., 23.
83. Ibid.
84. Ibid., 26.
85. Ibid., 133.
86. Ibid., 12–13.

by him, and he was forced out of the church.[87] Another factor in his deconversion was that he became convinced of the scientific proof that the earth is older than creationists say it is.[88] This led him to critically examine the beliefs of fundamentalist Christianity and he found them wanting.

The major portion of his book is a synthesis of his in-depth study of such topics as the existence of God; the superstitious nature of ancient peoples; the pseudonymity of the Bible; the lack of archaeological proof of certain events such as the plagues; the lack of historical evidence for Christianity; unanswered prayer; the problem of evil; issues surrounding predictive prophecy and biblical authority; and beliefs in Jesus incarnation, bodily resurrection, heaven, and hell.

Loftus admits that atheism is an "unsettling conclusion" since he has no hope of resurrection, no hope "that there is someone outside the space-time matrix who can help me in times of need or give me any guidance."[89] He says that people are Christians because they are longing to make sense of their lives and to believe that there is some ultimate meaning to life, but he claims that there is no reason for hope in God and you don't have to have ultimate meaning, there is enough in life without God to make life good, "you don't need an 'ultimate' anything to live life in this world. . . . This life is all there is: a short blip of existence in the cosmos. . . . I should therefore be motivated to give all I have today, for this is all I have."[90]

John Marks, in *Reasons to Believe: One Man's Journey Among the Evangelicals and the Faith He Left Behind*, tells his story of becoming a fundamentalist as a teenager and then gradually losing his faith in God. While attending the University of Marburg in Germany, Marks took a trip to Israel and it was there, as he viewed the tourist-oriented sites relating to Jesus, that he lost his faith in Jesus, but kept his belief in God, "There was history everywhere . . . the story of Jesus had happened, but it began to feel less than divine. Christ began to feel less like God and more like the cornerstone of the dilapidated Church of the

---

87. Loftus, *Why I Became an Atheist*, 32.
88. Ibid., 26.
89. Ibid., 404.
90. Ibid., 412.

Holy Sepulchre, a shrine founded by the Empress Helena, mother of the Emperor Constantine."[91]

Later he went to the Balkans and saw the results of ethnic cleansing. He got "a small glimpse of the hell that human beings make for themselves on earth," he could "no longer reasonably believe in the existence of a sovereign being."[92] He believed that a God who could not stop the horror and violence in the world did not have a right to his loyalty. As a result he gave up his belief in God.[93]

Austin Miles in *Don't Call Me Brother: A Ringmaster's Escape from the Pentecostal Church* tells how he went from being a ringmaster in a circus to an ordained minister in the Assemblies of God. He then recounts his disillusionment with televangelists who not only used dishonest methods to raise funds, but were also child abusers.[94] This led him to leave the church.

INTERVIEWS AS CASE STUDIES

I will now look at three case studies, interviews I conducted with three people who left the fundamentalist evangelical movement. All three spent their childhood and teenage years in the movement. The first, Sandra Colter (not her real name), desperately tried to fit into the Christian culture around her. Yet when people asked how her prayer life was going, she couldn't honestly say that everything was just great. She wondered why she couldn't hear God's voice, why it wasn't working for her. People in her community would talk about how God spoke to them through their prayers, but it wasn't happening for her. She was despairing. She tried to make it seem like God was speaking to her, but she wondered if it was really true. Her questions about her belief system started with reading about science, other religions and books about fundamentalism. She no longer believes in heaven or hell, but she has found it difficult to let go of her community. She does not feel guilty about leaving, but she grieves the loss of the feeling of belonging

91. Marks, *Reasons to Believe*, 323.

92. Ibid., 11.

93. Ibid., 365.

94. Miles, *Don't Call Me Brother*, 149–50, 292.

and sometimes she is still plagued with the "what if" question, "What if there really *is* a hell?"[95]

The second interview was with Tim Stabler (not his real name). For him, the scariest thing was the command to witness to others about Jesus. He thought this would be the worst possible thing he would ever have to do. Heaven and hell seemed like science fiction to him. The fundamentals of the virgin birth, the second coming of Jesus, and Jesus' resurrection seemed unbelievable. For him, it was reading outside the fundamentalist circle that began his questioning about the belief system in which he had been raised. He read about other religions and about evolution. These made sense to him, so he gave up his fundamentalist evangelical beliefs and he has no regrets or misgivings about his decision. No guilt. He sees life as a journey and referring to the Buddhist concept that "you only need the boat to cross the river; once you cross the river you have no more use for the boat," he muses that maybe Christianity had served its purpose for him. He says, "Now that I don't use it, it's just one of those things you discard, it's not necessary to your life."[96]

The third interview was with Dora Astro (not her real name). For her, life as a fundamentalist evangelical is something she wants to forget. Her bad memories revolve around beliefs in the rapture, judgment, the threat of hell, self-flagellation, and condemnation. When she prayed, she didn't feel close to God and could never understand what it meant to have a personal relationship with Christ, "How could you have a personal relationship with somebody who, yes, they are supposed to be alive, but they are not really alive, so it was just totally perplexing to me and then I thought, what's wrong with me that this stuff doesn't make any sense?"[97] She found she had to limit her own thinking in order to make all the beliefs fit and there was no room for doubt. "You can't have questions, because then you are doubting. You can't be doubting because you wouldn't be a good Christian if you doubt."[98] Her departure from fundamentalist evangelicalism began when she started to study other points of view. She has left the movement and sometimes still feels angry about the psychological abuse she suffered. She feels that her religion contributed to low self-esteem; it prevented her from believing

95. Sandra Colter (not her real name), interview, June 18, 2007.

96. Tim Stabler, (not his real name), interview, June 18, 2007.

97. Dora Astro (not her real name), interview, July 6, 2007.

98. Ibid.

in herself. She is now a Universalist and believes that all religions can have some value.

STORIES IN EDITED WORKS

Besides the monographs and case studies referred to above, I consulted four edited works that contain stories of former fundamentalists. *Leaving Fundamentalism*, edited by G. Elijah Dann, contains stories of thirteen individuals who left Protestant fundamentalism, most of them Canadians. Among these individuals are those who were "born again" as early as at age four, as well as those who became fundamentalist evangelicals as university students. Some had difficulty experiencing the closeness of God. They also questioned fundamentalist interpretation of biblical texts and doctrines. They found no answers to their faith questions or to questions about inerrancy, hell, Jesus' status, sin, divorce, and homosexuality. After leaving fundamentalism, some remained within Christianity; others left but felt a loss of community and faith; and still others left feeling free.

The book, *Jesus Girls: True Tales of Growing Up Female and Evangelical,* edited by Hannah Faith Notess, tells stories of women who were raised in fundamentalist evangelical churches and struggled with beliefs they had been taught.

The stories in *Leaving the Fold: Testimonies of Former Fundamentalists*, edited by Edward T. Babinski, are divided into sections according to where the individuals ended up after they left fundamentalist evangelicalism. It has stories of fundamentalists who became moderate or liberal Christians, stories of those who became agnostics or atheists, and stories of people who embraced non-Christian spiritualities. Individuals write about their struggles with biblical interpretation, ethical issues, church politics, and the exclusive nature of fundamentalist evangelicalism.

In *Finding Faith, Losing Faith: Stories of Conversion and Apostasy,* Scot McKnight and Hauna Ondrey set out to discover what happens in the process of conversion. To do so, they examine stories of people who left their religion, sometimes to join another. They discuss the phenomenon of conversion from the perspective of those who left the church and found freedom outside of Christianity, those who left the

synagogue for the church, those who left Roman Catholicism for evangelicalism, and those who left evangelicalism for Roman Catholicism.

ANALYSIS OF WHY PEOPLE LEFT FUNDAMENTALIST EVANGELICALISM

Using the above sources, I will analyze the stories of seventy-three
individuals, examining their reasons for leaving fundamentalist evangelicalism and looking at the kind of spiritual expression/belief system
they embraced (if any) after they left. (See Appendix C for the names
of these people.)

Forty-seven of the individuals in the sample are male, twenty-five
are female, and one wrote anonymously. Seventeen of them were/are
ministers, priests, missionaries, preachers, teachers in seminaries or
evangelists in the movement: Charles Templeton, David Rattigan, Glen
Robitaille, Dewey Beegle, Tom Harpur, Keith Dixon, Farrell Till, M. Lee
Deitz, Skip Porteous, Robert Price, Austin Miles, Arch Taylor, Howard
Teeple, Julie Bogart, Ruth Tucker, Jon Sweeney, and Kenneth Daniels.

Some began their fundamentalist faith journey in childhood by
attending church either with or without their parents. Others joined
evangelical churches in their youth or adult life. Church traditions represented include Church of the Nazarene, Pentecostal, Open Brethren,
Methodist, Baptist, Church of God, the United Church, Christian and
Missionary Alliance, Mennonite Brethren, Presbyterian, Church of
Christ, New Apostolic Church, and Assemblies of God.

Using an inductive approach, I examined reasons why these individuals left fundamentalist evangelicalism. I determined several categories that mark their reasons for leaving. These include a literal-factual
reading of the Bible, issues with the fundamentals, questions and doubts
that were not addressed, the inability to have a certain prescribed spiritual experience, hard-line ethical standards, and the hypocrisy found in
other Christians.

Literal-Factual Reading of the Bible

The question of the literal-factual interpretation of the Bible was a major
issue for many of those leaving fundamentalist evangelicalism. Thirty-
one of those who left the movement expressed difficulty with the Bible,

its origin, its literal-factual interpretation, and its claims to inerrancy. They became convinced that the Bible was a human book, not a book dictated by God. Keith Dixon viewed the Bible as a poetic and mystical book, with God as a figment of people's imagination.[99] Along with the idea that the Bible was written by humans, many of those who left fundamentalism started to eventually doubt the claim of its inerrancy and infallibility, including Jeffrey Robbins, David Rattigan, Dewey Beegle, Ernest Heramia, Joe Barnhart, Arch Taylor, and Kenneth Daniels. Skip Porteous, a former Pentecostal minister, wondered, based on the large number of biblical manuscripts in existence, how one could know what the original said.[100] When Ernest Heramia learned that the book of Esther was based on the Babylonian myth of Ishtar and Marduk, he gave up the principle of biblical inerrancy.[101] During his translation of biblical texts, Greek scholar Joe Barnhart became convinced that the Bible was fallible and that it was the lack of education that kept fundamentalists believing in the infallibility of the Bible.[102] Glenn Robitaille's period of doubting began when he read Leviticus 21:18–20, "For no one who has a blemish shall draw near, one who is blind or lame, or one who has a mutilated face or a limb too long, or one who has a broken foot or a broken hand, or a hunchback, or a dwarf, or a man with a blemish in his eyes or an itching disease or scabs or crushed testicles." Robitaille could not believe that people with physical defects were unworthy to approach God.[103] His literal reading of the biblical text was the beginning of his study of higher biblical criticism.

Dewey Beegle, who had to leave his teaching post because he used biblical critical methods in his teaching, asserted that "the ultimate and perennial problem in right-wing Christianity is the failure to be inductive in its study of Scripture. . . . Some fundamentalists accept the insights of lower (textual) criticism, but in the area of higher criticism (who wrote the book; when, where, why, and to whom it was written) no findings are considered valid, even though formulated during millions of study hours over two centuries."[104]

99. Dixon, "The Ministry Revisited," 88.

100. Porteous, *Jesus Doesn't Live Here Anymore*, 158.

101. Heramia, "The Thorn-Crowned Lord," 196.

102. Barnhart, "Fundamentalism as Stage One," 234–35.

103. Robitaille, "From Fear to Faith," 164.

104. Beegle, "Journey to Freedom," 64.

A number of people were unable to reconcile Darwin's theory of evolution with the biblical account of creation, i.e., the literal-factual reading of the account.

A belief that several people found particularly difficult was the belief in hell. Among those who voiced this issue were David Rattigan, Kenneth Daniels, Julie Bogart, Alan Gil, John Loftus, Charles Templeton, and Helen Milderhall. They asked questions such as. "What about those who died before Christ?" and "Why would God want to punish what God created?"

Some saw contradictions, incorrect assertions and inconsistencies in the Bible. Jim Lippard noted the multiple creation accounts and subsequently collected ten pages of biblical errors and contradictions.[105] Edward Babinski noted that Jesus made an incorrect assertion when he said, "Immediately after the suffering of those days the sun will be darkened, and the moon will not give its light; the stars will fall from heaven. . . . They will see the Son of Man coming on the clouds of heaven. . . . Truly I tell you, this generation [meaning his own] will not pass away until all these things have taken place" (Matt 24:29–30, 34).[106] Since those things did not happen before Jesus' generation died, Babinski asserted that Jesus' claim was not true. He also read critiques about the belief, common in fundamentalism, that Old Testament prophecies are fulfilled in the New Testament.[107] Austin Miles, originally a "born again" Pentecostal, came to see that the Song of Solomon was not about Jesus' love, as he had been told, but about human love.[108] One of the contradictions that Skip Porteous saw was that the biblical assertion that the Jews killed Jesus did not correspond with the biblical claim that the Jews were the chosen people.[109] Christine Rosen questioned the use of the Bible as the only textbook used in school and subsequently questioned all the doctrines that flowed from that book, such as creationism, the end times, and the belief in heaven and hell.[110] Bible teacher Arch Taylor came to see that those who claimed the inerrancy of the Bible were not really defending the "Word of God," as they claimed, but

---

105. Lippard, "From Fundamentalism to Open-ended Atheism," 325.

106. Babinski, "If It Wasn't for Agnosticism," 219.

107. Ibid., 220.

108. Miles, "Don't Call Me Brother," 265.

109. Porteous, *Jesus Doesn't Live Here Anymore*, 29.

110. Rosen, *My Fundamentalist Education*, 70–100.

were actually defending a system of belief they had devised themselves, doctrines formulated by using selective biblical texts as proof texts.[111] Virginia Ramey Mollenkott, at first believing that homosexuality was sin, conducted an extensive biblical critical study and came to see that the Bible does not condemn homosexuality, in fact, it supports and celebrates human diversity.[112] Pamela Grown-Seely, after experiencing the immoral behaviour of church leaders and the infidelity of her Christian husband, decided that she could not trust men to interpret the Bible, which had primarily been interpreted by males.[113]

Issues with the Fundamentals

Closely related to questions about the literal-factual reading of the Bible were questions about the fundamentals. Marlene Winell had to re-think her beliefs in original sin, salvation, and hell. When she worked with pre-school children, she couldn't understand how these children could be infected by sin at such a young age.[114] Joseph Simons wondered why a God would need to have sin paid for.[115] Charles Templeton tackled fundamentals such as of the virgin birth of Jesus, Jesus' resurrection, the plan of salvation, and the belief in hell, devoting most of his book to dispelling these and other fundamentalist evangelical beliefs.[116] John Loftus discusses these same beliefs as well as the issues of the authority of the Bible and the existence of God.[117] When writing of his deconversion, Kenneth Daniels devotes one of his chapters to "The Reliability of the Bible," in which he demonstrates that "the Bible is not the product of divine inspiration; it is the product of human composition, just like all other books."[118]

---

111. Taylor, "The Bible, and What It Means to Me," 167.

112. Mollenkott, *Sensuous Spirituality*, 190.

113. McKnight and Ondrey, *Finding Faith, Losing Faith*, 27.

114. Winell, *Leaving the Fold*, 36.

115. Simons, "Rapture, Community, and Individualist Hope," 35.

116. Templeton, *Farewell to God*, 89–93, 117–23, 138–9, 223–6.

117. Loftus, *why I became an atheist*, 78–105, 289–316, 317–28, 344–51, 351–382, 387–398.

118. Daniels, *Why I Believed*, 237–70.

Unanswered Questions

Many individuals who left fundamentalist evangelicalism had a lot of questions for which they received no answers. Is it my fault that I can't believe? How can AIDS be a punishment from God when that is not the God of the New Testament? They say I'm a sinner, but I can't figure out what my sin is. Why is God quiet when I pray? Why are some prayers not answered? Why must truth be sought in a God whom we cannot see and with whom we cannot speak? If only the Elect are saved, why is it important to evangelize, if God doesn't want everyone to be saved anyway? How could warm feelings about the opposite sex be sinful? If God is real, why isn't he more present? Why would God want African men to divorce all but one of their wives when they are converted to Christianity? Where does this leave the women who have been divorced?

When people had questions about their faith, there was generally no way to discuss them with their fundamentalist friends and leaders. The only concern of the fundamentalist community was to put them straight, to convince them to believe without questioning. Some found that when they were confronted with questions about the Bible, they were unable to find answers. They came to see the weakness of traditional arguments for certain beliefs and views. And it was only admissible to ask "safe" questions, those questions that were not a challenge to the fundamentalist belief system.

The questions individuals asked often caused them to look elsewhere for answers, studying other religions, such as Buddhism, and reading broadly in a variety of disciplines. This led them to think inclusively. William Bagley discovered that the Tao Te Ching had existed five hundred years before Jesus and contained teachings that were similar to his.[119] So Jesus' teachings were maybe not as unique as he had assumed. Ernest Heramia studied Norse mythology and in it discovered the concept of "letting The Weirdness in," which to him meant welcoming his greatest fears.[120] He found many similarities between these myths and Bible stories and discovered that "the teachings and actions of the Jesus I loved had been preceded by the teachings and actions of others who lived long before the events depicted in the Gospels."[121] Others read

---

119. Bagley, "Reflections on a Christian Experience," 189.

120. Heramia, "The Thorn-Crowned Lord," 203.

121. Ibid.

in the fields of philosophy, theology, science, psychology, evolution, business, social sciences, mathematics, history, and physics and found that what they had learned in church had ignored discoveries in these disciplines. For some, these readings led them to discredit Christianity. For others, it made them dig deeper, leaving their unquestioning faith tradition behind, yet not rejecting Christianity completely.

People wrote about the emotions that went along with their doubts and questions. Guilt was a common emotion. They felt guilty that they were not working hard enough "for the Lord," guilty because they thought they were bad, and guilty for having questions about faith. There was also anger, anger about narrow-mindedness, anger about exclusion, and anger about abuse. People felt pain, the pain of not being accepted for who they were, the pain of being left out of the community, the pain of being fired from the community. And they felt sadness; they grieved the loss of their community, which had given them so much security, recognition, and connection.

People who had questions about fundamentalist evangelicalism were judged by other Christians. Jacob Shelley was warned by his pastor not to study religion at university because it might result in loss of faith.[122] Fundamentalist communities seemed exclusive, shutting people out who didn't believe as they did. Dewey Beegle resigned from seminary teaching because he got into trouble with the President for upsetting the students with his views on biblical interpretation.[123] As a result of narrow mindedness, people were not able to process their questions. Sandra Colter felt guilty that prayer wasn't answered. She asked, "Why isn't it working for me? Why don't I get it?"[124] She thought there was something wrong with her.

Lack of a Prescribed Spiritual Experience

Many of those who left fundamentalist evangelicalism had difficulty experiencing God in ways prescribed by the movement, such as a sudden, emotional conversion; answers to prayer; feeling close to God; and bringing others to Jesus. They asked God for help, but no help came,

122. Shelley, "Life Stages," 130.

123. Beegle, "Journey to Freedom," 73.

124. Sandra Colter, (not her real name), interview, June 18, 2007.

"I kept trusting God would someday come through. He never did."[125] They prayed and read their Bible but God seemed far away. They read their Bible so much that everything seemed old; they already knew it all. They were not able to experience the love of God. There was no sense of awe in their experience of God. They found that giving themselves to God didn't change anything in their lives. They tried to witness to others, bring them to Jesus, but they were not successful, and they felt uncomfortable doing it.

For me there was a link between behaviour and "being saved." If I was "saved," if Jesus had really "come into my heart," then my behaviour should show it. And I didn't seem to behave much differently after I was "saved" than before the experience. I knew I was a bad girl because I talked back to my parents and I didn't feel like witnessing about my faith. I didn't get any feedback that my behaviour was Christ-like, so I judged myself as bad and unchristian. Obviously, the salvation experience hadn't worked for me. I thought I would feel different, but I didn't. It was all about doing the right thing so that I could go to heaven. But I never felt like I was doing the right thing. And because I was convinced that being "saved" hadn't worked, I tried again and again to be "saved," "going forward" at evangelistic meetings, keeping up with daily "devotions," and praying for forgiveness constantly. Even though I seemed to have done everything by the book, I was living with an internal emotional contradiction. I didn't seem to measure up to the ways a true Christian should act. I was guilty. I pled for assurance of salvation but it never came.

Timothy William Grogan, taken in at first by Hal Lindsey's *The Late Great Planet Earth*, witnessed many prophecies and healings, only to discover that "none of these prophecies and healings turned out to be genuine."[126]

Some were told that they were supposed to be "slain in the Spirit" and speak in tongues, but it didn't always work. In David Rattigan's case, he was successful in receiving the Holy Spirit (proven by the fact that he fell over when the leader touched his forehead) and in speaking in tongues, but he later believed these events were "more the result of human manipulation than of genuine spiritual power."[127]

---

125. Barker, "Losing Faith in Faith," 301.

126. Grogan, "Lies, Damn Lies, and Boredom," 315.

127. Rattigan, "Fantastic Voyage," 59.

Ethical Standards

For some, leaving fundamentalist evangelicalism came as a result of ethical issues. Divorce was sin. One pastor was fired because of his divorce. There was obvious racism and rigging of votes to get the more conservative men (and it was men, not women) into church positions. There were also unethical methods of fundraising in some churches.

One individual reported that handouts, provided by James Dobson, were given to parents, advising them not to dress children in the "wrong" clothes, lest they turn to homosexuality.[128] Fundamentalism saw homosexual feelings as the work of the devil.

Hypocrisy

Another factor responsible for people leaving fundamentalist evangelicalism was hypocrisy and disappointment in the behaviour of other Christians. Conrad Hyers saw inconsistency between what fundamentalists said was important (love) and their actions.[129]

Disagreements over doctrines and ethical matters led to schisms. Austin Miles was disillusioned with the behaviour of ministers and evangelists who were guilty of child abuse.[130] Some left the movement because they had been sexually abused by church leaders.

Along with the disappointment in other Christians, Kevin Henke, Marlene Winell, Joseph Simons, and John Loftus observed that people who were not Christians exhibited just as good behaviour and sometimes better behaviour than that of Christians. This too figured into their reasons for leaving the movement.

THE PROCESS OF DECONVERSION

Just like the disbelief in Santa Claus happens gradually, I wondered if it was similar for people leaving their faith. Did they experience one thing after another until finally they were convinced to give up their fundamentalist beliefs?

128. Rak, "Looking Back at Sodom," 98–99.
129. Hyers, "The Comic Vision," 104.
130. Miles, "Don't Call Me Brother," 267.

It turns out that people did not usually give up their faith over night. The process was often slow and there were generally a number of issues over a period of years that were instrumental in the decision to leave the fundamentalist community. What began as a doubt or question for one person was sometimes the final straw for another. For example, Leia Minaker's first point of questioning about the faith was when her boyfriend asked her how she would feel if Muslims, Hindus, and Buddhists would achieve heaven too.[131] For William Bagley it was the reflection and study of other religions that made him realize there was a problem with the exclusivity of fundamentalist evangelicalism.[132] For Leia Minaker, the issue of the validity of other religions was what initiated her doubts about fundamentalist evangelicalism, whereas this issue was the final factor that convinced William Bagley to walk away from faith.

People gave up friends, a comfortable evangelical sub-culture, security, and recognition within the group. For some it was a reluctant leaving. For James Fieser, "my entire fundamentalist experience is a part of my past I'd prefer to forget, but that has proven difficult."[133] David Rattigan wrote: "leaving fundamentalism is a lengthy process of pain and frustration."[134] For Julie Rak the painful part was leaving what was positive about the church, especially the sense of community.[135] Ten years after she left the church, Beverly Bryant still had an uncomfortable, separated relationship with the church. She missed theological discussions and had good childhood memories of church experiences such as the Christmas pageant.[136] For Leia Minaker, fundamentalism had given her comfort and safety, but the process of leaving it was the most painful time in her life, "My family, once so close-knit, was torn. Conversations with my parents and siblings led to tears and broken hearts. . . . While my family stood together praying for my soul, I stood alone, begging to be understood and accepted for my changing way of thinking."[137] Dan Barker, a former evangelist, felt the pain both of

131. Minaker, "Are You a 'Real' Christian?", 187.
132. Bagley, "Reflections on a Christian Experience," 189.
133. Fieser, "The Jesus Lizard," 183.
134. Rattigan, "Fantastic Voyage," 67.
135. Rak, "Looking Back at Sodom," 106.
136. Bryant, "Inching Along," 160.
137. Minaker, "Are You a 'Real' Christian?", 188.

letting people down who believed in him and his message, as well as the inner pain of giving up all that he believed, "It was like tearing my whole frame of reality to pieces. . . . All of my bases for thinking and values had to be restructured."[138] When he walked away, he wrote a letter to colleagues, friends, and family members, explaining his decision; and in that letter he explained how difficult it had been for him: "the child in me still sometimes wishes to regain the comforts and reassurances of my former beliefs. . . . The Bible says those who seek will find. . . . I am constantly seeking. And I have not found. Right now I am somewhere between the agnostic and the atheist."[139]

The steps in the process of deconversion are similar to the steps in joining a religion. Scot McKnight and Hauna Ondrey in *Finding Faith, Losing Faith: Stories of Conversion and Apostasy*, claim that the process of conversion has six dimensions: the individual's own *context*, a *crisis*, a *quest* prompted by the crisis, an *encounter* with persons or ideas that promote the religion, a *commitment* to the new faith, and *consequences* of doing so.[140] They say that deconversion carries the same aspects. These stages are evident in the stories I analyzed of people leaving fundamentalism.

First, the context. By context is meant the particular situation in which individuals find themselves culturally, religiously, and socially. There is always a context for an individual's experience. Before they left the fundamentalist evangelical movement, people found their primary identity within fundamentalist evangelical churches. This was their context. Some taught in fundamentalist schools or colleges. What was expected of them, with regard to both belief and behaviour, was clear. Doctrines about original sin, salvation, and hell could not be questioned. It was a black and white world. A few who are gay or lesbian had the added judgment that homosexuality was considered sin. No belief systems outside of those that were fundamentalist evangelical were seen as valid, nor were they encouraged to read material that fell outside the fundamentalist evangelical world view. This was their context while within the movement.

When they started to raise questions about the fundamentalist evangelical belief system, about the inerrancy of the Bible, and about

138. Barker, *godless*, 39.
139. Ibid., 47.
140. McKnight and Ondrey, *Finding Faith, Losing Faith*, 5.

the exclusivity of that brand of Christianity, their context changed. Now they did not feel as connected to the church community. Asking questions about faith was not encouraged. Friends and family did not understand why they were questioning the fundamentals. They were being prayed for because, in the mind of their faith community, they were starting down a slippery slope leading to unbelief. They were "backsliding."

Next, the crisis. When people converted to fundamentalist evangelicalism as children, the crisis often had to do with fear of hell. If they were "born again" later in life, it could have been as a result of a personal failure, an addiction, a catastrophe, a lack of meaning, or an illness. This made them open to a conversion in which they could be assured that God cared for them and heard their prayers. The belief system assured them of forgiveness and a future home in heaven when they die.

In deconversion, according to the stories I read, moments of crisis that led to deconversion were intellectual, physical, and/or emotional. On the intellectual front, people found contradictions, inconsistencies, and errors in the biblical text. And the scientific fact of evolution went against the believed literal-factual interpretation of the Genesis creation story. For some, arguments for the existence of God didn't seem to hold. For others, accidents, devastation by war, and unnecessary deaths begged the question of where God was in suffering.

Knowledge of other faiths changed their belief that there was only one true faith. It made God too small. Restrictions in women's roles were taught as biblical, but women saw this as biased interpretation by men. Some within the Pentecostal tradition questioned the practices of prophesying, healing, and speaking in tongues when these did not happen for them. They saw these as human manipulation.

Some who taught Bible courses or worked in translation of biblical texts came to believe the Bible to be fallible. This insight brought on an intellectual crisis.

At the physical level, some experienced or witnessed sexual abuse by ministers, priests, and evangelists. Others, as a result of faith issues, had panic attacks and were forced to dig deeper to see what was causing them. It turned out that when they left their faith behind, their panic attacks ceased. Some women struggled with their sexuality and this led them to re-examine the fundamentalist evangelical belief that homosexuality was sinful and unnatural. Julie Rak concluded that "if the price of obedience is your dignity and integrity as a person, then obedience to a tradition that marginalizes the essence of who you are is going to result in spiritual death."[141]

At the emotional level, several wrote of their serious efforts to connect with God, but to no avail: God was silent. Prayers were left unanswered. They felt abandoned.

The third and fourth dimensions referred to by McKnight and Ondrey are quest and encounter. Because of the crisis, people go on a quest for a new meaning system, for truth, a quest for answers: "A crisis in one's faith precipitates a quest for resolution, for no one desires to live in crisis."[142] In the process of conversion, this quest led them to talk with others who appeared to have found a meaningful faith in God. In the process of conversion, some in crisis read the Bible for answers. They had encounters with God, whom they believed could save them from sin through Jesus' death on the cross.

For those who eventually left fundamentalist evangelicalism, their quest was for intellectual coherence and their encounters were with people of other faith traditions and exposure to literature outside of the fundamentalist evangelical mindset. When they embarked on in-depth studies of biblical texts, read books on evolution, and explored other denominations and spiritualities, they saw a bigger world than they had previously imagined. A few people spoke of their deconversion as a "born again" experience.

The fifth dimension evident in both conversion and deconversion is commitment. There is a commitment to a new way of thinking. When people were converted, their commitment was first of all to God, and then to a fundamentalist evangelical church. They were committed to pray, read the Bible, leave sinful practices behind, attend church regularly, and associate with other fundamentalist evangelicals.

In many cases the commitment of those leaving fundamentalist evangelicalism was to join more moderate and liberal Christian denominations. In other cases, it meant a commitment to freedom away from Christianity altogether, to atheism, agnosticism, humanism, or to non-Christian spiritualities. Others said they were happy to simply live in the present and remain open to the spiritual dimension of their lives.

141. Rak, "Looking Back at Sodom," 106.

142. McKnight and Ondrey, *Finding Faith, Losing Faith*, 42, 46.

The final dimension of both conversion and deconversion is that of consequences that may affect one's thinking, behaviour, and emotions. Inevitably there are consequences to any decision. Conversion resulted in a change of mindset. Jesus became the all important number one in their lives, as they sought to please him in every way. And their behaviour changed, especially if they felt that prior to conversion they had participated in activities that now were deemed to be sinful. And emotionally, they sometimes felt on a high at the time of conversion; their sins were forgiven and they had a relationship with God.

In the experience of deconversion, the consequences proved in some cases to be positive and in others, not so positive. As they left fundamentalist evangelicalism, people found acceptance of who they were and freedom from injustice, inequality, fear, and guilt. David Rattigan found that he now had room for "ambiguity, doubt and uncertainty without fear."[143] They were free to explore faith as they wished, "free to question and challenge, think and explore, without fear or condemnation."[144] Jeffrey Robbins, who left fundamentalist evangelicalism but retained a Christian identity, put his experience this way, "Securities offered by a self-certain faith have been closed to me, but not without opening a window into the integrity of the human experience, and by extension, into the soul of the mystery of God."[145]

On the less positive side some wrote of their loss of a close community. Leaving it behind brought them pain. There were things they missed, like participation in church activities and roles they formerly had in the church. Some lost friendships. There was depression and a loss of meaning and purpose in life. And then there was the "what if" factor that still plagued some ex-fundamentalist evangelicals. What if the teachings of fundamentalist evangelicalism were true after all? What if there really is a hell? Some found that the fundamentalist evangelical tape running in their heads was difficult to turn off. All of these were consequences of their deconversion.

143. Rattigan, *"Fantastic Voyage,"* 68.
144. Shelley, "Life Stages," 134.
145. Robbins, "The Slippery Slope of Theology," 120.

WHAT HAPPENED TO THOSE WHO LEFT

When the fundamentalist framework did not stand up anymore, people left the movement. It didn't mesh with their reality and what they learned from other disciplines, religions, and experiences. James Barr's understanding is that "in order to escape from fundamentalism one needs not only to see that the Bible points in a different direction but also to see that the outside world of thought has a very different character from that which fundamentalists suppose it to have."[146] And this is what happened as fundamentalist evangelicals stepped outside of their religious context. The world outside of fundamentalism was not as evil as they had once been led to believe. But where did they go? Did they retain a connection within the Christian world or did they walk away from all religion and spirituality?

Of the seventy-three stories of people leaving fundamentalist evangelicalism, twenty-six individuals stayed within Christianity and twenty-six indicated they became either agnostics or atheists. Thirteen were left with unanswered questions, they wrestled with old beliefs, and they were unsure of what they believed. Eight still considered themselves to be spiritual, but not necessarily Christian. They went to other religions or spiritualities, such as Buddhism, Wicca, or Universalism.

People who remained within Christianity changed to denominations in which there was more freedom of belief, more equality, and freedom of lifestyle: places where they were accepted as they were and where questions and doubts were not seen as weaknesses. Jacob Shelley felt he didn't have to conform to a prescribed kind of Christianity anymore. He was "completely liberated, free to question and challenge, think and explore, without fear or condemnation."[147] He felt that "leaving fundamentalism doesn't necessarily lead to agnosticism, atheism, or scepticism . . . leaving fundamentalism doesn't mean leaving faith—if anything, it allows for a sincere pursuit of faith."[148] Some have remained ministers, but changed to more liberal churches. Robert Price became left-wing neo-orthodox. For him "the anxiety of doubt had passed into the adventure of discovery. It was like being born again."[149] An

146. Barr, *Escaping From Fundamentalism*, viii.
147. Shelley, "Life Stages," 134.
148. Ibid., 123.
149. Price, "Beyond Born Again," 145.

anonymous writer indicates that she/he is free of fundamentalism, but has not separated from the people or institutions, "I choose to flirt with the possibilities of the future rather than untangle the complexities of the past or grapple with the tasks and pains of separation."[150] Harvey Cox became interested in ecumenical-evangelical dialogue.[151] Mike and Karla Yaconnelli established their own church, the Grace Community Church, for "people who don't like to go to church."[152] Virginia Ramey Mollenkott still believed that "the Ultimate, the Sacred, God Herself is everywhere at the core of everything and everyone."[153] She talked about experiencing a "holy instant" during meditation, when she saw herself as "a sinless Self traveling through eternity and temporarily having human experiences in a body known as Virginia Ramey Mollenkott."[154]

James Barr indicated that his purpose in writing *Escaping from Fundamentalism* was "to offer help to those who have grown up in the world of fundamentalism or have become committed to it but who have in the end come to feel that it is a prison from which they must escape."[155] The feeling of needing to escape was very strong for the individuals who gave up Fundamentalism. Several indicated they were much happier and felt a sense of freedom. Charles Templeton wrote that "when finally I shook free of Christianity, it was like being born again."[156] Skip Porteous stopped believing in sin and it set him free.[157] Kirsten Cruzen, upon realizing the humanity of those who interpret the Bible, said, "I lost the faith I needed to surrender it all."[158]

A number had difficulty forgetting their prior religious experiences in fundamentalism. They looked back with nostalgia to their experiences as fundamentalist evangelicals and wished to recover elements of what they left behind. Austin Miles wrote that one day he might find God, "I lost God in church. Maybe by leaving the church, I will get back

---

150. Anonymous, "The Naked Empress," 205.

151. Cox, "An Ecumenical/Evangelical Dialogue, 93.

152. Yaconnelli, "Behind the Wittenburg Door," 181.

153. Mollenfott, *Sensuous Spirituality*, 3.

154. Ibid.

155. Barr, *Escaping From Fundamentalism*, vii.

156. Templeton, "Inside Evangelism," 285.

157. Skip Porteous, "How I Walked Away," 1995, http://www.skeptictank.org /files//fw/porteous.htm.

158. Noless, *Jesus Girls*, 117.

to God."[159] Christine Wicker wrote that "in some buried part of my soul, I still miss that sweet safety, that sense of being chosen, of having an in with God that would withstand anything in life."[160] Edward Babinski, in studying near-death experiences, indicated that the evidence he found for life after death made him a happier man.[161] Kevin Henke defined agnosticism as the assertion that there is "not enough evidence to commit oneself to a faith that is based on accepting the existence of deities that cannot be readily seen or even detected. On the other hand, the agnostic is not so bold as to deny the possibility that one or more deities may exist somewhere."[162] He left the door open for believing in a deity.

There were those who were unsure of what they believed after they left fundamentalist evangelicalism and some were left with nagging doubts and uncertainty. Although Keith Dixon talked of his "quiet joy of being," which he achieved by living in the present, he admitted to having no clear answers, but taking care not to give in to pain, fear, and confusion, "the path is blissfully uncharted."[163] Julie Rak, now outside of evangelical faith, was no longer sure what her faith meant to her.[164] Leia Minaker didn't think there was any proof that God exists, but admitted she might be wrong. She was no longer sure of her beliefs and didn't think there were any pat answers.[165] Patton Dodd considered himself to be in middle territory, which he claimed to be the only honest way. Not having given up on Christianity completely, he wrote, "Once an evangelical, always an evangelical. If not in terms of belief or practice, then at least in terms of mental residue. They say you can never go home again, but you can never really leave home, either."[166] Jon Sweeney, who joined the Episcopal Church, no longer believed in a literal hell, but the old tapes were still playing in his head. He wrote, "My heart still fears it . . . I have wondered many times if I could or should renounce every ounce of questioning thought and turn back to fundamentalism."[167]

159. Miles, *Don't Call Me Brother*, 316.

160. Wicker, *God Knows My Heart*, 3.

161. Babinski, "If it Wasn't for Agnosticism," 224.

162. Henke, "A Little Horse Sense," 251.

163. Dixon, "The Ministry Revisited," 94.

164. Rak, "Looking Back at Sodom," 107.

165. Minaker, "Are You a 'Real' Christian?", 190.

166. Dodd, *My Faith So Far*, xi.

167. Sweeney, *born again and again*, 149.

Christine Rosen wrote that she learned a lot from her years as a fundamentalist, and although she lives a secular life, she still sometimes reads the Bible.[168] Joseph Simons wrote that "God may be there, but probably not in the way many of us imagine. . . . I do concede that a part of us may apprehend God, leaving us with a sense of the divine."[169]

For those leaving fundamentalist evangelicalism it can mean leaving friends, a close-knit community, and a certain security that comes from knowing what you believe. For those who find an alternate community to join, there is freedom from the guilt and fear that was instilled in them when they were part of the fundamentalist evangelical movement.

Another way of understanding the process of leaving fundamentalism is to consider the relationship of deconversion to stages of faith and levels of consciousness, which leads us to the next chapter.

168. Rosen, *My Fundamentalist Education*, 173.

169. Simons, "Rapture, Community, and Individualist Hope," 37.

9

Stages of Faith and Levels of Consciousness

RESEARCHERS SUCH AS JEAN Piaget have determined that humans develop through different stages. Eventually the concept of growth through stages was applied to a number of aspects of human development: cognitive, moral, emotional, etc. James Fowler has done pioneer work in applying the concept of stages of development to faith. Others have since built on his work.

The stages of faith are not necessarily linear. People may go back and forth from one stage to another or they may be in several stages at once. Even though they have left the mentality associated with one stage, they may still be emotionally drawn to that stage, as in Jon Sweeney's case. He writes, "While I may no longer believe in a literal place of hell with my head, my heart still fears it. . . . Fundamentalist clergy . . . often teach that people like me will be going to hell when they die. I have wondered many times if I could or should renounce every ounce of questioning thought and turn back to fundamentalism."[1] How can we make sense of Sweeney's experience?

In the model that Ken Wilber calls the "integral model," he writes about levels of consciousness that are "milestones of growth and development."[2] In the area of spiritual development, Wilber indicates the word "spiritual" can take on four different meanings: (1) spirituality as the highest level of any developmental line; (2) spiritual consciousness as its own developmental line; (3) spirituality as a special peak

1. Sweeney, *born again and again*, 149.
2. Wilber, *Integral Spirituality*, 5.

experience; or (4) spirituality as an attitude, such as a feeling of love.[3] In this chapter, I will discuss the stages of spiritual growth and development using the second meaning. In other words, within the context of the Christian tradition, how can we understand spiritual growth as a line of development from childhood to adulthood? What are the stages through which people can progress from an initial understanding of spirituality or religious belief to a more complex, nuanced understanding? And what effect does this have on the nature of one's belief system? What is involved in the process of moving from one stage to another and how does this help to understand what Sweeney was going through?

I will examine two theories of stages of faith/levels of consciousness, that of James Fowler and Jim Marion and then propose my own stages and discuss how these relate to the experiences of those who have left fundamentalist evangelicalism.

In Fowler's books, *Stages of Faith: The Psychology of Human Development and the Quest for Meaning*; *Becoming Adult, Becoming Christian: Adult Development and Christian Faith*; and *Faith Development and Pastoral Care*, he describes six stages of faith.[4] Even though his theories of stages of faith were developed twenty-five years ago, I still find them applicable to the discussion of the process of people leaving their fundamentalist faith.

Jim Marion, in *Putting on the Mind of Christ: The Inner Work of Christian Spirituality*, draws on the work of Ken Wilber and discusses levels of consciousness as they relate to one's journey within the Christian tradition.[5] In the Foreword to Marion's book Wilber says that Marion's work is the "first book to clearly describe the entire Christian spiritual path" in terms of levels of consciousness.[6] Based on Wilber's stages of consciousness, Marion describes nine levels of consciousness as they relate to Christian spiritual development.

What follows is an examination of how Fowler's stages of faith relate to Marion's levels of consciousness, and a discussion of what happens as people transition from one stage/level to another.

---

3. Ibid., 100–2.

4. Fowler, *Stages of Faith, Becoming Adult,* and *Faith Development and Pastoral Care.*

5. Marion, *Putting on the Mind of Christ*, xi.

6. Ibid., xi–xiii.

FOWLER: PRIMAL STATE (A PRE-STAGE)
MARION: ARCHAIC CONSCIOUSNESS

Fowler refers to the "primal state" or "undifferentiated faith" as a pre-stage from in utero to two years old.[7] The infant does not differentiate between herself/himself and the mother. Marion says that within the first two years the infant develops both physical and emotional differentiation. When children are in a nurturing home, they have a basic trust in the parent(s) during this time and this can pay great dividends for their faith development later on.

FOWLER: INTUITIVE-PROJECTIVE FAITH
MARION: MAGICAL CONSCIOUSNESS

Fowler calls the first stage the "intuitive-projective faith," which emerges with language at around two years old. This is the stage of the pre-schooler until around age seven. It is a time of self-awareness, imagination, and impulsiveness. Children see the world according to their own needs and interests. Their world centers on themselves. They want to be independent, yet they are dependent on their authority figures and learn about rewards and punishments from them. They cannot sort things out for themselves.

They have an uncomplicated acceptance of what they are told about faith. They can be "powerfully and permanently influenced" and for the children who are immersed in Christian fundamentalism, complete with teachings on sin and hell, it is not unusual for them to have a conversion experience before the age of seven.[8] In fundamentalist evangelicalism, conversion of children is seen as a good thing, after all, we don't want children to go to hell, do we? This is the reason for summer camps where children are regularly encouraged to give their hearts to Jesus. *My spouse "asked Jesus into his heart" at three years old and I did it at seven years old. At that time, I believed in a literal hell and definitely didn't want to go there. If saying the prayer to accept Jesus would keep me from hell, I was all for it.*

Philip Helfaer believes that in instances where children are taught these conservative beliefs, there is a risk they will take on a "precocious

7. Fowler, *Stages of Faith*, 121.
8. Fowler, *Stages of Faith*, 132–33.

identity" in which they internalize an adult Christian identity that involves commitment to Jesus, an exclusiveness with respect to their own faith tradition, and a preoccupation with doing God's will.[9] If this happens, it is difficult for children to develop their own identity in adolescence. Helfaer claims that "there is, in one sense, no adolescence in the life of the individual who typifies the pattern of precocious identity formation."[10]

Transition to the Next Stage

Children transition to the next stage when they begin to think concretely and are trying to sort out the difference between reality and fantasy.

FOWLER: MYTHIC-LITERAL FAITH
MARION: MYTHIC CONSCIOUSNESS

Between ages seven and ten, children enter the second stage of faith, what Fowler calls the "mythic-literal faith." They are beginning to understand cause and effect. They know there are consequences for their behaviour. They want to believe and behave in such a way as to please God. At this stage there is complete confidence in the tradition they have appropriated.

They are not tolerant of any views except their own, views they have learned from parents, schoolteachers, and religious leaders. If these contradict each other, the child has to choose which one will be authoritative for them. They may also believe in other mythic entities, such as Santa Claus, the Easter bunny, and the tooth fairy, believing that if they are good, they will be rewarded. For the child raised in the Christian tradition, Christianity is seen as the only true religion and God is the "Sky-God" (the God living up there in sky) who is there to give them what they ask for. They believe the Bible stories in a literal-factual way, i.e., the star really did stop over Bethlehem to indicate to the magi where Jesus was born and God really did create the world in six days.

9. Helfaer, *The Psychology of Religious Doubt*, 129.
10. Ibid., 136.

Farrell Till writes of his strong childhood belief in the literal-factual interpretation of the Bible, "As a child, I was dutifully taken to Sunday School by my mother and cousins. I heard the doctrine of biblical inerrancy proclaimed in Bible classes and from the pulpit, so I grew up believing what I had been taught: the Bible was a perfectly harmonious book from cover to cover; over forty men, writing over a period of 1,500 years, living in different cultures and speaking different languages, had produced a collection of sixty-six books that contained no inconsistencies or contradictions. I really believed it!"[11] Till's experience shows how the first fundamental, authority of Scripture, can cement the belief into consciousness. The belief in the Bible as absolute authority provides certainty. Following from this, other fundamentals are held with the same confidence.

Christians operating at the level of mythic consciousness believe the Christian way is the only true way to God. Others need to be converted to Christianity in order to save them from hell. There is little tolerance for other religious traditions. Fowler says "from this stage on, we are dealing with ways of being in faith that can typify adults as well as the age groups where they most typically have their rise."[12] Marion believes that Christianity has, for the most part, remained at this level for the last two thousand years.[13]

At this stage people value the Bible stories and beliefs and are not able to stand back and critically reflect on what they believe. *As an adolescent, I believed the stories in the Bible were true and that they happened exactly in the way they were written. I believed that my faith tradition was the only true one; even all those who belonged to other Christian denominations were bound for hell.*

Kirsten Cruzen writes, "I began to identify with my mother's desire to surrender all. I embraced my faith radically and vigilantly. My friends and I challenged each other to remember Jesus' imminent return. Would we be ready? Would we have saved enough souls?"[14] As a teenager, Cruzen, whose parents were missionaries, had completely bought into their belief system, including giving all to Jesus, expecting his return to earth, and taking on the responsibility of saving souls.

11. Till, *From Preacher to Skeptic*, 293.
12. Fowler, *Becoming Adult, Becoming Christian*, 57.
13. Marion, *Putting on the Mind of Christ*, 47.
14. Cruzen, *Surviving the Call to Missions*, 112.

In this stage, if people do have doubts and questions, they assume it is because they don't have enough faith. In fundamentalist evangelicalism, this stage may continue into the teenage years, as was the case for me. *In high school I listened daily to a religious radio broadcast called "Back to the Bible." On one broadcast they were advertising a pamphlet that told how you could be sure you were saved. This struck an immediate chord with me. I had been struggling with this question for some time and was very tempted to write in and ask to receive the pamphlet. I thought this might give me assurance of salvation. In the end I didn't send for it. It is clear to me now that at the time I was beginning the transition to the next stage of faith, but I was still stuck in the mythic-literal level of consciousness.*

Many people go through adulthood at this level.

Transition to the Next Stage

One of the reasons it is so difficult to leave this stage of faith is that there is a lot of security in believing that there is a Sky-God who is in full control and who cares for you personally. Sweeney writes of the challenge to leave this stage when he says, "The old-time paradigm for God in the world still makes sense to me; I cannot shake it. I know that we are supposed to take on a more scientific worldview in which God leaves heaven above and becomes a force in the world all about us; in which God is no longer waiting to listen like a friend or a kindly grandparent to our needs and troubles. . . . But, I cannot completely do it."[15]

In the transition to the next stage, the child asks questions of meaning and begins to see the limitations of taking the Bible in a literal way. This may result in becoming disillusioned with those who taught them. Because the literal-factual way of understanding the Bible is so forcefully engrained in fundamentalist evangelicals, this stage may come later in life.

It was not until my late teenage years that I began to have questions about what the Bible said. For this reason, I took a course in Koine Greek in my first year college, thinking this would give me access to the New Testament in its original language.

---

15. Sweeney, *born again and again*, 51.

FOWLER: SYNTHETIC-CONVENTIONAL FAITH

Children generally move into the third stage of faith, the "synthetic-conventional faith," in early adolescence.[16] By synthetic, Fowler means that people tend to synthesize their values and beliefs to create an integrated identity.[17] These values come from peers, the media, school, and the religious community. And by conventional he means that the values and beliefs they hold are those of the group or groups to which they belong and are not examined critically. They cannot reflect on their values objectively. When adults are at this stage of faith, they have a strong sense of community, hold onto their faith, and work hard in the church. For fundamentalist evangelicals, their identity is formed primarily by association with their religious community.

There is still a strong attachment to the fundamentals. However, these start to be held in a somewhat nuanced way with greater complexity of thought. This can be manifest in two ways. First, there is an indwelling of other worlds of meaning, such as science, sports, business, the arts, or whatever might be of particular interest to individuals. Since it may be difficult to fit these worlds into the fundamentalist worldview, the question becomes, "How can I lead a Christian life as an artist or a business woman or a football player?" There may be ethical issues at stake. Second, Christian apologetics start to be important as people try to harmonize the Bible with science, history, and psychology.

Transition to the Next Stage

When people see contradictions in biblical narratives and when they start to question the community's values and beliefs, they are ready to move on to the next stage. Fowler says that two things have to happen in the transition to the fourth stage of faith. First, individuals start to critically examine the beliefs that were tacitly held before, and second, they start believing in their own truth that they find within instead of being guided by external authorities, "the self . . . must struggle with the question of identity and worth, apart from its previously defining connections. . . . Persons must take into themselves much of the authority

16. Fowler, *Becoming Adult, Becoming Christian*, 57.
17. Ibid., 59.

they previously invested in others for determining and sanctioning their goals and values.[18]

Fowler says that "many religious groups reinforce a conventionally held and maintained faith system, sanctifying one's remaining in the dependence on external authority."[19] This is certainly the case in fundamentalist evangelicalism where the hope of heaven and the fear of hell is explicitly tied to a prescribed way of believing. It takes a bold step to question these beliefs.

As an adult I attended the Mennonite Brethren Biblical Seminary. Here I continued my study of Koine Greek, translating portions of the New Testament for myself. And it was here that I first questioned the fundamentalist evangelical view of the role of women in the home and in the church. I did not agree with the interpretation of biblical texts that indicated women should be subordinate to their husbands and should not give religious instruction in situations where men were present. This did not seem right to me but since I still had a literal view of the Bible, I was unable to come to terms with it. It wasn't until a number of years later that I conducted an exegesis on 1 Timothy 2:8–15, (see chapter 6), the text that was used in fundamentalist evangelical communities to prevent women from holding leadership positions in church. But even after I had done the exegesis of this text, I still had difficulty viewing the Bible metaphorically. The teaching of the literal truth of the Bible was too entrenched in my mind and body. But the transition had begun and there was no going back.

The transition may be difficult and painful and it may take years to move from one stage to the next. In some cases, people may lose an entire community of Christians with whom they were closely connected for many years. In terms of their identity needs, they may lose their need for *connection*. They may, in fact, no longer feel connected to God. And their need for *recognition* may fade because the community will realize they do not believe quite the same way as they do. If anything, they may get negative recognition, which brings shame. Their need to *take action* may diminish because they may no longer feel comfortable participating in many of the community's activities, especially as they pertain to leadership roles. They may experience a feeling of loss and loneliness, both the loss of the *security* that came with beliefs held so dearly and the loss of relationships and community as they begin to question firmly held values

18. Fowler, *Faith Development and Pastoral Care*, 68.

19. Fowler, *Stages of Faith*, 178.

and beliefs. The literal-factual way of seeing religious beliefs no longer satisfy them. Even though most of their identity needs are not currently being met in their present community, it may still be difficult to leave it, unless there is an alternative that will meet their needs for meaning, connection, recognition, action, and security.

In this transition people may have disagreements with church leaders. They may also have an identity crisis of faith in which they no longer know what to believe. Sandra Colter, who was part of a ministry team as a young adult, felt closely bonded to the others on the team.[20] Even though she had questions about the efficacy of prayer and she doubted whether God really could speak to people, she remained in the community for some time, pretending that she was experiencing the same kind of spirituality evident in the others. Sandra was in a transition period, and, as it turned out, she soon moved to the next stage of faith.

There can also be confusion and guilt for not believing the teachings as they were taught. When Julie Rak discovered that her church believed homosexuality to be a sin, she had to leave the church. She writes that "if the price of obedience is your dignity and integrity as a person, then obedience to a tradition that marginalizes the essence of who you are is going to result in spiritual death." [21] Rak did not leave happily and she was left with not knowing what her faith meant to her.

It wasn't until much later in my own life that I realized I had to say good-bye to the security of a literal faith, even though it actually hadn't provided me much security for a long time. I questioned commonly held interpretations of biblical texts and began to hold interpretations differently than the others in my church community.

FOWLER: INDIVIDUATIVE-REFLECTIVE FAITH
MARION: RATIONAL CONSCIOUSNESS

Fowler says that people may enter the fourth stage of faith, the "individuative-reflective faith," in young adulthood. This is when the shift has been made from dependence on external authorities to reliance on the self as authority. They do not accept leadership if they are not allowed to also think for themselves. This is what happened to Dewey Beegle,

20. Sandra Colter (not her real name), interview, June 18, 2007.
21. Rak, *Looking Back at Sodom*, 106.

who had to leave his church as a result of his view of biblical inspiration: "I could not honestly sign the creedal claim of 'inerrancy' because it meant accepting the theories developed during the modernist-fundamentalist battle in the late nineteenth and early twentieth centuries."[22] *While I no longer depended on the authority of church leaders, I was not sure whether I could rely on myself as the authority.*

Beliefs once tacitly held are now critically examined. At one point in his life, Keith Dixon, formerly a church minister, realized he no longer believed the doctrines he had been taught, "Claims that could not be scientifically verified were dubious to me. The Bible had become for me a collage of historical, poetic, and mystical writings."[23] At this stage, one is able to take a step back and reflect on one's belief system. Religious symbols formerly taken at face value are now demythologized. *As I conducted more biblical research, I came to understand biblical story as metaphor and that the Bible was written by people who wrote about their experience of the Divine, rather than a book in which God told people what to believe.*

People start to think more abstractly and realize that there are different ways of knowing and believing. They put aside the idea that God lives in the sky. The Sky-God consciousness they are leaving includes the idea that God is a personal entity who acts decisively in the world. The idea that God is out punishing evildoers in a manner reminiscent of a literal reading of biblical texts is now untenable. But churches are often not prepared to answer their questions. This is corroborated in the stories I read. Christine Rosen questioned the Keswick Christian School's teaching on fundamentalist beliefs, but she quickly discovered there were certain questions she was not allowed to ask.[24]

But this is also the level at which one struggles for meaning. There is obviously no Sky-God for those at this stage and for many "God is dead. And we may know of no other God to replace the one that has been lost."[25] Kenneth Daniels, upon reading about other religious perspectives, became a humanist. He had been desperate to remain a fundamentalist Christian, writing that "I was far from eager to give it up, praying and

22. Beegle, *Journey to Freedom*, 70.

23. Dixon, *The Ministry Revisited*, 88.

24. Rosen, *My Fundamentalist Education*, 108.

25. Marion, *Putting on the Mind of Christ*, 66.

seeking reading material to convince myself it had to be true."[26] But it didn't happen for him. He writes that, after leaving Christianity, he sometimes felt that his life lacked the significance it once had.[27]

The church wants people to remain at the mythic level. When individuals within the Christian tradition try to make sense of their Christian beliefs from a rational perspective, they may not get the support they need from the community. As a result they may leave the Christian faith. But Marion makes the point that, in doing so, they have actually progressed to the next level of consciousness and have become more like Jesus in that they have become "more tolerant, less judgmental, more compassionate, more inclusive."[28] Marion asserts that fundamentalism has remained at the mythic level, "In religion, that most conservative of human institutions, not only millions of adherents but many in leadership positions lag behind in the mythic level. Fundamentalist religions, in no matter what religion it is found . . . is chiefly characterized by its holding on to the mythic worldview and its exclusion from 'salvation' of those who do not adhere to that worldview."[29]

Many fundamentalist evangelicals remain in the third stage of faith, the Synthetic-Conventional, where authority for their beliefs and interpretation of the Bible rests solely in the church leadership. They never let go of the Sky-God. For some, letting go of the image of God that captivated their religious identity is devastating. They can become depressed, thinking there is no longer any meaning in life. Some even commit suicide. When one cannot find a place of support, considering that fundamentalist evangelical churches view such people as a threat, it becomes a lonely journey. They may be viewed as intellectuals, rebels, backsliders, and on the side of the devil. They are demonized by fundamentalist evangelicals.

Transition to the Next Stage

In the transition to the next stage of faith, people begin to be open to other faith traditions. They start to doubt that their own tradition is the only true way as they begin to take into account the perspectives

26. Daniels, *Why I Believed*, 97.

27. Ibid., 317.

28. Marion, *Putting on the Mind of Christ*, 55.

29. Ibid., 60.

of other people and other groups. This transition could take years, a contact here and a contact there, a letting go of defensiveness about their own faith tradition and letting go of the idea that there is only true way of believing. Susan Campbell, who struggled with the misogyny of the church, found this transition difficult. She was left with a feeling of aloneness. She realized that "the real Jesus wouldn't have loved me less because of my gender," but she called herself a floater within Christianity, "I am still seeking. I will arm-wrestle with God for a while longer."[30]

FOWLER: CONJUNCTIVE FAITH
MARION: VISION-LOGIC CONSCIOUSNESS

From approximately age thirty-five and beyond, a person may reach the stage of "conjunctive faith." In this stage the individual realizes that life is more complex than they formerly thought. They can hold polarities together, they can see both their masculine and feminine sides, they can hold both a conscious and a shadow self. They can live with ambiguities and paradoxes, yet they have a receptivity that opens the way for symbolic and mystical experiences. Body, emotions, and mind are fully integrated.

They develop a global perspective and an openness to the truths of other traditions, religions, cultures, and philosophies, and while they may stay within their own faith tradition, they are not single-mindedly devoted to it.[31] Fowler writes that "one begins to make peace with the tension arising from the fact that truth must be approached from a number of different directions and angles of vision."[32] They have a humility about the beliefs they formerly held as true because they know "that the symbols, stories, doctrines, and liturgies offered by its own or other traditions are inevitably partial, limited to a particular people's experience of God and incomplete."[33] There is a readiness for dialogue with people of other faith traditions, believing that this can enrich their own faith. Sweeney, a former Baptist missionary, came to see that other Christian traditions than Baptist were acceptable. He came to believe that "souls . . . no longer looked so desperate. I was no longer convinced

---

30. Campbell, *Dating Jesus*, 205.
31. Fowler, *Becoming Adult, Becoming Christian*, 64–67.
32. Fowler, *Faith Development and Pastoral Care*, 72.
33. Fowler, *Stages of Faith*, 186.

that they were in fact dying."[34] Sweeney joined the Episcopalian tradition and he became open to accepting other religious traditions as valid.

This stage can lead to "a deepened quality of spirituality in which one hungers for ways to relate to the otherness in self, God, and fellow humans."[35] *When I began to see the validity of other faith perspectives and spiritualities, I no longer felt that Christianity was the only "true" religion. I had contact with Muslims, Jewish people, and Aboriginal people. I learned that these traditions have a lot to offer and that knowledge of these can enrich one's own spirituality. I learned that there are many valid worldviews and spiritual paths.*

With this development the despair and grief over the loss of the Sky-God is replaced with a spiritual growth that is nurtured by wisdom and insight from a variety of places, ideologies, other religious traditions.

FOWLER: UNIVERSALIZING FAITH
MARION: PSYCHIC CONSCIOUSNESS, SUBTLE CONSCIOUSNESS, CHRIST CONSCIOUSNESS AND NONDUAL CONSCIOUSNESS

In Fowler's sixth and final stage, "universalizing faith," the self is no longer at the centre. People have given up the self in order to understand the world through others' eyes. The self is completely relinquished to God, the ground of Being.[36] Fowler indicates that very few actually reach this stage, referring to Gandhi, Martin Luther King, Jr., and Mother Teresa as some who have achieved it.

Marion adds four final levels of consciousness: "psychic," "subtle," "Christ," and "nondual." At the psychic level of consciousness, information is received from the extrasensory. Marion claims that the person at this level has "awakened to the deeper part of self, the permanent part of self that transcends space and time."[37] Subtle consciousness is what Marion says is achieved by mystics. They may feel energy vibrations and communicate with spiritual beings, like angels, who become their spiritual guides. In Christ consciousness and nondual consciousness

34. Sweeney, *born again and again*, 97.

35. Fowler, *Faith Development and Pastoral Care*, 74.

36. Fowler, *Faith Development and Pastoral Care*, 75.

37. Marion, *Putting on the Mind of Christ*, 70.

there is a total surrender to God and the individual's divinity is fully realized. This person can "live solely in the present, curiously detached from everyday struggles and anxieties."[38] Marion says that some mystics have achieved this level. It is a place of bliss. These last three levels of consciousness appear to be similar to Fowler's stage of universalizing faith, in which the person and the Divine are one.

NEUFELD REDEKOP STAGES

As I reflected on the experiences of those who had left fundamentalist evangelicalism in the light of the Fowler and Marion analysis, a new paradigm of stages of spiritual growth emerged, stages specific to those growing out of fundamentalist evangelicalism. My model is informed by the stories of former fundamentalist evangelicals. The table below shows Fowler's and Marion's models as well as my own.

TABLE 5. MODELS OF STAGES OF FAITH AND LEVELS OF CONSCIOUSNESS

Fowler Stages	Marion Levels of Consciousness	Neufeld Redekop Stages
Primal State (a pre-stage)	Archaic	
Intuitive–Projective	Magical	
Mythical-Literal	Mythic	Literal-Factual
Synthetic-Conven-tional		
Individuative-Reflective	Rational	Complex-Questioning
Conjunctive	Vision-Logic	Integrative
Conjunctive (continued)	Vision-Logic (continued)	Inclusive
Universalizing	Psychic	
	Subtle	
	Christ	
	Nondual Consciousness	

38. Ibid., 183.

Introducing the Neufeld Redekop Model

In my analysis of individuals' stories, I found that the journey within and out of the fundamentalist evangelical movement can take place within a range of at least four stages, which I have named "literal-factual," "questioning," "integrative," and "inclusive." I found that faith is possible at all these stages, and people can be secure or insecure in their faith at all stages, but the nature of faith evolves and changes if people move from one stage to the next. I will first describe these four developmental stages and then show how they are brought to life in the stories of the "witnesses" introduced in the previous chapter.

Literal-Factual Stage

When people join the fundamentalist evangelical movement, whether they have been in the community since birth or whether they became members of a fundamentalist evangelical church later in life, they usually enter a community of faith at the literal-factual stage of faith, comparable to Fowler's mythical-literal stage and Marion's mythic consciousness level. For them, the Bible is the only spiritual authority and it is believed in a literal-factual way. This means that what is written in the Bible is historical fact and it is literally true when read at face value. Eve was created from Adam's rib and it was Eve who started Adam on the road to sin by offering him a piece of fruit from the tree of which they were told by God not to eat. Noah really did build the ark and took male and female of every animal with him into the ark. Daniel was in the lion's den. Mary was a virgin when she conceived Jesus; God was the father of Jesus. Jesus is the only way to God, just like Jesus says in John 14:6, "I am the way, and the truth, and the life. No one comes to the Father except through me." By Jesus' death he atoned for the sins of all people and on the third day he was physically resurrected. He went back "up" to heaven, "as they were watching, he was lifted up, and a cloud took him out of their sight" (Acts 1:9). They believe the Sky-God, a God who lives up there somewhere. Songs like "Face to Face" reinforce this belief, "Face to face shall I behold him, far beyond the starry sky," and "When My Life-Work is Ended": "How my full heart will praise him for the mercy, love, and grace that prepare for me a mansion in the sky."

They see Jesus as the Son of God and the only way to God. Everyone is in need of salvation through Jesus' crucifixion because all have sinned. They believe that one day Jesus will come back to earth to get his people. This will happen at the sound of a trumpet and then Jesus will come in the clouds where his people will meet him in the air (1 Thess 4:16–17). Those who are not saved will go to hell, a fiery place, a place of punishment for unforgiven sin. Those who have been converted will go to heaven, a place where God and Jesus are and where all will be bliss.

People live out their faith by their upright lives and generous spirit. They practice what they believe. They strive to live in a way consistent with literal-factual interpretations of some parts of the Bible, such as the admonition to be patient, loving, slow to anger, compassionate, etc. They experience love in the community of faith.

God answers believers' prayers. That's what the Bible says. If God does not answer a particular prayer, it means that either the person's faith was not strong enough or it was not God's will to answer that prayer. Any verse in the Bible can be believed exactly as it is written. For all intents and purposes, God wrote the Bible and it makes sense just as it was written.

The spiritual practices of the faith seem to work for them. They attend church regularly. They pray. They read their Bible. They believe they can receive direct guidance from God. God can speak to them.

They are not encouraged to try to understand other systems of belief or read literature outside of the fundamentalist evangelical perspective. Doing so might cause them to "backslide" out of the movement, which would be bad, because then they would be on the road to hell.

Figure 4. Don't Ask Don't Think

If fundamentalist evangelicals are questioned by someone who points out any inconsistencies or contradictions in the Bible, this does not disturb them. They are quite content to leave the "problems" others see in the Bible in God's hands. They know that God is in control and even though they may not understand, God does, and some day when they see Jesus face to face, they will understand too.

The first understanding children have of the Bible is at the literal-factual stage. They do not question what they are taught. If they begin to have doubts about the validity of the teachings received at this stage, and if their questions are not answered to their satisfaction, they may move to the questioning stage. But this is not necessarily a matter of age. As children grow up to be teenagers and then adults, they may stay at the literal-factual stage or they may start to ask questions about what they have been taught.

The Complex-Questioning Stage

At the complex-questioning stage, which is similar to Fowler's individuative-reflective stage and Marion's rational consciousness level,
the Bible is still significant, and perhaps authoritative to a degree, but
people begin to see inconsistencies and contradictions in the Bible and
try to make sense of them. They ask questions, explore new insights,
and start to become more tolerant and less defensive. When Dennis
Ronald MacDonald saw inconsistencies in the Bible, he decided to
study Greek and he began to interpret the New Testament for himself,
concluding that "the New Testament is not the revelation of a divine
plan for humankind that can be captured somehow in a system. . . . The
New Testament is a witness to how some early Christians themselves
constructed meaningful symbolic worlds."[39]

At this stage people may do some reading outside the scope of
fundamentalist evangelicalism and as a result, they may question what
they have been told by their religious authorities, like parents, teachers, and preachers. When Pamela Brown-Seely observed the demise of
televangelists and the immoral behaviour of other church leaders, she
lost her confidence in their interpretation of the Bible.[40]

When Christine Rosen started to question what she had been told
about evolution and wanted to read more on the subject, her Christian
teachers restricted the kinds of books she was allowed to read.[41] In the
mind of the teachers she might become confused about what to believe.
She may find they do not have all the answers to the questions their
friends or colleagues are asking about the Bible. She may also become
disillusioned when observing fundamentalist evangelical Christians
who are not living up to the values that have been instilled by the movement. At this stage, people are starting to question whether, indeed,
Jesus is the only way to God. And they are questioning the reality of
heaven and hell. They are not so sure that people are born in sin nor
that they need to be saved.

Usually the questioning stage commences when children become
adolescents and teenagers. Fundamentalist evangelicals call this "rebel-
ling." The fundamentalist evangelical church has no answers for them,

---

39. MacDonald, "From Faith to Faith," 115.

40. McKnight and Ondrey, *Finding Faith, Losing Faith*, 27.

41. Rosen, *My Fundamentalist Education*," 79.

because adult members themselves have not questioned what they were taught. Every effort is made to keep teenagers in the church, but without taking their questions seriously. These teens will either be convinced that their questions are inappropriate and thus stop asking, or they will keep on asking. If they don't get satisfactory answers, they may leave the church. Since fundamentalist evangelical indoctrination is so powerful, people may not reach this stage until they are adults.

The last two stages in my model are comparable to Fowler's conjunctive stage and Marion's vision-logic level of consciousness with the difference being that in the integrative stage, the Bible may still be seen as an important source of wisdom and inspiration, but people examine biblical texts using insights from biblical scholarship and higher criticism, and in the inclusive stage people accept other religions as valid ways of knowing God.

The Integrative Stage

At the third stage, the "integrative stage," people are not afraid to become informed by scholars who are outside fundamentalist evangelicalism. When they do this, their minds are opened up to new ways of thinking and being. When Sweeney studied the Bible for himself, appropriating higher criticism, he found that he had to rethink the doctrines of atonement and hell.[42]

They are open to learning from other disciplines, such as history, biology, physics, sociology, psychology, and anthropology and relate what they have learned to what they believe about the Bible. They realize that the Bible is not a historical book, but a religious book, a book written by fallible human beings who were providing their own versions of their experiences and what they understood of the character and actions of their God.

They no longer believe in a Sky-God, realizing that in this vast universe, there is no God "up in the sky." They do not see hell as a place of fire, nor heaven as a place of mansions where God and Jesus dwell.

They no longer see Jesus as the only way to God. They may see "sin" as simply messing up and salvation as a way to get out of the messed up situation. This is how Jon Sweeney sees it, "We all need saving—again

42. Sweeney, *born again and again*, 147, 149.

and again—from greed, hate, selfishness, and all of the other vices that consume us. . . . The formula was not as simple as I was led to believe."[43]

The Inclusive Stage

The fourth stage, the "inclusive stage," is the stage at which people do not believe that Christianity is the only way to God. The Bible may still be seen as a source of wisdom, enlightenment, and spiritual direction but not authoritative in the sense that they have to abide by the literal-factual words of the text. It doesn't matter to them from where their insights come; they come from many different sources.

They accept all peoples unconditionally, regardless of religion, gender, race, ethnicity, ability, or sexual orientation. This is what happened to Christine Wicker, when as a religious reporter she had to interview people from other religions.[44] This opened her mind to the validity of all religions. At this stage, whether people remain within Christianity or whether they do not, they are open to learning from other religious traditions and incorporating these ideas and practices into their own spiritual life.

When people who are at the inclusive stage are part of a community that is at the literal-factual stage they are confronted with the choice of remaining in their community, even though they disagree with certain practices and policies, or of leaving the community. People at the literal-factual stage are often unable to accept what those at the inclusive stage are perceiving and experiencing.

God is no longer seen as a personal being, but rather in everything that exists. Jesus may be seen as a prophet with spiritual powers. There is no need for salvation and therefore no need for the doctrine of atonement, so firmly believed in the literal-factual stage. There is no hell nor heaven.

It is important to realize that people may be perfectly happy at any stage and that the movement from one stage to another, for whatever reason, may not necessarily be smooth. They may be partially in one stage and partially in another. They may move to one stage and then go back to the previous one. Or they may be in transition.

43. Ibid., 105.

44. Wicker, *God Knows My Heart*, 106–7, 123–26.

LEAVING FUNDAMENTALIST EVANGELICALISM AND STAGES OF DYING

Jim Marion, in *The Death of the Mythic God: The Rise of Evolutionary Spirituality*, introduces another way to think of the transition out of mythic consciousness, what I call the literal-factual stage. Using Elisabeth Kübler-Ross's stages of dying,[45] he compares her five stages of dying with what people experience when they leave their belief in the Sky-God (the mythic God). He shows how historically, the Roman Catholic Church has exhibited the first three stages, those of denial, anger, and bargaining.[46]

In the stage of denial, people are shunned if they don't believe the official church doctrine. This is what happened to Galileo. The Bible, literally understood, spoke of the earth as flat, with the heaven as a dome above, so Galileo's assertion that the earth was not the centre of the universe, but in fact revolved around the sun, was a huge threat to Christian orthodoxy. The new discovery was denied by the Church and Galileo was punished. When science continued to prove Galileo's discovery, it could no longer be denied and anger was the result. Pope Pius IX, in the mid 1800s produced a list of errors in which he condemned what science was proving to be true. Then in the next century, biblical criticism and evolution began to be accepted. This was the stage of bargaining. The Church accepted some aspects of the new, while holding on to the old. In many ways, this is the stage we are still at today. Creeds have not changed since they were written. The hymns of the 1700s and 1800s are still being sung. The message remains the same. Jesus came "down" from heaven to die for the sins of humanity and has gone back "up" to heaven to prepare a place for those who accept him.

Denial

Relating the stages associated with dying to those of leaving the fundamentalist evangelical movement, we see that the first stage, that of denial, may be evident when individuals at the literal-factual stage begin to have doubts about what they have been taught. Not wanting to leave the security they experience in their belief system, they may at first be

45. Kübler-Ross, *On Death and Dying*.
46. Marion, *The Death of the Mythic God*, 31–32.

tempted to deny their doubts, to put them out of their minds. They realize what they might have to give up. Their friends and families may not have the same doubts and there are tacit pressures for them to keep silent about questions of faith. Beverly Bryant was taught that it was sin to have a same-sex partner, and when she first realized her strong feelings for a woman, she did not want to believe what was happening to her.[47] When my spouse's grandma decided to take seminary classes in her eighties, she was confronted with new theological methods. This was difficult for her to accept. She was in denial when she asked herself, "How could so many men of faith be wrong?"

Anger

People may then move on to anger; they may be angry that people in their community of faith do not see what they see, i.e., contradictions in the Bible, fallibility of the Bible, validity of science, etc. If they continue to attend church, they may become angry with the singing or the sermons, and they may experience what is sometimes called, "white knuckle Sundays," when they drive home from church with clenched hands over the steering wheel. *While in seminary, when I first became aware of the patriarchal nature of the Bible, the prevalence of biblical interpretation by men, and the general refusal in Christian communities to use inclusive language in hymns and public reading of the Bible, I became angry. I found that if the language used was male, I couldn't concentrate on any truths that might be gained from what was being said.*

Bargaining

The third stage, that of bargaining, can be a time when individuals accept what science says and accept biblical scholarship, yet still hold on to beliefs and practices firmly enough to stay within the fundamentalist evangelical community. This way, they do not lose their community; they can stay within it, although likely not as actively as they once were. Marion writes that "Christians go to church on Sunday as if entering a time warp, putting the modern rational worldview aside for an hour or two to submit to the old mythic worldview. Then they re-emerge into

47. Bryant, "Inching Along," 157.

the rational worldview by which they operate their lives and professions during the week."[48]

I was at this stage for many years. I tried to believe the old beliefs but I constantly had to reframe what I was hearing so that it matched my own evolving world view. I remained within the community but feeling less and less satisfied and more and more disconnected from the old system of belief.

Depression and Mourning

Kübler-Ross's fourth stage of the experience of dying is that of depression and mourning. At this stage you know you are going to die and the thought of it brings you to a state of depression. Relating this to the death of a belief system, or the death of belief in the Sky-God, Marion says that those at this stage may still continue to attend church, but they are already mourning the inevitable loss of their beliefs and community.[49] They know that they cannot go back to what they once believed. Susan Campbell misses the community, "I miss the fellowship, and even in my isolation, I miss that feeling of belonging to something—or trying to belong. I know I am wrapping my years in the church in a big bow of nostalgia."[50]

While still remaining part of my community, the old story and hymns did not speak to me anymore. Sometimes I benefited little from the gathering of the community for worship. I mourned the loss of faith as I once knew it.

Acceptance

The fifth stage, that of acceptance, happens when a person has finally accepted their own death. In relation to faith, when they have accepted the loss of belief in the Sky-God and the fact that they will never be able to fully participate in the fundamentalist evangelical community again, they then have reached the stage of acceptance.

---

48. Marion, *The Death of the Mythic God*, 32.

49. Ibid.

50. Campbell, *Dating Jesus*, 199.

It is important to note that just as persons who are dying may experience these stages over and over again, or several all at once, so it is with faith. There is not necessarily a linear progression from stage to stage. Individuals can be bargaining and mourning at the same time. Or, they can move from acceptance one day, back to anger the next, and then to depression the following day. There may not be a smooth transition from one stage to the next and there is no guarantee that all will arrive at the stage of acceptance.

INTERSECTION OF STAGES OF DYING WITH STAGES OF FAITH

So how do these stages of dying relate to the stages of faith discussed above? At the literal-factual stage there is full acceptance of the fundamentalist evangelical belief system, but as individuals move into the questioning stage with questions about faith, they may at first put aside these questions because they don't want to face the repercussions of doubting what they have been taught. Instead, they may deny themselves answers to the questions and keep silent about them. When they voice their questions and when the church community has no answers, or worse, chastises them for having questions, they may move into a stage of anger. At this stage, they may become angry at the hypocrisy or failure of others in the community to understand what they are going through. As they transition into the integrative stage, they may do some bargaining, accepting higher biblical criticism while still remaining in the faith community, looking the other way with regard to certain beliefs and practices. As they move to the integrative stage, they may experience depression and mourning as they realize they will not be able to retain their old beliefs and they may not be able to remain in their community of faith. This brings them sadness. If they arrive at the inclusive stage, they will likely have reached the final stage of the death of the old system that they once knew and believed, the stage of acceptance. The Sky-God has died, along with belief in the fundamentals previously held dear, and the individual believes it and accepts it.

Table 6 below shows how the stages of dying intersect with stages of faith.

TABLE 6. STAGES OF FAITH AND STAGES OF DYING AS THEY RELATE TO FUNDAMENTALIST EVANGELICALISM

Literal-Factual Stage	Complex-Questioning Stage	Integrative Stage	Inclusive Stage
	Denial and Anger	Bargaining and Mourning	Acceptance
They are not confronted with the death of their faith. They don't question.	They deny their doubts. They are angry others don't see what they see.	They leave some beliefs but hold onto others. They mourn the loss of belief and community.	They accept the loss of beliefs and community.

STORIES THAT EXEMPLIFY THE INTERSECTION OF STAGES OF DYING WITH STAGES OF FAITH

When examining the stories of those who left fundamentalist evangelicalism, we see both the pathos of loss and the joy of new beginnings. In the end, for the individual who is leaving the belief system, the stages exemplify a movement towards freedom from guilt and fear. As people move from the literal-factual stage to the complex-questioning stage, they may move on to the integrative stage or they may remain at the complex-questioning stage. This progression is shown in Figure 5.

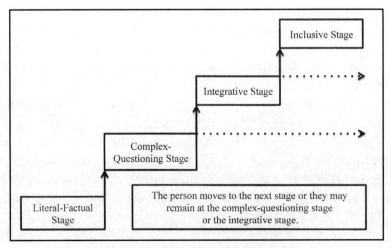

Figure 5. Stages of Faith from the Perspective of the Former Fundamentalist Evangelical

The fundamentalist evangelical church is saddened as people leave the literal-factual stage for the complex-questioning stage. From the church's perspective, shown in Figure 6, when someone progresses through the stages, it is actually seen as a regression. They are back-sliding. They are moving away from the community and the church believes the individual may even end up in hell if they continue to question their beliefs.

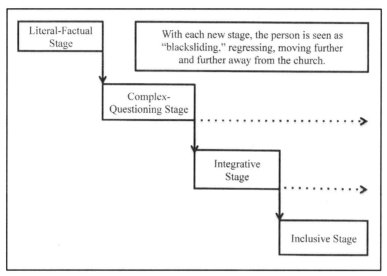

Figure 6. Stages of Faith from the Perspective
of the Fundamentalist Evangelical Church

Examining stories of those who were formerly operating at the literal-factual stage, we see that they started their journey away from fundamentalist evangelicalism because of questions and doubts. Those who questioned literal-factual interpretations of the Bible wondered about such aspects as the nature of Jesus, inerrancy of the text, original sin, belief in hell, the sinfulness of divorce, the meaning of prophecy, the position on homosexuality, and the assertion that AIDS was a punishment from God.

Some who were troubled by literal-factual biblical interpretations embarked on their own research. Howard Teeple, who was confronted with the theory of evolution at university and was troubled about the recorded words of Jesus, set out to learn what the Bible really said. Later, as a Greek scholar, and as one of the members of the International

Greek New Testament Project, he examined Greek New Testament manuscripts in libraries across Europe.[51] Others studied the history of fundamentalism, other religious traditions, philosophy, theology, science, and psychology. Their worldviews broadened as they travelled, studied other cultures, and became involved in non-fundamentalist organizations. After travelling to other countries and observing people practising other religions, Tom Harpur could no longer believe in one true faith, "tragically, each sect, cult, and denomination seems convinced that it alone is the truth in its entirety. All others are heretics."[52] People saw that their God was too small. And they started to doubt the exclusivity of Christianity.

Others were bothered by questions of an existential nature, such as the existence of God and the efficacy of prayer. They had inner spiritual conflicts. Marlene Oaks writes "Jesus, I want to believe you. . . . Oh, Jesus, where are you? With all of my heart I want to find the answer. . . . I read and reread, seeking, searching. I prayed daily and tried to talk with Jesus."[53] God seemed far away. Others saw nothing new in the Bible. They questioned the genuineness of charismatic prophecies and healings. David Rattigan, who at first didn't fall to the ground (as was expected) when hands were laid on him, became disillusioned with charismatic prophecies, believing that they were simply a result of human manipulation.[54]

Those individuals who began to question and seek answers to their questions about their faith were beginning to function at the complex-questioning stage. In transitioning from the literal-factual stage they sometimes experienced the first two stages of dying, the stages of denial and anger. At the beginning of the transition, some denied that they had any questions rather than face the fact that the answers they would be given would not satisfy them. Robert Price writes: "I was reluctant to find any weaknesses in the various arguments in favour of the resurrection of Christ, or the historicity of the gospels." [55]

Stories indicate that some were angry that their questions were left unanswered. For Jacob Shelley, "most troubling was the use of spiritual

51. Teeple, "I Started to be a Minister," 351.
52. Harpur, "Heaven and Hell," 99.
53. Oaks, "Old Time Religion is a Cult," 138.
54. Rattigan, "Fantastic Voyage," 59, 66.
55. Price, "Beyond Born Again," 147.

rhetoric either to buttress claims of authority or to discredit those—such as myself—who were dissatisfied with the rigid fundamentals and who were questioning their legitimacy. . . . The more I was exposed to the posturing, the angrier I became." [56]

Some saw inconsistencies between belief and practice. And when observing the behaviour of people who were not Christians, they saw that often these people were more upright than Christian folk. They were angry when they saw the hypocrisy of Christians. Austin Miles was horrified when he found out that Assemblies of God ministers were molesting children, and when they were discovered, they were simply moved to another district, where they repeated the crime. [57]

Some individuals felt abandoned by God, family, and friends. Leia Minaker writes that leaving fundamentalism was the most painful time in her life because it tore her family apart, a family that had been very close before, "conversations with my parents and siblings led to tears and broken hearts. . . . While my family stood together praying for my soul, I stood alone, begging to be understood and accepted for my changing way of thinking." [58] Others felt guilty about their doubts and were afraid to ask questions. At the beginning of their journey out of the literal-factual stage, they would sometimes rather deny that they had questions, than face the fact that they didn't know the answers.

In the stories I read, many individuals moved from the questioning stage to the integrative stage and later, some to the inclusive stage. Generally speaking, those who sought to integrate their new learnings into their Christian faith, remained within Christianity, while those who were unable to integrate their questions and doubts, left the church. At the integrative stage, some changed to other Christian denominations, which they felt were non-fundamentalist. These included the United Church, the Anglican Church, Greek Orthodox, Lutheran, and a left-wing neo-orthodox community. This provided them with opportunities to raise their questions openly without fear. They could happily live with ambiguities; everything was not black and white. David Rattigan writes, "Today I inhabit a different story. . . . It is a story that is not afraid to engage with those whose stories are different from mine. My world now has room for ambiguity, doubt, and uncertainty

56. Shelley, "Life Stages," 129.

57. Miles, "Don't Call Me Brother," 267.

58. Minaker, "Are You a 'Real' Christian?, 188.

without fear. I am a liberal Anglican . . ."[59] Dennis Ronald MacDonald learned to appreciate the symbolic language in the Bible without believing in its infallibility. He came to believe that "the New Testament is not the revelation of a divine plan for humankind that can be captured somehow in a system," but rather "a witness to how some early Christians themselves constructed meaningful symbolic worlds against the backdrop of mystery."[60] Individuals were able to integrate both belief and unbelief into their Christian experience. Ruth Tucker writes, "It is a mystery to me that belief and unbelief exist in ever-present tension in my life. . . . I accept the conflicts and questions as part of my psychological and spiritual makeup."[61]

At the integrative stage, people can experience both bargaining and the depressing/mourning stages of death. An anonymous writer tells of her/his decision to stay connected to the community without holding its fundamentalist beliefs, "Though I consider myself free from the enslavement of fundamentalism, I am not separated from its people and its institutions. I am . . . not formally banished from the circles of those whose perception of the universe I no longer share."[62]

A number of people talked about the slow painful process of leaving their fundamentalist evangelical church. For Marlene Winell it was a reluctant leaving; it took ten years before she stopped calling herself a Christian.[63] Charles Templeton, former evangelist, writes that "the reader should be aware that one feels a profound sense of loss when one abandons any belief system held from childhood. Those months of indecision during which I struggled with my beliefs and finally decided to demit the ministry remain the most troubled and trying of my life.[64]

People mourned the loss of their community and the loss of a sense of purpose. John Loftus admits that his decision to become an atheist was very unsettling for him, "I have no hope in a resurrection. . . . I no longer have the hope that there is someone outside the space-time matrix who can help me in times of need or give me any guidance."[65]

59. Rattigan, "Fantastic Voyage," 68.
60. MacDonald, "From Faith to Faith," 115.
61. Tucker, *Walking Away From Faith*, 11, 26.
62. Anonymous, "The Naked Empress," 205.
63. Winell, *Leaving the Fold*, 33.
64. Templeton, *Farewell to God*, 220.
65. Loftus, *why I became an ATHEIST*, 404.

They mourned the fact that they just were not able to believe like the others and that the church could not allow them to question. They remembered the joy they had felt in "knowing" they were on the right path. When Dan Barker left his faith, he wrote in his letter to fifty colleagues, friends, and family members that "the little child in me still sometimes wishes to regain the comforts and reassurances of my former beliefs."[66] Some wrote about recalling good theological discussions, music, and an active social life among community members.

There was a vacuum now. This was the case with David Stamos, who left the New Apostolic Church, "I was filled with profound disillusionment, not knowing in which direction to turn. I was filled with a tremendous vacuum. My life seemed meaningless. What had filled my life with meaning, what I had believed all my life, crumbled to dust."[67] Some were no longer certain of what they believed. They wrestled with the old powerful belief system and found it difficult to re-construct a new spiritual reality. Patton Dodd writes that he is somewhere in the middle, "not rejecting completely, not embracing uncritically. . . . Working on my doubt from a position of faith."[68]

Those who could not integrate their new way of being often left Christianity completely. For some, even if they accepted the loss of their belief system, they were still at times plagued with questions and doubts. James Fieser talks about his deconversion and evicting Jesus from his heart but he also says that "my entire fundamentalist experience is a part of my past I'd prefer to forget, but that has proven difficult."[69]

Others experienced a complete liberation, sometimes even expressed as another "born again" experience, an experience that gave them the freedom to think and believe in a way that was consistent with who they had become. This is how it was for William Bagley, who writes that "the key was to study fundamentalism very deeply. . . . When clarity is reached, one does not have to even take it (fundamentalism) off, it falls off."[70] For some, there was freedom from believing in sin. They came to understand that Christianity was not the only true way to God. They were now at the inclusive stage. They no longer saw the Bible as the

66. Barker, *godless*, 47.

67. Stamos, "Why I Am Not a New Apostolic," 344.

68. Dodd, *my faith so far*, 172.

69. Fieser, "The Jesus Lizard," 180–83.

70. Bagley, "Reflections on a Christian Experience," 185.

highest authority on the subject of spirituality. They no longer had fixed ideas about God. They accepted that they did not have all the answers. The arguments that Edward Babinski had used to defend Christianity seemed to him no longer valid; he realized that his fundamentalist God was too small. While he still could acknowledge that parts of the Bible could be inspiring, Babinski no longer saw it as the highest authority, "I have learned that many of the ideas it contains owe a significant debt to the cultural milieu out of which they arose. There are in the Bible . . . Old Testament verses lifted out of context and misapplied to Jesus' life, contradictions, redundancies, omissions . . ."[71]

At the inclusive stage, individuals accepted the death of the Sky-God and the loss of the fundamentalist evangelical belief system. Beyond that, they discovered that Christianity was not the only way to God. They were at the acceptance stage of the death of the belief system. Kevin Henke claims that he has finally found the peace he had been wanting for years, "the freedom to think for yourself, without limitations, is the most precious 'good news' that I can give to my children or anyone else who asks!"[72] From his perspective, the journey out of fundamentalist evangelicalism was without question a freeing experience. And for many of those whose stories I analyzed, even though transitions through the stages of faith might have been difficult, they had a sense of freedom when they left the movement.

71. Babinski, "If it Wasn't for Agnosticism," 221–22.
72. Henke, "A Little Horse Sense," 252.

10

Dealing with the Effects of Leaving Fundamentalist Evangelicalism

THE WORLD OF FUNDAMENTALIST evangelicalism can be a comfortable world for those who embrace it. Leaving it can be difficult.

Some people who wholly and fully believe all the fundamentals feel secure. They have a sense of purpose. They feel they have a place within the church community; they feel welcome there. They know that God loves them and that he is in control of not only their own lives, but of everything that happens to them and everything that happens in the world. They have a personal relationship with Jesus. They believe God talks to them and that his presence with them is real. Keith Dixon writes of his experience when he says: "Euphoria flooded my body, bathing me in warmth and light. . . . A Presence that actually filled the sanctuary, my body, my thoughts. . . . No boundary existed between my being and the Presence. I was one with It. Filled with awe, it dawned on me: *This must be God!*"[1]

God gives them guidance in decision-making. They believe God answers their prayers, even if the outcome is not exactly as they had hoped. "God knows best for me" is their attitude in prayer. Some have an unshakable belief in a personal God who acts on their behalf, as one individual stated, "I believe very strongly in God's power to change lives and any problems you have."[2] They have a firm belief that "the Bible is the final authority. It is God speaking to us."[3]

1. Dixon, "The Ministry Revisited," 83.
2. Celeste Confiance (not her real name), interview, September 28, 2008.
3. Ibid.

When asked about potential problems with biblical interpretation they answer that they don't need to know; they trust that God has everything under control. God knows and that's all that matters. When Celeste was asked whether she ever had any questions or doubts, she answered, "I am solid in my beliefs."[4]

They have a compulsiveness to share the faith because people who do not believe as they do are bound for hell. But this is not usually a burden to them. They love to share what they have found to be so wonderful.

Their whole identity is wrapped up in their faith. They listen to Christian music at home. They attend church on Sunday morning and evening and mid-week services if they are available. They participate in conferences and retreats offered by their church. They read the Bible daily and pray often. John Loftus writes that he "thought these were God's words and that he was speaking directly to me every time I read them."[5] They are connected both with God and with the church community. Beverly Bryant writes that "my life was for the Lord . . . I went to Bible study in the day and Bible study at night. I prayed, I learned about God, and I began to use my gifts in His service."[6] This gives them a feeling of well-being and the surety that they are on the right path that will give them a good, purposeful life, and a glorious future in heaven. As Ralph Hood, et al., observe, "Religious fundamentalism provides a unifying philosophy of life within which personal meaning and purpose are embedded. In short, *for fundamentalists, religion is a total way of life* [emphasis mine]."[7]

If one truly believes all the fundamentals of faith, one belongs within the closed system of fundamentalist evangelicalism, a system reinforced by preaching, music, printed material, and religious institutions.

There are others who are suffering with anxiety, guilt, and fear while still continuing in fundamentalist evangelicalism. Some of these remain in the movement, while others decide to leave. Those who remain do not have the feeling of security and assurance that others around them seem to have. Although they may not leave the movement, they suffer

4. Ibid.

5. Loftus, *why i became an ATHEIST*, 20.

6. Bryant, "Inching Along," 155.

7. Hood et al., *The Psychology of Religious Fundamentalism*, 15–16.

some of the negative impacts of staying in the church community. God seems far away. Their prayers are not answered. They feel guilty when they cross the boundary lines of what they are told is right and wrong. They have questions about the belief system but do not receive satisfactory answers or they may be told that to doubt is sin. Some may eventually leave, while others remain and conform to the pressure of believing a certain way, repressing their questions about the accepted beliefs of the community. Someone who writes anonymously says that he/she is not willing to take the energy to leave: "I choose to flirt with the possibilities of the future rather than untangle the complexities of the past or grapple with the tasks and pains of separation."[8]

David Johnson and Jeff VanVonderen suggest that a belief system (specifically a spiritually abusive system) can be like a trap, easy to get in but hard to get out, "leaving the system is equal to leaving God and His protection. Paranoia about the evils outside the system makes people afraid to leave."[9] Johnson and VanVonderen suggest that the trap needs to have attractive bait. And we have seen that there is plenty of good bait in fundamentalist evangelicalism: security, recognition, connection within a caring community, assurance of sins forgiven, eternal salvation, and the promise of heaven in the life hereafter.

THE EXPERIENCE OF LEAVING

For those who leave the movement, such as those we examined in chapter 8, they can be affected in a variety of ways. Some feel a great sense of relief and never look back. The impact on them when they leave seems negligible and even positive. Robert Price expresses his departure as a feeling akin to being "born again": "the anxiety of doubt had passed into the adventure of discovery. It was like being born again."[10] Some make the transition to what they believe is a non-fundamentalist Christian denomination and find in it a faith they can accept and a new church community to which they can belong. Lori-Ann Livingston found "freedom of belief, of lifestyle, of choice, freedom from injustice and

---

8. Anonymous, "The Naked Empress," 205.

9. Johnson and VanVonderen, *The Subtle Power of Spiritual Abuse*, 183–4.

10. Price, "Beyond Born Again," 145.

inequality. . . . So it is in this environment that I feel I have a home. . . . We feel accepted—just as we are, no more and no less."[11]

Others turn to agnosticism or atheism and seem to suffer no negative consequences from leaving fundamentalist evangelicalism. They feel they have simply grown out of the old belief system. This was the case with Skip Porteous, a former Pentecostal minister, who felt set free when he stopped praying and stopped believing in sin.[12]

But there are also those who are impacted psychologically in a negative way. For them leaving fundamentalism can be a traumatic experience and sometimes a long painful process. Jeffrey Robbins writes that when he began to think for himself, "the security offered by a self-certain faith was no more. . . . To be a fundamentalist is not only to accept the laudable responsibility of knowing what you believe, but more dangerously, believing that you know with an absolute certainty."[13] Decisions that used to be made by reading the Bible (applying the biblical text to their current situation) and prayer now have to be made with their own intelligence. They have to use their own judgment instead of relying on divine intervention. And they may discover that they have difficulty trusting their own judgment, since they have until now relied so heavily on an external voice to tell them what to do.

The code of what is right and what is wrong was clearly defined in fundamentalist evangelicalism. When people leave, this is no longer defined for them. But the tape of what is wrong may still play in their minds. They may have left the belief system, but not the guilt and fear that went along with it. What intensifies this is the notion, within fundamentalist evangelicalism, that when you have doubts, or morally stray from the prescribed path, you have "backslidden" and need to return to the right way. Leia Minaker writes of the guilt she felt when she left fundamentalism, since her action of leaving alienated her from her family and relationships were torn apart.[14]

When people leave, they may feel they have lost a community of people who thought the same as they did. A community in which they were accepted, loved, and recognized for their ideas. A community in which they could take significant action. A community where

11. Livingston, "From There to Here," 53.

12. Porteous, *Jesus Doesn't Live Here Anymore*.

13. Robbins, "The Slippery Slope of Theology," 119–20.

14. Minaker, "Are You a 'Real' Christian?", 188.

they were connected with many like-minded people. They are on their own now. This may result in feelings of isolation and emptiness. They may feel incomplete and lose their sense of purpose in life. When Jacob Shelley started to think differently than those in his church, he was ostracized. There were accusations and character attacks; he had pushed "the boundaries of accepted norms."[15] Shelley says that "all of this has had far-reaching implications, affecting friendships and other social relationships."[16]

Even though ex-fundamentalist evangelicals may no longer believe in a literal heaven and hell, they may suffer, from time to time, from the "what if" factor. Kenneth Daniels writes about this factor when he says ". . . there remained a nagging 'what if?' in the back of my mind during the course of my struggle with doubt . . . if I was somehow mistaken about my growing doubt, and if I persisted in my doubt, I not only risked losing the things I held dear in this life, but I also subjected myself to the possibility of endless torment in the hereafter without possibility of reprieve."[17]

The belief in a real hell is so engrained that it is difficult to shake the emotional effects and ex-fundamentalist evangelicals wonder if the whole system may be right after all. This is especially true if they were taught the beliefs as children; they may have taken on a "precocious identity," in which they internalized, as children, an adult Christian identity (as referred to in chapter 9). Believing adult concepts at a young age, concepts such as forgiveness and salvation, made it difficult for them to develop their own identity as young people.

There are challenges associated with leaving. We are going to look at these from a number of different perspectives, including the trauma of leaving, the recovery from addiction, and the paradigm shift that takes place. Then we will describe several supports that are available to those leaving fundamentalist evangelicalism.

15. Shelley, "Life Stages," 133.
16. Ibid.
17. Daniels, *Why I Believed*, 86.

THE TRAUMA OF LEAVING

For some, the trauma of leaving fundamentalist evangelicalism compels them to seek help. Dixon writes that "it took nearly a year for the anxiety attacks to fade."[18] David Stamos says that when he gave up fundamentalism, "I was filled with profound disillusionment, not knowing in which direction to turn. I was filled with a tremendous vacuum. My life seemed meaningless. What had filled my life with meaning, what I had believed all my life, crumbled to dust, and by my own hands. I fell into a period of great depression. I don't think a day passed without my thinking about suicide."[19] After two years, says Stamos, he was cured "of a very difficult disease and addiction."[20]

In *Narrating Our Healing: Perspectives on Working Through Trauma*, Chris N. van der Merwe and Pumla Gobodo-Madikizela say that "the essence of psychological trauma is loss: loss of language, meaning, order and sense of continuity. Trauma is a shattering of the basic organizing principles necessary to construct meaningful narratives about ourselves, others, and our environment."[21] The ex-fundamentalist evangelical may certainly experience this kind of trauma. The language they once used to speak of God is no longer part of their vocabulary. The clichés they once used now give them pause. They have lost the meaning they had when they communicated with God and connected with other like-minded people. If they no longer attend church functions, the order and continuity their lives once had are gone. They may experience a crisis of belief, as described by J. LeBron McBride, who claims, in *Spiritual Crisis: Surviving Trauma to the Soul,* that belief transitions can bring on crisis: "Many belief changes come as a result of the old structure no longer providing adequate answers or satisfying deeper longings for spirituality. . . . The initial result can be very disturbing as people realize that what they have believed is no longer true or no longer works for them."[22]

On her website, Marlene Winell refers to the concept of Religious Trauma Syndrome (RTS) and defines it as " the condition experienced

18. Dixon, "The Ministry Revisited," 88.

19. Stamos, "Why I Am Not a New Apostolic," 344.

20. Ibid.

21. Merwe and Gobodo-Madikizela, *Narrating Our Healing*, 39.

22. McBride, *Spiritual Crisis*, 72.

by people who are struggling with leaving an authoritarian, dogmatic religion and coping with the damage of indoctrination."[23] Her site can assist those who need help dealing with the consequences of RTS.

In her on-line article, "Why Religious Trauma Syndrome is so Invisible," Winell states that "while leaving one's religion can be a discrete period of adjustment, it can also mean a long-lasting upheaval. Some of the damage that is Religious Trauma Syndrome (RTS) can be deep, intractable, and life-long. It can have disastrous results similar to severe forms of PTSD."[24]

In 1985, due to the trauma some people experienced when they left fundamentalist evangelicalism, an organization called Fundamentalist Anonymous (F.A.) was established in the United States. Its formation was due to a discussion of the concept of "religious addiction" on an Oprah Winfrey show, after which seventeen thousand people phoned in to ask for help.[25] Thirty thousand people became members of F.A. and there were forty-two self help groups across the United States. Richard Yao, founder of the organization wrote a book, *There is a Way Out*, which was the foundation of F.A.[26] and in which the twelve steps of Alcoholics Anonymous were adapted to make them suitable for those who had walked away from their addiction to fundamentalism.

In 1987, at their annual convention, the American Psychological Association organized a panel on religious addiction, which was followed by an article in *The Journal of Religion and Health* entitled "Fundamentalist Religion and its Effect on Mental Health."[27] Subsequently, articles appeared that revealed a link between leaving that belief system and mental health issues. As recently as 2002, in the manual, *Diagnostic and Statistical Manual of Mental Disorders-DSM-IV-TR™*, one condition listed under the category of "Additional Conditions That May be a Focus of Clinical Attention" is "Religious or Spiritual Problem" with examples including "distressing experiences that involve loss or

---

23. Marlene Winell, "Journey Free: Resources for recovery from harmful religion," last modified 2011, http://journeyfree.org.

24. Ibid.

25. Sam and Annaka Harris, "Project Reason: spreading science and secular values," last modified 2012, http://www.project-reason.org/archive/item/fundamentalists_anonymous/

26. "Ex-Fundamentalists Anonymous," http://fundamentalistsanonymous.word press.com/founder-richard-yao/

27. Hartz and Everett, "Fundamentalist Religion and its Effect on Mental Health."

questioning of faith."[28] The manual indicates that if this is the condition the psychiatrist is dealing with, they are to use code V62.89 in their medical record keeping.[29] What this shows is that the medical world has recognized that leaving one's belief system can lead to a serious mental health condition.

FUNDAMENTALIST EVANGELICALISM AS AN ADDICTION

There are a number of resources that discuss fundamentalism as an addiction. In *Toxic Faith: Understanding and Overcoming Religious Addiction*, Stephen Arterburn and Jack Felton explore the characteristics of a toxic faith.[30] They say that "because of the lack of self-worth and the need to feel good about self, addictions develop. Addictions are about finding safety and relief from feelings of worthlessness and pain."[31] In fundamentalist evangelicalism, with its emphasis on sin and the need to be cleansed from sin, it is easy for individuals to feel worthless and be susceptible to becoming addicted to the belief system. When they start to doubt the sacrificial system that assures them of salvation, they can feel lost.

In *The Addictive Organization*, Anne Wilson Schaef and Diane Fassel argue that "an addiction is any substance or process that has taken over our lives and over which we are powerless. . . . The concept of process addictions refers to a series of activities or interactions that 'hook' a person, or on which a person becomes dependent"[32] and that "anything can be addictive when it becomes so central in one's life that one feels that life is not possible without the substance or the process."[33] When this substance or process is removed, for instance when people leave fundamentalism, which was their central focus, there can be a tremendous void.

Fundamentalist evangelicalism can become an addiction because it is all consuming and there is the sense that if you miss reading your

28. American Psychiatric Association, *Diagnostic and Statistical Manual*, 741.

29. Ibid.

30. Arterburn and Felton, *Toxic Faith*.

31. Ibid., 207

32. Schaef and Fassel, *The Addictive Organization*, 57–58.

33. Ibid., 119.

Bible one day or if you fall asleep while you are praying, you have failed God. Schaef and Fassel say that addictive organizations create rigid boundaries that control the people within the organization. They make the point that in closed systems "information that cannot be processed within the existing paradigm will not be allowed in or recognized. . . . It is closed because it presents very few options to the individual in terms of roles and behaviours, or even the thinking and perceptions a person can recognize and pursue. . . . It acknowledges that divergent ideas exist but will not let them into the frame of reference of the system, and it refuses even to recognize the existence of processes that are threatening to it.[34]" Fundamentalist evangelical churches tend to be closed systems in that discussion of beliefs outside of the fundamentalist paradigm are discouraged and any viewpoints outside of that paradigm are seen as a threat to what is believed to be true Christianity.

In a church that is fundamentalist evangelical, there are boundaries that must not be questioned, whether they are boundaries about behaviour or belief. When I was baptized and became a church member, I had to agree not to go to movies, not to dance, drink, or smoke. I had to agree to attend church regularly. And in a fundamentalist evangelical community, church leaders ensure that other authorities brought in to speak to the congregation are of the same persuasion.

Schaef and Fassel list a number of characteristics of the addictive organization, some of which can be applied to the fundamentalist evangelical movement. One of these characteristics is perfectionism: "They are obsessed with not being good enough, not doing enough, and not being able to be perfect as the system defines perfect. . . . In the addictive system, perfectionism means always knowing the answers . . . and never making a mistake. . . . Mistakes are unacceptable in the perfectionistic system."[35] This is certainly true for those within fundamentalist evangelicalism. One never feels good enough; there are always more sins to confess. Perfection is even condoned in the Bible, if understood literally, for in the book of Matthew it is reported that Jesus said, "Be perfect, therefore, as your Heavenly Father is perfect" (Matt 5:48). And "mistakes" are seen as sin, for which people need to be cleansed. They tend to feel guilty even for the smallest mistake they have made.

34. Ibid., 60–61, 71.
35. Ibid., 64–65.

Another characteristic of an addictive system is that people within the system are always looking for more: "the 'fix' of the addictive substance or process is never enough. . . . We begin to look to outward symbols for inner assurance."[36] In fundamentalism, people are always looking for more assurance, more peace, and more contentment by participating more and more in the life and practices of the fundamentalist community. And there is a lot in fundamentalist evangelical rhetoric that prescribes the kinds of spiritual experiences one should have. As people start to feel uneasy about their faith it drives them to another "fix"—another church service, prayer, music—instead of searching within for the reason for the incongruence between what they are learning to be true and what they are told they should believe.

A third characteristic of addictive systems is that feelings get frozen: "The purpose of the addiction is to block whatever goes on inside addicts that they fear they cannot handle. This includes a whole range of feelings such as rage, anger, fear and anxiety. . . . As we are more and more removed from our feelings and awareness, we are removed from information about who we are and what we really believe."[37] The fundamentalist evangelical may block fear and anxiety, choosing to deal with them by praying more and giving themselves more fully to God.

Fourthly, in the addictive process there is a promise of something good that will happen in the future; people focus on expectations of a future good, instead of living in the here and now.[38] For the fundamentalist evangelical this promise is the promise of heaven and a better world after they die. There is an emphasis on the necessity to believe in Jesus' resurrection and their own. They take literally and seriously the Apostle Paul's observation: "For if the dead are not raised, then Christ has not been raised. If Christ has not been raised, your faith is futile and you are still in your sins. . . . If for this life only we have hoped in Christ, we are of all people most to be pitied" (1 Cor 15: 16–17, 19).

There is, finally, in the addictive process, what Schaef and Fassel call "external referencing," meaning that "we learn who we are and what we value by reliance on outside authorities."[39] When this happens in fundamentalist evangelicalism, people lose touch with their own

36. Ibid., 65.
37. Ibid., 66.
38. Ibid., 69.
39. Ibid., 70.

judgment and intuition, in fact, they are taught that they are to learn what God wants, not to look within themselves for validation. And the way they learn what God wants is to hear what church leaders have to say, leaders who have been immersed in the Bible and are trusted to pass on the right interpretation.

In addictive organizations, difficult issues and problem solving are avoided and if they are dealt with to any extent, this is done by management, those in control of the organization.[40] In fundamentalist evangelicalism, this is often the case. When conflict arises, the leadership deals with it, or more often than not, denies its existence. Sermons may be preached about forgiveness or getting along together as a community, but the issues themselves might never be addressed together with the congregation.

When belonging to the fundamentalist evangelical movement is experienced as an addiction, it may not be an easy matter to leave.

THE PARADIGM SHIFT

Schaef and Fassel make the point that recovery has to involve a paradigm shift and that it usually occurs over time.[41] In an organization that is not addictive in nature, people are not afraid to have their beliefs challenged, they encourage participation at all levels, and management is not hesitant to share their own misgivings, insecurities, and mistakes.[42] In fundamentalist evangelicalism people are afraid to have their beliefs challenged and leaders seldom admit their own misgivings and insecurities.

A paradigm shift involves a radical change in how things are viewed. This was seen in the chapter on levels of consciousness, each level demanding a paradigm shift. There is often a gradual letting go of the old frame of reference as a new one develops. These transitions are not easy. Emergence out of fundamentalist evangelicalism is a move to another level of consciousness; as people transition, they find their own way of moving out of it.

William Bridges has written extensively about transitions. In *Transitions: Making Sense of Life's Changes* and *Managing Transitions:*

40. Ibid., 142, 169.
41. Ibid., 201.
42. Ibid., 220–21.

Making the Most of Change he writes about the process of transition, elaborating on three phases: the ending or letting go, the neutral zone, and the new beginning.[43] While he writes primarily about change and transitions within organizations, his analysis is quite applicable to the process of leaving fundamentalism.

At the time of leaving fundamentalist evangelicalism, a person may not have yet articulated any new ways of beginning. All they know is that the old is not working for them anymore. The former way is ending and they need to let go of it.

Letting Go

When one first begins to have questions about fundamentalist evangelicalism, the ending, or letting go process, figures largely. There is a lot to process. Bridges offers suggestions as to what an individual might do in the letting go stage, suggestions to enable the letting go process. He emphasizes that it is important to determine and articulate "just what it is to say good-bye to."[44]

The "letting go" or the ending can happen in several stages. Bridges identifies five aspects.[45] While he relates these primarily to the ending of jobs and relationships, I believe it can also be applied to leaving one's religion, and in this case, leaving fundamentalist evangelicalism.

Bridges identifies five "dis's" that he believes need to take place in the ending phase and he makes the point that these five do not necessarily take place in any specific order and that they could overlap with each other. The five phases are disengagement, dismantling, disidentification, disenchantment, and disorientation.[46] As one experiences these phases, one enters the neutral zone, a place that is "a nowhere between two somewheres, and . . . forward motion seems to stop while you hang suspended between *was* and *will be*."[47]

So let's examine how these five "dis's" might relate to leaving fundamentalist evangelicalism. What is it that people are leaving? They are leaving a clearly defined system with its fundamental beliefs. They

43. Bridges, *Transitions* and *Managing Transitions*.

44. Bridges, *Managing Transitions*, 33.

45. Bridges, *Transitions*, 109.

46. Ibid.

47. Bridges, *Managing Transitions* 40.

are leaving a literal approach to the Bible that formerly was reassuring. They are leaving a community together with its sub-culture and they are likely leaving a particular church.

Now, to the phases. First, disengagement. It means too disengage "either willingly or unwillingly from the activities, the relationships, the settings, and the roles that have been important to us."[48] Applying this to letting go of fundamentalist evangelicalism, it may mean people step down from serving on church committees. They may stop singing in the choir or teaching Sunday School. They may no longer support the church financially. They may stop attending church.

The second phase is dismantling, taking apart "my old world and the identity I had built in it."[49] Former Fundamentalist evangelicals look at what they have left behind; they unpack each piece of the package. They dismantle former beliefs and look at why they were part of the movement. They examine why they had to leave it behind.

Third, in disidentification, you "lose your old ways of defining yourself."[50] Former Fundamentalist evangelicals no longer define themselves as members in a fundamentalist evangelical community. They no longer identify with the movement, the roles they formerly played, the beliefs they had, and they may no longer identify with the people who still are in the movement.

Fourth, disenchantment. There is something enchanting about a belief system where prayers are supposed to be answered miraculously and where people are healed. We can compare this to the belief in Santa Claus, which is fun while it still rings true to the child, but when the child finds out there is no Santa Claus, she can become disenchanted. Relating this to leaving fundamentalist evangelicalism, they may start to question aspects of their former belief system and the literal-factual approach to the Bible. They have become disenchanted.

The fifth phase is disorientation. When people are disoriented, they feel they have lost their bearings and they may be uncertain as to which way to go, "the old sense of life as 'going somewhere' breaks down."[51] *As a child, I played "Pin the tail on the donkey." First, we were blindfolded and spun around. When we started to walk we felt disoriented*

---

48. Bridges, *Transitions*, 110–11.

49. Ibid., 115.

50. Ibid., 115–16.

51. Ibid., 122.

and were not able to walk in a straight line towards the donkey. When people walk away from fundamentalist evangelicalism they may feel disoriented and not sure of which direction to go. They may feel lonely, confused, isolated, and lost. Before they knew exactly where they were headed, but now they are not sure.

During this process of ending, people may already be entering the neutral zone, a zone of waiting and surrendering: "one must give in to the emptiness and stop struggling to escape it."[52]

The Neutral Zone

As one is able to let go more and more, the neutral zone becomes more prominent. This is a time when many of the fundamentalist beliefs don't make sense anymore, but the belief system has not yet been replaced with something new. The new beginning phase is hardly perceptible at this point. But it is the neutral zone that is the stage of transition, a stage in which people often feel anxious and immobilized because "neither the old ways nor the new ways work satisfactorily."[53] It is a time when a person is letting go of the old but has not yet obtained full grasp of the new. See figure 7 below.

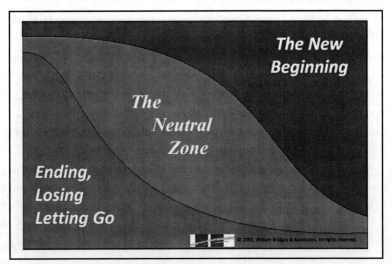

Figure 7. The Three Phases of Transition

52. Ibid., 140.

53. Bridges, *Managing Transitions*, 39.

As former fundamentalist evangelicals spend more and more time in the neutral zone, they may start to feel more comfortable living with uncertainty. They begin to feel at home in the world, at ease within the world, without feeling they have to convert people or that they will get contaminated by beliefs that are alien to the fundamentalist evangelical worldview. They are becoming more open to experimenting, testing, and exploring. When Keith Dixon was in the neutral zone, he explored the teachings of Buddhism, psychic phenomena, and Transcendental Meditation.[54]

It is quite possible that people can stay in the neutral zone for years, especially when they are leaving fundamentalist evangelicalism, because there has been so much indoctrination about what is perceived as the only way to God, that is, through Jesus' death on the cross. It is interesting that Bridges uses an illustration from the Bible to explain how difficult it can be to get through the neutral zone.[55] Referring to Moses who was with his people for forty years in the wilderness, Bridges makes the point that the forty years was the transition between the ending phase (when the people were in Egypt) and the beginning phase (when they would enter the Promised Land).[56] It took a long time. As we look further into the Moses story, we recall that during those forty years, the people struggled a lot with the transition. Throughout their time in Egypt life was difficult and they were treated poorly; however, they longed for the good food in Egypt as they travelled through the dessert with only manna and quails to eat. They were tempted to go back to Egypt. They could not yet see how good the Promised Land would be; they were in the neutral zone. It is the same for those leaving fundamentalist evangelicalism. Looking back to the security, recognition, and connection they had when they were part of the community, they may be tempted to go back because the neutral zone is a lonely place to be and they have not yet seen the "promised land" of their new spirituality.

54. Dixon, "The Ministry Revisited," 88–91.
55. Bridges, *Managing Transitions*, 43.
56. Ibid.

New Beginnings

Bridges states that "beginnings involve new understandings, new values, new attitudes, and—most of all—new identities."[57] Some former fundamentalist evangelicals make radical new beginnings. Others retain an aspect of their previous identity, but approach life within a new paradigm. For example, some may still have a love for the Bible, but the way they read it and understand it may be entirely different than before. Virginia Ramey Mollenkott realized that her departure from fundamentalist evangelicalism needed to begin with biblical research, because when she was a fundamentalist she loved the Bible.[58]

Bridges writes that in order to enter into a new beginning there needs to be a "purpose . . . a picture of how the outcome will look and feel . . . a plan for phasing in the outcome . . . ," and there needs to be a part to play for each individual.[59] The purpose or goal in the new beginning stage of leaving fundamentalist evangelicalism will not be the same for everyone. For those who want nothing more to do with any form of religion or spirituality the purpose in beginning anew may be to find something outside of religion entirely. For those who wish to retain a form of religious spirituality, their purpose may be to enter into a spirituality that rings true to them.

Next, Bridges says people need an image of the new way in their minds, a picture. As people talk with others who have experienced the new way, "they can begin to visualize and feel at home with the new way."[60] People leaving fundamentalism may start to visualize new ways of being that they might be able to indwell. It may be in the field of art or music or exploring different spiritual traditions. They start to think about which direction they would like to grow. They may have new insights and accept a new paradigm of belief. This was the case, for example for those who joined the Orthodox Church, in which they found a sense of mystery that, for them, replaced the need to believe doctrinal elements of fundamentalist evangelicalism. John Selby found that the idea of the presence of Jesus as indwelled Spirit, with no doctrine

---

57. Ibid., 58.

58. Mollenkott, *Sensuous Spirituality*, 190.

59. Bridges, *Managing Transitions*, 60.

60. Ibid., 65.

attached, was meaningful to him and provided him with a new way of believing.[61]

Third, Bridges talks about making a plan for change. He says that this plan "starts with the outcome and then works backward, step by step, to create the necessary preconditions for that outcome."[62] For the person leaving fundamentalism the outcome they hope to achieve may be to feel connected to the Spirit of the universe. Knowing that, they would need to figure out the steps they needed to take to arrive at that outcome. They might meditate, spend time in nature, read about, or talk with those who have achieved this.

The final aspect of a new beginning is to learn what part the person has to play in the emergence of the new beginning. The person who leaves fundamentalism will, of course, need to be an actor in the plan. It probably won't just happen on its own. They might seek out others to talk with, or read about spiritual ways of being or other topics that coincide with their desired outcome. In the stories I read, those who were thriving were those who felt settled about what they had embraced and who they had become. Some got to this stage on their own, but others needed support.

GETTING SUPPORT

Some who leave fundamentalist evangelicalism need extra support doing so. It is unlikely that they will get help from within the fundamentalist evangelical community, since according to them, the one leaving needs to be brought back into the fold. They may find other groups to join that are not fundamentalist in nature. Others seek counselling to assist in the process of leaving and the anxiety associated with it. There is probably no one program or method that can guarantee freedom from fundamentalist evangelicalism. Individuals need to discover the methods that will be most helpful to them in leaving the movement.

61. Selby, *Jesus for the rest of us.*
62. Bridges, *Managing Transitions*, 67.

Websites That Offer Support

There are websites that people can visit for support. There is an online group called "Fundamentalist Religion Recovery," a group intended "for people with a fundamentalist religious background, who now find the beliefs destructive and would like a safe space to recover."[63] This group was founded on February 3, 2010.

The "Recovering from Religion" website says that the purpose of the site is "to link together sites which provide support and promote healing for those who have left religious fundamentalism."[64]

The "Walk Away From Fundamentalism" website states that it is "a support forum for those who have left or are in the process of leaving fundamentalist Christianity."[65] One of the questions asked on the site is "What have been the hardest challenges in leaving your religion"? One individual answered that he/she "began the exit from my fundamental belief system ten years ago after nearly fifty years of deep involvement. The biggest challenge for me has been getting it out of my system. Leaving it at a head/choice/believing place is different than having all the body responses and deeper places gone. I can still shake with fear and guilt and anger."[66]

There is a "Leaving Born-Again Fundamentalism Christianity Email List" where "you may freely discuss spiritual conflicts, guilt, fear of losing good friends, dealing with Christian family members, fear of losing salvation." [67] Steve Locks, who developed the site, says in his preface:

> The deconversion experience is one of the most dramatic trans-
> forming experiences that can happen to a religious person for
> which there is no "exit counselling" from the church. Where does
> one go with such a life-changing discovery? Our Christian friends
> do not want to look that deeply into our lives, preferring only to
> coach us back to Christianity, believing we must be mistaken.
> Often they condemn us as hell-bound for "turning our backs on
> Christ," rather than facing the possibility that we have just found

63. Daily Strength, "Fundamentalist Religion Recovery," support group, created February 3, 2010, http://www.dailystrength.org/groups/fundamentalist-religion-recovery.

64. "Recovering from Religion," created 2001, http://recoveringfromreligion.org/

65. Support Forum, "Walk Away from Fundamentalism," founded 2001, http://forum1.aimoo.com/walkaway.

66. Ibid., April 30, 2011.

67. Support group, "Leaving Born Again Fundamentalist Christianity E-Mail List," created June 16, 1999. http://www.angelfire.com/pa/greywlf/leaving.html.

that the Christian belief system is untenable. The Internet is one of the few places where those who leave Christianity can turn easily for help and find people who have already been through this leaving process. Often new deconverts feel that they are in a very lonely situation as there is nobody around who will sympathetically listen to their thoughts. Therefore it can be a great thrill and relief to find others with similar stories to tell.[68]

The site is a collection of people's stories and resources available to assist those leaving the movement.[69] It references more than sixty links to other helpful websites and it lists newsgroups, forums, and discussion groups that people can join. This is a great resource for people who are looking for support as they leave fundamentalist evangelicalism.

The Twelve Step Program

The Twelve Step Program, adapted for assistance in leaving fundamentalist evangelicalism, is a method some have found helpful in their recovery. Schaef and Fassel say that for recovery "total abstinence (meaning total change of systems) is required. However, abstinence is done a day at a time, sometimes, even a minute at a time."[70] This is the reason why Fundamentalist Anonymous groups were organized in the 1980s. People felt that, in order to stay out of fundamentalist evangelicalism, they needed the consistent support of others. Fundamentalism was seen as an addiction and it was felt that the twelve steps could be used as a way to become free from fundamentalism.

Let us look at two versions of the twelve steps used by those who wished to leave fundamentalist evangelicalism. The following steps were developed for the 1980s Fundamentalist Anonymous groups:

1. I realize that I had turned control of my mind over to another person or group, who had assumed power over my thinking.

2. That person or group persuaded me of the inerrancy of the Bible, in spite of its many internal contradictions.

---

68. "Leaving Christianity," http://sites.google.com/site/leavingxtianity/home.user type:5 tt= 1

69. Ibid.

70. Schaef and Fassel, *The Addictive Organization*, 183.

3. I became addicted to the Bible as the supreme focus of my faith, in spite of the commandment that God should come first.

4. I admit to God, to myself and to another person the shortcomings of my belief in the unbelievable.

5. I have made an inventory of my false claims about the Bible.

6. I have made a list of those whom I led into confusion about the Bible.

7. I am willing to make amends to all those whom I may have led astray.

8. I realize that I have the inner power to restore sanity to my life and to search Scripture for the truth.

9. I will reach out to friends who can help me clarify my thinking about the Bible, God, and Jesus.

10. I confess that only with God's help can my mind grasp the truth.

11. I will seek through prayer and meditation to improve my conscious contact with God, praying for knowledge of God's will for me, and the power to carry that out.

12. Having had a spiritual awakening as the result of these twelve steps, I will offer these steps to other former biblical fundamentalists.[71]

These steps were obviously a help to many people, since so many F.A. groups were operative in the 1980s.

Another set of twelve steps, quite different from those above, are based on "reality and rationality."[72] These steps apply to any religious addiction. While the previous twelve steps assumed a continued belief in God, these do not.

71. Lee Adams Young, "Fundamentalists Anonymous: Twelve Steps to Sanity," October 2009, http://www.oocities.org/church_of_hank/fundamentalists_anonymous.html.

72. Ed, "The 12 Steps of Fundamentalists Anonymous," S.W.O.G. (blog), n.d., http://secular-sobriety-chat.blogspot.com/2010/05/12-steps-of-fundamentalists-anonymous.html.

1. We admit we were oppressed by religion and that our lives had become incomprehensible and unmanageable under the guise of faith.

2. We came to understand through common sense, education and critical thinking that our own inner strength can restore us to sanity and help us break free of the tyranny of religion.

3. We made a decision to accept complete responsibility for our lives and our will, instead of giving that free will to a god that never made sense.

4. We made a fearless searching inventory of ourselves and our beliefs, and discarded what was not logical and not ours.

5. We admitted to ourselves and others the true nature of our beliefs, stripped of the lies of faith and religion.

6. We were entirely ready to remove the illogical defects of skewed faith from our beliefs through education, common sense, and critical thought.

7. We humbly realized we are all human and make mistakes, and take personal responsibility for our shortcomings, and strive to be a good person.

8. We made a list of all beliefs that have harmed us and those around us, and willingly removed them from our lives.

9. We made direct amends to all persons we tried to control with religious indoctrination.

10. We continue to take personal inventory of ourselves and our beliefs through logical thinking, and when we are wrong, learn from our mistakes and correct them accordingly.

11. We sought through education and critical thinking to improve our understanding of our developing beliefs and disconnection from religion, empowering ourselves to carry out our renunciation of faith.

12. Having had an intellectual awakening as a result of these steps, we carry our lack of faith humbly and consciously, and offer to educate others when they are ready to break free of the tyranny of religion, and to practice these principles in all our affairs.[73]

The primary difference between these two versions of the twelve steps is that one retains a belief in God and the other does not. I would think that not all steps would suit everyone, since people who leave fundamentalist evangelicalism are at different places in their journey. For those who become atheists or agnostics, the second version of twelve steps might be quite appropriate. For those who still believe in God or a higher Power, the first version may be suitable. However, a person may have to write their own twelve steps, since not all of the steps may apply to them. I sat down to write twelve steps that I felt could help me and this is was the result:

1. I realize that I was oppressed by fundamentalist evangelicalism, believing to be true what I was told by church leaders; believing the inerrancy of the Bible and that it was literally true; believing that it was the only way to God. All who did not believe in this way were doomed.

2. I became addicted to making decisions only through prayer and reading the Bible. I became addicted to looking for a religious "fix" whenever I felt discouraged.

3. Through research and study I came to understand that there are different approaches one can take to understanding the Bible and belief systems.

4. I admit that my fundamentalist evangelical beliefs were narrowly based and that I had not taken into consideration other approaches to the Bible and the many other ways that people believe in a higher Power.

5. I made an inventory of the tenets of faith I could no longer believe.

6. I came to recognize that I could make conscious choices about my beliefs.

73. Ibid.

7. I removed beliefs that harmed me and others.

8. I realize that I have the strength and power to find a spiritual path that is right for me.

9. I will communicate with others who can help provide me with spiritual clarity that is not fundamentalist in nature. I claim my freedom to join new communities that enable me to grow.

10. As I learn more about spirituality, the Universe and higher Powers, I will incorporate these learnings into my changing belief paradigm.

11. Through research, meditation, music, and community I will seek to improve my conscious spiritual empowerment.

12. As I learn more about a conscious spirituality, I will share this with others who desire to be free from fundamentalist evangelicalism.

A version of the Twelve Step Program may be helpful to former fundamentalist evangelicals in working through what they believe. The steps may assist them in the process of leaving, either as a basis of reflection or action.

Exercises and Visualizations

Psychologist Marlene Winell, in *Leaving the Fold: A Guide for Former Fundamentalists and Others Leaving Their Religion*, writes of five phases in recovery, emphasizing that these are not linear; individuals might weave in and out of these phases or they may be in several phases at the same time.[74] The first phase is *separation*, separation from the church community to which they belonged. It may even mean separation from family and friends who don't understand the individual's exit from fundamentalism. This is similar to Bridge's disengagement phase. In Winell's second stage, that of *confusion*, people may question the actions they took to leave the movement. They may have second thoughts, but they know they cannot go back. They are disenchanted with fundamentalist evangelicalism. In *avoidance*, the third phase, they

74. Winell, *Leaving the Fold*, 16–19.

might avoid religion completely; they might withdraw from all belief. They have stopped identifying with the movement and likely with their community as well. In the fourth phase, *feeling and emotion*, they may have mixed feelings about leaving. They may be disoriented. They may experience anger, grief, depression, fear, loneliness, and disconnection.[75] And the fifth state is *rebuilding*, perhaps with a goal to find a spirituality that works for them. This is similar to the new beginning phase described by Bridges.

Winell suggests a number of exercises that can support people as they go through the phases of recovery.[76] These exercises can assist people to move through what Bridges calls the neutral zone to the new beginning phase. First, Winell suggests that readers take several inventories as they reflect on their fundamentalist experience. These include inventories of benefits they had when they were members of a fundamentalist community; aspects of fundamentalism they felt were mentally and emotionally manipulative; and family characteristics that were dysfunctional.[77] Winell then moves on to suggesting healing and recovery exercises, first of all noting that the inner child, who was taught she was a sinner, needs to be affirmed. She suggests a visualization exercise as well as affirmations that can be repeated each day in order to affirm oneself, both one's inner child and adult.[78] She provides exercises to help ex-fundamentalists recover a sense of self-worth, emotional wellness, and independent thinking. These exercises include visualizations, journaling, art, and music.

Learning About the History of the Movement

Another way people have found that helps them leave fundamentalist evangelicalism is to study the history of the movement. As we look at the history of fundamentalist evangelicalism, we can ask questions of it that can result in releasing us from the emotional hold it can have on us. We can ask about the historical circumstances under which the beliefs were formulated; why it was so important for boundary lines to be drawn around "fundamental" beliefs; why people felt it necessary to

75. Ibid., 105.
76. Ibid., 87–256.
77. Ibid., 43–132.
78. Ibid., 142, 162–64.

use these beliefs to demarcate who was "in" and who was "out"; who decided what beliefs should be included; how the beliefs became so pervasive that the result was a closed world view and separate sub-culture; what people gained from believing this way; and why they remained within the system.

As discussed in chapter 3, fundamentalist evangelicalism emerged at a time in history when North American Christianity had to respond to the issues raised by biblical scholarship brought to North America from Europe and to Charles Darwin's evolutionary theory. Questions arising out of biblical criticism and science threatened to undermine the foundations of Christian faith. Those who did not think it right to incorporate these new ideas into Christian faith felt the need to outline clearly the beliefs they thought to be essential.

Elijah Dann tells of his experience studying the history of Protestant fundamentalism and evangelicalism in graduate studies.[79] He writes that "it had never been suggested to me during all my time in church, by any of the people I had spoken with or listened to, that the version of Christianity I clung to was an invention borne of historical circumstances and traceable to political and theological quarrels in twentieth-century American culture.[80] And as a result of his studies his worldview changed; he was no longer attached to his previous beliefs.

Like many of those whose stories I have read, my own departure from fundamentalist evangelicalism happened gradually, and like Dann, learning about the origins of the movement has helped me understand my own personal journey within it. And with the writing of this book, I can now say that I have left the movement. Having done so, I sometimes look back on that belief system with a certain amount of nostalgia. Appearing to provide security, meaning, and connection for so many people, it seems to give hope in this life and for the next. While I had some memorable and meaningful experiences within it, it was never fully satisfying.

As a child and young person, I felt my life was too full of "sin" to be accepted by God, and so I never knew for sure if I would be going to heaven. And I was unable to experience the spiritual "high" that others seemed to have. As I grew older, I came to realize the patriarchal nature of the Bible, its translators, and those who wrote commentaries to interpret

79. Dann, "Confessions of an Ex-Fundamentalist," 220–21.
80. Ibid., 220.

the Bible. *This led me to a hermeneutics of suspicion with respect to the Bible and I started to question all the "fundamentals."*

Today I believe the Bible is a book that tells us about how people *experienced the Sacred. I view it as people's words about God. I still read and value the Bible, interpreting it as not literally, factually true, but as a book with wisdom and insight. But this is not easy to do, as David Rattigan writes,* "The old stories are so deeply ingrained, so much a part of our version of reality for so long, that thinking in terms of those stories is a habit of mind we still have to shake off. It was our reality for so long that thinking outside its conventions is not something we can all of a sudden just decide to do. It's a process."[81] *And that is the process I am in right now.*

Today I believe in the innocence of children and that there is no need to evangelize them or tell them that if they continue being "bad" they will go to hell. I have come to believe that there is no hell except what we make for ourselves in this life. I believe in an afterlife, but it remains a mystery to me.

Having given up the Sky-God, I even struggle with a belief in the existence of any kind of God. Like Ruth Tucker, "I wish the big question was not, at least unconsciously, ever before me: Is there really a God out there, or is my faith tradition a concoction . . . ?"[82] *So I live with uncertainty, drawing hope and meaning where I can find it. There no longer is "one door and only one," as I sang in my childhood and youth. There are many ways to God.*

I often experience the Sacred through music. I still sing some of the old gospel songs (and other Christian songs), reframing the words I cannot believe literally. At any time, you might find me sitting at my piano, playing and singing spiritual songs.

Sometimes, still in the stage of grieving the loss of fundamentalist evangelicalism, I find that I miss singing in the choir, sitting on church committees, and just being an important part of the church community. But for the most part I have accepted it. I am in the neutral zone, closer to a new beginning than to the letting go stage. I look toward new ways of perceiving spiritual reality. My hope is for connection with the Sacred, the Great Spirit of the universe. I find hints of this connection through music, Aboriginal teachings, and sometimes, even through what I hear in the church.

81. Rattigan, "Fantastic Voyage," 68.
82. Tucker, *Walking Away from Faith*, 26.

Appendix A

NAMES OF SELECTED SONGS
WRITTEN BETWEEN 1860 AND 1920

SONG NUMBER	SONG TITLE AND YEAR WRITTEN
1	All for Jesus (1861)
2	All the Way My Savior Leads Me (1875)
3	All Things Are Thine (1872)
4	All Things in Jesus (1915)
5	Almost Persuaded (1871)
6	Anywhere with Jesus (1887)
7	Are You Washed in the Blood? (ca.1878)
8	Be Ye Strong in the Lord (1887)
9	Blessed Assurance (1873)
10	Break Thou the Bread of Life (1877)
11	Bring Them In (1885)
12	Bringing in the Sheaves (1874)
13	Christ for the World We Sing (1869)
14	Christ Our Redeemer Died on the Cross (late 1800s)
15	Close to Thee (1874)
16	Come Every Soul by Sin Oppressed (1869)
17	Come Holy Spirit, Come Spirit of Pow'r! (late 1800s)
18	Come to the Savior, Make No Delay (1870)
19	Come with Thy Sins to the Fountain (1894)
20	Conquering Now and Still to Conquer (1890)
21	Constantly Abiding (1908)
22	Count Your Blessings (1897)

23	Dare to Be a Daniel (1873)
24	Day Is Dying in the West (1877)
25	Do You Hear Them Coming? (1892)
26	Does Jesus Care? (1901)
27	Down at the Cross (1878)
28	Face to Face (1898)
29	Faith Is the Victory (1891)
30	Far and Near the Fields Are Teeming (1885)
31	Far Away in the Depths of My Spirit (1889)
32	Far, Far Away in Heathen Darkness (1886)
33	For God So Loved the World (1920)
34	Free from the Law (1873)
35	Gather Them In for Yet There Is Room (late 1800s)
36	Give of Your Best to the Master (1902)
37	Give Me a Passion for Souls Dear Lord (1914)
38	God Be with You Till We Meet Again (1882)
39	God Loved the World of Sinners Lost (1871)
40	God of Our Fathers (1876)
41	God of the Earth, the Sky, the Sea (1864)
42	God Will Take Care of You (1904)
43	Hallelujah! What a Savior (1875)
44	Hark! The Voice of Jesus Calling (1868)
45	Have Thine Own Way Lord (1907)
46	Have You Any Room for Jesus? (1878)
47	Have You Sought for the Sheep? (late 1800s)
48	He Hideth My Soul (1898)
49	He Is So Precious to Me (1902)
50	He Leadeth Me (1862)
51	Hide Thou Me (1880s)
52	Hiding in Thee (1876)
53	Holy Holy Holy Is the Lord (1869)
54	I Am Coming Home (1911)
55	I Am Coming to the Cross (1869)
56	I Am Happy in the Service of the King (1912)
57	I Am Thine O Lord (1875)

58	I Can Hear My Savior Calling (1890)
59	I Hear Thy Welcome Voice (1872)
60	I Heard the Bells Christmas Day (1863)
61	I Know Whom I Have Believed (1883)
62	I Must Tell Jesus (1893)
63	I Need Thee Every Hour (1872)
64	I Shall See the King (1915)
65	I Stand Amazed in the Presence (1905)
66	I Surrender All (1896)
67	I Wandered in the Shades of Night (1897)
68	I Will Sing of My Redeemer (1876)
69	I Will Sing the Wondrous Story (1886)
70	I Would Be Like Jesus (1911)
71	I Would Be True (1906)
72	I'll Go Where You Want Me to Go (1892)
73	I'm Pressing on the Upward Way (1898)
74	In Shady Green Pastures (1902)
75	In the Harvest Field There Is Work to Do (1867)
76	In the Shadow of His Wings (after 1874)
77	Is It the Crowning Day? (1910)
78	Is My Name Written There? (1876)
79	Is Your All on the Altar? (1905)
80	It Is Well with My Soul (1873)
81	It May Be at Morn (1878)
82	It May Be in the Valley (1908)
83	I've Wandered Far Away from God (1892)
84	Jesus Blessed Jesus (1906)
85	Jesus Has Lifted Me (1916)
86	Jesus Is All the World to Me (1904)
87	Jesus Is Tenderly Calling Thee Home (1883)
88	Jesus My Lord, to Thee I Cry (ca.1870)
89	Jesus Paid It All (1865)
90	Jesus Saves (1882)
91	Jesus Savior Pilot Me (1871)
92	Jesus What a Friend for Sinners (1910)

93	Joyful Joyful We Adore Thee (1908)
94	Just When I Need Him Most (1907)
95	King of My Life, I Crown Thee Now (1900)
96	Lead On O King Eternal (1888)
97	Leaning on the Everlasting Arms (1887)
98	Leave It There (1916)
99	Let Jesus Come into Your Heart (1889)
100	Listen to the Blessed Invitation (1888)
101	Look to the Lamb of God (late 1800s to early 1900s)
102	Love Lifted Me (1912)
103	Low in the Grave He Lay (1874)
104	Marvellous Grace (1911)
105	Moment by Moment (1893)
106	More About Jesus (1887)
107	More Like the Master (1906)
108	My Jesus I Love Thee (1864)
109	My Life, My Love, I Give to Thee (1882)
110	My Lord Has Garments So Wondrous Fine (1915)
111	My Song Shall Be of Jesus (1875)
112	Near the Cross (1869)
113	Nearer Still Nearer (1898)
114	Nearer the Cross (1893)
115	No Not One (1895)
116	Nor Silver nor Gold (1900)
117	Not So in Haste My Heart (1875)
118	Nothing Between (1905)
119	Nothing but the Blood (1876)
120	O Beautiful for Spacious Skies (1904)
121	O Little Town of Bethlehem (1868)
122	O Master Let Me Walk with Thee (1879)
123	O That Will be Glory for Me (1900)
124	O Wonderful Words of the Gospel (late 1800s)
125	One Day When Heaven Was Filled with His Praises (1908)
126	One More Day's Work for Jesus (1869)
127	Only a Sinner (1905)

128	Open My Eyes, That I May See (1890s)
129	Out of My Bondage, Sorrow and Night (1887)
130	Pass Me Not Oh Gentle Savior (1870)
131	Praise Him Praise Him (1869)
132	Precious Promise God Hath Given (1873)
133	Redeemed How I Love to Proclaim It (1882)
134	Rescue the Perishing (1869)
135	Safe in the Arms of Jesus (1868)
136	Saved by the Blood of the Crucified One (1902)
137	Saved to the Uttermost (1875)
138	Savior, Tis a Full Surrender (1903)
139	Savior Thy Dying love (1862)
140	Send the Light (1890)
141	Shall We Gather at the River (1864)
142	Simply Trusting Every Day (1876)
143	Since the Fullness of His Love Came In (1880)
144	Sing the Wondrous Love of Jesus (1898)
145	Softly and Tenderly Jesus Is Calling (1880)
146	Sometime We'll Understand (1891)
147	Sons of God Beloved in Jesus (after 1870)
148	Standing on the Promises (1886)
149	Stepping in the Light (1890)
150	Sunshine in my Soul (1887)
151	Sweet Are the Promises, Kind Is the Word (1885)
152	Sweetly Lord Have We Heard Thee Calling (1871)
153	Take the Name of Jesus with You (1870)
154	Take the World but Give Me Jesus (1879)
155	Tell It to Jesus (1876)
156	Tell Me the Story of Jesus (1880)
157	The Banner of the Cross (1885)
158	The Cross Is not Greater (1892)
159	The Crowning Day (1881)
160	The Haven of Rest (1889)
161	The Light of the World Is Jesus (1875)
162	The Name of Jesus Is So Sweet (1902)

163	The Old Rugged Cross (1913)
164	The Way of the Cross Leads Home (1906)
165	There Comes to My Heart a Sweet Strain (1887)
166	There Is a Place of Quiet Rest (1903)
167	There Is Glory in My Soul (late 1800s)
168	There Is Never a Day So Dreary (1892)
169	There Is Power in the Blood (1899)
170	There Shall Be Showers of Blessing (1883)
171	There's a Land That Is Fairer Than Day (1868)
172	There's a Song in the Air (1872)
173	There's within My Heart a Melody (1910)
174	This Is My Father's World (1901)
175	Throw Out the Life-Line (1888)
176	Thy Word Is a Lamp to My Feet (1908)
177	Tis the Blessed Hour of Prayer (1880)
178	To the Millions Living O'er the Deep Deep Sea (1899)
179	To the Work (1869)
180	Under His Wings (1896)
181	Upon a Wide and Stormy Sea (1908)
182	We Have an Anchor (1882)
183	What a Wonderful Savior (1891)
184	What If It Were Today? (1912)
185	When My Life-Work Is Ended (1891)
186	When the Roll Is Called Up Yonder (1893)
187	When We Walk with the Lord (1887)
188	While Jesus Whispers to You (1878)
189	Whiter Than Snow (1872)
190	Will Jesus Find Us Watching? (1976)
191	Will You Come, Will You Come? (ca.1889)
192	Wonderful Grace of Jesus (1918)
193	Wonderful Words of Life (1874)
194	Would You Live for Jesus? (1898)
195	Ye Must Be Born Again (1877)
196	Yield Not to Temptation (1868)

Appendix B

NAMES OF SONG WRITERS OF SELECTED SONGS WRITTEN BETWEEN 1860 AND 1920

NAMES OF SONG WRITERS	NUMBER OF SONGS WRITTEN
Ackley, Alfred Henry	2
Atchinson, Jonathan Burtch	1
Babcock, Maltbie Davenport	1
Barraclough, Henry	1
Bates, Katharine Lee	1
Baxter, Lydia Odell	1
Bennard, George A.	1
Bennett, Sanford Filmore	1
Bilhorn Peter Philip	1
Black, James Milton	1
Blackall, Christopher Rube	1
Blandy, Ernest William	1
Bliss, Philip Paul	7
Booth, Ballington	1
Breck, Carrie Elizabeth Ellis	1
Bridgers, Luther Burgess	1
Brooks, Phillips	1
Brown, Mary Haughton	one-half*
Carter, Russell Kelso	1
Chapman, John Wilbur	2
Christiansen, Avis Marguerite Burgeson	1
Cornelius, Maxwell Newton	1
Cornell, Warren D.	1

Crosby, Fanny	28
Cushing, William Orcutt	2
Davis, Grace Weiser	1
Featherston, William Ralph	1
Gabriel, Charles Hutchinson	7
Gilmore, Joseph Henry	1
Gilmour, Henry Lake	1
Gladden, Washington	1
Graeff, Frank Ellsworth	1
Gray, James Martin	2
Grose, Howard Benjamin	1
Hall, Elvina Mable	1
Hamilton, Eliza H.	1
Hartsough, Lewis	1
Hawks, Annie Sherwood	1
Henderson, S.J.	1
Hewitt, Eliza Edmund	8
Hoffman, Elisha Albright	8
Holland, Josia Gilbert	1
Hopper, Edward	1
Hudson, Ralph Erskine	2
Hussey, Jennie Evelyn	1
Jackson, Henry Godden	1
James, Mary Dagworthy	1
Johnston, Julia Harriette	1
Jones, Lewis Edgar	1
Kidder, Mary Ann Pepper	1
Kirkpatrick, William James	2
Lathbury, Mary Artenesia	2
Lillenas, Haldor	1
Loes, Harry Dixon	1
Longfellow, Henry Wadsworth	1
Longfellow, Samuel	1
Lowry, Robert	3
March, Daniel	1
Martin, Civilla Durfee	1
Martin, William Clark	1

McAfee, Cleland Boyd	1
McDonald, William	1
McGranahan, James	1
Miles, Austin	1
Morris, Leila Naylor	3
Murphy, Anne May Sebring	1
Nicholson, James L.	1
Niles, Nathaniel	1
Nusbaum, Cyrus Silvester	1
Oatman, Johnson	3
Ogden, William Augustine	1
Ostrom, Henry (pseudonym: George Walker Whitcomb)	1
Owens, Priscilla Jane	2
Palmer, Horatio Richmond	1
Phelps, Sylvanus Dryden	1
Pollard, Adelaide Addison	1
Pollard, Rebecca S.	1
Poole, William Charles	2
Pounds, Jessie Brown	2
Prior, Charles Edward	one-half*
Rankin, Jeremiah Eames	2
Roberts, Daniel Crane	1
Root, George Frederick	1
Rowe, James	2
Rowley, Francis Harold	1
Russell, Anna Belle	1
Sammis, John Henry	1
Scott, Clara H. Fiske	1
Sellers, Ernest Orlando	1
Shaw, Knowles	1
Shurtleff, Ernest Warburton	1
Slade, Mary Bridges Canedy	1
Sleeper, William True	2
Spafford, Horatio Gates	1
Stites, Edgar Page	1
Stockton, John Hart	1

Stockton, Martha Matilda Brustar	1
Thomas, Alexcenah	1
Thompson, James Oren	1
Thompson, Will Lamartine	2
Tindley, Charles Albert	2
Torrey, Bradford	1
Tovey, Herbert George	1
Turner, H.L.	1
Ufford, Edwin Smith	1
Van DeVenter, Judson Wheeler	2
Van Dyke, Henry Jackson	1
Walter, Howard Arnold	1
Warner, Anna Bartlett	1
Whittier, John Greenleaf	1
Whittle, Daniel Webser	7
Witter, William Ellsworth	1
Wolcott, Samuel	1
Yates, John Henry	1
Young, George A.	1

* Charles Edward Prior and Mary Haughton Brown each wrote one verse of the same song.

Appendix C

NAMES OF FORMER FUNDAMENTALIST EVANGELICALS

Name	Source of Their Story
Anonymous	*Leaving Fundamentalism*
Astro, Dora (not her real name)	Interview
Babinski, Edward T.	*Leaving the Fold*
Bagley, William	*Leaving the Fold*
Barker, Dan	*Leaving the Fold* and *godless*
Barnhart, Joe	*Leaving the Fold*
Beegle, Dewey M.	*Leaving the Fold*
Belt, Jessica	*Jesus Girls*
Bogart, Julie	*Finding Faith, Losing Faith*
Brown, Sally	*Finding Faith, Losing Faith*
Bryant, Beverley	*Leaving Fundamentalism*
Campbell, Susan	*Dating Jesus*
Coffin, David	*Leaving the Fold*
Colter, Sandra (not her real name)	Interview
Cox, Harvey	*Leaving the Fold*
Cruzen, Kirsten	*Jesus Girls*
Daniels, Kenneth	*Why I Believed*
Dann, G. Elijah	*Leaving Fundamentalism*
Deitz, M. Lee	*Leaving the Fold* and *Finding Faith, Losing Faith*
Dilley, Andrea Palpant	*Jesus Girls*

Dixon, Keith	*Leaving Fundamentalism*
Dodd, Patton	*my faith so far*
Fieser, James	*Leaving Fundamentalism*
Gil, Alan	*Finding Faith, Losing Faith*
Grogan, Timothy William	*Leaving the Fold*
Grown-Seely, Pamela	*Finding Faith, Losing Faith*
Harpur, Tom	*Leaving the Fold*
Henke, Kevin R.	*Leaving the Fold* and *Finding Faith, Losing Faith*
Heramia, Ernest	*Leaving the Fold*
Hyers, Conrad	*Leaving the Fold*
Keen, Sam	*Leaving the Fold* and *Finding Faith, Losing Faith*
Lippard, Jim	*Leaving the Fold*
Livingston, Lori-Ann	*Leaving Fundamentalism*
Loftus, John W.	*why I became an ATHEIST*
MacDonald, Dennis Ronald	*Leaving the Fold*
Marks, John	*Reasons to Believe*
McAteer, Anastasia	*Jesus Girls*
McCall, Harry H.	*Leaving the Fold*
Mildenhall, Helen	*Finding Faith, Losing Faith*
Miles, Austin	*Leaving the Fold* and *Don't Call Me Brother*
Minaker, Leia	*Leaving Fundamentalism*
Mollenkott, Virginia Ramey	*Sensuous Spirituality*
Montoya, David	*Leaving the Fold*
Moore, Robert	*Leaving the Fold*
Notess, Hannah Faith	*Jesus Girls*
Oaks, Marlene	*Leaving the Fold*
Porteous, Skip	*Jesus Doesn't Live Here Anymore*
Price, Robert M.	*Leaving the Fold*
Rak, Julie	*Leaving Fundamentalism*
Rattigan, David	*Leaving Fundamentalism*

Robbins, Jeffrey W.	*Leaving Fundamentalism*
Robitaille, Glenn A.	*Leaving Fundamentalism*
Rosen, Christine	*My Fundamentalist Education*
Schaeffer, Frank	*Crazy for God*
Shelley, Jacob	*Leaving Fundamentalism*
Simons, Joseph	*Leaving Fundamentalism*
Stabler Tim (not his real name)	Interview
Stamos, David N.	*Leaving the Fold*
Steiner, Jason	*Finding Faith, Losing Faith*
Sweeney, Jon M.	*born again and again*
Taylor, Arch B., Jr.	*Leaving the Fold*
Teeple, Howard M.	*Leaving the Fold* and *I Started to be a Minister*
Templeton, Charles	*Leaving the Fold*
Till, Farrell	*Leaving the Fold*
Tucker, Ruth	*Walking Away From Faith*
Wicker, Christine	*God Knows My Heart*
Winell, Marlene	*Leaving the Fold: A Guide for Former Fundamentalists*
Yaconnelli, Karla	*Leaving the Fold*
Yaconnelli, Mike	*Leaving the Fold*
Zindler, Frank R.	*Leaving the Fold*

Bibliography

Addison, Steve. "How the West Was Won—Methodists and Baptists on the American Frontier," The World Changers' Library. Online: http://www.movements.net/wp-content/02-How-the-West-was-Won.pdf.

Aland, Kurt, et al., eds., *The Greek New Testament*. New York: United Bible Societies, 3rd ed., 1975. First published in 1966.

American Psychiatric Association. *Diagnostic and Statistical Manual of Mental Disorders, Fourth Edition – Text Revision (DSMIV-TRTM)*. Washington DC: American Psychiatric Publishing, 2002.

Ammerman, Nancy. "North American Protestant Fundamentalism." Chap. 1 in *Fundamentalisms Observed*. The Fundamentalism Project. Chicago: University of Chicago Press, 1991.

Anonymous. "The Naked Empress, Queen of Fundamentalism." In Dann, *Leaving Fundamentalism: Personal Stories*, 193–205.

Armstrong, Karen. *The Battle for God*. New York: Ballantine Books, 2000.

———. *A History of God*. New York: Ballantine Books, 1993.

———. *A Short History of Myth*. Toronto: Alfred A. Knopf Canada, 2005.

Arndt, William F. and F. Wilbur Gingrich. *A Greek-English Lexicon of the New Testament and Other Early Christian Literature*. 2nd ed., rev. ed. Chicago: The University of Chicago Press, 1979.

Arterburn, Stephen and Jack Felton. *Toxic Faith: Understanding and Overcoming Religious Addiction*. Nashville: Tomas Nelson, 1991.

Astro, Dora (not her real name). Interview conducted on July 6, 2007.

Averill, Lloyd J. *Religious Right, Religious Wrong*. New York: Pilgrim Press, 1989.

Babinski, Edward T. "If It Wasn't for Agnosticism, I Wouldn't Know *What* to Believe!" In Babinski, *Leaving the Fold: Testimonies of Former Fundamentalists*, 207–31.

———, ed. *Leaving the Fold: Testimonies of Former Fundamentalists*. Amherst: Prometheus Books, 2003.

Bagley, William. "Reflections on a Christian Experience." In Babinski, *Leaving the Fold: Testimonies of Former Fundamentalists*, 185–92.

Baker, Sharon L. *Razing Hell: Rethinking Everything You've Been Taught about God's Wrath and Judgment*. Louisville: Westminster John Knox, 2010.

Balmer, Randall. *Encyclopedia of Evangelicalism*. Louisville: Westminster John Knox, 2002.

Barker, Dan. *godless: How an Evangelical Preacher Became One of America's Leading Atheists*. Berkeley: Ulysses, 2008.

———. "Losing Faith in Faith." In Babinski, *Leaving the Fold: Testimonies of Former Fundamentalists*, 299–303.

Bibliography

Barnhart, Joe, "Fundamentalism as Stage One." In Babinski, *Leaving the Fold: Testimonies of Former Fundamentalists*, 233–38.

Barr, James. (1984). *Escaping from Fundamentalism*. London, SCM Press.

———. *Fundamentalism*. London: SCM, 1977.

———. "Fundamentalism and Evangelical Scholarship." *Anvil* 8, no, 2 (1991): 143.

Barrett, C. K. *The New Testament Background: Selected Documents*. New York: Harper & Row, 1961.

Beale, David O. *In Pursuit of Purity: American Fundamentalism Since 1850*. Greenville: Unusual Publications, 1986.

Bebbington, David W. *The Dominance of Evangelicalism: The Age of Spurgeon and Moody*. Downers Grove: InterVarsity, 2005.

Beegle, Dewey M. "Journey to Freedom." In Babinski, *Leaving the Fold: Testimonies of Former Fundamentalists*, 63–81.

Belt, Jessica. "Dead End." In *Jesus Girls: True Tales of Growing Up Female and Evangelical*. Eugene: Cascade, 2009, 97–105.

Bender, Harold S. and C. Henry Smith., eds. *The Mennonite Encyclopedia: A Comprehensive Reference Work on the Anabaptist-Mennonite Movement*. Hillsboro: Mennonite Brethren Publishing House, 1955.

Bernard, J.H. *The Pastoral Letters*. Grand Rapids: Baker, 1980.

Bernstein, Alan E. *The Formation of Hell: Death and Retribution in the Ancient and Early Christian Worlds*. Ithaca: Cornell University Press, 1993.

Block, Alvina. "Family History." Unpublished manuscript, last modified July 16, 2007, Microsoft Word file.

Boone, Kathleen C. *The Bible Tells Them So: The Discourse of Protestant Fundamentalism*. New York: State University of New York Press, 1988.

Borg, Marcus J. and John Dominic Crossan. *The First Christmas: What the Gospels Really Teach About Jesus' Birth*. New York: HarperOne, 2007.

Bray, Gerald, ed., *Documents of the English Reformation*, Minneapolis: Fortress, 1994.

Bridges, William. *Managing Transitions: Making the Most of Change*, 3rd ed. Philadelphia: Da Capo, 2009. First published 1991.

———. *Transitions: Making Sense of Life's Changes*, 2nd ed. Updated and expanded. Philadelphia: Da Capo, 2004.

Brock, Rita Nakashima. *Journeys By Heart: A Christology of Erotic Power*. New York: Crossroad, 1998.

Broughton, Vic. *Too Close to Heaven: The Illustrated History of Gospel Music*. London: Midnight Books, 1996.

Brown, Candy Gunther. *The Word in the World: Evangelical Writing, Publishing, and Reading in America, 1789–1880*. Chapel Hill: The University of North Carolina Press, 2004.

Brown, Francis. *The New Brown Driver Briggs Gesenius Hebrew and English Lexicon*. Lafayette: Associated Publishers and Authors, 1980.

Bryant, Beverley. "Inching Along." In Dann, *Leaving Fundamentalism: Personal Stories*, 151–60.

Bruce, F.F. *The Books and the Parchments: Some Chapters on the Transmission of the Bible*. Old Tappan: Fleming H. Revell, 1963.

Buchanan, George Wesley. *To the Hebrews*, vol. 36. The Anchor Bible, edited by W.F. Albright and David Noel Freedman. Garden City: Doubleday, 1972.

Campbell, Susan. *Dating Jesus: A Story of Fundamentalism, Feminism, and the American Girl*. Boston: Beacon Press, 2009.

Campus Crusade for Christ. "Four Spiritual Laws." New Life Publications, 2008. No pages. Online: http://www.campuscrusade.com/fourlawseng.htm.

Canadian Conference of Catholic Bishops. "Declaration on the Question of the Admission of Women to the Ministerial Priesthood," Sacred Congregation for the Doctrine of the Faith. Ottawa: Canadian Conference of Catholic Bishops Publications Service, 1976.

Carpenter, Joel A., ed. *Fundamentalism in American Religion: 1880–1950*. New York: Garland, 1988.

"Chicago Statement on Biblical Inerrancy," International Council on Biblical Inerrancy Committee, 1978. Online: http://www.bible-researcher.com/chicago1.html.

Clark-Soles, Jaime. *Death and the Afterlife in the New Testament*. New York: T & T Clark, 2006.

Coffin, David. "Fundamentalism: A Blessing and a Curse." In Babinski, *Leaving the Fold: Testimonies of Former Fundamentalists*, 83–88.

Cole, Stuart G. *The History of Fundamentalism*. New York: Harper & Row, 1971. First published 1931 by Richard R. Smith, Inc.

Colter, Sandra (not her real name). Interview conducted on June 18, 2007.

Confiance, Celeste (not her real name). Interview conducted on September 28, 2008.

Court, John and Kathleen. *The New Testament World*. Englewood Cliffs: Prentice Hall, 1990,

Cox, Harvey. "An Ecumenical/Evangelical Dialogue." In Babinski, *Leaving the Fold: Testimonies of Former Fundamentalists*, 91–94.

Crisafulli, Chuck and Kyra Thompson. *Go to Hell: A Heated History of the Underworld*. New York: Simon Spotlight Entertainment, 2005.

Cruzen, Kirsten. "Surviving the Call to Missions." In *Jesus Girls: True Tales of Growing Up Female and Evangelical*. Eugene: Cascade, 2009, 107–17.

Cusic, Don. *The Sound of Light: A History of Gospel Music*. Bowling Green: Bowling Green State University Popular Press, 1990.

Cyber Hymnal, last modified 2011. Online: www.hymntime.com/tch/.

Daily Strength. "Fundamentalist Religion Recovery," support group, created February 3, 2010, http://www.dailystrength.org/groups/fundamentalist-religion-recovery.

Dana, H. E. and Julius R. Mantey. *A Manual Grammar of the Greek New Testament*. Toronto: Macmillan, 1927.

Daniels, Kenneth W. *Why I Believed: Reflections of a Former Missionary*. Duncanville: Kenneth W. Daniels, 2009.

Dann, G. Elijah, ed. *Leaving Fundamentalism: Personal Stories*. Waterloo: Wilfrid Laurier University Press, 2008.

———. "Confessions of an Ex-Fundamentalist." In Dann, *Leaving Fundamentalism: Personal Stories*, 207–222.

DeBerg, Betty A. *Ungodly Women: Gender and the First Wave of American Fundamentalism*. Minneaoplis: Augsburg Fortress, 1990.

Deitz, L. Lee. "My Conversion from Fundamentalism." In Babinski, *Leaving the Fold: Testimonies of Former Fundamentalists*, 305–11.

Dibelius, Martin and Hans Conzelmann. *The Pastoral Epistles*. Philadelphia: Fortress, 1972.

Dilley, Andrea Palpant. "Why Isn't God like Eric Clapton?" In *Jesus Girls: True Tales of Growing Up Female and Evangelical*. Eugene: Cascade, 181–191.

Dixon, Keith. "The Ministry Revisited." In Dann, *Leaving Fundamentalism: Personal Stories*, 81–94.

Dodd, Patton. *My Faith So Far: A Story of Conversion and Confusion*. San Francisco: Jossey-Bass, 2005.

Dollar, George W. *A History of Fundamentalism in America*. Greenville: Bob Jones University Press, 1973.

Ed, "The 12 Steps of Fundamentalists Anonymous," S.W.O.G. (blog), n.d., http://secular-sobriety-chat.blogspot.com/2010/05/12-steps-of-fundamentalists-anonymous.html.

Edwards, Jonathan. "A Faithful Narrative of the Surprising Work of God." Report sent to England, November 6, 1736. Online: http://www.jonathan-edwards.org/Narrative.html.

———. "Sinners in the Hands of an Angry God." Sermon given in Enfield, CT, July 8, 1741. Online: http://www.ccel.org/ccel/edwards/sermons.sinners.html.

Ellis, William T. *"Billy" Sunday: The Man and His Message*. Philadelphia: L.T. Myers, 1914.

Esau, Mrs. H.T. *First Sixty Years of M.B. Missions*. Hillsboro: Mennonite Brethren Publishing, 1954.

Estep, William R. *The Anabaptist Story*. Grand Rapids: William B. Eerdmans, 1963. Revised 1975.

Evangelical Outreach. "Hell and the LAKE OF FIRE are Waiting for YOU!" Evangelical Outreach, 1999. No pages. Online: http://www.evangelicaloutreach.org/heavenhell.pdf.

Evans, Rod L. and Irwin M. Berent. *Fundamentalism: Hazards and Heartbreaks*. La Salle: Open Court, 1988.

"Ex-Fundamentalists Anonymous," http://fundamentalistsanonymous.wordpress.com/founder-richard-yao/

Falwell, Jerry, et al. *The Fundamentalist Phenomenon: The Resurgence of Conservative Christianity*. Garden City: Doubleday, 1981.

"Fanny Crosby," Christian History, http://www.christianitytoday.com/ch/131 christians /poets/crosby.html.

Fieser, James. "The Jesus Lizard." In Dann, *Leaving Fundamentalism: Personal Stories*, 171–83.

Finke, Roger and Rodney Starke. *The Churching of America 1776–2005: Winners and Losers in Our Religious Economy*. New Jersey: Rutgers University Press, 2005.

Fowler, James. *Becoming Adult, Becoming Christian: Adult Development and Christian Faith*. New York: Harper & Row, 1984,

———. *Faith Development and Pastoral Care*. Philadelphia: Fortress, 1986.

———. *Stages of Faith: The Psychology of Human Development and the Quest for Meaning*. New York: Harper & Row, 1981.

Furnish, Victor Paul. *II Corinthians*. The Anchor Bible, vol. 32A. Garden City: Doubleday, 1984.

Gasper, Louis. *The Fundamentalist Movement: 1930–1956*. Twin Books Series. Grand Rapids: Baker Book House, 1963. Reprinted 1981.

General Conference of Mennonite Brethren Churches. "Resolution on the Ministry of Women in the Church." *Yearbook of the General Conference of Mennonite Brethren Churches*. Hillsboro: Mennonite Brethren Publishing, 1981.

George, Timothy, ed. *Mr. Moody and the Evangelical Tradition*. New York: T & T Clark, 2004.

Grogan, Timothy William. "Lies, Damn Lies, and Boredom." In Babinski, *Leaving the Fold: Testimonies of Former Fundamentalists*, 313–19.

Hallote, Rachel S. *Death, Burial and Afterlife in the Biblical World: How the Israelites and Their Neighbours Treated the Dead*. Chicago: Ivan R. Dee, 2001.

Hankins, Barry, ed. *Evangelicalism and Fundamentalism: A Documentary Reader*. New York: New York University Press, 2008.

Hanson, Anthony Tyrrell. *The Pastoral Epistles*. The New Century Bible Commentary. Grand Rapids: Eerdmans, 1982.

Harpur, Tom. "Heaven and Hell." In Babinski, *Leaving the Fold: Testimonies of Former Fundamentalists*, 97–100.

Harris, Harriet A. *Fundamentalism and Evangelicals*. London: Clarendon Press, 1998.

Harris, Sam and Annaka, "Project Reason: spreading science and secular values," last modified 2012, http://www.project-reason.org/archive/item/fundamentalists_anonymous/

Hart, D.G. et al., eds. *The Legacy of Jonathan Edwards: American Religion and the Evangelical Tradition*. Grand Rapids: Baker Academic, 2003.

Hartz, Gary W. and Henry C. Everett (Fall 1989). "Fundamentalist Religion and its Effect on Mental Health." *Journal of Religion and Health* 28, no. 3 (Fall 1989): 207–217.

Hassey, Janet. *No Time for Silence: Evangelical Women in Public Ministry Around the Turn of the Century*. Grand Rapids: Zondervan, 1986.

Hebert, Gabriel. *Fundamentalism and the Church*. London: SCM, 1957.

Helfaer, Philip. *The Psychology of Religious Doubt*. Boston: Beacon, 1972.

Henke, Kevin R. "A Little Horse Sense Is Worth a Thousand Inerrant Doctrines." In Babinski, *Leaving the Fold: Testimonies of Former Fundamentalists*, 241–52.

Heramia, Ernest. "The Thorn-Crowned Lord/The Antler-Crowned Lord." In Babinski, *Leaving the Fold: Testimonies of Former Fundamentalists*, 195–203.

Herntrich, Volkmar. "*krinō*" in Kittel, Gerhard, ed. *Theological Dictionary of the New Testament*, vol. 3. 10 vols. Grand Rapids: Eerdmans, 1965, 921–33.

Hood, Ralph W., Jr., et al. *The Psychology of Religious Fundamentalism*. New York: The Guilford Press, 2005.

Howard, J. Keir. "Neither Male nor Female: An Examination of the Status of Women in the New Testament," *The Evangelical Quarterly* 55 (1983): 81–91.

Hustad, Donald P. *Jubilate! Church Music in the Evangelical Tradition*. Carol Stream: Hope Publishing, 1981.

Hyers, Conrad. "The Comic Vision." In Babinski, *Leaving the Fold: Testimonies of Former Fundamentalists*, 103–7.

International Council on Inerrancy, http://www.kulikovskyonline.net/herme.

Jenkins, Jerry B. and Tim F. Lahaye. *Left Behind Series*. Carol Stream: Tyndale House, 1999.

The Jewish Publication Society. *Tanakh: A New Translation of the Holy Scriptures*. Philadelphia: The Jewish Publication Society, 1985.

Johnson, David and Jeff VanVonderen. *The Subtle Power of Spiritual Abuse: Recognizing and Escaping Spiritual Manipulation and False Spiritual Authority Within the Church.* Minneapolis: Bethany House, 1991.

Kant, Immanuel. *The Critique of Pure Reason.* Translated by Norman Kemp Smith. London: Macmillan, 1929.

Kauffman, Daniel. *The Conservative Viewpoint.* Scottdale: Mennonite Publishing, 1918.

Kee, Howard Clark. *Understanding the New Testament.* Englewood Cliffs: Prentice Hall, 1993.

Keen, Sam. "To a Dancing God." In Babinski, *Leaving the Fold: Testimonies of Former Fundamentalists*, 255–59.

Kegan, Robert. *In Over Our Heads: The Mental Demands of Modern Life.* Cambridge: Harvard University Press, 1994.

Keswick Christian School. "Mission and Philosophy," 2010. No pages. Online: http://keswickchristian.org/mission-and-philosophy/.

Koester, Helmut. *History and Literature of Early Christianity: Introduction to the New Testament.* Philadelphia: Fortress Press, 1982.

Krentz, Edgar. *The Historical-Critical Method.* Philadelphia: Fortress, 1975.

Kübler-Ross, Elizabeth. *On Death and Dying.* New York: Simon & Schuster, 1969.

Leaves, Nigel. *The God Problem: Alternatives to Fundamentalism.* Santa Rosa: Polebridge, 2006.

"Leaving Christianity," http://sites.google.com/site/leavingxtianity/home.

Lehtipuu, Outi. *The Afterlife Imagery in Luke's Story of the Rich Man and Lazarus.* Leiden: Brill, 2007.

Lindsey, Hal with Carole C. Carlson. *Late Great Planet Earth.* Grand Rapids: Zondervan, 1970.

Lippard, Jim. "From Fundamentalism to Open-ended Atheism." In Babinski, *Leaving the Fold: Testimonies of Former Fundamentalists*, 321–27.

Livingston, L.A. "From There to Here." In Dann, *Leaving Fundamentalism: Personal Stories*, 41–54.

Loftus, Jon W. *why i became an ATHEIST: a former preacher rejects Christianity.* Amherst: Prometheus, 2008.

MacDonald, Dennis Ronald. "From Faith to Faith." In Babinski, *Leaving the Fold: Testimonies of Former Fundamentalists*, 109–16.

McBride, J. Lebron. *Spiritual Crisis: Surviving Trauma to the Soul.* New York: Haworth Pastoral Press, 1998.

McCall, Harry H. " 'Who Do Men Say That I Am?' " In Babinski, *Leaving the Fold: Testimonies of Former Fundamentalists*, 329–34.

McIntosh, Steve. *Integral Consciousness and the Future of Evolution: How the Integral Worldview is Transforming Politics, Culture and Spirituality.* St. Paul: Paragon House, 2007.

Marion, Jim. *The Death of the Mythic God: The Rise of Evolutionary Spirituality.* Charlottesville: Hampton Roads, 2004.

———. *Putting on the Mind of Christ: The Inner Work of Christian Spirituality.* Charlottesville: Hampton Roads, 2000.

Marks, John. *Reasons to Believe: One Man's Journey Among the Evangelicals and the Faith He Left Behind.* New York: Harper Collins, 2008.

Marsden, George M. *Fundamentalism and American Culture.* New York: Oxford University Press, 2006.

———. *Understanding Fundamentalism and Evangelicalism*. Grand Rapids: Eerdmans, 1991.

Marty, Martin E. and R. Scott Appleby, eds. *Accounting for Fundamentalisms*. The Fundamentalism Project. Chicago: University of Chicago Press, 1994.

———. *Fundamentalism and Society*. The Fundamentalism Project. Chicago: University of Chicago Press, 1993.

———. *Fundamentalism and the State*. The Fundamentalism Project. Chicago: University of Chicago Press, 1993.

———. *Fundamentalisms Comprehended*. The Fundamentalism Project. Chicago: University of Chicago Press, 1995.

———. *Fundamentalisms Observed*. The Fundamentalism Project. Chicago: University of Chicago Press, 1991.

McKnight, Scot and Hauna Ondrey. *Finding Faith, Losing Faith: Stories of Conversion and Apostasy*. Waco: Baylor University Press, 2008.

McAteer, Anastasia. "Exorcizing the Spirit." In *Jesus Girls: True Tales of Growing Up Female and Evangelical*. Eugene: Cascade, 2009, 69–76.

Mennonite Brethren Church of North America. *General Conference Yearbook 1879*. Medford, OK: Mennonite Brethren Publishing, 1879.

———. "Resolution on the Ministry of Women in the Church." Yearbook of the General Conference of Mennonite Brethren Churches. Newton: General Conference of Mennonite Brethren Churches, 1981.

Merwe, Chris N. Van der and Pumla Gobodo-Madikizela. *Narrating Our Healing: Perspectives on Working Through Trauma*. Newcastle: Cambridge Scholars, 2007.

Miles, Austin. "Don't Call Me Brother." In Babinski, *Leaving the Fold: Testimonies of Former Fundamentalists*, 261–72.

———. *Don't Call Me Brother: A Ringmaster's Escape from the Pentecostal Church*. Buffalo: Prometheus, 1989.

Miller, Steve. "Inerrancy and Authority." *Direction* 12, no. 1 (January 1983): 3–9.

Minaker, Leia. "Are You a 'Real' Christian?" In Dann, *Leaving Fundamentalism: Personal Stories*, 185–205.

Mollenkott, Virginia Ramey. *Sensuous Spirituality: Out From Fundamentalism*. Revised and expanded. Cleveland: Pilgrim, 2008. First published 1992.

Montoya, David. "The Political Disease Known as Fundamentalism." In Babinski, *Leaving the Fold: Testimonies of Former Fundamentalists*, 119–34.

Moore, Robert. "From Pentecostal Christianity to Agnosticism." In Babinski, *Leaving the Fold: Testimonies of Former Fundamentalists*, 275–82.

Mullan, David George, ed. *Women's Life Writing in Early Modern Scotland: Writing the Evangelical Self, c.1670-c.1730*. Contemporary Editions. Burlington: Ashgate, 2003.

Nelson, Cyrus N., compiler. *Sunday School Sings*. Mound, MN: Praise Book Publications, 1957.

———. *Youth Sings*. Mound, MN: Praise Book Publications, 1951.

Neufeld Redekop, Gloria. "Let the women learn: I Timothy 2:8-15 reconsidered." *Studies in Religion/Sciences Religieuses* 19, no. 2 (1990): 235–45.

———. *The Work of Their Hands: Mennonite Women's Societies in Canada*. Waterloo: Wilfrid Laurier University Press, 1996.

Nichols, Stephen J. *Jonathan Edwards: A Guided Tour of His Life and Thought*. Phillipsburg: P&R Publishing, 2001.

Noll, Mark A. *A History of Christianity in the United States and Canada.* Grand Rapids: Eerdmans, 1992.

———. *The Rise of Evangelicalism: The Age of Edwards, Whitefield and the Wesleys.* A History of Evangelicalism: People, Movements and Ideas in the English-Speaking World edited by David W. Bebbington and Mark A. Noll, 5 vols. Downers Grove: Inter-Varsity, 2003.

———. *Turning Points: Decisive Moments in the History of Christianity.* 2nd edition. Grand Rapids: Baker Academic, 2000.

Notess, Hannah Faith. *Jesus Girls: True Tales of Growing Up Female and Evangelical.* Eugene: Cascade, 2009.

———. "Quick and Powerful." In *Jesus Girls: True Tales of Growing Up Female and Evangelical.* Eugene: Cascade, 79–88.

Oaks, Marlene. "Old Time Religion Is a Cult." In Babinski, *Leaving the Fold: Testimonies of Former Fundamentalists,* 137–42.

O'Meara, T. F. *Fundamentalism: A Catholic Perspective.* New York: Paulist, 1990.

Padgett, Alan. "Wealthy Women at Ephesus: 1 Timothy 2:8–15 in Social Context." *Interpretation* 41 (1987): 25–27.

Patte, Daniel. *Early Jewish Hermeneutic In Palestine, SBL Dissertation.* Series 22. Missoula: Society of Biblical Literature, 1975.

Payne, Philip. "Liberation Women at Ephesus: A Response to Douglas J. Moo's Article 1 Timothy 2:11–15: Meaning and Significance." *Trinity Journal* (1981): 169–170.

Pohle, E. E. *Dr. C.I. Scofields' Question Box.* Chicago: Bible Institute Colportage, 1917.

Porteous, Skip. "How I Walked Away," 1995. No pages. Online: http://www.skeptictank. org/files//fw/porteous.htm.

———. *Jesus Doesn't Live Here Anymore: From Fundamentalist to Freedom Writer.* Buffalo: Prometheus, 1991.

Price, Robert M. "Beyond Born Again." In Babinski, *Leaving the Fold: Testimonies of Former Fundamentalists,* 145–50.

Rak, Julie. "Looking Back at Sodom: My Evangelical and Lesbian Testimonies." In Dann, *Leaving Fundamentalism: Personal Stories,* 95–107.

Rattigan, David L. "Fantastic Voyage: Surviving Charismatic Fundamentalism." In Dann, *Leaving Fundamentalism: Personal Stories,* 55–68.

Rawlyk, George A. and Mark A. Noll, eds. *Amazing Grace: Evangelicalism in Australia, Britain, Canada, and the United States.* Montreal: McGill-Queen's University Press, 1994.

———. *The Canada Fire: Radical Evangelicalism in British North America 1775–1812.* Montreal & Kingston: McGill-Queen's University Press, 1994.

"Recovering from Religion," created 2001, http://recoveringfromreligion.org/.

Redekop, Vern Neufeld. *From Violence to Blessing: How an Understanding of Deep-Rooted Conflict Can Open Paths to Reconciliation.* Ottawa: Novalis, 2002.

Richert, Herbert C. et al., compilers. *Mennonite Brethren Church Hymnal.* Hillsboro: Mennonite Brethren Publishing, 1953.

Robbins, Jeffrey W. "The Slippery Slope of Theology." In Dann, *Leaving Fundamentalism: Personal Stories,* 109–20.

Robitaille, Glenn A. "From Fear to Faith: My Journey into Evangelical Humanism." In Dann, *Leaving Fundamentalism: Personal Stories,* 161–70.

Rosen, Christine. *My Fundamentalist Education: A Memoir of a Divine Girlhood.* New York: Public AffairsTM, 2005.

Routley, Erik. *The Music of Christian Hymns*. Chicago: G.I.A. Publications, 1981.

Sacred Congregation for the Doctrine of the Faith. "Declaration on the Question of the Admission of Women to the Ministerial Priesthood." Rome, 1976.

Sandeen, Ernest R. *The Origins of Fundamentalism: Toward a Historical Interpretation.* Facet Books, Historical Series–10, edited by Richard C. Wolf. Philadelphia: Fortress, 1968.

———. *The Roots of Fundamentalism: British and American Millenarianism 1800–1970.* Chicago: University of Chicago Press, 1970.

Sandys-Wunsch, J. *What Have They Done to the Bible? A History of Modern Biblical Interpretation.* Collegeville: Liturgical Press, 2005.

Schaef, Anne Wilson and Diane Fassel. *The Addictive Organization.* San Francisco: Harper & Row, 1988.

Schaeffer, Frank. *Crazy for God: How I Grew Up as One of the Elect, Helped Found the Religious Right, and Lived to Take All (or Almost All) of It Back.* Cambridge: Da Capo Press, 2007.

Schüssler Fiorenza, Elizabeth. "The Study of Women in Early Christianity: Some Methodological Considerations." In *Critical History and Biblical Faith New Testament Perspectives.* Edited by Thomas J. Ryan. Villanova: College Theology Society, 1979, 30–58.

Scofield, C. I. *Rightly Dividing the Word of Truth.* New York: A.C. Gaebelein, 1888.

———. *Scofield Reference Bible.* New York: Oxford University Press, 1909.

———. *Synthesis of Bible Truth*, vol. III. *The Scofield Bible Correspondence School Course of Study.* N.p.,: C.I. Scofield, 1907.

Selby, John. *Jesus for the rest of us.* Charlottesville: Hampton Roads, 2006.

Shelley, Jacob. "Life Stages." In Dann, *Leaving Fundamentalism: Personal Stories*, 121–35,

Sim, David C. "The Gospel of Matthew and the Gentiles." *Journal for the Study of the New Testament* 57, no.2 (July 1995): 19–48.

Sim, Stuart. *Fundamentalist World: The New Dark Age of Dogma.* Cambridge: Icon Books, 2004.

Simons, Joseph. "Rapture, Community, and Individualist Hope." In Dann, *Leaving Fundamentalism: Personal Stories*, 25–39.

Sims, Walter Hines, ed. *Baptist Hymnal.* Nashville: Convention Press, 1956.

Singer, Isadore and George A. Barton. "Moloch (Molech)." *Jewish Encyclopedia.* Online: www.jewishencyclopedia.com.

Slevidge, Maria J., ed. *Fundamentalism Today: What Makes It So Attractive.* Elgin: Brethren Press, 1984.

Spong, John Shelby. *A New Christianity for a New World: Why Traditional Faith is Dying and How a New Faith is Being Born.* San Francisco: Harper Collins, 2001.

———. *Rescuing the Bible from Fundamentalism.* New York: Harper Collins, 1991.

Stabler, Tim (not his real name). Interview conducted on June 18, 2007.

Stackhouse, John G., Jr. *Canadian Evangelicalism in the Twentieth Century: An Introduction to its Character.* Vancouver: Regent College, 1999.

———. "Women in Public Ministry in 20th-Century Canadian and American Evangelicalism: Five Models." *Studies in Religion/Sciences Religieuses*, 17, no. 4 (1988): 481.

Stamos, David N. "Why I Am Not a New Apostolic." In Babinski, *Leaving the Fold: Testimonies of Former Fundamentalists*, 337–45.

"Statement of Faith," The Evangelical Fellowship of Canada, last modified 2012, http://www.evangelicalfellowship.ca/page.aspx?pid=265.

Support Forum, "Walk Away from Fundamentalism," founded 2001, http://forum1.aimoo.com/walkaway. April 30, 2011.

Support group, "Leaving Born Again Fundamentalist Christianity E-Mail List," created June 16, 1999. http://www.angelfire.com/pa/greywlf/leaving.html.

Sweeney, Douglas A. *The American Evangelical Story: A History of the Movement.* Grand Rapids: Baker Academic, 2005.

Sweeney, Jon M. *born again and again: surprising gifts of a fundamentalist childhood.* Brewster: Paraclete, 2005.

Tabor, Britton H. *Skepticism Assailed, Or, The Stronghold of Infidelity Overturned.* Toronto: J. L. Nichols and Company, 1895.

Taylor, Arch B., Jr. "The Bible, and What It Means to Me." In Babinski, *Leaving the Fold: Testimonies of Former Fundamentalists*, 153–68.

Teeple, Howard M. "I Started to Be a Minister." In Babinski, *Leaving the Fold: Testimonies of Former Fundamentalists*, 347–57.

———. *I Started to be a Minister: From Fundamentalism to a Religions of Ethics.* Evanston: Religion and Ethics Institute, 1990.

Templeton, Charles. *Farewell to God: My Reasons for Rejecting the Christian Faith.* Toronto: McClelland & Stewart, 1996.

———. "Inside Evangelism." In Babinski, *Leaving the Fold: Testimonies of Former Fundamentalists*, 285–91.

Thompson, Frank Charles, ed. *The New Chain-Reference Bible.* Indianapolis: B.B. Kirkbride Bible, 1964. 48th reprint.

Till, Farrell. "From Preacher to Skeptic." In Babinski, *Leaving the Fold: Testimonies of Former Fundamentalists*, 293–95.

Toews, J. A. *A History of the Mennonite Brethren Church: Pilgrims and Pioneers.* Fresno: General Conference of Mennonite Brethren Churches, 1975.

Toews, J. B. *JB: The Autobiography of a Twentieth Century Mennonite Pilgrim.* Fresno: Center for Mennonite Brethren Studies, 1995.

Tomlinson, David. *The Post-Evangelical.* London: Triangel, 1995.

Torrey, R. A. *Difficulties and Alleged Errors and Contradictions in the Bible.* New York: Fleming H. Revell, 1907.

———. *Personal Work: How to Work for Christ, A Compendium of Effective Methods.* Montrose: Montrose Christian Literature Society, 1901.

———. *What the Bible Teaches.* New York: Fleming H. Revell, 1898.

Torrey, R. A. et al., eds. *The Fundamentals: A Testimony to the Truth.* 12 vols. Los Angeles: Bible Institute of Los Angeles, 1917.

Tucker, Ruth A. *Walking Away From Faith: Unraveling the Mystery of Belief & Unbelief.* Downers Grove: InterVarsity, 2002.

Turner, Alice K. *The History of Hell.* Orlando: Harcourt Brace, 1993.

Utzinger, J. Michael. *Yet Saints Their Watch are Keeping: Fundamentalists, Modernist, and the Development of Evangelical Ecclesiology, 1887–1937.* Macon: Mercer University Press, 1983.

Verner, D. C. *The Household of God, The Social World of the Pastoral Epistles.* Missoula: Society of Biblical Literature, 1983.

Vidler, Alec R. *The Church in an Age of Revolution.* New York: Penguin Books, 1961.

Warner, Laceye C. *Saving Women: Retrieving Evangelistic Theology and Practice*. Waco: Baylor, 2007.

Wenger, J.C. ed. *The Complete Writings of Menno Simons c. 1496–1561*. Translated by Leonard Verduin with a biography by Harold S. Bender. Scottdale: Mennonite Publishing, 1956.

Wicker, Christine. *God Knows My Heart: Finding a Faith That Fits*. New York: St. Martin's, 1999.

Wilber, Ken. *Integral Spirituality: A Startling New Role for Religion in the Modern and Postmodern World*. Boston: Integral Books, 2006.

Winell, Marlene. "Journey Free: Resources for recovery from harmful religion," last modified 2011, http://journeyfree.org.

———. *Leaving the Fold: A Guide for Former Fundamentalists and Others Leaving Their Religion*. Oakland: New Harbinger, 1993.

Wright, Keith. *The Hell Jesus Never Intended*. Kelowna: Northstone, 2004.

Yaconnelli, Mike and Karla. "Behind the Wittenburg Door." In Babinski, *Leaving the Fold: Testimonies of Former Fundamentalists*, 171–81.

Young, Lee Adams. "Fundamentalists Anonymous: Twelve Steps to Sanity," October 2009, http://www.oocities.org/church_of_hank/fundamentalists_anonymous.html.

Zindler, Frank R. "Biography." In Babinski, *Leaving the Fold: Testimonies of Former Fundamentalists*, 359–63.

General Index

A

African Methodist Episcopal Zion
    Church, 50
afterlife, 10–11, 29, 83, 96, 98, 138,
    180–84, 186–87, 193, 195–97,
    210–11, 215, 217, 225, 312
Age of Reason, 5, 40
Ahura Mazda, 182
Alexander, Archibald, 74
Alexander, Charles, 91
Alexander, Helen, 37
Alline, Henry, 47
Alphonse, Jean, 154
altar call, 12, 13, 70–72, 86
American Bible Society, 49
American Psychological Association,
    293
American Tract Society, 49
Ammerman, Nancy, xx, 47, 59, 76, 78
Anabaptism, xix, 3, 33, 35
Anglican tradition, 34, 48, 50–51, 69,
    84, 283
Angra Mainyu, 178, 182
Antioch, 147, 190–91
anxious bench, 47
apataō, 169
Apocalypse of Paul, 211
Apocalypse of Peter, 211
apocalyptic literature, 186, 209
Arius, 147
Armstrong, Karen, 65
Arndt, Johann, 38
Asbury, Francis, 48
Associated Gospel Churches, 69
Athanasius, 147
atonement, xxiii, 7, 23, 58–59, 99, 226,
    274

Augustine, 178, 212–13
authentein, 168

B

Babinski, Edward T., 238, 241, 254, 286
backsliding, 12, 37, 249
Bagley, William, 243, 247, 285
Baker, Sharon, 177, 179, 190, 195–96,
    210
Balmer, Randall, 26
baptism, xix, 9–10, 33, 35, 49, 212
Baptist Bible Union of North America,
    69
Baptist tradition, 3, 7, 22, 24, 35–36,
    49–50, 53, 57, 63, 69, 121, 128–
    29, 132, 225–27, 232, 239, 267
Barker, Dan, 227–28, 245, 247–48, 285
Barnhart, Joe, 240
Barr, James, 23–24, 26, 252–53
Barrows, Cliff, 92
Barton, George A., 189
Bauer, F.C., 62
Bebbington, David, 22, 24, 34
Beegle, Dewey M., 239–40, 244, 264–65
Bernard, J.H., 170
Bernstein, Alan E., 176, 179–80, 205,
    211
Bible Institute of Los Angeles, 67, 69,
    74, 132
Bible, the
    authority of, xxii, 18, 23–27, 29,
        33–34, 51, 70, 137, 139, 154,
        158–59, 205, 217, 242, 260, 270,
        286–87

Simons, Joseph, 242, 246, 255
Simons, Menno, 34
Simpson, Albert Benjamin, 68
sin
    original, 5, 51, 61, 214, 226, 242,
        248, 281
    punishment for, 7, 38, 176, 178–84,
        187, 195, 201–202, 205, 208,
        211–14, 243, 258, 271
Singer, Isadore, 189
singing
    folksong melodies, 84
    gospel songs, 1, 71, 82–134, 231,
        312
    Hebrew melodies, 83
    musical structure, 88
    psalms, 83–87
Sleeper, William True, 133
social justice, 34, 50, 201
Socrates, 180
Sodom and Gomorrah, 194, 203
sōphrosynē, 164
Spafford, Horatio G., 127
Spener, Philip Jakob, 38–40
Spinoza, Baruch, 35, 153
Spinoza, Benedict, 153
Spong, John Shelby, 157
Stackhouse, John G., Jr., 159
stages of faith, xxiii, 218, 255–286
Stamos, David N., 285, 292
Stebbins, George, 133
Stewart Evangelistic Fund, 77
Stewart, Lyman and Milton, 77
Stoddard, Solomon, 43, 45–46
Strachan, John, 51
Straton, John Roach, 63
Strauss, David, 62
Sunday School, 3, 4, 13–14, 21, 49, 61,
    70–71, 76–77, 93, 121–22, 132,
    232, 260, 299
Sunday, Billy, 66, 69, 71–73, 89, 91
Sweeney, Jon, 20, 225–27, 239, 254,
    256–57, 261, 267–68, 274
Swinden, Tobiz, 213
Synod of Carthage, 147

T

Tabor, Britton, 84
targum, 170
Tartarus, 177–78, 182, 184, 208
Taylor, Arch B., Jr., 239–42
Teeple, Howard M., 233, 239, 281–82
teknogonia, 170
Templeton, Charles, 223–24, 239, 242,
    253, 284
testimonies, 9–10, 70, 77, 219
theosebeia, 165
Thomas, William Henry Griffith, 69
Tibetan Book of the Dead, 182
Till, Farrell, 239, 260
Tindley, Charles Albert, 130
Tomlinson, Dave, 21, 141
Torrey, R.A., 59–61, 67–69, 74, 77–79,
    91
Tovey, Herbert George, 121, 132
Tucker, Ruth, 233–34, 239, 284, 312
Turner, Alice K., 213
Tyndale, William, 148–50

U

Ukranian Catholic tradition, 51
Ulrich, Zwingli, 33
underworld,
    and justice, 179
    appearance of, 178
    location of, 177
    names for, 177
    rulers of, 178
    type of existence in the, 182
Unitarian tradition, 63, 121
United Church of Canada, 51

V

Van DeVenter, Judson Wheeler, 129
Van Vonderen, Jeff, 289
Verner, D.C., 160
Virgil, 182–83, 212
virgin birth, 24, 58–59, 63, 77–78, 237,
    242, 270
Vulgate, 35, 148, 150

Index of Song Titles

A

A Mighty Fortress is Our God, 32
All for Jesus, 107
All the Way My Savior Leads Me, 110, 124
All Things in Jesus, 97
Almost Persuaded, 91, 132
Anywhere with Jesus, 101, 123
Are You Washed in the Blood?, 101
Arise My Soul Arise, 85

B

Be Ye Strong in the Lord, 112
Blessed Assurance, 99–101, 125
Break Thou the Bread of Life, 94
Bring Them In, 113, 115
Bringing in the Sheaves, 114

C

Christ Our Redeemer Died on the Cross, 100
Close to Thee, 110, 124
Come Every Soul By Sin Oppressed, 99–100, 118
Come to the Savior, Make No Delay, 100–101
Come with Thy Sins to the Fountain, 101
Conquering Now and Still to Conquer, 112
Constantly Abiding, 89, 110, 126

D

Do You Hear Them Coming?, 118
Does Jesus Care?, 89
Down at the Cross, 99–100

F

Face to Face, 118
Faith is the Victory, 111–12
Far and Near the Fields Are Teeming, 113–14
Far Away in the Depths of My Spirit, 110
Far, Far Away in Heathen Darkness, 113–14
Free from the Law, 97, 101

G

Gather Them In for Yet There Is Room, 113–14
Give of Your Best to the Master, 113, 115
Give Me a Passion for Souls Dear Lord, 16, 114, 132–33
God Be with You Till We Meet Again, 119
God Loved the World of Sinners Lost, 97, 99, 102
God Will Take Care of You, 110, 123

CPSIA information can be obtained at www.ICGtesting.com
Printed in the USA
LVOW100124060912

297544LV00004B/4/P